SALES MANAGEMENT

This tenth edition of *Sales Management* continues the tradition of blending the most recent sales management research with the real-life "best practices" of leading sales organizations. The authors teach sales management courses, and interact with sales managers and sales management professors on a regular basis. Their text focuses on the importance of employing different sales strategies for different customer groups, as well as integrating corporate, business, marketing, and sales strategies. *Sales Management* includes coverage of the current trends and issues in sales management, along with numerous real-world examples from the contemporary business world that are used throughout the text to illuminate chapter discussions.

Key changes in this edition include:

- Updates in each chapter to reflect the latest sales management research, and leading sales management trends and practices;
- Revised end-of-chapter cases;
- Revised ethical dilemma boxes;
- All new chapter opening vignettes about well-known companies that illustrate key topics from that chapter; and
- New or updated comments from sales managers in "Sales Management in the 21st Century" boxes.

An online instructor's manual with test questions and PowerPoints is available to adopters.

Thomas N. Ingram is a Department Chair Emeritus and Professor of Marketing Emeritus at Colorado State University, USA.

Raymond W. (Buddy) LaForge is the Brown-Forman Professor of Marketing Emeritus at University of Louisville, USA.

Ramon A. Avila is the George and Frances Ball Distinguished Professor of Marketing and the founding director of the Center for Professional Selling at Ball State University, USA.

Charles H. Schwepker, Jr. is the Randall and Kelly Harbert Distinguished Marketing Professor at University of Central Missouri, USA.

Michael R. Williams is the American Floral Services Chair in Marketing and is Professor of Marketing and Associate Dean for Academic Affairs at Oklahoma City University, USA.

Sales Management
Analysis and Decision Making

TENTH EDITION

Thomas N. Ingram

Raymond W. LaForge

Ramon A. Avila

Charles H. Schwepker, Jr.

Michael R. Williams

Routledge
Taylor & Francis Group

NEW YORK AND LONDON

Tenth edition published 2020
by Routledge
52 Vanderbilt Avenue, New York, NY 10017

and by Routledge
2 Park Square, Milton Park, Abingdon, Oxon, OX14 4RN

Routledge is an imprint of the Taylor & Francis Group, an informa business

© 2020 Taylor & Francis

The right of Thomas N. Ingram, Raymond W. LaForge, Ramon A. Avila, Charles H. Schwepker, Jr., and Michael R. Williams to be identified as authors of this work has been asserted by them in accordance with sections 77 and 78 of the Copyright, Designs and Patents Act 1988.

Eighth edition published by M.E. Sharpe 2012
Ninth edition published by Routledge 2015

Library of Congress Cataloging-in-Publication Data
A catalog record has been requested for this book

ISBN: 978-0-367-25273-1 (hbk)
ISBN: 978-0-367-25274-8 (pbk)
ISBN: 978-0-429-28692-6 (ebk)

Typeset in Galliard
by Servis Filmsetting Ltd, Stockport, Cheshire

Visit the companion website: www.routledge.com/cw/ingram

BRIEF CONTENTS

CONTENTS

Our objective in writing the tenth edition of *Sales Management: Analysis and Decision Making* was to continue to present comprehensive and rigorous coverage of contemporary sales management in a readable, interesting, and challenging manner. Findings from recent sales management research are blended with examples of current sales management practice into an effective pedagogical format. Topics are covered from the perspective of a sales management decision maker. This decision-making perspective is accomplished through a chapter format that typically consists of discussing basic concepts, identifying critical decision areas, and presenting analytical approaches for improved sales management decision making. Company examples from the contemporary business world are used throughout the text to supplement chapter discussion.

STRENGTHS OF THIS EDITION

The tenth edition of *Sales Management: Analysis and Decision Making* continues what has been effective in previous editions, but contains changes that improve the content and pedagogy in the book. The authors teach sales management courses, are involved in sales management research, and interact with sales managers and professors on a regular basis. These activities ensure that the text covers the appropriate sales management topics and employs the most effective pedagogy. The key strengths of the tenth edition include:

- The 10 chapters and paperback format from the previous edition have been maintained. This makes it easy for professors to cover the text in a semester or quarter, and still have sufficient time to use active learning exercises throughout the course. Students can purchase the tenth edition for much less than the cost of a typical hardcover sales management book.

- New Opening Vignettes generate student interest in the chapter content by providing recent examples of leading sales organizations employing the chapter material.

- "Sales Management in the 21st Century" boxes include new sales executives or updated personal comments that reinforce important sales management concepts in each chapter.

- Revised "Ethical Dilemma" boxes provide students the opportunity to address important ethical issues facing sales managers with many set up as role-play exercises.

- Revised chapter cases with related role plays put students in the role of a sales manager in a specific sales organization situation. The cases require students to analyze the situation, decide on the appropriate action, and then implement their decisions through role-play scenarios.

- New and revised pedagogy is available in the "Developing Sales Management Knowledge" and "Building Sales Management Skills" activities at the end of each chapter.

- All chapters have been updated to incorporate the latest findings from sales management research and the best practices from leading sales organizations. Topics receiving new or expanded coverage include: using social networking in recruiting and selecting; virtual reality in training; evaluation of training; coaching; and ethical leadership.

LEVEL AND ORGANIZATION

This text was written for the undergraduate student enrolled in a one-semester or one-quarter sales management class. However, it is sufficiently rigorous to be used at the MBA level.

A sales management model is used to present coverage in a logical sequence. The text is organized into five parts to correspond with the five stages in the sales management model.

Part One, "Describing the Personal Selling Function," is designed to provide students with an understanding of personal selling prior to addressing specific sales management areas. We devote one chapter at the beginning of the text to this topic.

Part Two, "Defining the Strategic Role of the Sales Function," consists of two chapters. One discusses important relationships between personal selling and organizational strategies at the corporate, business, marketing, and sales levels. This chapter focuses on how strategic decisions at different organizational levels affect sales management decisions and personal selling practices.

The second chapter in this part investigates alternative sales organization structures and examines analytical methods for determining salesforce size, territory design, and the allocation of selling effort.

Part Three, "Developing the Salesforce," changes the focus from organizational topics to people topics. The two chapters in this part cover the critical decision areas in the recruitment and selection of salespeople and in training salespeople once they have been hired.

Part Four, "Directing the Salesforce," continues the people orientation by discussing the leadership, management, and supervisory activities necessary for successful sales management and examining important areas of salesforce motivation and reward systems.

Part Five, "Determining Salesforce Effectiveness and Performance," concludes the sales management process by addressing evaluation and control procedures. Differences in evaluating the effectiveness of the sales organization and the performance of salespeople are highlighted and covered in separate chapters.

PEDAGOGY

The following pedagogical format is used for each chapter to facilitate the learning process.

- *Learning Objectives.* Specific learning objectives for the chapter are stated in behavioral terms so that students will know what they should be able to do after the chapter has been covered.

- *Opening Vignettes.* All chapters are introduced by an opening vignette that typically consists of a recent, real-world company example addressing many of the key points to be discussed in the chapter. These opening vignettes are intended to generate student interest in the topics to be covered and to illustrate the practicality of the chapter coverage.

- *Key Words.* Key words are highlighted in bold type throughout each chapter and summarized in list form at the end of the chapter to alert students to their importance.

- *Boxed Inserts.* Each chapter contains two boxed inserts titled "Sales Management in the 21st Century." The comments in these boxes are provided by members of our Sales Executive Panel and were made specifically for our text.

- *Figure Captions.* Most figures in the text include a summarizing caption designed to make the figure understandable without reference to the chapter discussion.
- *Chapter Summaries.* A chapter summary recaps the key points covered in the chapter by restating and answering questions presented in the learning objectives at the beginning of the chapter.
- *Developing Sales Management Knowledge.* Ten discussion questions are presented at the end of each chapter to review key concepts covered in the chapter. Some of the questions require students to summarize what has been covered, while others are designed to be more thought-provoking and extend beyond chapter coverage.
- *Building Sales Management Skills.* Application exercises are supplied for each chapter, requiring students to apply what has been learned in the chapter to a specific sales management situation. Many of the application exercises require data analysis. Many chapters also have an Internet exercise to get students involved with the latest technology. Role plays are also included in most chapters.
- *Making Sales Management Decisions.* Each chapter concludes with two short cases. Most of these cases represent realistic and interesting sales management situations. Several require data analysis. Most are designed so that students can role-play their solutions.

CASES

The 18 short cases at the end of the chapters can be used as a basis for class discussion, short written assignments, or role plays. These are designed to help bring the material in each chapter to life for students by illustrating how chapter concepts can be applied in practice.

SUPPLEMENTS

Instructor's Resources

The Instructor's Resources (at www.routledge.com/cw/ingram) deliver all the traditional instructor support materials in one handy place. Electronic files are provided for the complete Instructor's Manual, Test Bank, and chapter-by-chapter PowerPoint presentation files that can be used to enhance in-class lectures.

Instructor's Manual

The Instructor's Manual for the tenth edition of *Sales Management: Analysis and Decision Making* contains many helpful teaching suggestions and solutions to text exercises to help instructors successfully integrate all the materials offered with this text into their class. Each chapter includes the following materials designed to meet the instructor's needs.

- Learning objectives
- Chapter outline and summary
- Ideas for student involvement
- Possible answers to review sections in the text, *Developing Sales Management Knowledge* and *Building Sales Management Skills*
- Ideas for how to incorporate the role-play exercises found in the text into the classroom setting, as well as suggestions for conducting the role plays

(The Instructor's Manual files are located at: www.routledge.com/cw/ingram)

Test Bank

The revised and updated Test Bank, with over 100 new questions, includes a variety of multiple choice and true/false questions, which emphasize the important concepts presented in each chapter. The Test Bank questions vary in levels of difficulty so that each instructor can tailor his/her testing to meet his/her specific needs. The Test Bank files are located at: www.routledge.com/cw/ingram

PowerPoint Presentation Slides

This package brings classroom lectures and discussions to life with the Microsoft PowerPoint presentation tool. Extremely professor-friendly and organized by chapter, these chapter-by-chapter presentations outline chapter content, and generally include a link to a short related video. The eye-appealing and easy-to-read slides are, in this new edition, tailored specifically to the *Sales Management* text from the Ingram author team. The PowerPoint presentation slides are available at: www.routledge.com/cw/ingram.

ACKNOWLEDGMENTS

We are delighted to publish the tenth edition of *Sales Management: Analysis and Decision Making* with Routledge. Our hope is that this is one of many editions we work on together. A great deal of credit for this edition should go to all of the wonderful people at Routledge. Their expertise, support, and constant encouragement turned an extremely difficult task into a very enjoyable one. We are thankful for the expertise and support of the many publishing professionals who have worked with us on previous editions of this book. In particular, we appreciate the efforts of Harry Briggs, Rob Zwettler, Mike Roche and Becky Ryan. We would also like to thank our senior editor, Meredith Norwich, and editorial assistant, Alston Slatton for their work on the tenth edition of this book. Without their efforts this edition would not have seen the light of day. However, we also want to thank the many individuals with whom we did not have direct contact but who assisted in the development and production of this book.

We are also very appreciative of the support provided by our colleagues at Colorado State University, the University of Louisville, Ball State University, University of Central Missouri, and Oklahoma City University.

Thomas N. Ingram
Raymond W. LaForge
Ramon A. Avila
Charles H. Schwepker, Jr.
Michael R. Williams

Thomas N. Ingram (Ph.D., Georgia State University) is the Department Chair Emeritus and Professor of Marketing Emeritus at Colorado State University. Before commencing his academic career, Tom worked in sales, product management, and sales management with ExxonMobil. Professor Ingram has received numerous awards for contributions to sales research and teaching, most recently as a recipient of the Lifetime Achievement Award from the American Marketing Association Selling and Sales Management Special Interest Group. He has also been honored as the Marketing Educator of the Year by Sales and Marketing Executives International (SMEI), as a Distinguished Sales Educator by the University Sales Center Alliance, and as the first recipient of the Mu Kappa Tau National Marketing Honor Society Recognition Award for Outstanding Scholarly Contributions to the Sales Discipline. Tom has served as the Editor of *Journal of Personal Selling & Sales Management*, Chair of the SMEI Accreditation Institute, and as Editor of the *Journal of Marketing Theory and Practice*. Professor Ingram's published work has appeared in *Journal of Marketing, Journal of Marketing Research, Journal of Personal Selling & Sales Management,* and *Journal of the Academy of Marketing Science,* among others. One of his co-authored articles which appeared in the *Journal of Marketing* was recognized by the American Marketing Association Selling and Sales Management Special Interest Group as one of the "Top Ten Articles of the 20th Century" in the sales discipline.

Raymond W. (Buddy) LaForge (DBA, University of Tennessee) is the Brown-Forman Professor of Marketing Emeritus at the University of Louisville. He is the founder of the *Marketing Education Review*; has co-authored *Marketing: Principles and Perspectives,* 5th ed. (2007); *Professional Selling: A Trust-Based Approach,* 4th ed. (2008); *Sell,* 4th ed. (2015); *The Professional Selling Skills Workbook* (1995); *Strategic Sales Leadership: Breakthrough Thinking for Breakthrough Results* (2006); and co-edited *Emerging Trends in Sales Thought and Practice.* His research is published in many journals, including the *Journal of Marketing, Journal of Marketing Research, Decision Sciences, Journal of the Academy of Marketing Science, International Journal of Research in Marketing,* and *Journal of Personal Selling & Sales Management.* Buddy has received numerous awards, including the Outstanding Sales Scholar Award from Mu Kappa Tau, a Special Recognition Award from the American Marketing Association Sales Interest Group, a Top Thirteen Faculty Favorite Award from the University of Louisville, the Distinguished Scholar Award from the Research Symposium on Marketing and Entrepreneurship, the Distinguished Sales Educator Award from the University Sales Center Alliance, the Undergraduate Teaching Award from the College of Business, the Beta Alpha Psi Outstanding College of Business Faculty Award, and the American Marketing Association Sales Interest Group Lifetime Achievement Award. The Sales Program at the University of Louisville has been recognized as a Top University Sales Education Program by the Sales Education Foundation from 2007 to 2014.

Ramon A. Avila (Ph.D., Virginia Polytechnic Institute and State University) is the George and Frances Ball Distinguished Professor of Marketing and the founding director of the Center for Professional Selling, and earned his bachelor's degree and MBA from Ball State University. He completed his Ph.D. at Virginia Polytechnic Institute and

State University in 1984. He joined the Ball State faculty in 1984. Before coming to Ball State, he worked in sales with the Burroughs Corporation. Dr. Avila was presented with Mu Kappa Tau's Outstanding Contributor to the Sales Profession in 1999 and is the only the third person to receive this award. Dr. Avila has also received the University's Outstanding Faculty award in 2001, the Outstanding Service award in 1998, the University's Outstanding Junior Faculty award in 1989, the College of Business's Professor of the Year, and the Dean's Teaching award every year it was given from 1987 to 2002. Dr. Avila has presented numerous papers at professional conferences and has been the program chair and the director for the National Conference in Sales Management, and has published research in *Journal of Marketing Research, Journal of Euromarketing, Industrial Marketing Management, Journal of Management, Journal of Marketing Theory and Practice, Journal of Personal Selling & Sales Management,* and *Journal of Marketing Education.* A frequent consultant, he has worked with major corporations, including AT&T, Burroughs, Honeywell, Indiana Gas, Indiana Michigan Power, Indiana Bell, and Midwest Metals. Dr. Avila serves on the editorial review boards of four business-related journals. He is also the former associate editor for the *Mid-American Journal of Business.* Dr. Avila's teaching focuses on industrial marketing, professional selling, and sales management.

Charles H. Schwepker, Jr. (Ph.D., University of Memphis) is the Randall and Kelly Harbert Marketing Professor at the University of Central Missouri. He has experience in wholesale and retail sales. His primary research interests are in sales management, personal selling and marketing ethics. Dr. Schwepker's articles have appeared in the *Journal of the Academy of Marketing Science, Journal of Business Research, Journal of Public Policy and Marketing, Journal of Personal Selling & Sales Management, Journal of Service Research,* and *Journal of Business Ethics,* among other journals, and various national and regional proceedings. Edited books in which his articles have appeared include *Marketing Communications Classics* (2000), *Environmental Marketing* (1995), *The Oxford Handbook of Sales Management and Sales Strategy* (2011) and the *Handbook of Unethical Work Behavior* (2013). He has received several honors for both teaching and advising, including the Hormel Teaching Excellence award, Byler Distinguished Faculty Award and the Alumni Foundation Harmon College of Business Administration Distinguished Professor award. Dr. Schwepker received the James Comer award for best contribution to selling and sales management theory awarded by the *Journal of Personal Selling & Sales Management* and three "Outstanding Paper" awards at the National Conference in Sales Management, among others. He is on the editorial review boards of the *Journal of Personal Selling & Sales Management, Journal of Marketing Theory & Practice, Journal of Business & Industrial Marketing, Journal of Relationship Marketing,* and *Journal of Selling* , and has five times won an award for outstanding reviewer. Dr. Schwepker is a co-author of *Sell,* 6th ed. (2020).

Michael R. Williams (Ph.D., Oklahoma State University) is the American Floral Services Chair in Marketing and is Professor of Marketing and Associate Dean for Academic Affairs at Oklahoma City University. His previous academic associations include Professor of Marketing at Illinois State University and Director of the Professional Sales Institute. Prior to his academic career, Dr. Williams established a successful 30-plus-year career in industrial sales, market research, and sales management and continues to consult and work with a wide range of business organizations. He has co-authored *Sell,* 6th ed. (2020); *Professional Selling: A Trust-based Approach,* 4th ed. (2008); *The Professional Selling Skills Workbook* (1995); and a variety of executive monographs and white papers on sales performance topics. Dr. Williams' research has been published in national and international journals including *Journal of Personal Selling & Sales Management, International Journal of Purchasing and Materials Management, Journal of Business and Industrial Marketing, Quality Management Journal,* and *Journal of Industrial Technology.* His work has also received numerous honors, including Outstanding Article for the Year in *Journal of Business and Industrial Marketing,* the AACSB's Leadership in Innovative Business Education award, the

Marketing Science Institute's Alden G. Clayton competition, and the Mu Kappa Tau Marketing Society recognition award for Outstanding Scholarly Contribution to the Sales Discipline. He has also received numerous university, college, and corporate teaching and research awards including Old Republic Research Scholar, the presentation of a seminar at Oxford's Brasenose College, *Who's Who in American Education,* and *Who's Who in America*. Mike has and continues to serve in leadership roles as an advisor and board member for sales and sales management associations and organizations.

Sales Management
Analysis and Decision Making

CHANGING WORLD OF SALES MANAGEMENT

Personal selling is an important component of the marketing strategies for many firms, especially those operating in business-to-business markets. The 500 largest U.S. salesforces employ almost 25 million salespeople, with the 200 largest manufacturing salesforces consisting of over 528,000 salespeople. Each manufacturing salesperson produces an average of about $7.8 million in annual sales and supports over 15 other jobs in their company.[1] These statistics illustrate the large size and significant impact of personal selling in today's business world.

Sales Management is concerned with managing a firm's personal selling function. Sales managers are involved in both the strategy (planning) and people (implementation) aspects of personal selling, as well as evaluating and improving personal selling activities. Research indicates that sales managers can increase profitable sales growth by 5 percent to 20 percent or more by moving from average to excellent salesforce effectiveness.[2] Sales managers are involved in a variety of activities and must be able to interact effectively with people in the personal selling function, with people in other functional areas in their firm, and with people outside their company, especially customers and other business partners.

Most sales organizations employ sales managers at various levels within the sales organization. These sales managers have different titles and may not have direct responsibility for specific salespeople, but all perform sales management activities that affect the salespeople in a sales organization. Illustrative titles for sales managers include chief sales officer, vice president of sales, divisional sales manager, regional sales manager, sales leader, branch manager, area director, and field sales manager.

Our objective in this chapter is to introduce the exciting world of sales management. We begin by identifying challenges in the sales organization environment and suggesting effective sales management responses to these challenges. Then, the characteristics of the best sales organizations and most effective sales managers are discussed. We conclude by presenting a general sales management model that provides a framework for the book, describing the format of each chapter, and introducing the members of our Sales Executive Panel. The goal is to "set the stage" for your journey into the dynamic and exciting world of sales management.

CHALLENGES IN THE SALES ORGANIZATION ENVIRONMENT

Sales organizations operate in a complex and turbulent environment. Political, social, and economic trends in the global business environment and rapid advances in technology have produced an extremely competitive marketplace. Many of these changes have had an especially significant impact on organizational purchasing. The purchasing and supply function has increased in importance at many firms, because it is viewed as an effective way for firms to lower costs and increase profits. Therefore, organizational buyers are more demanding, better prepared, and more skilled. Sales organizations must understand this situation to be able to generate business with new customers and to keep and expand business with existing customers.

Several significant changes in the organizational purchasing process are directly relevant to sales organizations. Organizational buyers have higher expectations in terms of customized products and services that solve their problems and improve their business performance. More organizations are using a formalized purchasing process, with more individuals from different functional areas and management levels involved at different stages of the process. Many buyers do not want to talk to a salesperson until they have gathered the relevant information about their purchasing situation and expect salespeople to provide information and insights they do not have. The net result is a much longer purchasing process.[3]

The costs of maintaining salespeople in the field are escalating, and a longer purchasing process increases selling costs even more. Thus, a critical challenge for sales organizations is to increase sales while decreasing selling costs. Sales organizations must find effective ways to facilitate the emerging buying process of organizational buyers in a manner that generates profitable sales growth. Achieving this objective typically requires many sales organizations to make appropriate adjustments to their personal selling process and in sales management practices.

SALES MANAGEMENT RESPONSES

Sales organizations are responding to these challenges in different ways. Many firms are implementing a marketing orientation with the sales organization viewed from a more strategic perspective. Market-oriented firms typically develop customer-centric cultures and focus efforts more toward customers rather than just products. Market segmentation and prioritizing customers within target markets becomes increasingly important. Sales is also viewed more as a core business process rather than a tactical activity. This strategic perspective considers the sales organization as critical in delivering value to customers and generating profits for the firm. Salespeople, sales managers, and other business functions need to change many of their activities to be successful in implementing a more strategic role.[4]

One emerging approach guiding many firms is to create and implement a *sales enablement* perspective. The sales enablement area is in the early stage of its development, so there is no universally accepted definition. However, most discussions of a comprehensive sales enablement program include several key elements:

- A buyer-focused function driven by a firm's top-level executives.
- An alignment of the steps in the sales process to deliver value at each stage of the buying process.
- An integration and coordination of the efforts of executives, sales managers, salespeople, and personnel from other business functions that directly impact customers to create value in all interactions with buyers.
- An incorporation of the appropriate training, technology, performance metrics, and reward programs to guide and support the execution and achievement of sales enablement and sales organization objectives.

There is increasing evidence that firms creating and executing a sales enablement function perform better than firms without them.[5]

Sales enablement is beginning to develop as a discipline. The Sales Enablement Society (sesociety.org) was established in 2015 as a volunteer organization of professionals from diverse industries, companies, and business functions. The organization provides a variety of networking opportunities for members. The major purpose is to increase the knowledge base and identify the best practices for a successful sales enablement function. One ongoing effort is to establish an official definition of sales enablement.

Firms employing a comprehensive sales enablement function are making dramatic changes in their sales operations and transforming most aspects of sales management. Others are focusing on improving a few sales management areas to increase sales organization effectiveness. As indicated in Figure 1.1, these sales management responses

Sales Management Responses   FIGURE 1.1

Many sales organizations are responding to the challenges facing them by making changes in their sales operations.

emphasize ways to create customer value, increase sales productivity, and/or improve sales leadership.

Create Customer Value

Many sales organizations are moving from an emphasis on merely selling products to solving customer problems and adding value to customer businesses over the long term. The key is to identify value as defined by the customer and then to create, communicate, and deliver this value. For example, RS Medical sells physician-prescribed home electrotherapy devices. Salespeople typically focused on the key features of their products when meeting with physicians, because they thought this information was of most interest to the physicians. However, the physicians had more interest in information that would help improve their practice as a business. Once RS Medical salespeople identified what was really of value to physicians, they began to educate physicians on how to make their practices more efficient and more profitable by using RS Medical products. The value provided by this approach led to an increase in device sales for RS Medical.[6]

Changes in the business environment often result in changes in how customers define value. Salespeople and sales managers must identify the new value definitions and deliver the value desired by customers. For example, customers of Minnesota Thermal Science (MTS) used to be most interested in the technology of pharmaceutical packaging. The introduction of strict and costly regulations in the pharmaceutical industry drove many firms to become more interested in ways to reduce their costs. MTS salespeople responded to this change in value and began to present a much stronger business case for their packaging solutions, such as showing customers how their packaging and distribution costs could be reduced by using MTS packaging.[7]

The importance of creating customer value is likely to increase in the future. But, how customers define value is likely to change as well. The most successful sales organizations will be those that are able to identify how their customers define value over time and then communicate and deliver this value to them. Changes in value creation will typically require changes in many aspects of sales management.

Increase Sales Productivity

Even as sales organizations try to create more value for customers, sales managers are under pressure to increase sales productivity. The basic role of a sales organization has typically been to sell with sales managers and salespeople normally evaluated and rewarded for growing sales volume. Generating sales is still important, but the profitability of these sales is increasingly more important. Therefore, the focus for sales managers has moved from sales volume only to sales productivity. Sales productivity includes the costs associated with generating sales and serving customers and emphasizes producing more sales for a given level of costs. Sales managers must "do more with less" by being more effective and more efficient throughout the sales organization.

Many sales organizations are employing different types of technology to increase sales productivity. Improvements in existing technologies, the development of new technologies, and the opportunity to integrate different technologies provide many opportunities to automate some of the tasks currently performed by salespeople and sales managers. The use of salesforce automation (SFA), customer relationship management (CRM), and data analytics tools represent effective technologies for increasing sales productivity. The rapid development of artificial intelligence (AI) and more effective use of social media are especially likely to have important impacts on sales productivity in the future.

Existing and emerging AI technology products are expected to drive sales productivity improvements. AI technologies analyze data and learn from the ongoing data-analysis process to provide better results and guidance for salesperson and sales management actions.[8] AI applications can free salespeople and sales managers from spending time on many different tasks, such as providing price quotes, creating sales reports, data input to CRM systems, sales forecasting, and prescriptive insight for personalized sales presentations. By performing different tasks, AI technology can act as an efficient assistant for salespeople and sales managers.

Take prospecting as an example. Many salespeople spend large amounts of time identifying sales leads, qualifying the leads, prioritizing the prospects, and then making an appointment to talk with the prospect. This is a time-consuming process. Conversica offers an AI virtual Sales Assistant product that promptly responds to website inquiries, personalizes every message, asks questions to qualify the lead, and then sets up a time for a salesperson to call the prospect.[9] This use of AI automates many of the prospecting tasks with the salesperson only directly involved when a qualified prospect has been identified and an appointment established. The time a salesperson has saved by not having to be involved in most of the prospecting process can be used more productively, because the salesperson can spend more time interacting with qualified prospects, engaging in the sales process, and generating more sales.

The use of social media in sales organizations has increased significantly in recent years. Many salespeople are engaged in *social selling*, using social media to identify, understand, engage, and network with prospects and customers. Studies indicate that the best performing salespeople are involved in social selling.[10] Social selling is also being integrated with other technologies, such as CRM and AI, to increase sales productivity. For example, SAP has integrated social media with a variety of other technologies to identify and pursue selling opportunities by listening, learning, and engaging with prospects and customers throughout the sales process. This approach has produced large sales increases and efforts to continuously improve social selling efforts in the future.[11]

The pressure for sales organizations to increase sales productivity is likely to intensify in the future. Emerging technologies are expected to provide new avenues for creating customer value in cost effective ways. The challenge is to increase sales in a profitable manner by always looking for ways to get "more bang for the sales buck."

Improve Sales Leadership

Traditionally, sales organizations have utilized hierarchical, bureaucratic organization structures with a top-down approach to controlling and directing salespeople. In such structures, sales managers operate at different levels with direct supervisory control for the level below and direct accountability to the management level above. In these structures, sales managers are responsible for the performance of salespeople who report to them and they use various types of controls and incentives to produce desired results.

These hierarchical structures can be reasonably effective in stable business environments, but don't always allow an effective level of responsiveness in a complex, dynamic environment. To be competitive in a rapidly changing, unpredictable business environment, more progressive sales organizations have been "flattening" the hierarchy and empowering salespeople to make decisions in the field. The need to have responsive, empowered salespeople has changed the role of sales managers and their relationships with salespeople. Sales managers today must not only be managers and supervisors, but increasingly, they must be leaders.

As sales managers take on more leadership roles, they must focus more on collaboration rather than relying strictly on control mechanisms to achieve desired results. This means not only collaborating more with salespeople and customers, but also various functional areas within the organization such as marketing, customer service, and production to deliver competitive, timely solution in the marketplace. As noted by Maria Valdivieso de Uster, the director of marketing and sales practice for leading consulting firm McKinsey and Company, marketing and sales both have valuable insights about customers and collaboration is needed to better serve those customers. She says that marketing and sales leaders need to work together as equals since failure to collaborate is outmoded and detrimental to performance.[12]

Sales leaders develop their people more through coaching than criticism. Prior to entering college, most students have engaged in team sports and other goal-directed group activities. As a result, students have some idea of what it takes to have a successful (or not) team and the role of coaching in team success. While coaching styles vary, all good coaches have one thing in common: they know what they are talking about, and they know how to impart knowledge to individuals and to the entire team. According to CSO Insights, the research division of consulting firm Miller Heiman, coaching is one of the key best practices for global sales success.[13] Miller Heiman notes that employee development is ingrained in the culture of leading sales organizations. Training, coaching, and development is not limited to new employees or to correct performance problems. In the best sales organizations, it is an ongoing activity aimed at maximizing individual and team performance.

Sales leaders readily accept that an empowered salesforce is superior to one that must wait for direction in a fast-moving business environment. When salespeople are granted more decision-making authority, they can be more responsive to customers. Empowered salespeople are typically more satisfied with their jobs and more motivated than those who work under tight controls. By empowering salespeople, sales leaders are sharing managerial responsibility and helping prepare the next generation of managerial talent. Most importantly, empowered salespeople can be a key ingredient in fielding a world-class salesforce.[14]

Contemporary sales leaders collect and share information about customers and best practices rather than withholding it from others in the organization. This requires that sales leaders must be adept at analyzing complex information and distilling it into understandable language for use in researched, planned, customized, customer-focused encounters.[15]

As sales managers take on more leadership responsibilities, they must recognize individual differences in salespeople rather than treating them all the same. This is a balancing act, as group norms, policies, procedures and processes play a key role in productive sales organizations. However, sales leaders must find ways to coach, train, and motivate individuals as part of their jobs. An example of this practice is to develop and implement personal improvement plans for each salesperson with mutually agreed upon sales targets, activities, and sales competency goals.[16]

When sales managers take on more leadership roles in addition to their managerial duties, dramatic results can occur. For example, BMC, a global leader in software solutions, noticed that their sales growth was slowing. The company also observed that traditional sales techniques such as emailing and calling on prospects without prior contact (cold calling) were becoming less productive. Further, software purchasing decisions were no longer being made strictly by information technology personnel, but by multi-functional teams across customer organizations. BMC realized that buying power was shifting to new audiences, and that their sales teams were not always in contact with key decision-makers. BMC adopted the LinkedIn Sales Navigator program to automate and organize the front-end phase of its sales process of identifying and researching potential clients. As a result, BMC's salespeople were better prepared for sales calls, more credible in their initial contacts, and more productive in generating revenue. Within a year, BMC doubled the number of contacts with prospective customers and established a new market in Latin America.[17]

As sales managers expand their roles more into leadership, there is a trend to move from administrative activities to more of an entrepreneurial orientation throughout the sales organization. Sales managers and salespeople need to view themselves as entrepreneurs, with the sales function driving value creation and innovation within their firms. It is common knowledge that successful entrepreneurs are not bound by conventional thinking. They are visionaries who detect evolving patterns and market opportunities and develop creative responses to changing environments.[18]

In recent years, sales managers with a leadership orientation have successfully implemented new technologies and processes despite significant resistance to change. Notable examples include the widespread use of automation in customer relationship management systems (CRM), the integration of social selling into business-to-business selling and the rapid growth of sales enablement. As we look to the future, the best sales organizations will continue to embody an entrepreneurial perspective focusing on innovation, value creation, empowerment, strategy, technology, and collaboration.

BEST SALES ORGANIZATIONS[19]

Sales consulting firms and academic researchers have studied the best sales organizations to identify the practices that make them successful now and position them for success in the future. A synthesis of this research indicates that the best sales organizations tend to:

- Create a customer-driven culture throughout the sales organization and align sales operations with business and marketing strategies.
- Base market offerings on customer needs and deliver favorable customer experiences.
- Focus on customer value in sales messaging to minimize price-based competition.
- Learn the "why" behind lost customers and lost sales to improve the future wins.
- Ensure that the sales culture supports continuous development of salespeople and sales leaders.
- Train and coach the right skill sets, leveraging best practices of top performers to improve all others. Continually assess attributes of top sales performers.
- Recruit, hire, and retain the best talent for specific sales situations.
- When salespeople leave the organization, consistently determine why and take appropriate action.
- Develop and implement personalized performance improvement plans for all personnel in the sales organization.
- Use technology appropriately to learn about customers, build market intelligence, and enable salesperson and sales manager success.
- Integrate sales with other functional areas, especially marketing and customer service, to deliver maximum customer value.
- Develop an adaptable structure and formalize a relationship-building sales process dedicated to continuous improvement.

It is clear the best sales organizations address all stages of the sales management process. There is no secret recipe that will lead to high performance. The coordination of numerous activities is required to dramatically improve sales organization performance. For example, Avnet, one of the world's largest distributors of information technology, has invested heavily in capabilities and tools that impact customer relationships. Avnet introduced "always on" digital design service tool that lets customers evaluate various configurations and the related costs. The service proved successful for more than 700 projects in reducing customer design and purchase processes by two to five weeks. As a result, Avnet is rolling out the service worldwide. These enhanced service capabilities have strengthened Avnet's customer relationships and been instrumental in internal restructuring and realignment across all departments so that the entire company is now focused on customer outcomes.[20]

EFFECTIVE SALES MANAGERS

Sales managers work with the systems and processes and interact with the people involved in making a sales organization successful. Research indicates that the most effective sales managers possess specific skills and focus on particular activities. The most important sales management skills are: communication and listening skills; human relations skills; organization and time management skills; industry, company, product, and general business knowledge; coaching, motivating, and leadership skills; and honest and ethical tendencies.[21]

In addition to these general skills, the best sales managers focus on a number of specific activities in their interactions with salespeople:[22]

- Prepare their sales team for constant change by being a role model and mentoring salespeople.
- Earn the trust of salespeople by being dependable and competent, and exhibiting integrity.
- Give salespeople continuous feedback in a positive manner.
- Build enthusiasm throughout the sales team.
- Get involved by being accessible to salespeople and visible to customers.
- Grow and develop salespeople by emphasizing continuous job improvement and career development.

As you can see, sales management is a complex and constantly evolving field. The most effective sales managers possess a variety of skills and are involved in many different activities. We now present a sales management model that captures all aspects of sales management and provides a framework for the remainder of the book.

SALES MANAGEMENT PROCESS

The sales management model presented in Figure 1.2 illustrates the major stages in the sales management process. This model is valuable to sales organizations and provides the basic framework for the study of sales management. We discuss the components of each stage in the sales management process and indicate how the remaining chapters in the book address the important areas of sales management.

Describing the Personal Selling Function

Because sales managers are responsible for managing the personal selling function, they must thoroughly understand it. This text therefore devotes a chapter to that subject before discussing sales management activities. Chapter 2 (Overview of Personal Selling) provides background information about the personal selling function with an emphasis on customer dialogue, value, and relationships. This discussion captures the key changes in personal selling being implemented by many companies. These changes have a direct impact on sales management activities as examined throughout the text.

FIGURE 1.2   **Sales Management Model**

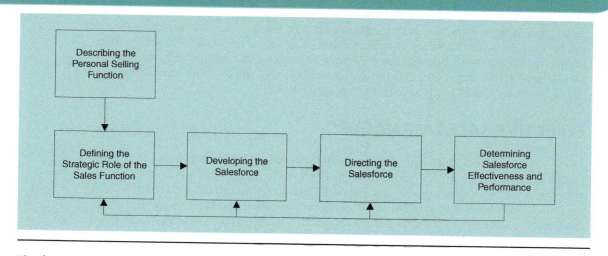

The four major stages of the sales management process and an understanding of personal selling are the focus of the book.

Defining the Strategic Role of the Sales Function

Many firms in the contemporary business world consist of collections of relatively autonomous business units that market multiple products to diverse customer groups. These multiple-business, multiple-product firms must develop and integrate strategic decisions at different organizational levels. Chapter 3 (Organizational Strategies and the Sales Function) discusses the key strategic decisions at the corporate, business, marketing, and sales levels and the basic relationships between these decisions and the personal selling and sales management functions. Corporate- and business-level strategic decisions typically provide guidelines within which sales managers and salespeople must operate. This is especially true for firms focusing on a CRM strategy. By contrast, personal selling is an important component of marketing strategies in specific product market situations. The role of personal selling in a given marketing strategy has direct and important implications for sales managers.

Strategic decisions at the corporate, business, and marketing levels must be translated into strategies for individual accounts. We discuss the major elements of a sales strategy: account targeting strategy, relationship strategy, selling strategy, and sales channel strategy. Because personal selling is typically important in organizational marketing situations, we provide an explanation of organizational buyer behavior as a foundation for the development of sales strategies.

Sales strategies are designed for individual accounts or groups of similar accounts. Therefore, an account targeting strategy is needed to identify and classify accounts into useful categories. Then, the type of relationship, the desired selling approach, and the most productive mix of sales channels are determined for each account category. These decisions result in an integrated sales strategy for each targeted account and account group.

The development and integration of corporate, business, marketing, and sales strategies establishes the basic strategic direction for personal selling and sales management activities. However, an effective sales organization is necessary to implement these strategies successfully. Chapter 4 (Sales Organization Structure, Salesforce Deployment, and Forecasting) presents the basic concepts in designing an effective sales organization structure: specialization, centralization, span of control versus management levels, and line versus staff positions. Different decisions in any of these areas produce different sales organization structures. The appropriate structure for a firm depends on the specific characteristics of a given selling situation. If strategic account selling programs are used, specific attention must be directed toward determining the best organizational structure for serving these major accounts.

Closely related to sales organization decisions are decisions on the amount and allocation of selling effort. We present specific methods for making salesforce deployment decisions. Because the decisions on selling effort allocation, salesforce size, and territory design are interrelated, they should be addressed in an integrative manner. A number of different analytical approaches can assist in this endeavor, but "people" issues must also be considered.

Developing the Salesforce

The sales strategy, sales organization, and salesforce deployment decisions produce the basic structure for personal selling efforts and can be considered similar to the "machine" decisions in a production operation. Sales managers must also make a number of "people" decisions to ensure that the right types of salespeople are available and have the skills to operate the "machine" structure effectively and efficiently.

Chapter 5 (Acquiring Sales Talent: Recruitment and Selection) discusses the key activities involved in planning and carrying out salesforce recruitment and selection programs. These activities include determining the type of salespeople desired, identifying prospective salesperson candidates, and evaluating candidates to ensure that the best are hired. Legal and ethical issues are important considerations in the recruitment and selection process. The ramifications of this process for salespeople's subsequent adjustment to a new job (socialization) are also examined.

Chapter 6 (Continual Development of the Salesforce: Sales Training) emphasizes the need for continuous training of salespeople and the important role that sales managers play in this activity. The sales training process consists of assessing training needs, developing objectives, evaluating alternatives, designing the training program, carrying it out, and evaluating it. Sales managers face difficult decisions at each stage of the sales training process, because it is not only extremely important but also expensive, and there are many sales training alternatives available.

Directing the Salesforce

Hiring the best salespeople and providing them with the skills required for success is one thing; directing their efforts to meet sales organization goals and objectives is another. Sales managers spend a great deal of their time in motivating, supervising, and leading members of the salesforce.

Chapter 7 (Sales Leadership, Management, and Supervision) distinguishes between the leadership, management, and supervisory activities of a sales manager. *Leadership activities* focus on influencing salespeople through communication processes to attain specific goals and objectives. *Management activities* include all aspects of the sales management process, such as recruiting, selecting, and training salespeople. *Supervisory activities* are concerned with day-to-day control of the salesforce under routine operating conditions. Key issues and problems in sales leadership, management, and supervision are discussed.

Chapter 8 (Motivation and Reward System Management) presents several content and process theories of motivation that attempt to explain how individuals decide to spend effort on specific activities over extended periods of time. Sales managers can use these theories as a foundation for determining the best ways to get salespeople to spend the appropriate amount of time on the right activities over a period of time. These theories provide the basis for specific salesforce reward systems. Both compensation and non-compensation rewards are examined. The advantages and disadvantages of different compensation programs are investigated, as well as methods for sales expense reimbursement. Specific guidelines for developing and managing a salesforce reward system are suggested.

Determining Salesforce Effectiveness and Performance

Sales managers must continually monitor the progress of the salesforce to determine current effectiveness and performance. This is a difficult task, because these evaluations should address both the effectiveness of units within the sales organization and the performance of individual salespeople.

Chapter 9 (Evaluating the Effectiveness of the Organization) focuses on evaluating the effectiveness of sales organization units, such as territories, districts, regions, and zones. The *sales organization audit* is the most comprehensive approach for evaluating the effectiveness of the sales organization as a whole. Specific methods are presented for assessing the effectiveness of different sales organization units with regard to sales, costs, profitability, and productivity. Skill in using these analyses helps a sales manager to diagnose specific problems and develop solutions to them.

Chapter 10 (Evaluating the Performance of Salespeople) changes the focus to evaluating the performance of people, both as individuals and in groups. These performance evaluations are used for a variety of purposes by sales managers. Specific criteria to be evaluated and methods for providing the evaluative information are examined, and the use of this information in a diagnostic and problem-solving manner is described. A method for measuring salesperson job satisfaction, which is closely related to salesperson performance, is presented as well.

CHAPTER FORMAT

Sales Management: Analysis and Decision Making was written for students. Therefore, its aim is to provide comprehensive coverage of sales management in a manner that students will find interesting and readable. Each chapter blends recent research results with current sales management practice in a format designed to facilitate learning.

At the beginning of each chapter, "Objectives" highlight the basic material that the student can expect to learn. These learning objectives are helpful in reviewing chapters for future study. An opening vignette then illustrates many of the important ideas to be covered in the chapter, using examples of companies in various industries to illustrate the diversity and complexity of sales management. Most of the companies described in the vignettes are well known, and most of the situations represent real actions by these firms.

Key words in the body of each chapter are printed in bold letters, and figures and exhibits are used liberally to illustrate and amplify the discussion in the text. Every figure contains an explanation so that it can be understood without reference to the text.

Each chapter contains two boxed inserts entitled **Sales Management in the 21st Century.** The examples in both boxes have been provided specifically for this textbook by sales executives from various companies whom we recruited to serve as a **Sales Executive Panel.** To ensure that the textbook includes the latest practices from leading sales organizations, each executive was asked to provide specific examples of "best practices" in their company. Backgrounds of each executive are provided at the end of this chapter.

Sales managers are confronted with various ethical issues when performing their job activities. Many of these ethical issues are addressed in the **Ethical Dilemma** boxes that appear in the remaining chapters. You will be presented with realistic ethical situations faced by sales managers and asked to recommend appropriate courses of action.

A chapter summary is geared to the learning objectives presented at the beginning of the chapter. **Understanding Sales Management Terms** lists the key words that appear in bold throughout the chapter. **Developing Sales Management Knowledge** presents 10 questions to help you develop an understanding of important sales management issues and relationships. **Building Sales Management Skills** consists of exercises in which you can apply the sales management knowledge learned in the chapter. **Making Sales Management Decisions** includes two interesting case situations that allow you to make important sales management decisions. If you understand sales management terms, develop sales management knowledge, and build sales management skills, you will be prepared to make successful sales management decisions.

CONCLUDING STATEMENT

This brief overview of contemporary sales management and summary of the contents and format of *Sales Management: Analysis and Decision Making* set the stage for your journey into the dynamic and exciting world of sales management. This should be a valuable learning experience as well as an interesting journey. All the information contained in this textbook should prove very relevant to those of you who begin your career in personal selling and progress through the ranks of sales management.

SALES EXECUTIVE PANEL

Chris Aiken started with Pfizer Pharmaceuticals as a sales representative in San Angelo, Texas in 1991 and is currently a Senior Professional Healthcare Representative in Oklahoma City. His primary customer base includes primary care and specialty physicians as well as group and account management. In addition, he serves on a variety of advisory boards both on a regional and national basis with Pfizer. Chris has a B.B.A. in Marketing from Texas Tech University and an MBA from Oklahoma City University.

Kim Davenport is a Regional Business Director with Acordia Therapuetics. He leads a team of nine sales representatives who sell in the southwest United States. Kim has a B.S. in Marketing from Ball State University.

Darlene Keppler has been in the family business (Keppler Steel) for over 25 years. She is a senior account manager. She graduated from Hanover College (Indiana).

Eric Nall is District Sales Manager for Epic Industrial Equipment where he leads a team of nine salespeople marketing heavy industrial and manufacturing equipment in the central U.S. Eric has a B.F.A. in Graphic Design and an M.S. in Industrial and Systems Engineering from the University of Tennessee.

James Richardson is the Western Division Sales Director for Addvance Medical—a distributor of medical equipment and supplies selling to hospitals, healthcare practice groups, and medical centers. James leads a team of ten salespeople. He has a B.S. in biology from University of Texas and M.S. in Mechanical Engineering from University of Oklahoma.

Marty Robbins has been in the printing industry for over 20 years. He is the Marketing Process Manager at LabelTech Inc. Marty is a graduate of Ball State University.

Nathan Schmidt is a Senior Account Executive for PCE Insurance. He has over 10 years' experience in the insurance industry and over 15 years' experience overall. Nathan is a Marketing graduate from Indiana Wesleyan University.

John Schwepker is the Vice President of Sales for Abstrakt Marketing group, one of the fastest growing marketing companies in the country. He has a diverse background of working for Fortune 500 companies, privately held companies as well as being an entrepreneur. He earned a Bachelor's degree in Marketing at Southeast Missouri State University as well as an MBA from the University of Phoenix and has over two decades of Sales and Sales Management experience. John has been instrumental in helping Abstrakt grow by over 384% in the four years he has been there. John grew up in St. Charles, Missouri eventually moving to Los Angeles, CA to train for the Olympics and then back to St. Louis. John sold his imaging business in 2008, where he was the Vice President of Sales and Marketing to Cintas where he became the General Manager, then National Business Development Manager for the Document Imaging Division. John is now the Vice President of Executive Sales for Abstrakt Marketing Group responsible for growing all sales divisions within the organization. John resides in O'Fallon with his wife Sheila and their three children.

Troy Secchio has been in industrial sales for over 31 years. Currently, Troy is the Sr. Business Development Manager with Worldwide Protective Products, a manufacturer of high performance hand, arm and body protection. Throughout Troy's career he has provided leadership in key areas of sales and marketing, including management of national strategic sales, directing both inside and outside sales, and setting corporate sales strategy. His successful experience within account, people, and product management has honed his leadership skills, enabling him to develop relevant value propositions that truly impact customer relationships, through value-added results. Troy is an alumnus of the University of Texas at Arlington with a B.S. in Business Administration—Marketing.

Tom Simpson is Vice President and COO for Elite PS. He leads the sales operation efforts for the company which includes more than 20 direct sales and support staff. Tom has a B.S. in Telecommunications from Ball State University.

Marty Zucker is Regional Office Coffee Services Manager for W.B. Mason Office Products, the largest independent Office Supply Company in the United States. He is responsible for Coffee and Water Sales and Service for 30 locations in New Jersey, New York, Pennsylvania, Delaware, Ohio and Maryland. Marty's main focus is on increasing sales and margins while maintaining all the equipment in the field. Marty works very closely with manufacturers such as Keurig, Starbucks and Newco. Marty has been in the Office Products industry for 48 years. He has held such positions as Regional Vice President National Accounts, Midwest Region, Vice President/General Manager Chicago, Vice President Sales New York/New Jersey and Director of Operations for the Long Island Division. Marty studied marketing and business administration at the State University New York, Delhi.

Describing the Personal Selling Function

The chapter in Part 1 describes the personal selling function. A clear understanding of personal selling is essential to gain a proper perspective of the issues facing sales managers. Chapter 2 discusses the role of personal selling in marketing, including the significance of personal selling, types of sales jobs, and the key job roles fullfilled by salespeople. The trust-based relationship selling process, with a focus on understanding, creating and communicating, and continually increasing customer value, is illustrated. This includes a discussion of knowledge, skills, and trust-building as foundations of the selling process. Selling strategy and several personal selling approaches such as consultative selling are also discussed as part of trust-based relationship selling. The chapter discusses sales professionalism with key themes of complexity, collaboration, and accountability and concludes with career insights for future salespeople and sales managers.

OVERVIEW OF PERSONAL SELLING

OBJECTIVES

After completing this chapter, you should be able to

1. Describe the role of personal selling in marketing.

2. Discuss the key roles of salespeople as financial contributors, change agents, communications agents, and customer value agents.

3. Explain the trust-based relationship selling process and how it differs from transactional selling.

4. Understand the concept of selling strategy with its key elements of customer value and alternative personal selling approaches.

5. Explain adaptive selling and five alternative approaches to selling: stimulus response, mental states, problem solving, needs satisfaction, and consultative.

6. Discuss current trends in sales professionalism: complexity, collaboration, and accountability.

IS THE CUSTOMER MISSING FROM YOUR SALES PROCESS?

In sales, a primary principle of success is to put the customer first. In practice, however, many salespeople fall short.

"Often when we work with salespeople, they say, 'I already talk to customers about their needs and provide them with solutions,'" says Mike Moorman, a Managing Principal at ZS Associates. "The reality is that sales professionals are rarely doing these things as well as they need to be."

Consequently, these companies follow a sales process that reflects the way they want to sell, not how the customer prefers to buy. That's one reason why, when working with B2B sales teams to help them improve sales effectiveness and drive organic sales growth, ZS Associates uses the term "customer engagement process" instead of "sales process."

"We want to highlight the fact that sellers must always align their efforts with how the customer wants to buy," says Kelly Tousi, a Principal at ZS Associates. "It reminds our clients to consider how they'll provide value for buyers."

What does it look like when sales teams do a better job of understanding value? Consider the experience of one ZS Associates client, an industrial manufacturer that sells injection-molding equipment. ZS found that, while the salespeople at this company knew the technical attributes of the product, they did little to really understand their customers' needs.

Not until the client's competitors made significant inroads did the sales team recognize that the larger issue for its customers was managing overall cost of ownership and minimizing business risk. By reengineering the customer engagement process, the ZS client was able to determine and quantify how its unique solution best addressed these larger needs for each customer's situation. Increased profitable organic growth soon followed.

Clearly, identifying this level of value via a customer engagement process has many advantages, including an ability to win more deals and command higher prices. Tousi says that companies also put themselves in a much better position to win new business with less effort. "Some sales teams find that customers decide to work with them without soliciting bids from other companies," she says.

The biggest challenge related to adopting a customer engagement process isn't formulating the process itself, but rather a culture change. "The quality of the customer engagement process is important, of course," Tousi says. "But it's not nearly as important as getting the buy-in from the organization and getting salespeople to execute it consistently. There's more value in that consistent execution than people realize."

Moorman agrees. "The technical design of the customer engagement process is only 15 percent of the challenge," he says. "The real challenge is getting people to understand, embrace, and rigorously execute it."

Companies that form a small, early-experience group that develops and refines the process will have implementations that are more successful than those initiated by companies that take a top-down approach. Participants among such groups become advocates and develop convincing success stories. These stories help change the sales organization's understanding of what it means to align its selling behaviors with customer needs.

"I have a client currently going through this," says Tousi. "They've talked for 10 years about the need to engage differently with their customers. They chose to do an early-experience team, and this really helped bring the skeptics on board. We started to hear things like, 'I don't know why I've never taken this approach before. It really works.'"

It's important to note that many customer-engagement skills among salespeople are best developed via coaching, not training. "Value-based selling and solution selling are apprenticed skills," Moorman says. "You become good by practicing them and being coached by someone who understands them. Training has its place, but without good coaching to support customer engagement, you'll have a hard time driving adoption and effective execution."

Buyers today don't want information; they want insight. Ditching the pitch is a much-needed step toward winning more deals and achieving higher levels of customer satisfaction. The fact is, customers don't want to be "sold to." They prefer that sellers engage them instead.

"Customers who experience a powerful customer engagement process almost always comment on how different the process feels," Moorman says. "As one customer recently shared, 'I thought you were going to come here and tell me about your products, but we came to this meeting and you only talked about our needs. This has been great.'"

Source: Selling Power Editors, June 28, 2013.

THE ROLE OF PERSONAL SELLING IN MARKETING

Marketing is the activity, set of institutions, and processes for creating, communicating, delivering, and exchanging offerings that have value for customers, clients, partners, and society at large.[1] **Personal selling,** a crucial part of marketing, involves interpersonal communications between buyers and sellers to initiate, develop, and enhance customer relationships. In the best sales organizations, salespeople earn the trust of their customers and utilize selling strategies that satisfy customer needs. In such organizations, salespeople help create customer value and, over time, increase the value delivered to customers.

The Significance of Personal Selling

Personal selling has always been an important part of marketing, particularly for companies that operate in business-to-business markets where purchasing situations often involve complex technical products, large dollar amounts, professional buyers, and

Selected Companies with Large Salesforces EXHIBIT 2.1		
Company	**Industry Sector**	**Approximate Number of Salespeople**
PepsiCo	Consumer Goods	36,000
American Express	Financial Services	23,400
AT&T	Communications	25,000
Microsoft	Computer & Office Equipment	16,000
Xerox	Computer & Office Equipment	15,000
IBM	Computer & Office Equipment	14,000
Citigroup	Financial Services	12,700
Johnson & Johnson	Medical Products	8,500
Pfizer	Pharmaceuticals	7,600

multiple parties who influence purchase decisions. The importance of personal selling is reflected in the numbers of salespeople employed by major companies as shown in Exhibit 2.1.[2] Consumer goods companies such as Coca-Cola, Procter & Gamble, and PepsiCo rely heavily on advertising and sales promotion to boost sales at the retail level. But these companies also have huge salesforces that sell to retailers, wholesalers, and other channel intermediaries. As shown in Exhibit 2.1, for example, PepsiCo has 36,000 salespeople.

In terms of money spent, personal selling is the most important part of marketing communications, especially in business-to-business markets. The general public is accustomed to seeing salespeople in some sectors, including retailing, automotive, real estate, insurance and financial services, and service organizations that serve the ultimate consumer. In the business-to-business arena, however, salespeople's significant contributions to marketing go largely unnoticed by the general public. Business purchases far exceed those in consumer markets, with wholesalers, retailers, government agencies, manufacturers, homebuilders, professional services firms, transportation providers, and schools and hospitals being among key customers in the business market.

Types of Sales Jobs

There is considerable variety among sales jobs, with distinctions sometimes made according to what is sold (products vs. services, industrial vs. consumer) or to whom the product is sold (e.g., ultimate consumers, manufacturers, resellers, institutions, the government). Sales jobs can also be classified according to the relative emphasis placed on gaining new customers versus servicing existing customers. Salespeople who focus on gaining new customers are sometimes referred to as **hunters, pioneers,** and **order-getters**. These salespeople increase market share for their companies by adding new customers. These new customers may subsequently be turned over to account-servicing salespeople referred to as **farmers** and *order-takers*. This latter category of salespeople try to increase sales as they build customer share, that is, they seek to improve the seller's position within each account.

Some salespeople are not responsible for making the actual sale, but support the sales effort by providing information and performing other supplemental services. For example, **missionary salespeople** support the overall sales effort by "spreading the gospel" at the grassroots level. An example of this in the pharmaceutical industry is the **detailer**, a salesperson who provides physicians, nurses, and other medical professionals with pertinent information about drugs to support the overall sales effort. In the retail sector, **merchandisers** support the sales effort by setting up point-of-purchase displays, rotating stock, and keeping store personnel informed about new products and sales promotions.

In many companies, salespeople combine these roles in a single job. For example, the national accounts salespeople for Tyco Integrated Security, a multinational company, are expected to contact and secure major new business and maintain existing business at a rate consistent with Tyco's strategic business plan. National accounts salespeople at Tyco also do sales support work such as providing current market information to their employer and attending trade shows and other customer events. In this case, the Tyco salesperson is a hunter for new business, a farmer, or cultivator, of existing business, and also fulfills a sales support role.[3] As a reference point for this book, when we use the term *salesperson*, we are typically referring to a business-to-business combination salesperson that has new business, existing business, and sales support responsibilities. It should also be noted that some salespeople work as part of a sales team. Team selling is discussed in Chapter 3.

Key Roles of Salespeople

To make their investment in personal selling pay off, companies expect a lot from their sales organizations. The expectations of salespeople can be viewed as achieving four key roles: financial contributor, change agent, communications agent, and customer value agent. Salespeople are important **financial contributors** to their organizations as they assume a key role in revenue production. An emphasis on achieving profit goals, i.e., a healthy bottom line, is well known in business. To support the bottom line, salespeople are expected to achieve revenue goals or a healthy "top line" on the profit and loss statement. Most salespeople are charged with specific dollar goals or quotas, and their job performance and compensation are typically tied closely to whether or not they achieve these revenue goals. While sales organizations are expected to achieve overall revenue targets, they are also increasingly being held accountable for improving overall profitability by enhancing sales organization productivity.

Salespeople are also expected to act as **change agents** as they stimulate sales cycles and help customers reach buying decisions as soon as reasonably possible. In this sense, salespeople are catalytic agents, that is, when they are added to the economic process, their role is to make something happen. More specifically, they are expected to educate potential customers and advance toward an ultimate sale. In their change agent role, salespeople are heavily involved in the diffusion of innovation, which frequently leads to improved quality of life for consumers and improved business practices. The change agent role can also positively impact economic cycles, assisting in recovery from slow economic periods and extending periods of relative prosperity.

Another key role fulfilled by salespeople is that of **communications agent**. Basic economics holds that information has utility, and the value of information is widely recognized in the business world. Salespeople are heavily involved as two-way communications agents between their customers and their employers. Customers depend on salespeople for their knowledge of products and services, as well as developments in the marketplace. Sales organizations typically rely on their salespeople to be the eyes and ears of the company, reporting back to the company on competitive activity, buyer preferences, and ideas for new products. Despite the possibility that such communications activities could take away from selling time, most companies find it extremely beneficial to rely on the salesforce to provide valuable information back to the company. Sales organizations consolidate market information from individual salespeople to get a larger picture about competitive activity across the entire market area. Thus it is important that salespeople are careful to report information accurately and in a timely fashion. See "An Ethical Dilemma" for a scenario in which the salesperson must think about upselling at the request of their sales manager.

The fourth key role fulfilled by salespeople is that of **customer value agent**, with salespeople helping to create, communicate, deliver, and continually increase customer value. **Customer value** previously discussed in Chapter 1, depends on the buyer's situations, needs, and priorities, but essentially it can be defined as the customer's perception of what they receive (e.g., products, services, information) in exchange for what they give up (e.g., time, effort, and money). Customer value is determined in part by product/service capabilities and the support given by the sales organization to the customer. In addition, salespeople's expertise and behaviors can

AN ETHICAL DILEMMA

Tom Carey sells corporate sponsorship packages for the South Bend Racers, a minor league hockey team in Northwest Indiana. The packages include advertising in game programs throughout the 30-game home season, LCD signage in the arena, and a block of season tickets. The packages range in price from $2,000 to $10,000, depending on the size of the ads and signs, and how many season tickets are included. Tom's sales manager is pushing the sales team to sell as many $5,000 and $10,000 packages as possible. Tom tries to match the sponsorships package to the budget and needs of each potential customer rather than pushing the $10,000 packages. Tom stated to a fellow Racer salesperson, "Let's face it, we are South Bend. There are not that many companies in South Bend that can afford our $10,000 package. We are not the Chicago market."

His sales manager is not happy and told Tom, "You need to get with the program and sell more of the $10,000 packages. You are leaving money on the table selling all of these $2,000 packages. The $10,000 packages are a good deal for sponsors. What's the matter, don't you believe in your product?"

What should Tom do?

a. Listen to his boss and sell the $5,000 and $10,000 packages.
b. Continue to sell each package that is a good fit for the customers budget.
c. Talk to his boss about a compromise.

also be an important dimension of customer value. Salespeople can add to or detract from customer value depending on criteria such as:

- Customer and market knowledge: is the salesperson knowledgeable about the customer's business, competition, and market conditions?
- Coordination: does the salesperson coordinate with others in their company to solve customer problems or provide opportunities to the customer?
- Efficiency: is time spent with this salesperson worthwhile, and can he or she get things done?
- Strategic alignment: does the salesperson understand and contribute to achieving the customer's strategic priorities?
- Trustworthiness: can the salesperson be trusted, i.e., is this person competent, customer-oriented, honest, dependable and compatible with customers?

TRUST-BASED RELATIONSHIP SELLING PROCESS

The sales process shown in Figure 2.1 is representative of sales processes that are customer-oriented. It is not representative of sales approaches that advocate putting pressure on the customer to "say yes" rather than truly satisfy the customer's needs. The latter approaches to selling are referred to as **transactional selling**. With transactional selling, salespeople focus on maximizing the outcomes of individual transactions rather than on longer-term relationships with customers. Put another away, transactional salespeople try to make a sale on every call, have little regard for the customer's unique needs or priorities, and typically are not very engaged in the service aspects that follow the sale. Transactional selling focuses more on one-way sales presentations, often called sales pitches, in which the salesperson strives to persuade the buyer to make an immediate purchase. These sales pitches vary little from customer to customer, and salespeople are not particularly interested in seeking feedback from buyers during their sales calls.

In contrast to transactional selling, **trust-based relationship selling**, as shown in Figure 2.1, seeks to initiate, develop, and enhance long-term customer relationships by

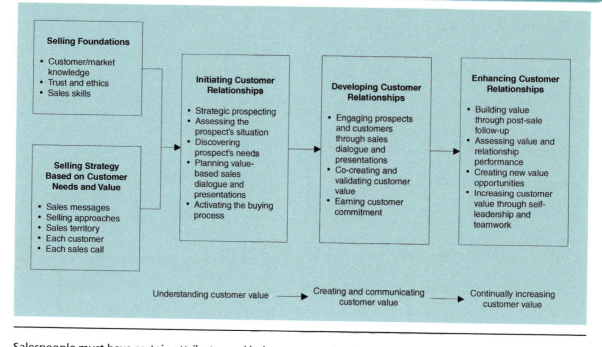

FIGURE 2.1   Trust-Based Relationship Selling Process

Salespeople must have certain attributes and behave appropriately to inspire trust in their customers and they must be able to adapt their selling strategies to the situation. One or more personal selling approaches are used in the sales process. The major phases in the sales process are initiating, developing, and enhancing customer relationships. Salespeople must understand, help create and communicate, and continually increase customer value during the sales process.

earning customer trust, focusing on customer needs, and having the salesperson play a key role in building the value received by the customer. With trust-based relationship selling, salespeople rely on questioning and listening to establish dialogue with customers. With this approach, communications between buyers and sellers are much more two-way and collaborative than with the transactional approach.

Selling Foundations: Knowledge, Skills, and Trust-Building

As shown in Figure 2.1, the trust-based sales process requires salespeople with the right knowledge and skills who employ an ethical, trust-building approach to selling. This process also requires salespeople whose actions are based on strategies that focus on customer needs and customer value.

Sales Knowledge and Skills

The particular knowledge and skill components required for successful selling will be somewhat dependent on the sales situation. For example, technical products typically require a different knowledge and skill base than would be necessary for selling simple products and selling to government buyers is different from selling to retailers. Despite situational differences, there are some skill and knowledge areas that are commonly required for success in a broad range of sales jobs. Salespeople must understand their customers, including what motivates their customers to make purchases and customer purchasing processes and protocols. They should be experts on their products and services, and be able to link the features (facts and specifications) and benefits (what those features do for their customers) of their offerings to buyer motives. Salespeople also need to be knowledgeable about their competitors and developments in the marketplace.

Specific skills that are important in the sales process include listening, questioning, sales dialogue skills, and sales presentation skills. Listening and questioning go hand in hand and are extremely important in understanding the buyer's viewpoint and determining their unique needs. Questioning methodologies such as SPIN (to be discussed later) and ADAPT are helpful to salespeople in determining relevant questions that can ultimately lead to productive interactions with buyers. The ADAPT method suggests that questions should be used to *A*ssess the buyer's situation, *D*iscover the buyer's needs, *A*ctivate the buying process, *P*roject the impact of solving a problem or realizing an opportunity, and make a *T*ransition to the sales presentation or the next step in the buying process.[4] One purpose of the ADAPT method is to develop an efficient, relevant line of questioning that will help both the salesperson and the buyer find common ground for sales dialogue and sales presentations.

In addition to questioning and listening, salespeople must have sales presentation and sales dialogue skills. The term *sales presentation* is traditionally used to describe the face-to-face interactions between buyers and sellers. The term implies more information flowing from the salesperson, though buyers certainly participate during most sales presentations. Key presentation skills include explaining the features and benefits of the product, producing additional information to reinforce claims made, using audiovisual sales aides, and, in some cases, demonstrating the product.

Sales presentation skills remain essential for salespeople, but **sales dialogue** skills are also important for an increasing number of salespeople. Sales dialogue involves business conversations that take place over time as salespeople attempt to initiate, develop, and enhance relationships with customers. Common sales dialogues include:

- determining if a prospective customer has the financial resources and an adequate interest in making a future purchase to warrant additional follow-up
- assessing the prospective customer's situation and buying processes
- discovering the prospective customer's specific needs and requirements
- confirming the prospective customer's strategic priorities
- illustrating how the sales organization can create and deliver customer value
- negotiating an agreement to do business
- building customer value by providing additional opportunities
- assessing the extent to which the customer is satisfied with the value received

These and other business conversations comprising sales dialogue should be driven by a clear purpose and should be customer-focused. Otherwise, time can be wasted, something both buyer and sellers would like to avoid. Sales dialogue features a back-and-forth, two-way conversation between buyers and sellers, with both parties benefiting from their participation.

Trust-Building as a Sales Foundation

To be successful at **trust-building** with their customers, research indicates that salespeople should demonstrate five key attributes: customer orientation, competence or expertise, dependability, candor or honesty, and compatibility.[5] Carew International, a leading sales training and consulting company, understands the importance of trust-building. Noting that business relationships seek mutual benefit, profits, efficiency, and growth for both buyers and sellers, Carew emphatically states that the foundation for these beneficial relationships is trust. Carew urges salespeople to demonstrate on a daily basis a firm commitment to doing the right thing. According to Carew, the right thing is a multidimensional concept, with telling the truth, being reliable, and dedication to the customer's well-being as key sales behaviors.[6] It is important to note that salespeople's trustworthiness and overall reputation is easily shared within buyers' networks of professional acquaintances. With communications technology making salespeople's actions more transparent, being trustworthy is more important than ever for sales success.

A **customer orientation** can be demonstrated through certain behaviors such as determining the buyer's unique needs before recommending a purchase, preventing and correcting problems, and sincere listening during sales calls. HR Chally, a large, widely respected sales consulting and training organization, has studied customer expectations of salespeople. The Chally findings reflect a strong customer orientation, as customers report that they appreciate salespeople who:

- are personally accountable for the customer's desired results
- understand the customer's business
- will be an advocate for the customer so the customer receives maximum value from the selling company
- will be a business consultant who thinks beyond the current transaction
- will solve customer problems
- will be creative in responding to customer needs[7]
- will be easily accessible

Having a strong customer orientation is necessary to build trust, but it is not enough. **Salesperson competence**, or expertise, is another important dimension required to build customer trust. While most customers will give new salespeople a little time to come up to speed, they rightfully expect salespeople to know what they are doing and to get answers if they don't already know the answer. In any interpersonal relationship, whether it is in the business world or not, **candor**, or honesty, is essential. Should a customer find that his or her salesperson has been dishonest, the relationship is likely ruined, perhaps never to be resurrected. **Dependability**, another important trust-builder, should be the easiest to achieve for all salespeople. It is as simple as doing what you say you will do. Yet many salespeople fail on this dimension by over-promising and under-delivering or simply forgetting to fulfill an obligation such as getting back to a customer with requested information by a specified time. Finally, **customer compatibility** can help build trust. Compatibility is less about the personal dynamics between buyers and sellers than it is about the salesperson being viewed as a good person to do business with. While some personal characteristics, e.g., pleasant personality and a positive attitude, can enhance compatibility, professionalism and making it easy for the customer to do business with the selling firm also determine compatibility. While we say that it is not necessary for a customer to like a salesperson in order to trust the salesperson, it is harder to trust someone whom one dislikes.

In addition to consistently exhibiting trust-building behaviors, it is important that salespeople be aware of pertinent laws and potentially troublesome ethical pitfalls. Some suggestions for playing it safe from an ethical and legal perspective are shown in Exhibit 2.2.

Selling Strategy

Selling strategy involves the planning of sales messages and interactions with customers. Selling strategy can be defined at three levels: for a group of customers, i.e., a sales territory; for individual customers; and for specific customer encounters, referred to as sales calls. Variations in selling strategy across these three levels are tied largely to how much alteration there is in sales messages at the territory, customer, and sales call levels and the extent to which unique customer needs and customer value are factored into these sales messages.

Personal Selling Approaches

Salespeople can use one or more personal selling approaches to interact with their customers. As shown in Figure 2.2, these approaches vary according to how much

Ethical and Legal Guidelines   EXHIBIT 2.2

1. Adhere to sales organization and company codes of ethics and codes of conduct.
2. Be truthful. Use facts and be able to substantiate performance claims made for products and services.
3. Accurately depict competitors. Do not disparage competitors.
4. Obtain competitive information only through ethical and legal means.
5. Be aware of and obey relevant laws and regulations, including local laws.
6. Do not create false expectations by over-promising. Remember that promises and verbal agreements can be as binding as a written contract.
7. Ensure that customers are aware of stipulations for proper usage of products and any safety issues and limitations.
8. Observe the need for confidentiality with sensitive information provided by customers and employers.
9. Avoid conflicts of interests, or even the appearance of conflicts of interests.
10. Avoid discussions with competitors that deal with pricing, profit margins, bids or intent to bid, terms of sale, discounts, promotional allowances, sales territories or markets to be served, and the rejection or termination of customers.
11. Do not make the purchase of one product a condition of making another product available to customers.
12. If selling to competing retailers or competing wholesalers who are buying similar quantities of like products, ensure a level playing field in terms of prices, terms of sale, and promotional support offered.
13. Be aware of and comply with customer codes of ethics, purchasing protocol and guidelines.
14. Report unethical and illegal activities to supervisors, and, if appropriate, to law enforcement and regulatory personnel.

salespeople adapt their messages from customer to customer, and the extent to which the sales message is based on unique buyer needs, customer value, and the customer's strategic priorities. The five personal selling approaches shown in Figure 2.2 are: stimulus response; mental states; problem solving; need satisfaction, and consultative selling.[8]

Since personal selling involves interpersonal communication, salespeople can practice **adaptive selling**, which means they can modify their sales messages and behaviors during a sales presentation or as they encounter unique sales situations and customers. Because salespeople often encounter buyers with different personalities, communications styles, and needs and goals, adaptive selling is an important concept. With adaptive selling, the salesperson could use one or more of the selling approaches shown in Figure 2.2 or could develop hybrid selling approaches that draw from the illustrated approaches.

Stimulus Response Selling

Of the five selling approaches shown in Figure 2.2, **stimulus response selling** is the least flexible and least focused on the buyer's unique needs and strategic priorities. With only minor variations, all customers get the same sales presentation. The logic behind stimulus response selling comes from lab experiments with animal behavior in which various stimuli would elicit desired behavior. Extended into the sales context, salespeople using this approach furnish the stimuli (words and actions) to produce the desired response (a customer purchase). Stimulus response selling is the dominant approach used by telemarketing salespeople, who work from a script or use a memorized canned sales presentation.

Buyers, especially professional buyers, do not like stimulus response sales approaches. Most buyers like to take an active role in the sales interaction, and stimulus response selling calls for the salesperson to do most of the talking. Further, buyers may have difficulty getting the information they want unless their questions and concerns fit the preplanned script. Should questions go unanswered, a positive purchase decision is unlikely.

FIGURE 2.2   Personal Selling Approaches

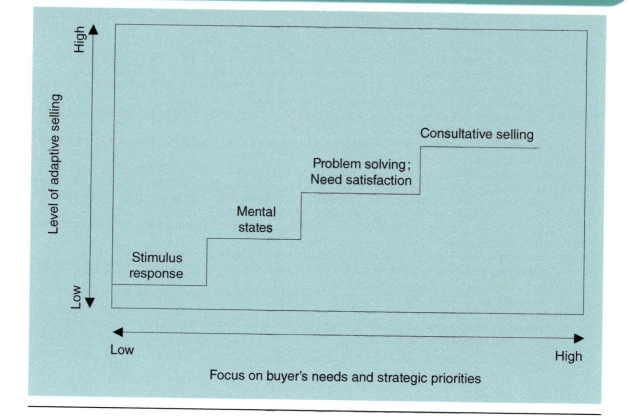

The five personal selling approaches are stimulus response, mental states, problem solving, need satisfaction, and consultative. These approaches vary according to how much the sales message focuses on unique customer needs and strategic priorities, and the level of adaptive selling from one customer to the next.

Stimulus response sales strategies offer some advantages to sellers. Through preplanning, key selling points can be sequenced in a logical order and likely questions and objections can be addressed before they are voiced by the buyer. Inexperienced salespeople may be able to use stimulus response approaches in some situations, and this experience may ultimately build more sophisticated sales expertise. Stimulus response methods can also be an efficient sales approach, as evidenced by the large telemarketing industry.

Considering the net effects of this method's advantages and disadvantages, it appears most suitable for relatively unimportant purchase decisions, when time is severely constrained and when professional buyers are not the prospects. Stimulus response methods are also more effective when the sales proposition is narrowly defined, as in the case of selling a single product rather than introducing an entire product line.

Mental States Selling

Mental states selling is essentially a sequential approach to selling in which the salesperson leads the customer through stages, or mental states, in the buying process. Commonly expressed as AIDA, the prescribed sequence is that the salesperson must first get the prospective customer's Attention, then secure their Interest, build the prospect's Desire for the product, and then convince the prospect to take Action by making a purchase. This approach to selling assumes that most buyers think alike and that salespeople can indeed lead buyers through the steps in the buying process. As buying decisions have become more complex, and multiple parties are often involved on the buying side, this assumption is frequently invalid.

Like stimulus response selling, the mental states approach is largely a one-way presentation with the salesperson doing most of the talking. Therefore, this method is not customer-oriented. Any tailoring of the sales presentation to individual customers is based on which mental state the customer is in, rather than particular customer needs or requirements. Further, it may be difficult for the salesperson to determine which stage a customer is in, or the customer may be moving back and forth through stages. Thus, the structure provided by the salesperson may be inappropriate and ineffective.

On the positive side, this method does force some pre-planning by the salesperson, who comes to realize that timing is an important aspect of the purchase process. Salespeople using this method are listening to the customer to determine what stage they are in. As the salesperson listens, it is highly likely that he or she will realize that a more customer-oriented approach is in order if customer needs are to be met. See "An Ethical Dilemma" for a situation in which the salesperson is contemplating the movement of the prospect into the "action" stage.

AN ETHICAL DILEMMA

Rhonda Thompson sells advertising for her college newspaper. One of her potential clients is contemplating buying an ad for an upcoming special issue featuring tanning salons, apartment complexes, bars, and restaurants. Over the past month, Rhonda has tried unsuccessfully to get a commitment from one of the newer restaurant owners to place an ad. Her sales manager has suggested that Rhonda call the prospect and tell him that there is only one remaining ad space in the special issue, and that she must have an immediate answer to ensure that the prospect's ad will appear in the special issue. The sales manager said, "Rhonda, this guy is stalling. You've got to move him to action, and this technique will do the trick. A gentle nudge never hurt anyone." Rhonda was troubled by her manager's advice since this special issue had plenty of ad space remaining. What should Rhonda do?

a. Follow her sales manager's advice.
b. Tell her client the truth, there is no hurry and plenty of ad space is available.
c. Talk to her sales manager about her ethical standards and this strategy does not fit in with how she likes to do business.

Need Satisfaction Selling

The logic of **need satisfaction selling** is that customers will be motivated to buy to satisfy particular needs. Salespeople using this method help customers identify their needs if customers are not already aware of their needs, and then sell customers products and services to meet the needs. In contrast to the stimulus response and mental states methods, need satisfaction selling focuses on the customer. Salespeople use questions to uncover buyer needs, and the customer typically dominates the sales interaction until needs have been established. At that point, the salesperson moves to a more active selling role, describing how his or her offering can satisfy the buyer's needs.

Customers appreciate this approach to selling, as they feel that their point of view and unique circumstances are being addressed. Although it may take a fair amount of time to fully define customer needs, both customers and salespeople think this is often time well spent, especially if a major purchase is pending. Also, this sales approach can minimize the resistance from the prospect that sometimes surfaces when a salesperson rushes to the persuasive part of the sales message without adequate attention to the buyer's needs. Just as it is when we visit our doctor, we appreciate diagnosis before prescription.

Problem-Solving Selling

Problem-solving selling extends need satisfaction selling beyond identifying needs to developing alternative solutions for satisfying these needs. This approach has been popularized by the commercial success of **SPIN selling**, conceived by Neil Rackham.[9] With SPIN selling, the salesperson investigates the customer's *Situation*, determines a *Problem*, discusses the *Implications* of the problem if it is left unattended, and shows how the salesperson's offering can solve the problem (*Need payoff*). An important reality for salespeople using problem-solving selling in a business world with competing priorities and limited resources is that not all customer problems are worth solving—at least in the short term. To be effective, the SPIN method and other problem-solving approaches typically require that salespeople clearly illustrate the significance of the existing problem and how the customer can receive significant customer value from the problem solution.

Consultative Selling

Consultative selling is the process of helping customers reach their strategic goals by using the products, services, and expertise of the sales organization.[10] Consultant Mack Hanan is credited with introducing the concept of consultative selling to the business world in 1970. In his most recent book on the topic, Hanan distinguishes between consultative sellers and suppliers or vendors by stating that "no matter what vendor suppliers make, they sell it; no matter what consultative sellers make, they sell the value that it adds."[11] Consultative selling requires that the salesperson be an expert on the customer's business, competitors, and market developments. This expertise ultimately puts the salesperson in a consultant, or advisor role, in which educating the customer is an important activity.

Consultative selling has become a popular approach across many industries, as indicated by job postings on employment Web sites. A recent review of a recent review of the popular job posting site www.indeed.com revealed more than 8,000 jobs in which consultative selling was specified as a key job activity. Hiring companies included FedEx, Microsoft, T-Mobile, Amtel, LLC, AT&T, and Liberty Mutual.[12]

Consultative selling is differentiated from other sales approaches because it focuses on achieving strategic goals of customers. A consultative process may also solve customer problems, meet customer needs, and provide additional customer opportunities. But unless the process is focused on strategic priorities of the customer, it is not truly a consultative process.

To illustrate consultative selling, consider how Wal-Mart screens out potential suppliers. Before a company has an opportunity to attempt to sell to Wal-Mart, it must answer key questions that would require some knowledge of Wal-Mart's strategic priorities. For example, one question is: "How can Wal-Mart gain market share with your product and, at the same time, control the cost of doing business to maximize sales?" Gaining market share and controlling costs have been and continue to be strategic priorities for Wal-Mart, facts that are readily available from annual reports, press releases, and other sources.

Consultative selling often requires that the salesperson be a coordinator, arranging for others in the selling company to play a role in the sales process. For example, logistics and manufacturing personnel might lend their expertise at the request of a software salesperson to help redesign the customer's supply chain. In this example, the customer might purchase the software for use in its supply chain, while the redesign of the supply chain helps the customer achieve a strategic priority of cutting overall operating expenses. The importance of consultative salespeople working with others within their own companies to create customer value is evident to Randall Murphy of Acclivus R3, a consulting firm whose clients include IBM, Shell, and Verizon. Mr. Murphy notes that it takes a high level of business expertise to practice consultative selling, and that salespeople and the sales organization typically need additional expertise and proactive support from coworkers and top management to succeed with a consultative approach. Mr. Murphy counsels sales managers to get buy-in from all-important parties within their own companies before implementing consultative selling.[13]

Consultative sellers must also commit to being partners with their customer over a long-time horizon rather than being focused on making short-term sales. Such a commitment means that the sales organization must also be committed to the consultative selling approach and design its salesperson performance evaluation and reward systems accordingly. Consultative selling is not appropriate for all sales situations. Some customers are not interested in such a collaborative approach and may not wish to share their strategic priorities with sellers. Some products, including many commodities, are purchased more on price basis. In such cases, unless value can be defined beyond price considerations, consultative selling is likely to be an inefficient sales approach. For more on consultative selling, see "Sales Management in the 21st Century: Consultative Selling."

SALES MANAGEMENT IN THE 21ST CENTURY

Consultative Selling

Nathan Schmidt, senior account executive for PCE Insurance, comments on consultative selling in commercial insurance markets.

My role as a strategic orchestrator is critical in consultative selling. The salesperson is at the hub of the interaction between sales, product management, marketing, underwriting and claims. At the point of impact with the customer, salespeople represent our combined expertise as a company and are expected to add to the customer's value equation.

The value of our salespeople is identified more by the information they gather from customers *than the information they dispense. We strive to be more than vendors to our customers. We want to be their trusted advisors. To accomplish trusted advisor status, we constantly focus on improving our efficiency and effectiveness so we can maximize customer value.*

If one of our clients has a disaster, everything must be in place for a smooth recovery. If a client's warehouse burns down, they trust me and my company will be there to handle all the challenges they are about to face. That is the real satisfaction in my job.

CURRENT TRENDS IN SALES PROFESSIONALISM

The current emphasis on **sales professionalism** has been widely embraced by progressive sales organizations, professional groups, sales consultants, educators, and sales trainers. The term has various meanings, but common elements of sales professionalism include the use of customer-oriented, truthful, non-manipulative sales strategies and tactics to satisfy the long-term needs of customers and the selling firm. Sales professionalism also requires that salespeople work from a dynamic, ever-changing knowledge base. New products, technologies, and market developments require a dedication to career-long learning to avoid obsolescence. There is an old saying that applies in this case: "If you think you have figured out the permanent formula for success, you are probably one step away from becoming obsolete."

As we look to the future of the sales profession, three key themes are evident. Sales organizations, including salespeople, sales managers, and sales executives must be:

- Capable of working in an increasingly complex business environment;
- Strong collaborators, both within their own organizations and with their customers;
- Accountable for their actions and results from an ethical and fiscal responsibility point of view.[14]

DHL Global Forwarding (DGF), an international airfreight company with headquarters in Bonn, Germany, typifies a successful sales organization dealing with complexity, collaboration, and accountability. DGF's 8,000 salespeople in the company's 850 branches deal with complex logistical projects in industrial settings across the globe. To remain competitive in a highly competitive marketplace, DGF invests heavily in sales training for different sales roles in 13 languages. A virtual team of 105 sales trainers work with the global salesforce to certify salespeople as specialists in international logistical operations. DFG's training utilizes a wide variety of delivery mechanisms, including online self-paced learning, classroom sessions, and sales management review sessions. Sales training is reinforced through newsletters, online magazines, video and email messages, and internal competitions inspire continual learning. Cigdem Wondergem, global head of sales training, received an international award from industry executives for her innovative sales training programs. To win the award, Ms. Wondergem exemplified the ability to deal with complexity, accountability, and collaboration. The CEO of DHL specifically praised Ms. Wondergem's strengths in communication and collaboration as keys to the successful sales training program.[15] For some of the key changes and salesforce responses related to the themes of complexity, collaboration, and accountability, see Exhibit 2.3.

EXHIBIT 2.3   Current Trends in Sales Professionalism: Complexity, Collaboration, and Accountability

Complexity Issues	Salesforce Responses
Increasing customer expectations driven by buyer dominance, slow-growth economies, and increasing competition	Focus on the customer; use salespeople to monitor market developments; emphasize trust-based, long-term customer relationships
Significant change occurring more frequently, e.g., sales technology advancing rapidly, markets often in a state of flux	Sales must become more strategic; sales organizations must become learning organizations; complement initial training with ongoing sales training; use sales specialists for specific customer types; develop multiple sales channels such as major accounts programs and electronic networks
Increasing customer diversity and globalization	Recruiting and developing salespeople who understand diverse cultures, languages, and business practices

Collaboration Issues	Salesforce Responses
More internal collaboration needed between sales, marketing, and other functional units	Implement cross-functional programs to foster communication and cooperation
Sales managers and salespeople need to collaborate more, rather than sales managers relying on authority to direct the salesforce	Sales managers should build trust with salespeople; ensure that salespeople know how to manage themselves and play a leadership role when required
Need for more customer-oriented selling	Focus on trust-based relationship selling; train salespeople in problem solving, conflict resolution, and how to recover from service failures

Accountability Issues	Salesforce Responses
Increasing the efficiency and effectiveness of sales operations	Appropriate use of sales technology; lower-cost contact methods, e.g., telemarketing for some customers; implementing more effective sales organization structures
Customer demands for ethical, trustworthy salespeople	Ensure that salespeople know the ethical and legal framework for their markets, including cultural and global market variations

Sources: Thomas N. Ingram, "Future Themes in Sales and Sales Management: Complexity, Collaboration, and Accountability," *Journal of Marketing Theory and Practice* (Fall 2004): 1–11; Thomas N. Ingram, Raymond W. LaForge, William B. Locander, Scott B. MacKenzie, and Philip M. Podsakoff, "New Directions in Sales Leadership Research," *Journal of Personal Selling & Sales Management* 25 (Spring 2005): 137–154.

Complexity

The business environment is becoming more complex, and, for sales organizations, increasing complexity is particularly acute. This is because sales organizations operate across organizational boundaries, working with customers and typically facing numerous competitors. Further, technology advances, growing dominance of large buyers such as Wal-Mart, slow-growth economies in much of the world, and increasing globalization and diversity in the customer base all contribute to a more complex sales environment. To succeed in such a complex setting, sales organizations must focus on the customer and strive for more trust-based, long-term relationships. Sales must become a "smarter" business function, meaning that sales strategy becomes more important. As will be discussed in Chapter 3, this often means developing new sales channels, or ways of reaching customers. To keep abreast of an ever-changing environment, sales organizations must become continual learning organizations and recruit salespeople who can adapt to diverse cultures, languages, and business practices.

Collaboration

The sales function is finding it increasingly important to collaborate with other functional areas within their companies and with customers. Within their own companies, the need for sales to integrate and cooperate more with production, finance, and marketing is getting a lot of attention in the business world. In particular, the importance of better alignment between sales and marketing is widely acknowledged as indicated by the American Marketing Association's training seminars on the topic. To improve collaboration between sales and marketing, the two parties should agree on critical customer issues such as identification of customer segments and the related needs, buying motives, purchasing processes, and relevant value dimensions within those segments.[16] Clearly, this need for more collaboration should be addressed by cross-functional training and communications programs.

Greater collaboration is also needed between sales managers and salespeople, and sales managers should strive to earn the trust of their salespeople rather than over-relying on the authority provided by their supervisory position. With customers, collaboration should extend the concept of customer-oriented selling to include problem solving and involving the salesforce in recovering from service problems that may arise. For more about the importance of collaboration, see "Sales Management in the 21st Century: The Importance of Teamwork."

SALES MANAGEMENT IN THE 21ST CENTURY

The Importance of Teamwork

Kim Davenport, Regional Business Director, Acordia Therapeutics, Inc., offers his perspective on Teamwork:

Our salespeople are the closest people to our customers. In the pharmaceutical field a lot of things must come together to get the right information and samples to our doctors. I believe the salespeople who are most effective long term are also an effective team player—he or she realizes they need coordinated involvement from many different areas of our organization in order to better serve the customer.

Our sales training philosophy stresses this team aspect: we tell our salespeople that they make the engine run, but they also need the rest of the car to get the job done.

Accountability

More than ever, sales organizations are being scrutinized under a sharp lens. The scrutiny focuses on two areas: ethics and fiscal responsibility. We have spoken at length in this chapter about the need for ethical, trustworthy salespeople. Companies and salespeople who do not practice ethical selling are increasingly subject to extreme criticism, customer dissatisfaction, and in some cases, legal sanctions.

Some of the current focus on sales ethics comes from unethical sales behavior. As an example, the Do Not Call restrictions imposed on telemarketers by the Federal Trade Commission were implemented primarily because unscrupulous sales organizations were acting contrary to the tenets of sales professionalism. Putting it bluntly, the incorporation of sales professionalism into an organization's sales practices is good business. To do otherwise puts the sales organization into a vulnerable position that may lead to its demise.

As we pointed out early in this chapter, the sales function represents a substantial investment for many firms. In the past, the sales function was more concerned about generating sales revenue than the costs of generating that revenue. Things have changed, and most sales managers and executives, along with an increasing number of salespeople, are being held accountable not only for achieving revenue targets, but doing so at a reasonable cost. The proper utilization of technology, careful travel planning, and control of other direct selling costs is definitely part of most sales managers' and salespeople's job.

SALES CAREER INSIGHTS

Since this is a college textbook, a few comments about sales careers are in order. Professional selling offers excellent career opportunities, and the U.S. Department of Labor projects growth over the next decade in the total number of salespeople in all industry categories. For many newly minted college graduates, professional selling is one of the most popular entry-level jobs. In larger companies, some new hires will make a career in sales and sales management and others will branch out into other areas, including marketing management and general management.

For new college graduates, starting in sales can be an attractive opportunity. The pay is good and can rapidly become great for those who excel, because pay is closely tied to performance in selling. In the early years of their careers, salespeople become experts on their company's products, competitive offerings, and customer behavior. They learn to work independently and as a team member while sharpening their communications skills and problem-solving skills. All of this helps prepare young salespeople for management positions should they want to move in that direction.

One of the most important elements of leadership is persuading others to your point of view, and salespeople are involved in persuasive communications on a daily basis. Further, running a sales territory has some parallels with running your own company in terms of achieving measurable outcomes, meeting obligations to others, and being accountable from a perspective that blends ethics and profitable business practices. For the many young people who aspire to be entrepreneurs, selling experience can be indispensable. Entrepreneurs spend a lifetime selling their ideas to others, including investors, resellers, and customers.

On a daily basis, salespeople encounter a great deal of variety in their jobs, calling on different customers, perhaps selling different products depending on the situation, and facing ever-changing competitive activities. Salespeople rarely complain about job boredom, as the variety and fast pace in most sales jobs make the job challenging rather than boring. Salespeople constantly know how they are doing in terms of job performance, as they are getting immediate feedback on every sales call. They play a critical role for their customers and their employers, so there is some pressure to perform at an acceptable level.

Like most professions, a key to success in sales and sales management is how well an individual is suited to a particular job. For those interested in learning more about sales careers, there are a variety of ways to proceed. Visit with professional salespeople and sales managers. Check out professional organizations such as the Sales Management Association (www.salesmanagement.org) and publications such as *Sales and Marketing Management* (www.salesandmarketing.com) and *Selling Power* (www.sellingpower. com). Read the free materials of leading sales training and consulting firms such as HR Chally (www.chally.com), Forum (www.forum.com), and Miller Heiman (www.miller heiman.com). Become familiar with a variety of sales positions and requirements of sales job applicants from university career centers and employment listing services such as Indeed (www.indeed.com). In addition, there are excellent books on professional selling available through university libraries and commercial bookstores for those who want to explore various dimensions of selling and sales management.

SUMMARY

1. **Describe the role of personal selling in marketing.** Personal selling involves interpersonal communications between buyers and sellers to initiate, develop, and enhance customer relationships. It is widely used in consumer goods companies, and plays an especially critical role in business-to-business markets. More money is spent on personal selling than any other form of marketing communications, including advertising and sales promotion. Some salespeople, referred to as hunters, pioneers, and order-getters, focus more on building market share with new customers, while others (e.g., missionary salespeople, detailers, and merchandisers) focus more on selling to existing customers. In many companies, salespeople have a combination of responsibilities to attract new customers, enhance relationships with existing customers, and perform some service activities to support the overall sales effort.

2. **Discuss the key roles of salespeople as financial contributors, change agents, communications agents, and customer value agents.** Salespeople perform a key role by making sales and thus generating revenue for their employers. Increasingly, salespeople are also expected to contribute to the bottom line by being more productive with their sales activities. Salespeople are change agents, meaning, when added to the process, they are expected to make positive things happen. In this role, salespeople facilitate diffusion of innovation and improved business practices. As communications agents, salespeople are involved in the two-way flow of information between their customers and their employer. Salespeople do more than communicate customer value. They can be part of customer value by impacting the value received by the customer. Salespeople can also be an important element in delivering increasing levels of customer value by providing additional opportunities to customers and by solving problems and providing ongoing service to their customers.

3. **Explain the trust-based relationship selling process and how it differs from transactional selling.** Transactional selling is focused more on the seller's desire to make an immediate sale than it is on the customer's needs and strategic priorities. Trust-based relationship selling, as shown in Figure 2.1, seeks to initiate, develop, and enhance customer relationships by earning customer trust, focusing on customer needs, and having the salesperson play a key role in building the value received by the customer. Communications with this approach are much more two-way and collaborative than with the transactional approach.

4. **Understand the concept of selling strategy with its key elements of customer value and alternative personal selling approaches.** Selling strategy involves the planning of sales messages and interaction with customers. Customer value is defined differently by different customers, but essentially it is what the customer gets (products, services, solutions) for what the customer gives up (typically time and money).

Selling strategies can be set for a group of customers or for a specific customer. In addition, selling strategies can vary from one sales call to the next as salespeople engage in sales dialogue with their customers. In developing selling strategies, salespeople may use various approaches as illustrated in Figure 2.2.

5. **Explain adaptive selling and five alternative approaches to selling: stimulus response, mental states, problem solving, need satisfaction, and consultative.** Adaptive selling takes place when salespeople modify their sales messages and behaviors during sales presentations and sales dialogues, or when they encounter unique sales situations and customers. Adaptive selling might draw from one or more of the basic approaches to personal selling, or the adaptive salesperson might develop a unique selling approach in a given sales situation. The approaches to personal selling shown in Figure 2.2 range from stimulus response (not focused on unique customer needs or strategic priorities, not adaptive) to consultative selling (high on both customer focus and level of adaptive selling). Between these two extremes, other approaches to selling are mental states, problem solving, and need satisfaction selling.

6. **Discuss current trends in sales professionalism: complexity, collaboration, and accountability.** The business world is becoming more complex, as indicated by increasing buyer expectations, slow-growth economies, and increasing levels of competitive activity. Significant change is occurring more frequently, and customers are increasingly diverse and global in their operation and perspectives. As a result, salesforces must focus on the customer and seek to build trust-based, long-term relationships. The sales function is becoming more strategic, and recruiting and training salespeople with the capacity to learn is important for success. More collaboration is needed within the selling company and with customers to ensure future success. More customer-oriented selling is required and salespeople should be trained in problem solving, conflict resolution, and how to recover from service failure. Salesforces are being held more accountable now than in the past. Accountability is important from efficiency/effectiveness and ethics/trust-building perspectives. Sales organizations are using new technologies, process improvements, and alternative sales organization structures to become more efficient and effective. Sales training on ethical and legal frameworks is recommended.

UNDERSTANDING SALES MANAGEMENT TERMS

personal selling
hunters
pioneers
order-getters
farmers
order-takers
missionary salespeople
detailer
merchandiser
financial contributor
change agent
communications agent
customer value agent
customer value
transactional selling
trust-based relationship selling
ADAPT

sales dialogue
trust-building
customer orientation
salesperson competence
candor
dependability
customer compatibility
selling strategy
adaptive selling
stimulus response selling
mental states selling
need satisfaction selling
problem-solving selling
SPIN selling
consultative selling
sales professionalism

DEVELOPING SALES MANAGEMENT KNOWLEDGE

1. Personal selling is especially critical for companies that sell to other businesses. Does this mean that personal selling is unimportant to retailers and others who sell directly to ultimate consumers?

2. Fielding a large salesforce is an expensive proposition. In terms of the key roles fulfilled by salespeople, how do companies make this investment pay off?

3. What is customer value? How can salespeople add to the value received by customers?

4. Review the five approaches to personal selling in Figure 2.2. Which of the five approaches require strong listening and questioning skills? Which of the five approaches would require sales dialogue?

5. How can salespeople earn the trust of their customers?

6. Explain how the ADAPT and SPIN questioning methods can be used in the sales process. How are the two methods similar? How are they different?

7. What is adaptive selling? Can a salesperson practice consultative selling without practicing adaptive selling?

8. How does consultative selling differ from problem-solving selling?

9. When do you think stimulus response selling would be most effective?

10. In consultative selling, how important is collaboration with the customer and within the sales organization?

BUILDING SALES MANAGEMENT SKILLS

1. Successful salespeople and sales managers must continue to learn about their profession, especially trends and best practices. One way to learn about new developments is to monitor leading sales training and consulting firms. Visit the following Web sites and develop a listing of the 10 ideas or trends that you think are particularly useful for improving the performance of a sales organization. The Web sites are:

   - HR Chally, www.chally.com
   - Forum Corporation, www.forum.com
   - Miller Heiman, www.millerheiman.com

2. Most entrepreneurs take on an active role in selling their ideas, products, and services to investors, customers, and future employees. However, many entrepreneurs have no prior sales experience and thus can benefit from learning about the sales process. *Entrepreneur Magazine* provides a free service through their Web site at www.entrepreneur.com with advice in virtually all business areas, including sales. From the home page, click on the video link, then browse by topic and click on the "Marketing link". Select one of the articles you think a sales manager might use to lead a discussion on buying or selling with their sales team. Be prepared to share your findings in a class discussion.

ROLE PLAY

3. **Role-Play**
   Situation: Review the ADAPT questioning method on p. 23.

   Characters: One student is the seller, and one student is the potential buyer.

   Scene: As the seller, you are trying to determine if one of your classmates has any unmet needs or problems with their cell phone or smart phone. Use ADAPT questions prepared in advance to see if your classmate would consider switching to another phone, coverage plan, or data plan. Afterwards, the buyer and seller should critique the seller's performance and discuss how thoughtful questions can be useful in the sales process. Repeat the exercise with the roles reversed.

ROLE PLAY

4. **Role-Play**

Situation: Review the ethical and legal guidelines in Exhibit 2.2.

Characters: One sales manager and one salesperson for ABC, an athletic shoe manufacturer that sells to sporting goods retailers.

Scene: The salesperson is a good performer in terms of meeting sales quotas, but the sales manager is concerned about some the salesperson's behaviors. Specifically, the salesperson sometimes makes promises that cannot be kept. Second, the salesperson tends to exaggerate the market growth and potential profitability of ABC's products when trying to secure new accounts. Role play a meeting in which the sales manager coaches the salesperson to take a trust-based approach to selling. The salesperson sees no harm in his/her current approach and sincerely believes that stretching the truth helps increase sales. Afterwards, discuss the pros and cons of trust-based selling in a competitive environment.

MAKING SALES MANAGEMENT DECISIONS

CASE 2.1: JORDAN WHOLESALE MARKETPLACE

Background

Jordan Wholesale Marketplace was founded in Los Angeles in 1965 to supply professional catering companies with a wide variety of institutional food products, including canned vegetables and meats. The company had grown steadily over the decades, and is now one of the largest full-service institutional food suppliers in the nation, selling perishable and non-perishable foods and foodservice supplies such as tablecloths, napkins, and tableware. In the past year, Jordan Wholesale Marketplace had begun an aggressive push into a new market segment, the hotel/motel restaurant market.

Current Situation

Tom Olivia is the Jordan Wholesale sales representative in Louisville, KY. Tom has been with the company for almost two years. He is a recent college graduate and looks forward to proving himself in his sales position, then moving into management with the company. Tom's sales manager, Grace Lamkin, has told Tom that if he finishes the year over 100 percent on his sales versus quota target that he would enter the pool of candidates for promotion sometime in the following 12 months. Tom is doing quite well with his existing accounts, and has added a couple of new accounts. He believes that he will finish the year a little over 100 percent of quota, but he needs to add some of the new hotel/motel business to be sure he achieves his sales goals.

Tom has been attempting to secure the restaurant business of Best Night Inn, a regional chain of 16 moderately priced motels in Kentucky. Best Night's corporate headquarters are in Louisville and the chain currently buys all of its food and restaurant supplies from Wick's Food Supply, a well-established wholesale restaurant supplier. Wick's has its own salesforce, most of whom are veteran salespeople who have established good relationships with the restaurant operators in their sales territories.

Jordan Wholesale has not been a supplier for Wick's for more than 10 years. Tom has been told that Jordan Wholesale and Wick's had some friction over service problems, with Wick's head buyer claiming that Jordan Wholesale was not a reliable supplier. The buyer reportedly withheld partial payment on several invoices, and ultimately Jordan Wholesale refused to sell to Wick's. Tom and the Jordan Wholesale sales representative who preceded him had tried to get reestablished with Wick's, but Wick's buyers had steadfastly refused to buy from Jordan Wholesale.

Tom was determined to get the Best Night Inn's business, so he made sales calls on the 16 motels to gauge their interest in switching to Good Food Wholesalers, another foodservice wholesaler with whom Tom had a strong working relationship. The Best Night operators were unanimous—they had no intention of leaving Wick's for Good Food Wholesalers. In making the rounds to the 16 motels, Tom learned that the individual hotel managers had no authority to buy from suppliers that had not been previously approved by their corporate headquarters in Louisville. Tom then called on Best Night's corporate headquarters, where he learned that becoming an approved supplier would take a minimum of 60 days—if approval was granted. Best Night's director of purchasing was frank with Tom, telling him: "We have been extremely satisfied with Wick's, and don't see much need to add Good Food Wholesalers to the list of approved suppliers. If I were in your shoes, I would try to sell through Wick's."

Tom went back to Wick's, trying once again to become one of their suppliers. He decided to use a foot-in-the-door strategy, meaning that he would only try to sell one small part of his product line, with hopes that if this proved to be successful, he would be able to expand his sales through Wick's. Tom presented the newest version of Jordan Wholesale, a very attractive tablecloth/napkin package that could be customized with Best Night's logo. Bill Wilson, the Wick's buyer, turned Tom down, saying, "Tom, don't take this personally, but we simply are not ready to do business with Jordan Wholesale again. You guys are doing some impressive things in the marketplace, and next year we may get together with you. But that's not in the plan for this year."

Disappointed, Tom felt he had but one choice if he wanted to make his year-end numbers. He arranged sales calls with the three Good Food Wholesalers sales representatives who called on Best Night Inns. Tom planned to work with the Good Food Wholesalers salespeople to present the Jordan Wholesale packages, cut the price to stimulate interest, and try to convince all 16 of the Best Night operators to buy the packages from Good Food Wholesalers. If the motel operators liked the packages, Tom figured he could use their interest to speed up the supplier approval process back at Best Night's headquarters and book the additional sales volume before year-end.

It was now Friday night, and Tom was heading home. It had been a tough week, and he was looking forward to the weekend. The Wick's situation with Best Night had not gone the way he hoped it would, but now that he had decided what to do, he was feeling better. Tom did not like to lose, and as he drove home, more than once he thought, "I'll show Wick's. If you don't play ball with me, I'll take the business through Good Food Wholesalers." Tom planned to call Grace Lamkin over the weekend and run the plan by her. Next week, he planned on hitting all of the Best Night Inns with the Good Food Wholesalers salespeople.

Questions

1. How likely is it that Tom Olivia will be successful in the short term with this strategy?
2. What are the longer-run implications of this strategy for Tom Olivia and Jordan Wholesale Marketplace?
3. If you were Grace Lamkin, what advice would you give Tom?

Role Play

Situation: Read Case 2.1.

Characters: Tom Olivia, Jordan Wholesale Marketplace sales representative; Grace Lamkin, Jordan Wholesale Marketplace sales manager.

Scene: *Location*—Tom and Grace talk on the phone on Saturday morning. *Action*—Grace expresses some concerns about Tom's plans for gaining the Best Night Inn business. She thinks that it is important that Jordan Wholesale Marketplace rekindle its relationship with Wick's and feels that Tom's plan could have a major negative impact on any chance of doing business with Wick's in the future. Tom is focused on making his numbers and thinks that Grace is unfairly holding him back.

ROLE PLAY

Upon completion of the role play, address these questions:

1. With an existing customer (Good Food Wholesalers) and two potential customers (wholesaler Wick's and end user Best Night Inn), how would you assess Tom's focus? Is it customer-oriented? Is it based on delivering customer value?
2. Assume that Tom proceeds with his plan to call on Best Night Inn with the Good Food Wholesalers salespeople. Would this preclude

any chance that he would be able to sell to Wick's in the future?

CASE 2.2: BURGAUER BUSINESS COMPUTERS

Background

Burgauer Business Computers (BBC) is a 20-year-old company operating throughout the United States, providing large retail customers with handheld computers and proprietary software to support the retail sales effort. The basic idea is that BBC works with electronics and home improvement retailers to store information that help retail salespeople as they attempt to make or facilitate sales in the store. Typical information includes product availability, specifications and technical information, pricing, product reviews and comparisons, and installation guidance when appropriate.

Current Situation

Olivia Hartsell is a major accounts representative for BBC, serving five states in the Midwest. She is responsible for sales to multi-store electronics retail chains that are headquartered in Illinois, Indiana, Ohio, Wisconsin, and Michigan. Olivia is responsible for securing new retail customers, upgrading and reselling to existing customers, and working with technical support personnel to ensure smooth installation and ongoing operations in the retail stores.

A month ago, Olivia heard about an interesting new sales opportunity. Brighter Office, a Web-based office supply retailer, had announced plans to build five stores in Illinois and Michigan over the next 18 months. In addition to office supplies, computers, and furniture, Brighter Office announced that its stores would move aggressively into several consumer electronics categories, including televisions and related audio-video items. BBC had not previously sold to office supply retailers, but Olivia had been given the go-ahead to pursue the Brighter Office account.

Olivia moved quickly to set up introductory meetings with several Brighter Office executives to explore the possible use of BBC handheld computers by Brighter Office salespeople. Over the course of two weeks, she met with Jim Denver, director of purchasing, MaryAnn Eden, director of management information systems, Bob Porter, director of retail sales operations, and Kirk Wolfe, chief financial officer. After meeting with these four people individually, she met with them together in an hour-long session to be sure that she fully understood what Brighter Office hoped to achieve with the electronics category and what they expected if a decision was made to utilize handheld computers as a retails sales tool.

Following the meeting, Olivia made some notes about her impressions of the key players from Brighter Office:

- Jim Denver, director of purchasing—Jim is the key contact person and was helpful in setting up the group meeting. He will not have much to say about the go or no-go decision on handhelds, but he will expect prompt delivery and installation, mistake-free billing, and reassurances before the sale that BBC will be a reliable source of supply.

- MaryAnn Eden, director of management information systems—she will be very influential in making the go or no-go decision and selecting a supplier if it is a go. She is an information technology expert and seemed rather impatient when other Brighter Office personnel expressed opinions about how the handhelds should be utilized. In particular, MaryAnn wants all the information stored on the corporate server and have it accessible on a password-protected portion of the Brighter Office home page. The handheld computers would be used only to access the Brighter Office home page. She thinks that handheld may be an unnecessary expense, and thinks that the retail sales associates can access the Brighter Office home page from a small number of stationary computers located in scattered positions in the stores.

- Bob Porter, director of retail sales operations—Bob couldn't care less about the details of the handheld technology, and he was quick to point out that he needed to know how these "gadgets" would increase sales and customer satisfaction. He seemed worried that retail operations would be charged for the expense of the handhelds and he is very interested in the payback. In a nutshell, will the handhelds be a worthwhile investment? He is somewhat concerned that, if Brighter Office does not go with the handhelds, the company may be perceived as lagging in technology.

- Kirk Wolfe, chief financial officer—hard to read him. He said very little during the meetings and would not reveal whether Brighter Office had a budget allocated for handhelds, or even a general category for retail sales support. He gave no indication if a lease arrangement might be a possibility if an outright purchase was not feasible.

Questions

1. What additional information does Olivia Hartsell need before she can attempt to make the sale to Brighter Office?

2. Using the ADAPT questioning method discussed in this chapter, develop 5–7 questions for the first two stages—A (assess the buyer's situation) and D (discover the buyer's needs)—that could be directed to MaryAnn Eden and Bob Porter. Note that there may be some questions that would be appropriate for both Eden and Porter, but some unique questions for Eden and Porter would definitely be appropriate.

Role Play

Situation: Read Case 2.2.   **ROLE PLAY**

Characters: Olivia Hartsell, BBC sales representative; MaryAnn Eden, Brighter Office director of management information systems.

Scene 1:   *Location*—MaryAnn Eden's office. *Action*—Using the questions previously developed for question 2, Olivia Hartsell tries to learn more about MaryAnn Eden's situation and her particular needs.

Scene 2:   *Location*—Bob Porter's office. *Action*—Using the questions previously developed for question 2, Olivia Hartsell tries to learn more about Bob Porter's situation and his particular needs.

Upon completion of the role play, answer these questions:

1. Did the Olivia Hartsell character adequately assess the situation and determine the buyer's needs for both MaryAnn Eden and Bob Porter?

2. What should Olivia Hartsell try to accomplish in her next sales calls on Brighter Office?

Defining the Strategic Role of the Sales Function

The two chapters in Part 2 discuss the sales function from a strategic perspective. Chapter 3 investigates strategic decisions at different levels in multibusiness, multiproduct firms. The key elements of corporate strategy, business strategy, marketing strategy, and sales strategy are described, and important relationships between each strategy level and the sales function are identified. Special attention is directed toward the role of personal selling in a marketing strategy and sales strategy development. Account targeting strategy, relationship strategy, selling strategy, and sales channel strategy are the key elements of a sales strategy.

Chapter 4 emphasizes the importance of sales organization design and sales-force deployment in successfully executing organizational strategies. The concepts of specialization, centralization, span of control, management levels, and line/staff positions are critical considerations in sales organization design. Special attention is directed toward the use of different sales organization structures in different selling environments. Salesforce deployment decisions include allocating selling effort to accounts, determining the appropriate salesforce size, and designing sales territories. The key considerations and analytical approaches for each of these decisions are discussed.

ORGANIZATIONAL STRATEGIES AND THE SALES FUNCTION

OBJECTIVES

After completing this chapter, you should be able to

1. Define the strategy levels for multibusiness, multiproduct firms.

2. Discuss how corporate and business strategy decisions affect the sales function.

3. List the advantages and disadvantages of personal selling as a marketing communications tool.

4. Specify the situations in which personal selling is typically emphasized in a marketing strategy.

5. Describe ways that personal selling, advertising, and other tools can be blended into effective integrated marketing communications programs.

6. Discuss the important concepts behind organizational buyer behavior.

7. Define an account targeting strategy.

8. Explain the different types of relationship strategies.

9. Discuss the importance of different selling strategies.

10. Describe the advantages and disadvantages of different sales channel strategies.

FIVE STRATEGIES FOR TRANSFORMING TO A BEST-IN-CLASS SALES ORGANIZATION

In a recent survey of more than 330 leading sales organizations, Aberdeen Group asked business leaders about what business pressures keep them awake at night. Not surprisingly, the number one issue is delivering revenue growth in increasingly competitive environments with lengthening sales cycles.

During these surveys, Aberdeen Group also gathered detailed performance metrics to rank the surveyed organizations in terms of overall corporate performance – identifying the key differentiated behaviors of best-in-class organizations (the top 20 percent of aggregate corporate performance scores). What strategies have worked for these high-performing organizations?

STRATEGY #1: USE CUSTOMER ENGAGEMENT DATA

The average sales cycle for best-in-class sales teams is 16 percent shorter than that of underperformers. The secret? For many, it's using analytics to track sales content effectiveness.

Top performers are three times more likely to use analytics to improve the quality of marketing content and overall sales effectiveness. In fact, best-in-class sales organizations are 1.2 times more likely than other organizations to have and use customer engagement data. With data-driven insights, reps can engage prospects with intelligence instead of guesswork—and course-correct in real time.

STRATEGY #2: IDENTIFY WHAT WORKS – AND MAKE SURE REPS REPEAT IT

Research by Sirius Decisions found that 65 percent of content created for sellers never gets used. Best-in-class organizations ensure marketing content resonates with customers—and doesn't got to waste. They ensure reps can quickly find and leverage content proven to be successful in closing deals, with 62 percent maintaining a central library of marketing-approved assets for different selling situations.

Best-in-class sales organizations are also 15 percent more likely than underperformers to use a formal selling methodology to identify optimal messaging and timing at each stage of the sales cycle—and 1.4 times more likely to align marketing content with specific stages of the sales cycle.

STRATEGY #3: PROVIDE ANYTIME-ANYWHERE-ANY-DEVICE ACCESS TO SALES CONTENT

The bottom line: Mobile access to sales content makes sales teams more productive and effective. Best-in-class organizations that provide mobile access to sales content achieve 2.75 times more reductions in their sales cycle than all other organizations. Their reps are also twice as likely to achieve their quotas.

STRATEGY #4: GIVE YOUR SELLERS MORE TIME TO SELL

Consider how much time your sales reps typically spend on administrative tasks, data entry, and searching for information when they could be selling. So it's no wonder that, according to an Accenture and CSO Insights sales performance optimization study, sales reps spend only 35 percent of their time interacting with customers.

As mentioned in Strategy #2 above, top-performing sales organizations make accessing and using effective marketing content faster and easier. Most of these organizations also maintain a central library of marketing—approved assets for different selling situations—and allow sales reps to customize for specific customers. Going even further, Aberdeen Group found that personalizing sales presentations with prepared content improved lead conversion by 1.3 times.

STRATEGY #5: KNOW WHEN TO WALK AWAY

Best-in-class organizations are better at prioritizing leads – and are 14 times more likely to walk away from deals unlikely to close. By making faster decisions to disqualify dead-end deals, sales reps can devote more time and energy to pursuing the most promising opportunities.

To learn more about these and other strategies employed by best-in-class sales organizations, view the webinar from Aberdeen Group and ClearSlide or download the white paper: "Transforming the Business of Selling" (www.sellingpower.com/2016/08/18/10537/five-strategies-for-transforming-to-a-best-in-class-sales-organization).

Source: Meera Mehta, *Selling Power* magazine (August 18, 2016).

The Aberdeen Group surveyed organizations in terms of overall corporate performance. The goal was to identify the key differentiated behaviors of best-in-class sales organizations and what strategies have worked for those high-performing organizations.

Customer driven data must be shared throughout the different levels of the organization. As Sirius Decision found, 65 percent of content created for sellers never gets used. From a strategic standpoint has the sales training department been included in the loop to train on using the content that has been created. Many firms consist of multiple business units that sell multiple products to different customer groups.

However, the strategies must be consistent with each other and integrated for the firm to perform successfully. We now examine the key strategic decisions at each organizational level and highlight the impact of these strategic decisions on the sales organization.

ORGANIZATIONAL STRATEGY LEVELS

The key strategy levels for multibusiness, multiproduct firms are presented in Exhibit 3.1. **Corporate strategy** consists of decisions that determine the mission, business portfoio, and future growth directions for the entire corporate entity. A separate **business strategy** must be developed for each **strategic business unit (SBU)** (discussed later in this chapter) in the corporate family, defining how that SBU plans to compete effectively within its industry. Because an SBU typically consists of multiple products serving different markets, each product/market combination requires a specific **marketing strategy.** Each marketing strategy includes the selection of target market segments and the development of a marketing mix to serve each target market. A key consideration is the role that personal selling will play in the marketing communications mix for a particular marketing strategy.

The corporate, business, and marketing strategies represent strategy development from the perspective of different levels within an organization. Although sales management may have some influence on the decisions made at each level, the key decision makers are typically from higher management levels outside the sales function. Sales management does, however, play the key role in sales strategy development. An example of one approach for strategy development at different organizational levels is presented in "Sales Management in the 21st Century: Integrating Organizational Strategy throughout Each Business Unit."

CORPORATE STRATEGY AND THE SALES FUNCTION

Strategic decisions at the topmost level of multibusiness, multiproduct firms determine the corporate strategy for a given firm, which is what provides direction and guidance for activities at all organizational levels. Developing a corporate strategy requires the following steps:

1. Analyzing the corporate situation to identify potential opportunities and threats

2. Determining corporate mission and objectives

Organizational Strategy Levels   EXHIBIT 3.1

Strategy Level	Key Decision Areas	Key Decision Makers
Corporate strategy	Corporate mission Strategic business unit definition Strategic business unit objectives	Corporate management
Business strategy	Strategy types Strategy execution	Business unit management
Marketing strategy	Target market selection Marketing mix development Integrated marketing communications	Marketing management
Sales strategy	Account targeting strategy Relationship strategy Selling strategy Sales channel strategy	Sales management

3. Defining strategic business units

4. Setting objectives and resource allocations for each strategic business unit

Once the corporate strategy has been developed, management is concerned with implementation, evaluation, and control of the corporate strategic plan. Although the corporate strategy has the most direct impact on business-level operations, each element does affect the sales function.

Corporate Mission

The development of a **corporate mission statement** is an important first step in the strategy formulation process. This mission statement provides direction for strategy development and execution throughout the organization. Sales managers and salespeople must operate within the guidelines presented in the corporate mission statement. Furthermore, they can use these corporate guidelines as a basis for establishing specific policies for the entire sales organization. Thus, in this way, the corporate mission statement has a direct effect on sales management activities.

Despite its importance, it has been estimated that only about 20 percent of companies have a clear mission statement that is articulated to salespeople by sales managers. The most successful corporate mission statements are simple, complete, and communicated directly to salespeople. Siebel Systems changed its mission statement to "Make one hundred percent customer satisfaction Siebel's overriding priority." This simplified version expressed the company's values succinctly and was easy for the salespeople to understand and adopt.[1]

Definition of Strategic Business Units

Defining strategic business units, often called SBUs, is an important and difficult aspect of corporate strategy development. The basic purpose is to divide the corporation into parts to facilitate strategic analysis and planning. An SBU is a designated unit within a corporation that operates like an individual business. SBUs typically consist of a single product or line of related products marketed to defined market segments. Most SBUs include all of the basic business functions with managers responsible for the performance of each function and the SBU. Some functions, however, might be provided at the corporate level and shared across SBUs. For example, centralizing parts of the purchasing function at the corporate level is a trend in many companies. Thus, an SBU usually has its own sales organization with sales managers and salespeople.

The definition of SBUs is an important element of corporate strategy. An example of defining strategy broadly to apply to all the operations of a corporation is presented in "Sales Management in the 21st Century: Integrating Organizational Strategies." Changes in SBU definition may increase or decrease the number of SBUs, and these changes typically affect the sales function in many ways. Salesforces may have to be merged, new salesforces may have to be established, or existing salesforces may have to be reorganized to perform different activities. These changes may affect all sales management activities from the type of salespeople to be hired to how they should be trained, motivated, compensated, and supervised.

Restructuring at General Electric (GE) provides a typical example. GE had considered lighting and appliances to be separate SBUs. The company, however, decided it could cut costs and better focus sales resources by combining lighting and appliances into a new business unit called GE Consumer Products. Except for some financial services at GE Capital Corp., all of the products GE sold to consumers were now included in GE Consumer Products. This change gave the GE sales organization more leverage in the consumer marketplace and increased the productivity of selling resources.[2] For example, Home Depot carried GE appliances, but not GE light bulbs. Wal-Mart sold many GE light bulbs, but few GE appliances. Because the same salesperson now sold both appliances and light bulbs, selling costs were reduced and the opportunity to get Home Depot to carry GE light bulbs and Wal-Mart to sell more GE appliances was increased.[3]

Integrating Organizational Strategies

Marty Robbins, marketing process manager at LabelTech, discusses the importance of integrating strategies at different levels in a company:

It is extremely important for large companies to develop effective strategies at different organizational levels. We focus a lot of attention on this process at LabelTech. The corporate strategy defines business units and determines strategic objectives and basic resource allocations for each business unit. Then, each business strategy will achieve its objectives. Next, another rigorous process is used to develop specific marketing strategies for the business unit's product/markets. Finally, strategies for selling to specific customer groups within each product/market are determined. This type of sequential process is intended to develop effective and consistent strategies at each organizational level.

Objectives for Strategic Business Units

Once SBUs have been defined, corporate management must determine appropriate strategic objectives for each. Many firms view their SBUs collectively as a portfolio of business units. Each business unit faces a different competitive situation and plays a different role in the **business unit portfolio.** Therefore, specific strategic objectives should be determined for each SBU. Corporate management has ultimate responsibility for establishing strategic objectives for each SBU. As illustrated in Exhibit 3.2, the strategic objective assigned to a business unit has a direct effect on resource allocations, as well as personal selling and sales management activities.

Determining strategic objectives for each SBU is an important aspect of corporate strategy. These strategic objectives affect the development of the sales organization's objectives, the selling tasks performed by salespeople, and the activities of sales managers. All sales organization policies are designed to help salespeople achieve the business unit strategic objective. However, too much emphasis on business unit objectives can place salespeople in uncomfortable situations, as illustrated in "An Ethical Dilemma."

SBU Objectives and the Sales Organization   EXHIBIT 3.2

SBU Objectives	Sales Organization Objectives	Primary Sales Tasks	Recommended Compensation
Build market share	Increase sales volume Expand distribution	Get new accounts Increase sales to existing accounts	Salary plus sales-based incentives
Hold market share	Maintain sales volume	Maintain sales to current accounts Replace lost sales with new accounts	Salary plus commission and/or bonus
Harvest market share	Reduce selling costs Target profitable accounts	Service most profitable accounts Eliminate unprofitable accounts Reduce service levels Reduce inventory	Salary plus profit-based incentives
Divest/liquidate market share	Minimize selling costs and clear out inventory	Dump inventory Eliminate service	Salary

Corporate Strategy Summary

Strategic decisions at the topmost levels of multibusiness corporations provide guidance for strategy development at all lower organizational levels. Even though the sales function is often far removed from the corporate level, corporate strategy has direct and indirect impacts on personal selling and sales management. The corporate mission, definition of SBUs, and determination of SBU objectives all affect sales organization operations. However, corporate strategy decisions have their most immediate impact on business unit strategies.

BUSINESS STRATEGY AND THE SALES FUNCTION

Whereas corporate strategy addresses decisions across business units, a separate strategy must be designed for each SBU. The essence of business strategy is competitive advantage: How can each SBU compete successfully against competitive products and services? What differential advantage will each SBU try to exploit in the marketplace? What can each SBU do better than their competitors? Answers to these questions provide the basis for business strategies.

Business Strategy Types

Although creating a business unit strategy is a complex task, several classification schemes have been developed to aid in this endeavor. One of the most popular is Porter's **generic business strategies**,[4] presented in Exhibit 3.3. Each of these generic strategies—**low cost, differentiation**, or **niche**—emphasizes a different type of competitive advantage and has different implications for a sales organization. The sales function plays an important role in executing a generic business strategy.[5] As indicated in Exhibit 3.3, the activities of sales managers and salespeople differ depending on whether the business unit is using a low-cost, differentiation, or niche business strategy. The sales function can often provide the basis for differentiation.

Many companies are adopting **customer relationship management (CRM)** as a business strategy:

> CRM is a strategy resulting in developing the most appropriate relationship with a customer, a process that is supported by technology and that may not necessarily yield deep or strategic partnerships with all customers. Technology is used to analyze customer and market information, automate specific business processes, and facilitate the development of customer

Generic Business Strategies and Salesforce Activities	EXHIBIT 3.3

Strategy Type	**Role of the Salesforce**
Low-cost supplier Aggressive construction of efficient-scale facilities, vigorous pursuit of cost reductions from experience, tight cost, and overhead control, usually associated with high relative market share.	Servicing large current customers, pursuing large prospects, minimizing costs, selling on the basis of price, and usually assuming significant order-taking responsibilities.
Differentiation Creation of something perceived industrywide as being unique. Provides insulation against competitive rivalry because of brand loyalty and resulting lower sensitivity to price.	Selling nonprice benefits, generating orders, providing high quality of customer service and responsiveness, possibly significant amount of prospecting if high-growth industry, selecting customers based on low price sensitivity, usually requires a high-quality salesforce.
Niche Service of a particular target market, with each functional policy developed with this target market in mind. Although market share in the industry might be low, the firm dominates a segment within the industry.	Becoming experts in the operations and opportunities associated with the target market, focusing customer attention on nonprice benefits and allocating selling time to the target market.

relationship strategies. The salesforce is imbedded in the context of an organization-wide focus on the customer as the center of the firm.[6]

A critical aspect of this definition is that CRM is a business strategy. However, the effective implementation of a CRM strategy requires integrated, cross-functional business processes, specific organizational capabilities, an appropriate business philosophy, and the right technology to make everything work.[7] AB Phone Works founder, Anneke Seley, states: "CRM is evolving to much more personalized and tailored capabilities." She believes "companies need to start from scratch with their CRM because social media fundamentally change the model that companies use for effective customer relationships."[8] Successful firms address the strategy, philosophy, process, and capability issues first, and then find the best technology for implementation. Unsuccessful firms tend to focus on the technology first and then try to adapt their strategy, philosophy, process, and capability to fit the technology.[9]

Deere & Company represents an example of a successful approach to CRM. Faced with the consolidation of customers within the agriculture industry, Deere responded by crafting a CRM strategy. The essence of the strategy was for its dealers to develop stronger relationships with the largest accounts using a consultative selling process. Different types of relationships and selling processes were used to serve smaller accounts. The strategic focus was to establish stronger relationships with fewer, but larger accounts. The appropriate technology to support the CRM strategy was then implemented by dealers. This approach produced strong sales and profit gains for Deere.[10]

Business Strategy Summary

Business strategies determine how each SBU plans to compete in the marketplace. Several strategic approaches are available, each placing its own demands on the sales function. The role of the sales function depends on how an SBU plans to compete in the marketplace, with the activities of sales managers and salespeople being important in executing a business strategy successfully.

MARKETING STRATEGY AND THE SALES FUNCTION

Because SBUs typically market multiple products to multiple customer groups, separate marketing strategies are often developed for each of an SBU's target markets. These marketing strategies must be consistent with the business strategy. For example, marketers operating in an SBU with a differentiation business strategy would probably not develop marketing strategies that emphasize low price. The marketing strategies for each target market should reinforce the differentiation competitive advantage sought by the SBU.

Figure 3.1 illustrates the major components of a marketing strategy and highlights the position of personal selling within the marketing communications portion of a marketing strategy. The key components of any marketing strategy are the selection of a **target market** and the development of a **marketing mix.** Target market selection requires a definition of the specific market segment to be served. The marketing mix then consists of a marketing offer designed to appeal to the defined target market. This marketing offer contains a mixture of product, price, distribution, and marketing communications strategies. The critical task for the marketing strategist is to develop a marketing mix that satisfies the needs of the target market better than competitive offerings.

Personal selling may be an important element in the marketing communications portion of the marketing mix. The marketing communications strategy consists of a mixture of personal selling, advertising, sales promotion, and publicity, with most strategies emphasizing either personal selling or advertising as the main tool. Sales promotion and publicity are typically viewed as supplemental tools. Thus, a key strategic decision is to determine when marketing communications strategies should be driven by personal selling or advertising. This decision should capitalize on the relative advantages of personal selling and advertising for different target markets and different marketing mixes.[11]

Advantages and Disadvantages of Personal Selling

Personal selling is the only promotional tool that consists of personal communication between seller and buyer, and the advantages and disadvantages of personal selling thus accrue from this personal communication. The personal communication between buyer and seller is typically viewed as more credible and has more of an impact (or impression) than messages delivered through advertising media. Personal selling also allows for better timing of message delivery, and it affords the flexibility of communicating different messages to different customers or changing a message during a sales call based on customer feedback. Finally, personal selling has the advantage of allowing a sale to be closed. These characteristics make personal selling a powerful tool in situations in which the benefits of personal communication are important (see Figure 3.2).

The major disadvantage of personal selling is the high cost to reach each member of the audience. Contrast this with the pennies that it costs to reach an audience member through mass advertising. The benefits of personal selling do not come cheap. They may, however, outweigh the costs for certain types of target market situations and for specific marketing mixes.

Target Market Situations and Personal Selling

The characteristics of personal selling are most advantageous in specific target market situations. Personal selling–driven strategies are appropriate when (1) the market consists of only a few buyers that tend to be concentrated in location, (2) the buyer needs a great deal of information, (3) the purchase is important, (4) the product is complex, and (5) service after the sale is important. The target market characteristics that favor personal selling are similar to those found in most business purchasing situations. Thus, personal selling is typically the preferred tool in **business marketing,**

Marketing Strategy and Personal Selling   FIGURE 3.1

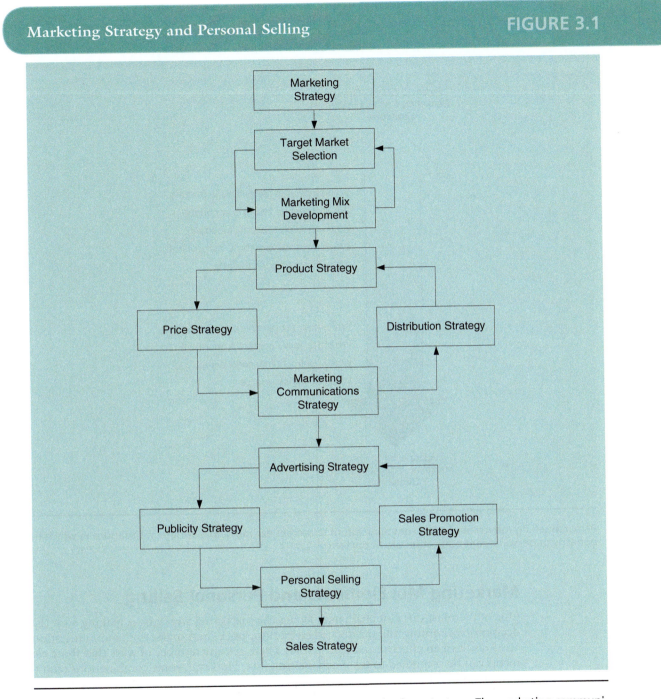

Personal selling is an important element of a marketing communications strategy. The marketing communications strategy is one element of a marketing mix designed to appeal to a defined target market. A marketing strategy can be defined in terms of target market and marketing mix components.

whereas advertising is normally emphasized in consumer marketing situations (see Figure 3.3).

An effective marketing communications mix capitalizes on the advantages of each promotional tool. Moreover, characteristics of the target market must be considered, and the promotional mix must also be consistent with the other elements of the marketing mix to ensure a coordinated marketing offer.

FIGURE 3.2

FIGURE 3.2   Personal Selling–Driven versus Advertising-Driven
                              Marketing Communications Strategies

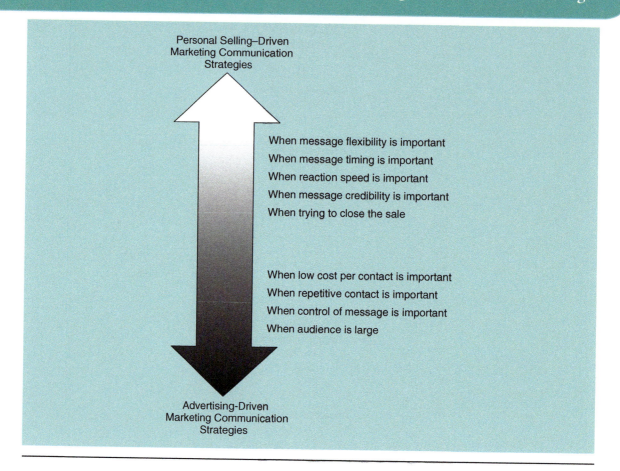

Personal Selling–Driven
Marketing Communication
Strategies

When message flexibility is important
When message timing is important
When reaction speed is important
When message credibility is important
When trying to close the sale

When low cost per contact is important
When repetitive contact is important
When control of message is important
When audience is large

Advertising-Driven
Marketing Communication
Strategies

Personal selling–driven marketing communications strategies are most appropriate in situations in which the benefits of personal communication are important.

Marketing Mix Elements and Personal Selling

One of the most difficult challenges facing the marketing strategist is making sure that decisions concerning the product, distribution, price, and marketing communications areas result in an effective marketing mix. There are any number of ways that these elements can be combined to form a marketing mix. However, some combinations tend to represent logical fits. Exhibit 3.4 shows when a personal selling emphasis might fit well with the other marketing elements. Again, these suggestions should be considered only as guidelines, because the development of unique marketing mixes may produce competitive advantages in the marketplace.

An interesting example is Best Buy. Best Buy is the largest consumer electronics retailer in the nation. It is, however, beginning to face increased competition from new sources. Wal-Mart, the world's largest retailer, is moving aggressively into high-end consumer electronics. In addition, Dell is also expanding its product mix to include MP3 players and flat-panel TVs. Best Buy's marketing strategy to compete with these giants is to focus more on the personal selling component of its marketing mix. Its salespeople, called "blueshirts," are implementing a CARE Plus sales process to increase sales by connecting more deeply with customers and providing attention, know-how, service, and complete solutions to meet customer needs. This personal selling–driven strategy is

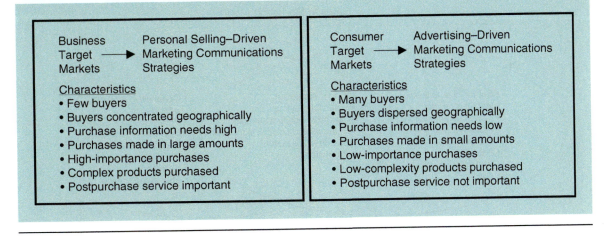

FIGURE 3.3

Targeting Market Characteristics and Marketing Communications Strategy

Business Target Markets → Personal Selling–Driven Marketing Communications Strategies

Characteristics
• Few buyers
• Buyers concentrated geographically
• Purchase information needs high
• Purchases made in large amounts
• High-importance purchases
• Complex products purchased
• Postpurchase service important

Consumer Target Markets → Advertising–Driven Marketing Communications Strategies

Characteristics
• Many buyers
• Buyers dispersed geographically
• Purchase information needs low
• Purchases made in small amounts
• Low-importance purchases
• Low-complexity products purchased
• Postpurchase service not important

Personal selling–driven marketing communications strategies are most appropriate for target markets that have characteristics typical of business markets.

EXHIBIT 3.4

Marketing Mix Elements and Personal Selling

Marketing Mix Area	Characteristics
Product or service	• Complex products requiring customer application assistance (computers, pollution control systems, stream turbines) • Major purchase decisions, such as food items purchased by supermarket chains • Features and performance of the product requiring personal demonstration and trial by the customer (private aircraft)
Channels	• Channel system relatively short and direct to end users • Personal selling needed in "pushing" product through channel • Channel intermediaries available to perform personal selling function for supplier with limited resources and experience (brokers or manufacturers' agents) • Product and service training and assistance needed by channel in intermediaries
Price	• Final price negotiated between buyer and seller (appliances, automobiles, real estate) • Selling price or quantity purchased enable an adequate margin to support selling expenses (traditional department store compared with discount house)

intended to differentiate Best Buy from Wal-Mart, with its low price strategy, and Dell, which has a direct selling Internet model.[12]

Integrated Marketing Communication

Although marketing communication strategies are typically driven by advertising or personal selling, most firms use a variety of tools in their marketing communication mix. The key task facing both business and consumer marketers is deciding how and

FIGURE 3.4   Marketing and Sales Activities

The coordination of sales and marketing activities is important to integrated marketing communication strategies.

when to use these tools. **Integrated marketing communication (IMC)** is the increasingly popular term used by many firms to describe their approach. IMC is the strategic integration of multiple marketing communication tools in the most effective and efficient manner. The objective is to use the most cost-effective tool to achieve a desired communication objective and to ensure a consistent message is being communicated to the market.

A typical approach is to use some form of advertising to generate company and product awareness and to identify potential customers. These sales leads might then be contacted and qualified by telemarketers. The best prospects are then turned over to the salesforce to receive personal selling attention. This approach uses relatively inexpensive tools (advertising and telemarketing) to communicate with potential customers early in the buying process and saves the more expensive tools (personal selling) for the best prospects later in the buying process.

One of the keys to integrating marketing communications successfully is greater coordination between the marketing and sales functions. Figure 3.4 presents the basic activities undertaken by the marketing function with input from sales on the left, and important sales tasks with input from marketing on the right.[13] The activities in the middle require the marketing and sales functions to work closely together. Although this may seem easy to achieve, it is often very difficult. Marketers tend to focus on products, analysis, projects, processes, the office, and take a long-term perspective. The sales function, in contrast, emphasizes customers, personal relationships, daily activity, results, the field, and a short-term perspective. Integrating these different orientations requires the creation of business structures, processes and systems, cultures, and employees designed to facilitate communication and coordination between the marketing and sales functions.

Marketing Strategy Summary

Selecting target markets and designing marketing mixes are the key components in marketing strategy development. Marketing strategies must be developed for the target markets served by an SBU and must be consistent with the business unit strategy. One important element of the marketing mix is marketing communications. The critical task is designing a mix that capitalizes on the advantages of each tool. Personal selling has the basic advantage of personal communication and is emphasized in target market situations and marketing mixes in which personal communication is important.

SALES STRATEGY FRAMEWORK

Corporate, business, and marketing strategies view customers as aggregate markets or market segments. These organizational strategies provide direction and guidance for the sales function, but then sales managers and salespeople must translate these general organizational strategies into specific strategies for individual customers.

A sales strategy is designed to execute an organization's marketing strategy for individual accounts. For example, a marketing strategy consists of selecting a target market and developing a marketing mix. Target markets are typically defined in broad terms, such as the small business market or the university market. Marketing mixes are also described broadly in terms of general product, distribution, price, and marketing communications approaches. All accounts within a target market (e.g., all small businesses or all universities), however, are not the same in terms of size, purchasing procedures, needs, problems, and other factors. The major purpose of a sales strategy is to develop a specific approach for selling to individual accounts within a target market. A sales strategy capitalizes on the important differences among individual accounts or groups of similar accounts.

A firm's sales strategy is important for two basic reasons. First, it has a major impact on a firm's sales and profit performance. Second, it influences many other sales management decisions. Salesforce recruiting, selecting, training, compensation, and performance evaluation are affected by the sales strategies used by a firm.

Because personal selling–driven promotion strategies are typical in business marketing, our discussion of sales strategy focuses on organizational (also called industrial or business) customers. Specific customers are referred to as accounts. Thus, a sales strategy must be based on the important and unique aspects of organizational buyer behavior. A framework that integrates organizational buyer behavior and sales strategy is presented in Figure 3.5.

ORGANIZATIONAL BUYER BEHAVIOR

Organizational buyer behavior refers to the purchasing behavior of organizations. Although there are unique aspects in the buying behavior of any organization, specific types of organizations tend to share similarities in their purchasing procedures (see Exhibit 3.5). Most of our attention is focused on business organizations classified as **users** or **original equipment manufacturers (OEM)**. However, we provide examples of **resellers**, **government organizations**, and **institutions** throughout the book.

As indicated in Figure 3.5, the development of sales strategy requires an understanding of organizational buyer behavior. The unique aspects of organizational buyer behavior revolve around the buying situation, buying center, buying process, and buying needs.

Buying Situation

One key determinant of organizational buyer behavior is the buying situation faced by an account. Three major types are possible, each representing its own problems for the buying firm and each having different strategic implications for the selling firm.

FIGURE 3.5

FIGURE 3.5   Sales Strategy Framework

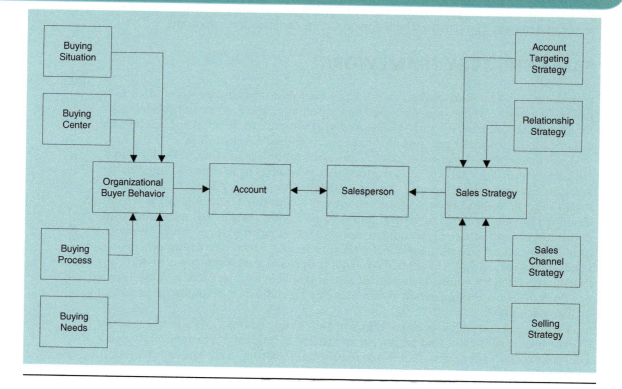

Salesperson interaction with accounts is directed by a sales strategy. The sales strategy, which defines how specific accounts are to be managed and covered, must be based on an understanding of the buying situation, buying center, buying process, and buying needs of the account.

EXHIBIT 3.5   Types of Organizations

Major Category	Types	Example
Business or industrial organizations	Users—purchase products and services to produce other products and services	HP purchasing facsimile machines from Sharp for their corporate offices
	Original equipment manufacturers (OEM)—purchase products to incorporate into products	HP purchasing microcomputer chips from Intel to incorporate into their personal computers
	Resellers—purchase products to sell	Best Buy purchasing HP personal computers to sell to organizations
Government organizations	Federal, state, and local government agencies	Virginia State Lottery purchasing HP personal computers for managers
Institutions	Public and private institutions	United Way purchasing HP personal computers for their offices

A **new task buying situation**, in which the organization is purchasing a product for the first time, poses the most problems for the buyer. Because the account has little knowledge or experience as a basis for making the purchase decision, it will typically use a lengthy process to collect and evaluate purchase information. The decision-making process in this type of situation is often called **extensive problem solving**.

A **modified rebuy buying situation** exists when the account has previously purchased and used the product. Although the account has information and experience with the product, it will usually want to collect additional information and may make a change when purchasing a replacement product. The decision-making process in this type of situation is often referred to as **limited problem solving**.

The least complex buying situation is the **straight rebuy buying situation,** wherein the account has considerable experience in using the product and is satisfied with the current purchase arrangements. In this case, the buyer is merely reordering from the current supplier and engaging in **routinized response behavior**.

SALES MANAGEMENT IN THE 21ST CENTURY

The Importance of the Buying Center

Kim Davenport, Regional Business Director, Acordia Therapeutics, INC., says he has to work with each of his sales representatives so they understand the importance of penetrating the different layers of the buying center:

It's not enough to be on a first name basis with the receptionist (potential gatekeeper). Many of our offices today have business managers and nurse practitioners that play a huge role in what products get prescribed, therefore, we can't just concentrate on the doctors. They are important and can be the decision maker but others in the office can play an equally important role. A big part of our selling is done during the noon hour where we provide the staff with lunch. The business manager in the office may be the one who sets these up. Nurse practitioners can be the decision makers and influencers on what products are prescribed. Nurses can also play an important role. If we ignore any of these buying center members we could be losing out to our competitors who may be talking to these key people. It is important for my sales reps to invite all these people to our lunches, ignoring any of them would be a huge mistake.

Buying Center

One of the most important characteristics of organizational buyer behavior is the involvement of the many individuals from the firm that participate in the purchasing process. The term **buying center** has been used to designate these individuals. The buying center is not a formal designation on the organization chart but rather an informal network of purchasing participants. (However, members of the purchasing department are typically included in most buying centers and are normally represented in the formal organizational structure.) The difficult task facing the selling firm is to identify all the buying center members and to determine the specific role of each.

The possible roles that buying center members might play in a particular purchasing decision are

- *initiators,* who start the organizational purchasing process
- *users,* who use the product to be purchased
- *gatekeepers,* who control the flow of information between buying center members
- *influencers,* who provide input for the purchasing decision
- *deciders,* who make the final purchase decision
- *purchasers,* who implement the purchasing decision

Each buying center role may be performed by more than one individual, and each individual may perform more than one buying center role.

EXHIBIT 3.6 Buying Center Members and Benefits Desired

Buying Center Member	Benefits Desired
Purchasing manager	Electronic ordering Competitive price Warranty
Logistics manager	Dependable delivery Order tracking
Chief financial officer	Competitive price Payment terms
Manufacturing manager	Dependable delivery Product quality Customized products

---

The members of a buying center are often from different functional areas and desire different benefits from a purchasing decision. Exhibit 3.6 presents an example. Notice that each function requires unique benefits, but some benefits are important to several functional areas. For example, a competitive price is important to both the chief financial officer and the purchasing manager, and the logistics manager and manufacturing manager are both interested in dependable delivery. The challenge is to understand both the role and benefits desired by each member of the buying center. Knowing the functional area of buying center members can help determine the relevant benefits.

Buying Process

Organizational buyer behavior can be viewed as a **buying process** consisting of several phases. Although this process has been presented in different ways, the following phases represent a consensus.

Phase 1. Recognition of a problem or need

Phase 2. Determination of the characteristics of the item and the quantity needed

Phase 3. Description of the characteristics of the item and quantity needed

Phase 4. Search for and qualification of potential sources

Phase 5. Acquisition and analysis of proposals

Phase 6. Evaluation of proposals and selection of suppliers

Phase 7. Selection of an order routine

Phase 8. Performance feedback and evaluation

These buying phases may be formalized for some organizations and/or for certain purchases. In other situations, this process may only be a rough approximation of what actually occurs. For example, government organizations and institutions tend to have more formal purchasing processes than most business or industrial organizations. Viewing organizational buying as a multiple-phase process is helpful in developing sales strategy. A major objective of any sales strategy is to facilitate an account's movement through this process in a manner that will lead to a purchase of the seller's product.

Buying Needs

Organizational buying is typically viewed as goal-directed behavior intended to satisfy specific **buying needs**. Although the organizational purchasing process is made to satisfy organizational needs, the buying center consists of individuals who are also trying to satisfy individual needs throughout the decision process. Individual needs tend to be career related, whereas organizational needs reflect factors related to the use of the product.

Even though organizational purchasing is often thought to be almost entirely objective, subjective personal needs are often extremely important in the final purchase decision. For example, an organization may want to purchase a computer to satisfy data-processing needs. Although a number of suppliers might be able to provide similar products, some suppliers at lower cost than others, buying center members might select the most well-known brand to reduce purchase risk and protect job security.

We discussed how the influence of buying center members varies at different buying phases in the preceding section. Couple this with the different needs of different buying center members, and the complexity of organization buying behavior is evident. Nevertheless, sales managers must understand this behavior to develop sales strategies that will satisfy the personal and organizational needs of buying center members.

SALES STRATEGY

Sales managers and salespeople are typically responsible for strategic decisions at the account level. Although the firm's marketing strategy provides basic guidelines—an overall game plan—the battles are won on an account-by-account basis. Without the design and execution of effective sales strategies directed at specific accounts, the marketing strategy cannot be successfully implemented.

The success of Hill-Rom illustrates the importance of developing effective sales strategies. Hill-Rom markets beds and other medical equipment to medical care facilities. The salesforce typically treated all customers about the same, although larger facilities received more attention than smaller facilities. The company performed an extensive customer segmentation analysis and identified two types of customers: key customers and prime customers. These customer groups differed in their buying needs and processes, and not just in size. Hill-Rom found that their current approach provided too much attention to prime customers and not enough to key customers. Based on this analysis, the company developed a specific sales strategy for each customer group. Key customers were assigned multifunctional sales teams under the direction of an account manager. Prime customers were served by territory managers. The results from the new sales strategies are higher sales, more satisfied customers, and lower selling costs.[14]

Our framework suggests four basic sales strategy elements: account targeting strategy, relationship strategy, selling strategy, and sales channel strategy. We consider each of these as a separate, but related, strategic decision area. Sales strategies are ultimately developed for each individual account; however, the strategic decisions are often made by classifying individual accounts into similar categories.

Account Targeting Strategy

The first element of a sales strategy is defining an account targeting strategy. As mentioned earlier, all accounts within a target market are not the same. Some accounts might not be good prospects because of existing relationships with competitors. Even those that are good prospects or even current customers differ in terms of how much they buy now or might buy in the future, how they want to do business with sales organizations, and other factors. This means that all accounts cannot be effectively or efficiently served in the same way.

An **account targeting strategy** is the classification of accounts within a target market into categories for the purpose of developing strategic approaches for selling to each account or account group. The account targeting strategy provides the foundation for all other elements of a sales strategy. Just as different marketing mixes are developed to serve different target markets, sales organizations need to use different relationship, selling, and sales channel strategies for different account groups.

The experience of an electronic products distributor provides a good example of the value of account targeting. The 10 inside and 12 outside salespeople emphasized excellent service to all 5,000 customers. An analysis of the customer base indicated that the top 400 customers accounted for 80 percent of sales with a gross profit of $150/order. The bottom 3,800 customers accounted for 5 percent of sales with a gross profit of $8/order, with the remaining customers in between these extremes. A consultant helped the company develop an account targeting strategy with four segments:

1. Key accounts—top 400 accounts

2. Target accounts—next best 400 accounts

3. Maintenance accounts—next best 400 accounts

4. Why bother accounts—remaining 3,800 accounts

The new account targeting strategy provided the basis for developing sales strategies for each account segment.[15]

Relationship Strategy

As discussed in previous chapters, there is a clear trend toward a relationship orientation between buyers and sellers, especially in business markets. However, some accounts want to continue in a transaction mode, whereas others want various types of relationships between buyer and seller. A **relationship strategy** is a determination of the type of relationship to be developed with different account groups. A specific relationship strategy is developed for each account group identified by a sales organization's account targeting strategy.

Any number of relationship strategies might be developed, but typically an account targeting strategy defines three to five target groups, each requiring a specific relationship strategy. We illustrate with the general approach established by a large industrial manufacturer. The firm's account targeting strategy identified four different account groups and determined a specific relationship strategy for each group. Exhibit 3.7 presents the characteristics of each relationship strategy.

The relationship strategies range from a transaction relationship based on selling standardized products to a collaborative relationship in which the buyers and sellers work closely together for the benefit of both businesses. In between these extremes are intermediate types of relationships. A solutions relationship emphasizes solving customer problems, and a partnership relationship represents a preferred supplier position over the long term. As a sales organization moves from transaction to collaborative relationships, the time frame becomes longer, the focus changes from buying/selling to creating value, and the products and services offered move from simple and standardized to more complex and customized.

The different characteristics of the different relationship strategies are further illustrated in Figure 3.6. The move from transaction to collaborative relationships requires

EXHIBIT 3.7   Characteristics of Relationship Strategies

	Transaction Relationship	Solutions Relationship	Partnership Relationship	Collaborative Relationship
Goal	Sell products		→	Add value
Time frame	Short		→	Long
Offering	Standardized		→	Customized
Number of customers	Many		→	Few

Relationship Strategy Selling Costs   **FIGURE 3.6**

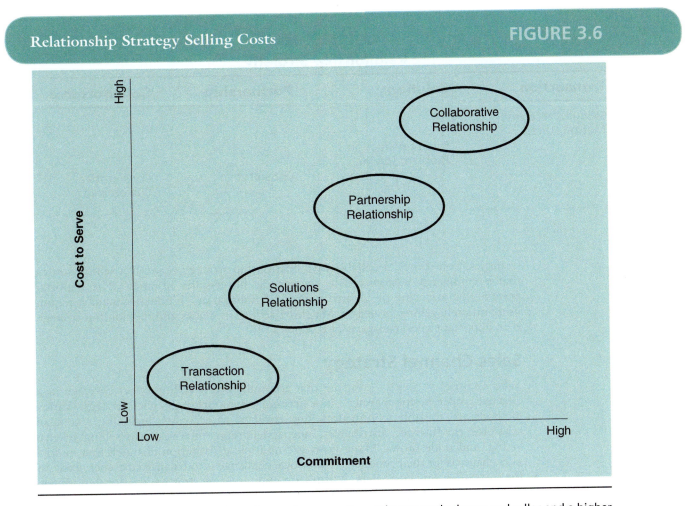

Each relationship strategy represents an increasing commitment between the buyer and seller and a higher cost to serve the customer.

a greater commitment between buyer and seller, because they will be working together much more closely. Some buyers and sellers are not willing to make the required commitments. In addition, the selling costs are increased to serve accounts with higher-level relationships. Therefore, sales organizations must consider the sales and costs associated with using different relationship strategies for different account groups. The critical task is balancing the customer's needs with the cost to serve the account.

Selling Strategy

Successfully executing a specific relationship strategy requires a different selling approach. A **selling strategy** is the planned selling approach for each relationship strategy. Chapter 2 presented five basic selling approaches: stimulus response, mental states, need satisfaction, problem solving, and consultative. These selling approaches represent different selling strategies that might be used to execute a specific relationship strategy. We illustrate this by continuing the example of the large industrial manufacturer and the relationship strategies presented in Exhibit 3.7 and Figure 3.6.

Exhibit 3.8 matches the appropriate selling strategy with the appropriate relationship strategy. As indicated, the stimulus response and mental states approaches typically fit with a transaction relationship strategy. The need satisfaction and problem-solving selling strategies are normally used with a solutions relationship strategy. The consultative approach is most effective with the partnership and collaborative relationship

EXHIBIT 3.8	Matching Selling and Relationship Strategies		
	Relationship Strategy		
Transaction	**Solutions**	**Partnership**	**Collaborative**
Stimulus response Mental states			
	Need satisfaction Problem solving		
		Consultative	Consultative Customized

strategies. Sometimes, a collaborative relationship strategy requires a selling strategy that is completely customized to the specific buyer-seller situation. The important point is that achieving the desired type of relationship in a productive manner requires using different selling strategies. Matching selling strategies and relationship strategies is an important sales management task.

Sales Channel Strategy

Sales channel strategy—ensuring that accounts receive selling effort coverage in an effective and efficient manner—is a necessary component of sales strategy. Various methods are available to provide selling coverage to accounts, including a company salesforce, the Internet, distributors, independent representatives, team selling, telemarketing, and trade shows. Many firms use multiple distribution channels and multiple sales channels for their products. The critical challenge is to balance customer needs and the costs of serving customers. A firm's account targeting strategy, relationship strategy, and selling strategy provide a basis for the sales channel strategy. In general, the most important account segments requiring the closest relationships and requiring the most complex sales process are served by the most expensive sales channels. In contrast, the least important, most transaction-oriented account segments receive the least expensive sales channels. The sales channel strategy for customers between these extremes should employ the most effective and efficient sales channel at each stage of the sales process. Because most of this book is concerned with management of a company field salesforce, our discussion of sales channel strategy focuses on alternatives to the typical company field salesforce.

The Internet

The Internet is rapidly becoming an important sales channel in selling to organizations. The focus is using this electronic channel in a way that meets customer needs and reduces selling costs. As technology continues to develop, opportunities to use the Internet effectively increase. Although the smallest accounts with the least profit potential might be served completely by electronic channels, most sales organizations integrate the Internet with other sales channels in various ways. The following examples illustrate different approaches:

- Cisco Systems uses field salespeople to generate new customers and then employs the Internet to serve customer needs for product information and reordering.[16]

- National Semiconductor uses a company salesforce for its largest accounts, but a distributor network for smaller accounts. However, private extranets are developed for each large account and distributor to access purchase information. Smaller accounts have access to an open Web site that links them to distributors.[17]

- Hewlett-Packard's Image and Printing Unit serving small and medium businesses uses customer support representatives to interact with customers trying to solve problems from its Web site. These potential customers can click a pop-up and will be connected with an HP representative online. This representative will try to help solve the problem or refer callers to another sales channel, such as an HP reseller, if appropriate.[18]

- Pragmatech asks Web site visitors five questions. Based on the responses to these questions and other information, the company determines whether the visitor represents a good potential opportunity or not. The best prospects are passed on to field salespeople. The others are interacted with electronically.[19]

These examples illustrate how the Internet is being used as an electronic sales channel by different companies. These and most other companies are focusing on ways to integrate the Internet into a multiple sales channel strategy that provides value to customers in a cost-effective manner. Thus, the Internet is being blended with field selling effort but also with other sales channels such as industrial distributors, independent representatives, and telemarketing.

Distributors

One alternative sales channel is **distributors**—channel middlemen that take title to the goods that they market to end users. These distributors typically employ their own salesforce and may carry (1) the products of only one manufacturer, (2) related but noncompeting products from different manufacturers, or (3) competing products from different manufacturers. Firms that use distributors normally have a relatively small company salesforce to serve and support the efforts of the distributor.

The use of distributors adds another member to the distribution channel. Although these distributors should not be considered as final customers, they should be treated like customers. Developing positive long-term relationships with distributors is necessary for success. Indeed, the development of a partnership with distributors can be the key to success.

Herman Miller, the furniture manufacturer, has 300 direct salespeople and 240 distributors. Herman Miller salespeople call on customers directly but also work with distributors to make sure customers are satisfied. In large markets, the salespeople are usually the lead on accounts, with the distributors responsible for smaller accounts. Herman Miller also provides the distributors with market information to help them succeed, and the salespeople maintain continuous contact to motivate the distributors to emphasize Herman Miller products.[20]

Dell represents an interesting example in the use of distributors in various ways. The cornerstone of its sales channel strategy has been to sell computers directly to customers through the Internet or by phone. However, personal computer sales from these channels have been decreasing and these channels are not well suited for developing countries. Dell is responding to this situation by adding kiosks in malls, creating its own stores, and selling its products through other resellers. This is a big change in sales channel strategy for the global leader in personal computer market share. Although this new strategy is intended to have a positive impact in the U.S., it should also help Dell increase sales in international markets, such as Russia, China, and Hungary, where customers are just learning to buy online and home delivery services do not support the direct sales model well.[21]

Independent Representatives

Firms using personal selling can choose to cover accounts with **independent representatives** (also called *manufacturers' representatives* or just *reps*). Reps are independent sales organizations that sell complementary, but noncompeting, products from different manufacturers. In contrast to distributors, independent representatives do not normally

---

EXHIBIT 3.9   Advantages of Independent Representatives

Independent sales representatives offer several advantages over company salesforces:

- Reps provide a professional selling capability that is difficult to match with company salespeople.
- Reps offer in-depth knowledge of general markets and individual customers.
- Reps offer established relationships with individual customers.
- The use of reps provides improved cash flow because payments to reps are typically not made until customers have paid for their purchases.
- The use of reps provides predictable sales expenses because most of the selling costs are variable and directly related to sales volume.
- The use of reps can provide greater territory coverage because companies can employ more reps than company salespeople for the same cost.
- Companies can usually penetrate new markets faster by using reps because of the reps' established customer relationships.

---

carry inventory or take title to the products they sell. Manufacturers typically develop contractual agreements with several rep organizations. Each rep organization consists of one or more salespeople and is assigned a geographic territory. It is typically compensated on a commission basis for products sold.

Most independent rep agencies are small with an average of six employees, although a few have up to 100 salespeople and support staff. Independent reps are typically compensated on a commission basis for products sold. There is, however, a trend toward paying larger commissions and even stipends for opening new territories and shifting some compensation toward paying for rep activities rather than just for sales results. Some rep agencies are performing direct mail, telemarketing, newsletter publishing, and Web-site design services for clients.[22]

Why would so many manufacturers use reps instead of company salesforces? As indicated in Exhibit 3.9,[23] reps have certain advantages over company salesforces, especially for small firms or for smaller markets served by larger firms. Because reps are paid on a commission basis, selling costs are almost totally variable, whereas a large percentage of the selling costs of a company salesforce are fixed. Thus, at lower sales levels a rep organization is more cost-efficient to use than a company salesforce. However, at some level of sales, the company salesforce will become more cost-efficient, because reps typically receive higher commission rates than company salespeople (see Figure 3.7).

Marley Cooling Tower capitalizes on the different cost structure between company salesforces and independent reps. Tim Wigger, vice president of sales, manages a company salesforce of 40, plus 70 manufacturers' reps. The company started with only a field salesforce but began adding reps to capitalize on growth outside the original salesperson territories. This approach has been a cost-effective way for Marley to grow in new geographic areas.[24]

Although reps may cost less in many situations, management also has less control over their activities. The basic trade-off is cost versus control. There are two aspects to control. First, because reps are paid a commission on sales, it is difficult to get them to engage in activities not directly related to sales generation. Thus, if servicing of accounts is important, reps may not perform these activities as well as a company salesforce. Second, the typical rep represents an average of 10 manufacturers or principals. Each manufacturer's products will therefore receive 10 percent of the rep's time if it is divided equally. Usually, however, some products receive more attention than others. The biggest complaints that manufacturers seem to have with reps is that they do not spend enough time with their products and thus do not generate sufficient sales. The use of reps limits the amount of control that management has over the time spent selling their products. The relationship with manufacturers' representative organizations can also produce some complex situations as indicated in "An Ethical Dilemma."

Independent Representatives versus Company Salesforce Costs   **FIGURE 3.7**

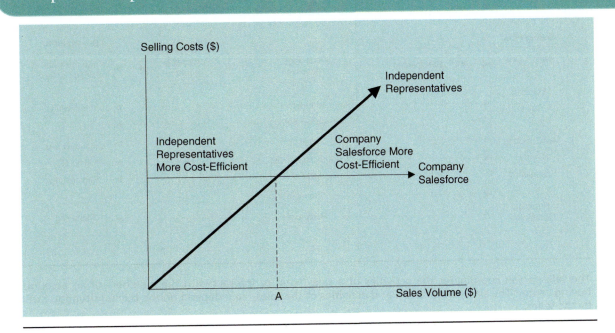

Independent representatives are typically more cost-efficient at lower sales levels, because most of the costs associated with reps are variable. However, at higher sales levels (beyond point A) a company salesforce becomes more efficient.

Team Selling

Our earlier discussion of organizational buyer behavior presented the concepts of buying centers and buying situations. If we move to the selling side of the exchange relationship, we find analogous concepts. As discussed in Chapter 1, firms often employ multiple-person sales teams to deal with the multiple-person buying centers of their accounts. Figure 3.8[25] illustrates the basic relationships between sales teams and buying centers. A company salesperson typically coordinates the activities of the sales

AN ETHICAL DILEMMA

You are the national sales manager for the Fabricated Wire Company (FWC). Your company sells to distributors and dealers throughout the United States. Most of your customers are located in big cities and these customers are located in big cities and these customers are served by your company salesforce. You also serve customers in rural areas with a manufacturer's representative agency (especially west of the Mississippi River). Your salesforce and your representative agency has done equally well in building your business throughout the country. To meet competitive pricing pressures you recently started selling direct to

those customers that are willing to buy direct from you. This helps FWC to plan their inventory more easily. Some of your salespeople and manufacturer representatives have been calling you and voicing their displeasure with the new channel strategy. What should you do?

a. Tell your salespeople that is the way it is and stop complaining.

b. Determine if this new sales strategy is costing the sales reps any commissions.

c. Tell your sales reps this strategy will help sell more overall and help our company be more profitable.

FIGURE 3.8   Team Selling and Buying Centers

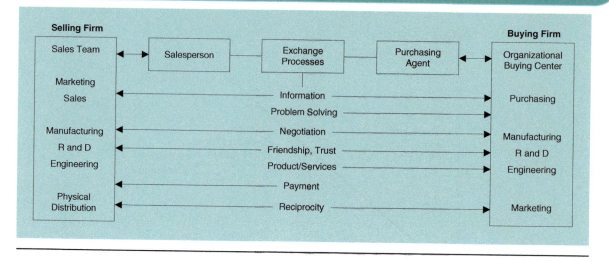

The salesperson coordinates the activities of a sales team to interact with the members of an account's buying center. The size, composition, and activities of the sales team depend on the buying situation faced by the seller.

team, whereas the purchasing agent typically coordinates the activities of the buying center. Both the sales team and buying center can consist of multiple individuals from different functional areas. Each of these individuals can play one or more roles in the exchange process.

The use of **team selling** is increasing in many firms, especially as a sales channel for a firm's most important prospects and customers (see Chapter 1). Generating the best new customers and expanding relationships with the best existing customers often requires the participation of many individuals from the selling firm. The software company DataCert provides an interesting example of team selling. The company employs sales teams consisting of employees from different departments to meet with prospects at crucial stages of the sales process. Regional sales managers determine which employees attend which meetings with each prospect. This is a very expensive sales channel approach, but prospects seem to appreciate the attention they receive. The team selling strategy has helped DataCert obtain top clients, such as UPS, Microsoft, and AT&T.[26]

Telemarketing

An increasingly important sales channel is **telemarketing** (also called *telesales*), which consists of using the telephone as a means for customer contact, to perform some of, or all, the activities required to develop and maintain account relationships. This includes both outbound telemarketing (the seller calls the account) and inbound telemarketing (the account calls the seller).[27]

Firms typically use telemarketing to replace field selling for specific accounts or integrate telemarketing with field selling to the same accounts (see Figure 3.9). The major reason for replacing field selling with telemarketing at specific accounts is the low cost of telemarketing selling. Telemarketing salespeople are able to serve a large number of smaller accounts. This lowers the selling costs to the smaller accounts and frees the field salesforce to concentrate on the larger accounts. Sometimes telemarketing can be used effectively to serve all accounts. For example, SecureWorks once used a field salesforce to bring its Internet security services to distributors and resellers. The company changed to salespeople selling directly to end users over the phone. Results of

Uses of Telemarketing   FIGURE 3.9

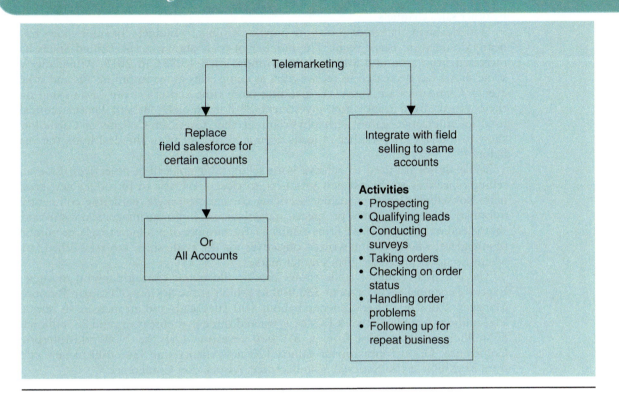

Telemarketing is typically used either to replace field selling or be integrated with field selling by performing specific activities.

the change have been spectacular, with the number of clients going from 50 to 850 and annual sales from $700,000 to over $8.5 million.[28]

More typical approaches are to use telemarketing to serve smaller accounts or to integrate telemarketing with other sales channels for most accounts. For example, infoUSA sells its lead development services to small businesses over the phone. Large companies receive the attention of field salespeople. Both the telemarketing and field salespeople focus on meeting customer needs, but the lower cost of phone sales produces more profit from smaller accounts.[29] A typical example of integrating telemarketing with other sales channels is for leads to be developed and appointments made by phone with field salespeople, distributor salespeople, or independent sales representatives making the personal sales call. Once a customer relationship is established, the telemarketing and field salespeople often share the responsibility for and perform different activities to build relationships with customers.

The development of telemarketing salesforces to serve some accounts or to support field selling operations can be difficult. One of the keys to success appears to be consistent communication with the field salesforce throughout all stages of telemarketing development. Field salespeople must be assured that the telemarketing operations will help them improve their performance. Specific attention must also be directed toward developing appropriate compensation programs for both salesforces and devising training programs that provide the necessary knowledge and skills for the telemarketing and field salesforces to be able to work effectively together.

Trade Shows

The final sales channel to be discussed here, **trade shows**, is typically an industry-sponsored event in which companies use a booth to display products and services to potential and existing customers. Because a particular trade show is held only once a year and lasts only a few days, trade shows should be viewed as supplemental methods for account coverage, not to be used by themselves, but integrated with and supported by other sales channels.

Statistics show that trade shows are popular. Company budgets for trade shows have nearly doubled in recent years. The number of trade shows in the United States has increased from around 4,500 in 1999 to more than 13,334 in 2018. Attendance at some shows has decreased in recent years as companies move to online ads and other events. Companies are, however, spending more time and effort on ways to improve their returns from trade show investments.[30] For example, Biovail Pharmaceuticals used an interactive game with physicians at the American College of Cardiology show to increase the number of leads generated to 900 from the 250 leads the year before.[31]

Trade shows are used to achieve both selling and nonselling objectives. Relevant selling objectives are to test new products, to close sales, and to introduce new products. Nonselling objectives include servicing current customers, gathering competitive information, identifying new prospects, and enhancing corporate image. Successful trade shows tend to be those where firms exhibit a large number of products to a large number of attendees, where specific written objectives for the trade show are established, and where attendees match the firm's target market.

The potential value of trade shows can be illustrated through several examples. Express Personnel Services spent $50,000 to exhibit at the Society of Human Resource Managers Conference and generated about 400 sales leads and an increase in sales of $1.2 million. Azanda Network Devices garnered three new customers and $3 million to $5 million in extra sales from a $70,000 investment at the NetWorld-Interprop Conference. Orion International gained 125 new clients and $245,000 in new sales from its exhibit at the National Manufacturers Association Conference.[32]

Channel Conflict

Developing an effective sales channel strategy is a challenging task. Sales managers must determine the right mix of sales channel alternatives to meet the needs of all their customers in a cost-effective manner. Once a sales channel strategy is created, sales managers are faced with managing multiple channels and the channel conflict that emerges. Channel conflict occurs when the interests of different channels are not consistent. Typical examples of channel conflict include introducing an Internet sales channel that takes sales away from distributors or independent reps, determining which accounts are served by the field salesforce and which accounts are served by a distributor, or taking accounts from field salespeople and turning them over to telemarketers. The development and integration of corporate, business, marketing, and sales strategies sets the strategic direction for a company and its sales organization. Sales strategies are of most direct concern to sales managers and salespeople. The effective implementation of sales strategies requires an appropriate sales organization structure and the productive deployment of selling resources. Chapter 4 examines these important areas.

SUMMARY

1. **Define the strategy levels for multibusiness, multiproduct firms.** Multibusiness, multiproduct firms must make strategic decisions at the corporate, business, marketing, and sales levels. Corporate strategy decisions determine the basic scope and direction for the corporate entity through formulating the corporate mission statement, defining strategic business units, setting strategic business unit objectives, and determining corporate growth orientation. Business strategy decisions determine how each business unit plans to compete effectively within its industry. Marketing strategies consist of the selection of target markets and the development

of marketing mixes for each product market. Personal selling is an important component of the marketing communications mix portion and business of marketing strategies and a key element in sales strategies.

2. **Discuss how corporate and business strategy decisions affect the sales function.** Corporate strategy decisions provide direction for strategy development at all organizational levels. The corporate mission statement, definition of strategic business units, determination of strategic business unit objectives, and establishment of the corporate growth orientation provide guidelines within which sales managers and salespeople must operate. Changes in corporate strategy typically lead to changes in sales management and personal selling activities. Business strategy decisions determine how each strategic business unit intends to compete. Different business strategies place different demands on the sales organization.

3. **List the advantages and disadvantages of personal selling as a marketing communications tool.** Personal selling is the only tool that involves personal communication between buyer and seller. As such, personal selling has the advantage of being able to tailor the message to the specific needs of each customer and to deliver complicated messages. The major disadvantage of personal selling is the high cost to reach individual buyers.

4. **Specify the situations in which personal selling is typically emphasized in a marketing strategy.** Marketing strategies tend to be either personal selling driven or advertising driven. Personal selling is normally emphasized in business markets where there are relatively few buyers, usually in concentrated locations, who make important purchases of complex products and require a great deal of information and service. Personal selling is also typically emphasized in marketing mixes for complex expensive products that are distributed through direct channels, or through indirect channels by using a "push" strategy, and when the price affords sufficient margin to support the high costs associated with personal selling.

5. **Describe ways that personal selling, advertising, and other tools can be blended into effective integrated marketing communications strategies.** Effective strategies typically consist of a mixture of personal selling, advertising, and other tools. Firms often use advertising to generate company and brand awareness and to identify potential customers. Personal selling is then used to turn these prospects into customers of the firm's products or services. Other tools are normally used to supplement the advertising and personal selling efforts.

6. **Discuss the important concepts behind organizational buyer behavior.** The key concepts behind organizational buyer behavior are buying situation, buying center, buying process, and buying needs. Buying situations can be characterized as new task, modified rebuy, or straight rebuy. The type of buying situation affects all other aspects of organizational buyer behavior. The buying center consists of all the individuals from a firm involved in a particular buying decision. These individuals may come from different functional areas and may play the role of initiators, users, gatekeepers, influencers, deciders, and/or buyers. Organizational purchasing should be viewed as a buying process with multiple phases. Members of the buying center may be involved at different phases of the buying process. Organizational purchases are made to satisfy specific buying needs, which may be both organizational and personal. These concepts are highly interrelated and interact to produce complex organizational purchasing phenomena.

7. **Define an account targeting strategy.** An account targeting strategy is the classification of accounts within a target market into categories for the purpose of developing strategic approaches for selling to each account or account group.

8. **Explain the different types of relationship strategies.** A sales organization might use any number of different relationship strategies to serve targeted accounts. Transaction, solutions, partnership, and collaborative relationship strategies are examples used by some sales organizations.

9. **Discuss the importance of different selling strategies.** A selling strategy is the planned selling approach for each relationship strategy. Selling strategies might include stimulus response, mental states, need satisfaction, problem solving, consultative, or a completely customized strategy. Different selling strategies are needed to successfully execute different relationship strategies.

10. **Describe the advantages and disadvantages of different sales channel strategies.** A sales channel strategy consists of decisions as to how to provide selling effort coverage to accounts. The sales channel strategy depends on the firm's marketing strategy. If indirect distribution is used, then distributors become the main focus of selling effort coverage. Firms might decide to employ independent representatives instead of having a company salesforce. The concept of team selling is analogous to the buying center concept. Depending on whether the seller faces a new task selling situation, a modified resell situation, or a routine resell situation, different individuals will be included in the sales team. Telemarketing is a sales channel that can be used to replace or support field selling operations. Finally, trade shows can be used to achieve specific objectives and supplement the other sales channels.

UNDERSTANDING SALES MANAGEMENT TERMS

corporate strategy
business strategy
strategic business unit (SBU)
marketing strategy
corporate mission statement
business unit portfolio
generic business strategies
low-cost strategy
differentiation strategy
niche strategy
customer relationship
 management (CRM)
target market
marketing mix
business marketing
integrated marketing
 communication (IMC)
user
original equipment
 manufacturer (OEM)
reseller

government organization
institution
new task buying situation
extensive problem solving
modified rebuy buying situation
limited problem solving
straight rebuy buying situation
routinized response behavior
buying center
buying process
buying needs
account targeting strategy
relationship strategy
selling strategy
sales channel strategy
distributors
independent representatives
team selling
telemarketing
trade shows
channel conflict

DEVELOPING SALES MANAGEMENT KNOWLEDGE

1. How does the corporate mission statement affect personal selling and sales management activities?

2. How can sales promotion and publicity be used to supplement a personal selling–driven strategy?

3. Why is personal selling typically emphasized in business markets and advertising emphasized in consumer markets?

4. Why do most firms use both personal selling and advertising in their strategies?

5. How would sales management activities differ for an SBU following a differentiation strategy versus an SBU using a low-cost strategy?

6. Discuss how the buying situation affects the buying center, the buying process, and buying needs.

7. How is the management of relationships with distributors different from the management of relationships with end-user customers?

8. How can trade shows be used to supplement other sales channels?

9. How might telemarketing be used when accounts are covered by distributors?

10. What are the most important organizational buyer behavior trends, and how might these trends affect sales strategies in the future?

BUILDING SALES MANAGEMENT SKILLS

1. Visit the library or use the Internet to find the annual report or similar information about a company of your choice. Try to choose a firm with whom you might like to work after graduation. Use the information in the annual report to describe the firm's corporate strategy, marketing strategy, and sales function.

2. You are the sales manager for WorldPub, a textbook publishing company. You believe it would be a good idea to get involved on the Internet to help move your company's line of college business textbooks. Discuss your strategy for using the Internet and other sales channels to sell textbooks.

3. Protech Athletics Manufacturing currently markets a line of sporting goods equipment through independent sales representatives. The company has grown considerably since its inception seven years ago. Recently, Protech has become frustrated with its independent reps. It believes its products are not getting the attention they deserve. Protech is wondering if there is something it can do to help motivate the reps. However, given its recent disappointment with the reps, Protech is entertaining the idea of developing its own salesforce. What do you suggest Protech do and why? What are the advantages and disadvantages associated with your solution?

4. A salesperson leaving a sales meeting was heard to remark, "If we didn't have to spend so much of our time with all this planning, we could spend our time on something productive like selling." What advice would you give this salesperson about the purposes of planning?

ROLE PLAY

5. **Role Play**

   Situation: Read An Ethical Dilemma on page 65.

   Characters: National Sales Manager for Fabricated Wire Company (FWC) and the president of your rep agency.

   Scene: *Location*—Conference room at FWC.
                    Action—Role Play the meeting between the two company representatives about selling directly to your customers.

MAKING SALES MANAGEMENT DECISIONS

CASE 3.1: COUSINS VIDEO AND PARTY STORES

Background

Cousins Video and Party Stores (CVPS) is a well-established company with over 150 outlets scattered along the West Coast. A little over 100 of their outlets are in California. Each outlet is a combination video store with a larger than usual party store. The party store side of the business has expanded over the past 10 years to carry almost anything a Celebration store might carry. The party store items can be anything from balloons and streamers for a birthday to seasonal holiday items. This combination has worked quite well for CVPS. Of the 150 stores, 47 are company-owned stores with the remaining stores leased to independent owners in a quasi-franchising agreement. The independent owners agree to buy their DVDs and party supplies from Cousins Video's parent company, Entertainment Inc. through their designated distributors. They also agree to uphold uniformity and facilitate appearance standards as set by Cousins Video. Every store's layout is exactly the same throughout the entire West Coast. The independent owners are encouraged to buy their convenience store merchandise from Cousins Video's designated distributor, but they are not required to do so. Lease payments are collected from independent owners when DVD deliveries are made each month when new releases come out.

Current Situation

In the past 12 months, Cousins Video and Party Store's growth rate has slowed considerably. This has been a major concern to CVPS's upper management, including Sophia Rones, vice president for sales. Rones has analyzed the declining growth rate and found that sales volume at company-owned stores is growing at a very acceptable 12 percent on an annualized basis. In contrast, stores run by independent dealers are lagging behind with an annual growth rate of only 2 percent. Rones believes the independent category is underperforming for three basic reasons. First, the independent stores are generally not kept as clean and professional looking as the company-owned stores. Second, many of the larger independent operators have begun buying a larger share of their party store merchandise from low-cost distributors other than CVPS's designated distributors. This hurts sales volume results, since CVPS's retail operation gets rebates from their designated distributors, which counts as sales volume in the Family Video financial system. Third, CVPS has suffered volume losses from closed outlets. Competition has intensified, and turnover among

dealers has become more commonplace. It was taking CVPS an average of 60 days to find new dealers when existing dealers decided to leave the business. When a dealer operation closed, CVPS rarely converted it to a company-owned store, as their aggressive growth strategy at the corporate level left little capital for acquisition of existing outlets.

Sophia Rones called her five regional managers into her California headquarters office to discuss the problem with declining sales volume and possible remedies to the problem. Given that the corporate strategy would continue to be to build market share and sales volume, Rones outlined the following five-point plan:

1. Each salesperson would continue to supervise company-owned stores and independent dealers.

2. Salespeople would be given specific objectives for facilities appearance and a percentage of sales of convenience store merchandise purchases from CVPS's designated distributors.

3. Salespeople would be given mandates that no retail outlet would remain closed for more than 30 days.

4. Sales volume objectives for salespeople would remain in place. Current year volume objectives would not change.

5. Regional sales managers' annual objectives would be revised to be consistent with salespeople's new objectives.

The regional managers saw the need for the revised strategy but raised several concerns. They felt that the corporate strategy focused on building market share, but that the sales organization was expected to both build and hold market share. They complained that the new-dealer team, a corporate group, should be adding new dealers at a faster rate, and that part of the volume shortfall was due to poor performance of the new dealer team, not the salesforce. They also pointed out that CVPS salespeople were paid on a straight salary basis, primarily because they had previously functioned more as managers of multiple retail outlets than as pure salespeople. The discussion became heated, and finally Lyle Holtzer spoke for the regional managers: "Look, Sophia, we know that corporate strategy can shift, and we know we have to adapt when that happens. But this drop in sales volume is partly the fault of the corporate new-dealer team. We don't see them having to change their ways. And we are really concerned that without some incentive pay, it will be hard to redirect our salespeople." Rones, having heard enough at this point, replied, "Tell your salespeople that their incentive is that if they succeed, they get to keep their jobs!" With that, the meeting quickly came to a conclusion.

Questions

1. Is it reasonable to charge CVPS' salesforce with simultaneously building and holding market share?

2. What are the pros and cons of Sophia Rones' five-point plan?

3. Since the meeting with the regional managers ended on a sour note, what should Gaines do now? What should the regional managers do?

Role Play

ROLE PLAY

Situation: Read Case 3.1.

Characters: Sophia Rones, Vice President of Sales; five regional managers.

Scene: *Location*—Conference room at Cousins Video and Party Stores Headquarters. *Action*—Role-play meeting among Sophia Rones and the five regional managers to discuss the five-point plan and to decide on a strategy to increase sales at independent stores.

CASE 3.2: NATIONAL COMMUNICATION MANUFACTURING

Background

National Communication Manufacturing (NCM) is a Kansas City-based manufacturer of GPS systems. In recent years, these devices have exploded in popularity as prices dropped to affordable levels. This is due to advancing technology and low-cost production outside the United States. Although NCM continues to manufacture a few of its own products, most production is outsourced to manufacturers in South Korea.

A key element in the NCM success story is the growth of dominant retail chains and club wholesalers such as Wal-Mart, Target, Best Buy, Sam's Club, and Costco. NCM uses major account teams to serve these and other large discounters, which accounts for 75 percent of NCM annual sales. The remaining 25 percent comes from smaller retail accounts that buy either from NCM's manufacture representative or directly from NCM's Web site.

Current Situation

Ann Culligan, NCM's national sales manager, is working on two major issues. First, she is fighting to keep NCM's direct cost of sales at 5 percent of total sales. The 5 percent target has been part of NCM's sales culture for more than 30 years, reflecting the belief that a low-cost operation translates into a more competitive position in the marketplace. Over the past few years, Ann's sales organization has reduced cost in various ways.

E-mail and texting, instead of long-distance phone calls, staying in budget motels, cutting overnight travel to a minimum were just a few of the measures taken to stay within the 5 percent guideline. In spite of Ann's diligent efforts, cost of sales was running at 7 percent for the major account team. Commissions remained fixed for several years at 4.5 percent.

The second issue currently demanding Ann's attention ironically stemmed from a NCM cost-cutting measure that was implemented one year ago. In an attempt to reduce manufacturer's representative costs, NCM has established a Web site as an alternative channel for smaller retailer customers. The reps have protested vehemently, but NCM insisted that selling on the Internet was an essential part of their selling strategy. Not all of NCM's products were available on the Web, a fact that did little to make happy the disgruntled representatives. Cost of sales of the Web site was a modest 2 percent of sales. Sales volume on the Web amounted to 3 percent of NCM's total sales during the past year, but current projections were for volume to increase to 5 percent of total sales this year and perhaps as much as 10 percent the following year. Some of the stronger reps were threatening to leave NCM in favor of the major competitor, which offered its reps a partial commission on all Web sales.

As Ann thought about the situation, she began to wonder if she could hit the 5 percent cost of sales target this year. Ninety percent of the cost of her major account teams was compensation-related salaries and incentive pay. Good salespeople were hard to find, and Ann had found that NCM had to pay the going rate or else NCM's top performers would look for new opportunities. Ann still regretted the recent loss of Barb Sherman, a major account manager, to a competitor who offered a better pay percentage. Sales volume at Sherman's former account had dropped 15 percent after her departure.

Ann didn't like to think about changing her major account strategy, but she wondered if she could move some of her large retail chain accounts to the manufacturers' rep organization. After all, representative commissions ran only 4.5 percent, and essentially there were no other direct sales costs associated with the reps. As she headed home after a long day at the office, Ann thought that the next morning she would try to build a case with the CEO of NCM to revise the 5 percent cost-of-sales target to reflect reality. If the answer is no, Ann thought she just might explore the idea of consolidating her major account teams and handing one selected large retail account to some of the more capable representative firms. She hated the idea of laying people off, but she told herself it may be necessary in this case.

Questions

1. Should Ann request a revision of the 5 percent cost-of-sales target? If so, what sort of information would she need to convince her CEO?

2. What factors should Ann consider as she contemplates a change in major account sales strategy, especially a change that assigns independent reps to some major accounts?

3. How would you assess NCM's alternative sales channel on the Web? Can you recommend any changes to minimize conflict with the independent reps?

ROLE PLAY

Role Play

Situation: Read Case 3.2.

Characters: Ann Culligan, NCM's National Sales Manager; CEO of GPP; President of Manufacturers' rep agency.

Scene 1:   *Location*—Office of NCM CEO. *Action*—Role-play meeting between Ann Culligan and NCM CEO to discuss 5 percent cost-of-sales target and to arrive at a decision.

Scene 2:   *Location*—Ann Culligan's office. *Action*—Role-play meeting between Ann Culligan and president of manufacturers' rep agency concerning the practice of selling over the Internet by NCM to arrive at a decision.

SALES ORGANIZATION STRUCTURE, SALESFORCE DEPLOYMENT, AND FORECASTING

OBJECTIVES

After completing this chapter, you should be able to

1. Define the concepts of specialization, centralization, span of control versus management levels, and line versus staff positions.

2. Describe the ways salesforces might be specialized.

3. Evaluate the advantages and disadvantages of sales organization structures.

4. Name the important considerations in organizing strategic account management programs.

5. Explain how to determine the appropriate sales organization structure for a given selling situation.

6. Discuss salesforce deployment.

7. Explain three analytical approaches for determining allocation of selling effort.

8. Describe three methods for calculating salesforce size.

9. Explain the importance of sales territories and list the steps in the territory design process.

10. Discuss the important "people" considerations in salesforce deployment.

11. Discuss the importance of forecasting and its role in sales force decision making.

USING INTELLIGENT FORECASTING TO ASSESS FUTURE SALES

If your sales forecast is cloudy—meaning you can't see the forest for the trees— here are some tips to make this essential element of every sales year a bit more transparent and accurate, even rewarding.

But first, some things to keep in mind:

1. Even the best forecasts will be wrong to some degree.

2. A sales forecast may become a goal that top management expects to be fulfilled.

3. There's always a temptation to underestimate to make the numbers look better down the road.

4. There's also a temptation on the part of new managers to over-promise.

5. What top management generally wants—and what managers should shoot for—is accuracy, no matter how difficult it is to achieve.

6. Top sales executives must know what they can expect from a far-flung field force that usually knows much more about the market than headquarters can.

Outside of the sales department, other company officials have a necessary interest in sales prospects.

While forecasting forces managers to confront, at the beginning of every year, the true nature of the coming sales challenge, this can be a very healthy exercise for a variety of reasons. It can flag problems or hurdles that must be overcome if satisfactory results are to be obtained. If difficulties lie ahead, it is better to know about them early, when solutions can still be found.

Mike Hemmer—a sales manager for a mid-sized wood materials, moldings, decorations, and door jambs company that sells through distributors to the home market—remembers when his job got a lot harder due to forces beyond his control. Forecasting became a huge challenge in Hemmer's market because a national homebuilder had entered and changed the market. "Much of our customer base was companies that supplied this homebuilder, and there was no loyalty or partnership," Hemmer says. "It's a commodity business. It comes down to price on many orders."

Elsewhere in the country, a variety of his company's wood products was more extensively used in new homes. But, in the sunny Southwest where Hemmer works, the moldings his company sells are less important—and they are fairly standard in configuration. That helps make price competition intense. "Yet we still have to make sales forecasts." For the firm must purchase its own products abroad, often three months ahead of delivery to customers.

And these customers want their products promptly, so Hemmer's company must keep millions of dollars of inventory on hand. Moreover, Hemmer must forecast sales to individual customers, because each customer often wants a different product.

Hemmer first tries to persuade his customers that there is still value in partnering, and he is sometimes successful in this effort. "When those guys are receptive to partnerships, we know what is coming up and we can crunch numbers and figure we will get 60 percent of that."

But, for other customers—the ones who must be won on price—Hemmer gets out his crystal ball. He looks at history and makes forecasts statistically. "We figure we will win one this week and then not the next week."

Hemmer works with his reps to do all the forecasts. "We use spreadsheets, and we spend a lot of time on it." Hemmer also uses proprietary software that helps with purchases, after he puts in the basic trends.

Even where price competition is not intense, forecasting can be very tricky. Jerry Aingsley forecasts revenue frequently and then must monitor sales activity very closely. Aingsley manages sales for a legal solutions firm that provides litigation support such as image scanning and electronic culling of millions of emails for legal discovery proceedings. It is not a simple, commodity business.

"It is a relationship sale," he says. Indeed, the average sales cycle is six visits before close. Aingsley starts each year by forecasting annual revenue broken down by month. He adjusts these monthly numbers every quarter. He relies chiefly on two bases for his forecast: the tenure of his sales reps and the company's project-tracking system. The project-tracking system lets Aingsley know when there is a large case coming down the road in, say, three months. Then the company will seek this business and look at all aspects of the case. "We need to decide who we need to sell to—the law firm or the client."

Rep experience is also crucial. Right now, Aingsley has mostly new reps on his team. "I cannot expect a brand-new rep to hit the street and sell $50,000 to $60,000 in his first month. It is possible, but not very likely." Aingsley does not expect a new rep to have any revenue in his first month. From the second to the fourth month he expects each rep to do perhaps $5,000 to $10,000 per month. By the sixth month, a rep should be in the $30,000 to $35,000 range.

"If I had a rep on my staff for five years, he might have built relationships that would add up to $60,000 per month. Then, if he has been tracking a large project, he might know that it is good for $40,000." So Aingsley could forecast $100,000 for the month with some confidence.

For new reps, Aingsley chiefly tracks visits: first-time, follow-up, and buyer visits. The first month, a new rep makes about 70 first-time visits; the next month, there will be follow-up visits; and only later will there be buyer visits, as relationships have developed. "I track all these activity measures on a daily basis."

Sometimes the business dictates the forecasts. Sarah Arnaud runs her own public relations company selling sponsorships for special events in communities that are bringing their old downtowns back to life. She seeks sponsorships from local businesses and has been at it for 15 years.

Arnaud starts her forecasts by figuring out how much she has to raise for each community. "I say we have $100,000 for this and $95,000 for that, and then another half million. I put it all down and see how much more we have to raise," she explains. Then she looks for logical buying times and where there are the concentrations of potential sponsors. "I end up juggling quite a bit," Arnaud says. "I want to go for low-hanging fruit. And, when we go after multiple events, I want to seek one sponsor for several events."

It is all a little rough. "I'd like to tell you it is brilliant and intelligent and I have an exact forecast, but I don't." Arnaud works mostly by experience. In 16 years, she has booked a quarter of her sponsors between Christmas and New Year's. "That is when executives are in their offices and there are no gatekeepers. You may not get through, but, if you do, it is to an executive."

Arnaud is really working on goals, not forecasts. "I have a little thermometer on the wall because I am very visual. I like to see where we are on things. I start out with an objective and try to see how to get to it."

Arnaud has developed a formula and knows it works. By September of any year, she already knew what events she would do for all of the next year. She does not take new clients for the following year after August 1. "And I am a fanatic about service. That makes hitting our goals much easier."

Source: Henry Canaday, *Selling Power* magazine, May 2018.

Chapter 3 discussed the close relationships among corporate, business, marketing, and sales strategies. The strategic levels must be consistent and integrated to be effective. Strategic changes at one organizational level typically require strategic changes at other organizational levels.

The development of effective strategies is one thing, successfully implementing them another. In one sense, the remainder of this book is concerned with the development and management of a sales organization to implement organizational strategies successfully. This chapter begins the journey into successful implementation by investigating the key decisions required in sales organization structure and salesforce deployment.

Appendix A discusses how forecasts provide the basis for critical sales decisions including: determining sales force size, determining territories, establishing sales quotas, setting budgets, and determining salesforce performance. The opening vignette discusses the importance of forecasting and how forecasting can flag problems or hurdles that must be overcome if satisfactory results are to be obtained. Forecasting can head off problems that may be ahead; it is better to know about them early when solutions can still be found.

SALES ORGANIZATION CONCEPTS

The basic problem in sales organization structure can be presented in simple terms. The corporate, business, marketing, and sales strategies developed by a firm prescribe specific activities that must be performed by salespeople for these strategies to be successful. Sales managers are also needed to recruit, select, train, motivate, supervise, evaluate, and control salespeople. In essence, the firm has salespeople and sales managers who must engage in a variety of activities for the firm to perform successfully. A sales organization structure must be developed to help salespeople and sales managers perform the required activities effectively and efficiently. This structure provides a framework for sales organization operations by indicating what specific activities are performed by whom in the sales organization. The sales organization structure is the vehicle through which strategic plans are translated into selling operations in the marketplace.[1]

The important role of a sales organization structure for a firm has been described as follows:

> The role of organization in sales has been compared to that of the skeleton in the human body; it provides a framework within which normal functions must take place. There is, however, a degree of uniformity in the human skeleton that does not characterize the sales organization. Each firm has its own objectives and problems, and the structure of the sales organization reflects this diversity.[2]

Developing a sales organization structure is difficult. Many different types of structures might be used, and many variations are possible within each basic type. Often the resultant structure is complex, with many boxes and arrows. The basic concepts involved are specialization, centralization, span of control versus management levels, and line versus staff positions.[3]

Specialization

Our earlier discussion suggested that a sales organization structure must ensure that all required selling and management activities are performed. In the simplest case, each salesperson could perform all selling tasks, and each sales manager could perform all management activities. Most sales organizations, however, are too complex for this structure and require instead some degree of **specialization**, in which certain individuals concentrate on performing some of the required activities to the exclusion of other tasks. Thus, certain salespeople might sell only certain products or call on certain customers. Some sales managers might concentrate on training, others on planning. The basic idea behind specialization is that, by concentrating on a limited number of activities, individuals can become experts on those tasks, leading to better performance for the entire organization. This approach can produce difficult situations as indicated in "An Ethical Dilemma."

A useful way to view salesforce specialization is from the perspective of the continuum presented in Figure 4.1. At one extreme, salespeople act as generalists, performing all selling activities for all the company's products to all types of customers. Moving toward the right of the continuum, salespeople begin to specialize by performing only certain selling tasks, selling only certain types of products, or calling on only specific types of accounts.

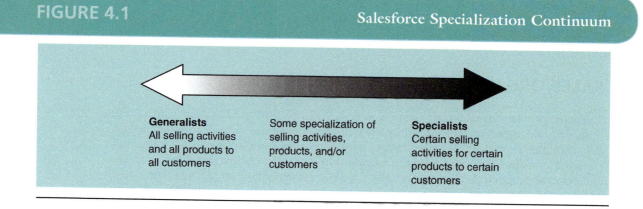

FIGURE 4.1   Salesforce Specialization Continuum

Generalists
All selling activities and all products to all customers

Some specialization of selling activities, products, and/or customers

Specialists
Certain selling activities for certain products to certain customers

A broad range of alternatives exists for specializing salesforce activities.

AN ETHICAL DILEMMA

Digital Electronic Computers (DEC) has spent a lot of money reorganizing their salesforce. From its beginning DEC's salespeople were responsible for all their products and all their customer types. The company had a huge growth spurt and the sales management team had decided their customers needed specific attention given to them depending on their size. DEC divided their salesforce into two groups: large accounts (LA sales team, companies that grossed $10,000,000 or more per year in sales) and small accounts (GA sales team, companies that grossed less than $10,000,000 in sales. On paper this looked good until the large account representatives started screaming they were not only selling against IBM, HP, and other computer giants, but now they were competing against one of their own (the GA salesforce). LA

sales manager, Tom Bradley, had to figure out what to do; his GA counterpart, Mary Thompson, thought all was fair and they should continue to let their salesforces go at it. DEC had small products like D-80 and D-800 that were meant to be sold to the small accounts. The D-1800 and D-2800 were built for large accounts. The GA sales team had been going after $8–12 million accounts to expand their market. The GA sales team had found a way to soup-up their D-800's to meet the needs of the larger accounts. What should Tom Bradley do?

a. Sit down with Mary Thompson and work out an agreement.
b. Tell his LA salesforce they need to work harder.
c. Maybe it is time to realign LA and GA accounts?

Centralization

An important characteristic of the management structure within a sales organization is its degree of **centralization**—that is, the degree to which important decisions and tasks are performed at higher levels in the management hierarchy. A centralized structure is one in which authority and responsibility are placed at higher management levels. An organization becomes more decentralized as tasks become the responsibility of lower-level managers. Centralization is a relative concept in that no organization is totally centralized or totally decentralized. Organizations typically centralize some activities and decentralize others. However, most organizations tend to have a centralized or decentralized orientation. There is no single greater influence over the success of the sales organization than how the sales leadership creates the sales culture and environment for the people who will work for them. In this regard, the best organizations have strong leaders who exercise authoritarian control, dictate team direction, and establish the codes of behavior that all team members must abide by. Although these tenets are similarly used within military units to enforce chain of command, sales leaders prefer to use motivation and the force of their personal character before employing the power associated to their title.

The senior leadership team typically does not micromanage its sales teams below. Instead, there is independent and autonomous local decision making that operates within the guidelines and protocols established by the leaders above. But rest assured, the actions of the lower levels of the organization always take into account the goals and desires of the senior leaders.[4]

The trends from transactions to relationships, from individuals to teams, and from management to leadership, are producing a more decentralized orientation in many sales organizations. Salespeople and other sales team members who have contact with customers must be able to respond to customer needs in a timely manner. They must be empowered to make decisions quickly. A decentralized structure facilitates decision making in the field and encourages the development of relationships with customers.

Span of Control versus Management Levels

Span of control refers to the number of individuals who report to each sales manager. The larger the span of control, the more subordinates a sales manager must supervise. **Management levels** define the number of different hierarchical levels of sales management within the organization. Typically, span of control is inversely related to the number of sales management levels. This relationship is illustrated in Figure 4.2.

In the flat sales organization structure, there are relatively few sales management levels, with each sales manager having a relatively large span of control. Conversely, in the tall structure, there are more sales management levels and smaller spans of control. Flat organization structures tend to be used to achieve decentralization, whereas tall structures are more appropriate for centralized organizations. The span of control also tends to increase at lower sales management levels. Thus, as one moves down the organization chart from national sales manager to regional sales manager to district sales manager, the number of individuals to be supervised directly increases.

FIGURE 4.2   Span of Control versus Management Levels

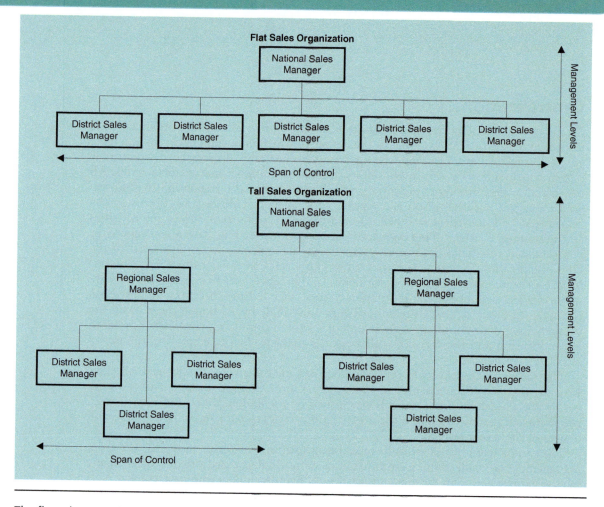

The flat sales organization has only two sales management levels, giving the national sales manager a span of control of 5. The tall sales organization has three sales management levels, giving the national sales manager a span of control of only 2.

Line versus Staff Positions

Sales management positions can be differentiated as to line or staff positions. **Line sales management** positions are part of the direct management hierarchy within the sales organization. Line sales managers have direct responsibility for a certain number of subordinates and report directly to management at the next highest level in the sales organization. These managers are directly involved in the sales-generating activities of the firm and may perform any number of sales management activities. **Staff sales management** positions, however, are not in the direct chain of command in the sales organization structure. Instead, those in staff positions do not directly manage people, but they are responsible for certain functions (e.g., recruiting and selecting, training) and are not directly involved in sales-generating activities. Staff sales management positions are more specialized than line sales management positions.

A comparison of line and staff sales management positions is presented in Figure 4.3. The regional and district sales managers all operate in line positions. The district sales managers directly manage the field salesforce and report to a specific regional sales manager. The regional sales managers manage the district sales managers and report to the national sales manager. Two staff positions are represented in the figure. These training managers are located at both the national and regional levels and are responsible for sales training programs at each level. The use of staff positions results in more specialization of sales management activities. Staff managers specialize in certain sales management activities.

In sum, designing the sales organization is an extremely important and complex task. Decisions concerning the appropriate specialization, centralization, span of control versus management levels, and line versus staff positions, are difficult. Although these decisions should be based on the specifics of each selling situation, several trends appear to be emerging. Many sales organizations are moving to some type of specialization, usually a

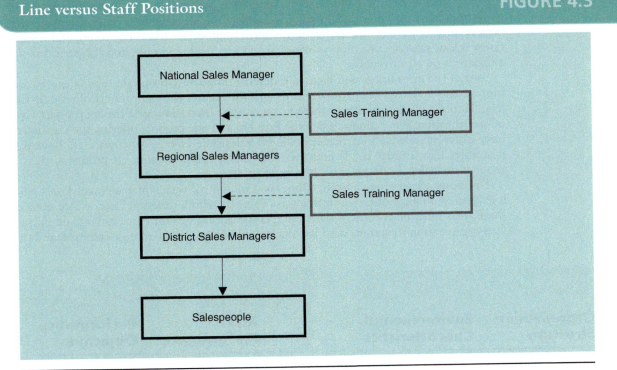

Line versus Staff Positions   FIGURE 4.3

The national, regional, and district sales managers occupy line positions, whereas the sales training managers represent staff positions.

structure that allows salespeople to concentrate on specific types of customers. The downsizing and restructuring of entire companies have affected the sales function. Sales management levels have been eliminated and replaced by sales organization structures that are flatter and that increase the span of control exercised by the remaining sales managers. This restructuring has influenced the trend toward more decentralized orientations and has resulted in the elimination of some staff positions. For example, some sales organizations have outsourced the sales training function to sales training firms, thereby either eliminating or greatly reducing the number of sales training staff positions.

SELLING SITUATION CONTINGENCIES

Determining the appropriate type of sales organization structure is as difficult as it is important. There is no one best way to organize a salesforce. The appropriate organization structure depends, or is contingent, on the characteristics of the selling situation. As a selling situation changes, the type of sales organization structure may also need to change. One key decision in sales organization design relates to specialization. Two basic questions must be addressed:

1. Should the salesforce be specialized?

2. If the salesforce should be specialized, what type of specialization is most appropriate?

The decision on specialization hinges on the relative importance to the firm of selling skill versus selling effort. Thus, if sales management wants to emphasize the amount of selling contact, a generalized salesforce should be used. If sales management wants to focus on specific skills within each selling contact, then a specialized salesforce should be used. Obviously, there must be some balance between selling effort and selling skill in all situations. But sales management can skew this balance toward selling effort or selling skill by employing a generalized or specialized salesforce.

Some guidelines for sales organization structure and selling situation factors are presented in Exhibit 4.1.[5] This exhibit suggests that a specialized structure is best when there is a high level of environmental uncertainty, when salespeople and sales managers must perform creative and nonroutine activities, and when adaptability is critical to achieving performance objectives. Centralization is most appropriate when environmental uncertainty is low, sales organization activities are routine and repetitive, and the performance emphasis is on effectiveness.

Two of the most important factors in determining the appropriate type of specialization are the similarity of customer needs and the complexity of products offered by the firm. Figure 4.4[6] illustrates how these factors can be used to suggest the appropriate type of specialization. For example, when the firm has a simple product offering but customers have different needs, a market-specialized salesforce is recommended. If, however, customers have similar needs and the firm sells a complex range of products, then a product-specialized salesforce is more appropriate.

Decisions concerning centralization, span of control versus management levels, and line versus staff positions, require analysis of similar selling situation factors. Decisions in these areas must be consistent with the specialization decision. For example, decentralized organization structures with few management levels, large spans of control, and the

---

EXHIBIT 4.1   Selling Situation Factors and Organizational Structure

Organization Structure	Environmental Characteristics	Task Performance	Performance Objective
Specialization	High environmental uncertainty	Nonroutine	Adaptiveness
Centralization	Low environmental uncertainty	Repetitive	Effectiveness

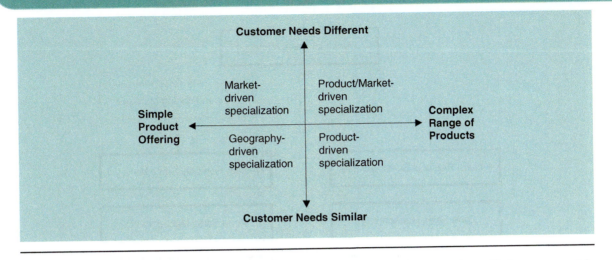

Customer and Product Determinants of Salesforce Specialization   FIGURE 4.4

Analysis of the similarity of customer needs and the complexity of a firm's product offering can provide general guidelines for determining the appropriate type of salesforce specialization.

use of staff positions may be consistent with a specialized salesforce in some selling situations but not in others.

Although the appropriate sales organization structure depends on the specific characteristics of a firm's selling situation, research evidence suggests that the structures need to change as a business goes through its life cycle. As firms move from start-up to growth to maturity to decline, the size and structure of the sales organization needs to adapt to the different situations at each life cycle stage. For example, specialization is most important in the growth and maturity stages and much less important at the start-up and decline stages. Sales managers should be alert to the need to examine their sales organization structure as their firm grows and matures.[7]

SALES ORGANIZATION STRUCTURES

Designing the sales organization structure requires integration of the desired degree of specialization, centralization, span of control, management levels, line positions, and staff positions. Obviously, there are a tremendous number of ways a sales organization might be structured. Our objective is to review several of the basic and most often used ways and to illustrate some variations in these basic structures.

To provide continuity to this discussion, each type of sales organization is discussed from the perspective of the ABC Company. The ABC Company markets office equipment (e.g., printers, furniture) and office supplies (e.g., paper, pencils) to commercial and government accounts. The firm employs 200 salespeople, who operate throughout the United States. The salespeople perform various activities that can be characterized as being related either to sales generation or account servicing. Examples of sales organization structures that the ABC Company might use are presented and discussed.

Geographic Sales Organization

Many salesforces emphasize **geographic specialization.** This is the least specialized and most generalized type of salesforce. Salespeople are typically assigned a geographic area and are responsible for all selling activities to all accounts within the assigned area.[8] There is no attempt to specialize by product, market, or function. An example of a geographic sales organization for the ABC Company is presented in Figure 4.5. Again, note

FIGURE 4.5   Geographic Sales Organization

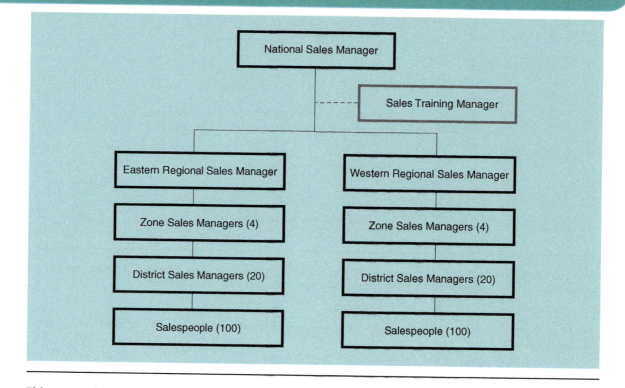

This geographic sales organization structure has four sales management levels, small spans of control, and a staff position at the national level.

that this type of organization provides no salesforce specialization except by geographic area. Because of the lack of specialization, there is no duplication of effort. All geographic areas and accounts are served by only one salesperson.

The structure in this example is a rather tall one and thus somewhat centralized. There are four levels of line sales management with relatively small spans of control, indicated in parentheses: national sales manager (2), regional sales managers (4), zone sales managers (5), and district sales managers (5). Note the sales management specialization in the sales training staff position. Because this staff position is located at the national sales manager level, training activities tend to be centralized.

Product Sales Organization

Product specialization has been popular in recent years, but it seems to be declining in importance, at least in certain industries. Salesforces specializing by product assign salespeople selling responsibility for specific products or product lines. The objective is for salespeople to become experts in the assigned product categories.

An example of a product sales organization for the ABC Company is presented in Figure 4.6. This organization structure indicates two levels of product specialization. There are two separate salesforces: One salesforce specializes in selling office equipment, and the other specializes in selling office supplies. Each of the specialized salesforces performs all selling activities for all types of accounts. The separate salesforces are each organized geographically. Thus, there will be duplication in the coverage of geographic areas, with both office equipment and office supplies salespeople operating in the same areas. In some cases, the salespeople may call on the same accounts.

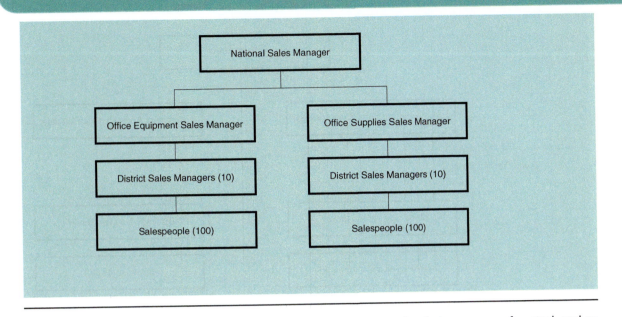

Product Sales Organization   FIGURE 4.6

This product sales organization structure has three sales management levels, large spans of control, and no staff positions.

The example structure in Figure 4.6 is flat and decentralized, especially when compared with the example presented in Figure 4.5. There are only three line management levels, with wide spans of control: national sales manager (2), product sales managers (10), and district sales managers (10). This structure has no staff positions and thus no management specialization beyond product specialization. The office equipment and office supplies salesforces are organized in exactly the same manner.

Market Sales Organization

An increasingly important type of specialization is **market specialization**. Salespeople are assigned specific types of customers and are required to satisfy all needs of these customers. The basic objective of market specialization is to ensure that salespeople understand how customers use and purchase their products. Salespeople should then be able to direct their efforts to satisfy customer needs better. There is a clear trend toward market specializations by many sales organizations.[9] For example, Yahoo! recently merged its search and display advertising salespeople into one salesforce. Instead of just selling search or display advertising, the salespeople now can focus on meeting all of the advertising needs of its customers from brand awareness to direct response.[10]

The market sales organization shown for the ABC Company in Figure 4.7 focuses on account types. Separate salesforces have been organized for commercial and government accounts. Salespeople perform all selling activities for all products but only for certain accounts. This arrangement avoids duplication of sales effort, because only one salesperson will ever call on a given account. Several salespeople may, however, operate in the same geographic area.

The example in Figure 4.7 presents some interesting variations in sales management organization. The commercial accounts salesforce is much more centralized than the government accounts salesforce. This centralization is due to more line management levels, shorter spans of control, and a specialized sales training staff position. This example structure illustrates the important point that the specialized salesforces within a sales organization do not have to be structured in the same manner.

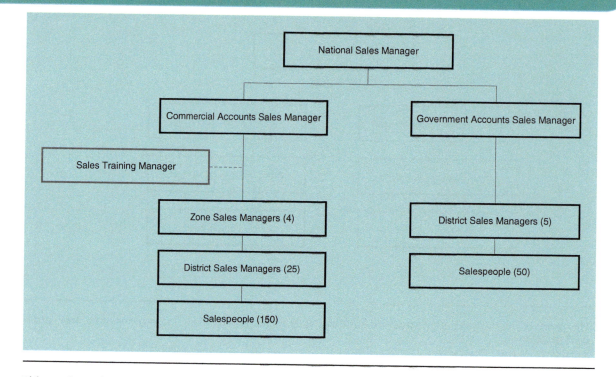

FIGURE 4.7   Market Sales Organization

This market sales organization structure organizes its commercial accounts salesforce differently from its government accounts salesforce. The commercial accounts salesforce has three sales management levels, small spans of control, and a staff position. The government accounts salesforce has two sales management levels, large spans of control, and no staff positions.

Functional Sales Organization

The final type of specialization is **functional specialization**. Most selling situations require a number of selling activities, so there may be efficiencies in having salespeople specialize in performing certain of these required activities. As already discussed in Chapter 3, many firms are using a telemarketing salesforce to generate leads, qualify prospects, monitor shipments, and so forth, while the outside salesforce concentrates on sales-generating activities. These firms are specializing by function.

An example of a functional sales organization for ABC Company is presented in Figure 4.8. In this structure, a field salesforce performs sales-generating activities and a telemarketing salesforce performs account-servicing activities. Although the salesforces will cover the same geographic areas and the same accounts, the use of telemarketing helps to reduce the cost of this duplication of effort. The more routine and repetitive activities will be performed by the inside telemarketing salesforce. The more creative and nonroutine sales-generating activities will be performed by the outside field salesforce.

The field salesforce is more centralized than the telemarketing salesforce, but both salesforces tend to be decentralized. The cost-effectiveness of telemarketing is illustrated by the need for only two management levels and three managers to supervise 40 salespeople. This example does not include any staff positions for sales management specialization.

Strategic Account Organization

Many firms receive a large percentage of their total sales from relatively few accounts. These large-volume accounts are obviously extremely important and must be considered

Functional Sales Organization   FIGURE 4.8

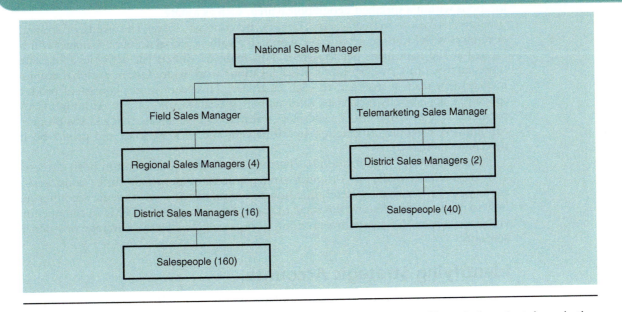

This functional sales organization structure organizes its field salesforce differently from its telemarketing salesforce. The field salesforce has three sales management levels, with small spans of control, and the telemarketing salesforce has two sales management levels, with large spans of control. Neither salesforce uses staff positions.

when designing a sales organization. The term **strategic account** is used to refer to large, important accounts that should receive special attention from the sales organization. Some firms use the terms *key account* or *major account* instead. Although the terms *strategic account*, *key account*, and *major account* are often used interchangeably, we emphasize strategic account, because the relevant professional association is named the Strategic Account Management Association (www.strategicaccounts.org). One approach for serving strategic accounts is presented in "Sales Management in the 21st Century: Organizing Strategic Accounts."

A **strategic account organization** represents a type of market specialization based on account size and complexity. Two types of strategic account organizations are of particular importance. **National account management (NAM)** focuses on meeting

SALES MANAGEMENT IN THE 21ST CENTURY

Organizing Strategic Accounts

Darlene Keppler, manager of account sales for Keppler Steel, a division of Keppler International, discusses her company's perspective for serving strategic accounts:

Keppler Steel is a manufacturer of fabricated metal wire. Keppler produces products for forging and stamping, architectural, structural metals, manufacturing, and spring and wire products. The forging and stamping are considered strategic accounts because they have a high potential for *product exposure and sales. Depending on the scope of the consumer product company, Keppler Steel has either a national or international sales account manager assigned to each customer. The manager is responsible for working with a team of Keppler colleagues to meet the high standards that strategic accounts require. Strategic account sales managers must be astute front-line managers, and have the ability to interface effectively with marketing, production planning, packaging, quality, and manufacturing departments.*

the needs of specific accounts with multiple locations throughout a large region or entire country. For example, Cintas has both national and regional accounts. National accounts have locations throughout the U.S. Regional accounts, in contrast, might have 10–15 locations within a specified geographical area, such as a state.

Global account management (GAM), by contrast, serves the needs of strategic customers with locations around the world. Typically, a global account manager will be located at the customer's headquarters. This manager directs the activities of account representatives in that customer's other locations worldwide. Often, a global account management team is assigned to each customer. This team might consist of product specialists, applications specialists, sales support specialists, and others. Although GAM programs take time and effort to develop, research results indicate that a GAM program can improve customer satisfaction by 20 percent and increase sales and profits by 15 percent or more.[11]

Strategic account organization has become increasingly important in both domestic and international markets. Although strategic account programs differ considerably across firms, all firms must determine how to identify their own strategic accounts and how to organize for effective coverage of them. Steve Andersen of PMI in the opening vignette describes his company's program to organize for effective coverage of strategic accounts.

Identifying Strategic Accounts

All large accounts do not qualify as strategic accounts. As illustrated in Figure 4.9, a strategic account should be of sufficient size and complexity to warrant special attention from the sales organization. An account can be considered complex under the following circumstances:[12]

- There are multiple buying locations.
- Top management heavily influences its purchasing decisions.
- Multiple functions are involved in buying decisions.
- Its purchasing process is complex and diffuse.
- Some purchasing activities are centralized.
- It requires special services.

FIGURE 4.9 **Identifying Strategic Accounts**

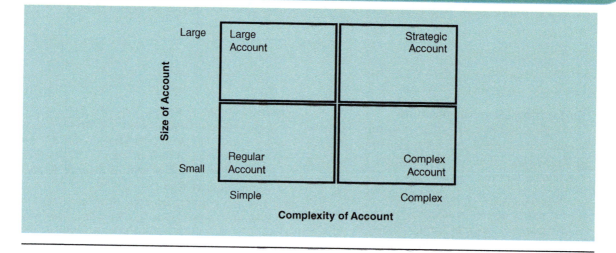

Strategic accounts are both large and complex. They are extremely important to the firm and require specialized attention.

Strategic Account Options   FIGURE 4.10

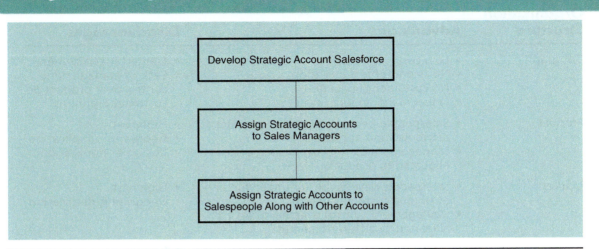

Once identified, strategic accounts can be served in three basic ways. The development of a strategic account salesforce is the most comprehensive approach and is being used increasingly often for customers in domestic and international markets.

Organizing for Strategic Account Coverage

Accounts that are not both large and complex are typically served adequately through the basic sales organization structure, but those identified as strategic accounts pose problems for organization design that might be handled in a variety of ways. The basic options are shown in Figure 4.10. In one option, strategic accounts, although identified, are assigned to salespeople, as are other accounts. This approach may provide some special attention to these accounts but is not a formal major account management program.

Many firms have found that formal strategic account management programs can strengthen account relationships and improve communications between buyers and sellers. These formal programs are designed in several ways. One approach is to assign strategic accounts to sales executives, who are responsible for coordinating all activities with each assigned account. This strategic account responsibility is typically in addition to the executives' normal management activities.

An increasingly popular approach is to establish a separate strategic account salesforce. This approach is a type of market specialization in which salespeople specialize by type of account based on size and complexity. Each salesperson is typically assigned one or more strategic accounts and is responsible for coordinating all seller activities to serve the assigned accounts. In other cases, formal sales teams are created to serve specific strategic accounts. Research indicates that the effectiveness of the strategic account salesforce depends on the esprit de corps of those serving the major account, access to sales and marketing resources, the number of activities performed with the strategic account, and top management involvement. Interestingly, the formalization of the strategic account salesforce approach was not related to effectiveness.[13]

COMPARING SALES ORGANIZATION STRUCTURES

The sales organization structures described in the preceding section represent the basic types of salesforce specialization and some examples of the variations possible. A premise of this chapter is that no one best way exists to structure a sales organization. The appropriate structure for a given sales organization depends on the characteristics of the selling situation. Some structures are better in some selling situations

EXHIBIT 4.2	Comparison of Sales Organization Structures

Organization Structure	Advantages	Disadvantages
Geographic	• Low cost • No geographic duplication • No customer duplication • Fewer management levels	• Limited specialization • Lack of management control over product or customer emphasis
Product	• Salespeople become experts in product attributes and applications • Management control overselling effort allocated to products	• High cost • Geographic duplication • Customer duplication
Market	• Salespeople develop better understanding of unique customer needs • Management control overselling effort allocated to different markets	• High cost • Geographic duplication
Functional	• Efficiency in performing selling activities	• Geographic duplication • Customer duplication • Need for coordination

than in others. Exhibit 4.2 summarizes much of what has been discussed previously by directly comparing the advantages and disadvantages of each basic sales organization structure.

As is evident from this exhibit, the strengths of one structure are weaknesses in other structures. For example, the lack of geographic and customer duplication is an advantage of a geographic structure but a disadvantage of the product and market structures. Because of this situation, many firms use **hybrid sales organization** structures that incorporate several of the basic structural types. The objective of these hybrid structures is to capitalize on the advantages of each type while minimizing the disadvantages.

An example of a hybrid sales organizational structure is presented in Figure 4.11. This structure is extremely complex in that it includes elements of geographic, product, market, function, and major account organizations. Although Figure 4.11 represents only one possible hybrid structure, it does illustrate how the different structure types might be combined into one overall sales organization structure. The example also illustrates the complex nature of the task of determining sales organization structure. As noted before, the task is an extremely important one; sales management must develop the appropriate sales organization structure for its particular selling situation to ensure the successful implementation of organizational and account strategies. This task becomes increasingly more difficult as firms operate globally.

SALESFORCE DEPLOYMENT

The important sales management decisions involved in allocating selling effort, determining salesforce size, and designing territories are often referred to as **salesforce deployment**. These decisions are closely related to the sales organization structure decisions. Changes in structure often require adjustments in all three areas of salesforce deployment—selling effort allocation, salesforce size determination, and territory design.

Salesforce deployment decisions can be viewed as providing answers to three interrelated questions.

1. How much selling effort is needed to cover accounts and prospects adequately so that sales and profit objectives will be achieved?

2. How many salespeople are required to provide the desired amount of selling effort?

Hybrid Sales Organization Structure   FIGURE 4.11

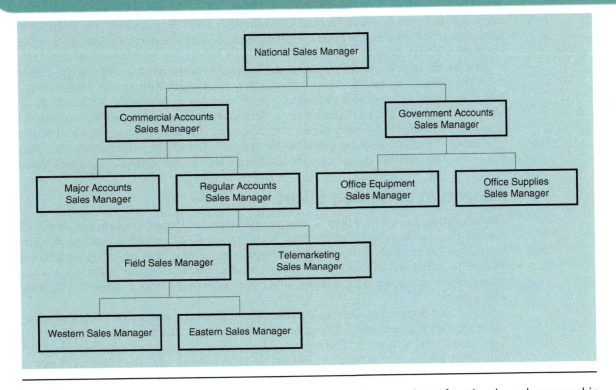

This complex sales organization structure incorporates market, product, functional, and geographic specialization.

Interrelatedness of Salesforce Deployment Decisions   FIGURE 4.12

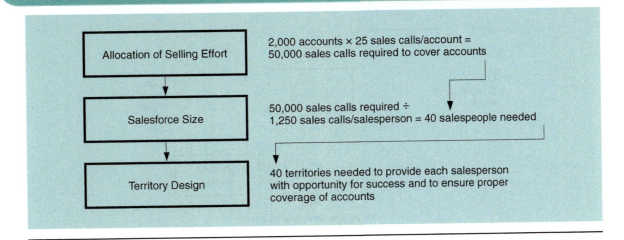

Determining how much selling effort should be allocated to various accounts provides a basis for calculating the number of salespeople required to produce the desired amount of selling effort. The salesforce size decision then determines the number of territories that must be designed. Thus, decisions in one deployment area affect decisions in other deployment areas.

3. How should territories be designed to ensure proper coverage of accounts and to provide each salesperson with a reasonable opportunity for success?

The interrelatedness of these decisions is illustrated in Figure 4.12. Decisions in one salesforce deployment area affect decisions in other areas. For example, the decision on allocation of selling effort provides input for determining salesforce size, which provides input for territory design.

Despite the importance of salesforce deployment and the need to address the deployment decisions in an interrelated manner, many sales organizations use simplified analytical methods and consider each deployment decision in isolation—an approach not likely to result in the best deployment decisions. Even such simplified approaches, however, can typically identify deployment changes that will increase sales and profits. The basic objectives of and approaches for determining selling effort allocation, salesforce size, and territory design are discussed separately in the remainder of this chapter.

Allocation of Selling Effort

The allocation of selling effort is one of the most important deployment decisions, because the salesforce size and territory decisions are based on this allocation decision. Regardless of the method of account coverage, determining how much selling effort to allocate to individual accounts is an important decision strategically speaking, because selling effort is a major determinant of account sales and a major element of account selling costs.

U.S. Paper Supply provides an excellent example of the impact of improved selling effort allocation to accounts. The company's salespeople had been spending about the same amount of time with all accounts. After analyzing customer data from its CRM technology system, clients were categorized based on revenue and sales potential. Based on these categories, salespeople plan the type and frequency of contacts with each customer

FIGURE 4.13   Analytical Approaches to Allocation of Selling Effort

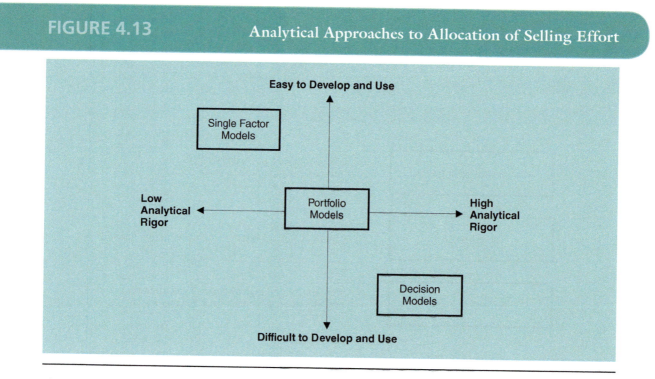

The single factor, portfolio, and decision model approaches for performing a deployment analysis differ in terms of analytical rigor and in ease of development and use. Typically, the more rigorous the approach, the more difficult it is to develop and use.

| | Examples of Single Factor Model   EXHIBIT 4.3 |

The single factor model was applied to evaluate the market potential of each account and then classify all accounts into A, B, C, and D market potential categories. The average number of sales calls to an account in each market potential category was calculated and evaluated. Based on this analysis, changes in the account effort allocation strategy were made. A summary of the results follows:

Market Potential Categories	Average Sales Calls to an Account Last Year	Average Sales Calls to an Account Next Year
A	25	32
B	23	24
C	20	16
D	16	8

for a 12-month period. The best accounts get the most face-to-face selling effort. Other accounts receive a blend of personal sales calls, telephone sales calls, e-newsletters, and product updates. This change in selling effort allocation produced a 25 percent increase in sales.[14]

Although decisions on the allocation of selling effort are difficult, several analytical tools are available to help. The three basic analytical approaches are single factor models, portfolio models, and decision models. These three are compared in Figure 4.13[15] and discussed in detail throughout the remainder of this section.

Single Factor Models

Easy to develop and use, **single factor models** do not, however, provide a very comprehensive analysis of accounts. The typical procedure is to classify all accounts on one factor, such as market potential, and then to assign all accounts in the same category the same number of sales calls. An example of using a single factor model for sales call allocation is presented in Exhibit 4.3.

Although single factor models have limitations, they do provide sales managers with a systematic approach for determining selling effort allocation. Sales managers are likely to make better allocation decisions by using single factor models than when relying totally on judgment and intuition. Because of their ease of development and usage, single factor models are probably the most widely used analytical approach for making these allocation decisions.

Portfolio Models

A more comprehensive analysis of accounts is provided by **portfolio models,** but they are somewhat more difficult to develop and use than single factor models. In a portfolio model, each account served by a firm is considered as part of an overall portfolio of accounts. Thus, accounts within the portfolio represent different situations and receive different levels of selling effort attention. The typical approach is to classify all accounts in the portfolio into categories of similar attractiveness for receiving sales call investment. Then, selling effort is allocated so that the more attractive accounts receive more selling effort. The typical attractiveness segments and basic effort allocation strategies are presented in Figure 4.14.[16]

Account attractiveness is a function of account opportunity and competitive position for each account. *Account opportunity* is defined as an account's need for and ability to purchase the firm's products (e.g., grocery products, computer products, financial services). *Competitive position* is defined as the strength of the relationship between the firm and an account. As indicated in Figure 4.14, the higher the account opportunity and the stronger the competitive positions, the more attractive accounts become.

FIGURE 4.14   Portfolio Model Segments and Strategies

Competitive Position

	Strong	Weak
High	**SEGMENT 1** **Attractiveness:** Accounts are very attractive because they offer high opportunity, and sales organization has strong competitive position. **Selling Effort Strategy:** Accounts should receive a heavy investment of selling effort to take advantage of opportunity and maintain/improve competitive position.	**SEGMENT 2** **Attractiveness:** Accounts are potentially attractive due to high opportunity, but sales organization currently has weak competitive position. **Selling Effort Strategy:** Additional analysis should be performed to identify accounts where sales organization's competitive position can be strengthened. These accounts should receive heavy investment of selling effort, while other accounts receive minimal investment.
Low	**SEGMENT 3** **Attractiveness:** Accounts are moderately attractive due to sales organization's strong competitive position. However, future opportunity is limited. **Selling Effort Strategy:** Accounts should receive a selling effort investment sufficient to maintain current competitive position.	**SEGMENT 4** **Attractiveness:** Accounts are very unattractive; they offer low opportunity, and sales organization has weak competitive position. **Selling Effort Strategy:** Accounts should receive minimal investment of selling effort. Less costly forms of marketing (for example, telephone sales calls, direct mail) should replace personal selling efforts on a selective basis, or the account coverage should be eliminated entirely.

Account Opportunity (vertical axis label)

Accounts are classified into attractiveness categories based on evaluations of account opportunity and competitive position. The selling effort strategies are based on the concept that the more attractive an account, the more selling effort it should receive.

Using portfolio models to develop an account effort allocation strategy requires that account opportunity and competitive position be measured for each account. Based on these measurements, accounts can be classified into the attractiveness segments. The portfolio model differs from the single factor model in that many factors are normally measured to assess account opportunity and competitive position. The exact number and types of factors depend on a firm's specific selling situation. Thus, the portfolio approach provides a comprehensive account analysis that can be adapted to the specific selling situation faced by any firm.

Sales organizations can apply the portfolio model approach in different ways. For example, one approach used successfully by firms in a variety of industries divides accounts into categories based on types of sales opportunities. The four account opportunity categories are: repurchase, replacement, expansion, and innovation. Each category requires different amounts and types of selling effort. Salespeople focus their selling effort on managing sales opportunities across accounts and not just on selling products. Companies employing this portfolio approach report significant sales increases.[17]

Portfolio models can be valuable tools for helping sales managers improve their account effort allocation strategy. They are relatively easy to develop and use (although more difficult than single factor models) and provide a more comprehensive analysis than single factor models.

Decision Models

The most rigorous and comprehensive method for determining an account effort allocation strategy is by means of a **decision model.** Because of their complexity, decision models are somewhat difficult to develop and use. However, today's computer hardware and software make decision models much easier to use than before. Research results have consistently supported the value of decision models in improving effort allocation and salesforce productivity.[18]

Although the mathematical formulations of decision models can be complex, the basic concept is simple—to allocate sales calls to accounts that promise the highest sales return from the sales calls. The objective is to achieve the highest level of sales for any given number of sales calls and to continue increasing sales calls until their marginal costs equal their marginal returns. Thus, decision models calculate the optimal allocation of sales calls in terms of sales or profit maximization.

Salesforce Size

Research results have consistently shown that many firms could improve their performance by changing the size of their salesforce. In some situations, the salesforce should be increased. In other situations, firms are employing too many salespeople and could improve performance by reducing the size of their salesforce. Determining the appropriate salesforce size requires an understanding of several key considerations as well as a familiarity with the analytical approaches that might be used.

Key Considerations

The size of a firm's salesforce determines the total amount of selling effort that is available to call on accounts and prospects. The decision on salesforce size is analogous to the decision on advertising budget. Whereas the advertising budget establishes the total amount that the firm has to spend on advertising communications, the salesforce size determines the total amount of personal selling effort that is available. Because each salesperson can make only a certain number of sales calls during any period, the number of salespeople times the number of sales calls per salesperson defines the total available selling effort. For example, a firm with 100 salespeople who each make 500 sales calls per year has a total selling effort of 50,000 sales calls. If the salesforce is increased to 110 salespeople, then total selling effort is increased to 55,000 sales calls. Key considerations in determining salesforce size are productivity, turnover, and organizational strategy.

Productivity

In general terms, *productivity* is defined as a ratio between outputs and inputs. One way the **sales productivity** of a salesforce is calculated is the ratio of sales generated to selling effort used. Thus, productivity is an important consideration for all deployment decisions. However, selling effort is often expressed in terms of number of salespeople. This suggests that the critical consideration is the *relationship* between selling effort and sales, not just the total amount of selling effort or the total level of sales. For example, sales per salesperson is an important sales productivity measure.

Sales will generally increase with the addition of salespeople, but not in a linear manner. With some exceptions, costs tend to increase directly with salesforce size. This produces the basic relationship presented in Figure 4.15. In early stages, the addition of

FIGURE 4.15	Sales and Cost Relationships

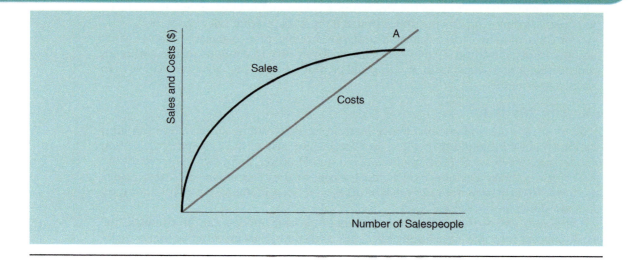

Although costs tend to increase in a linear manner with the addition of salespeople, the associated sales increases are typically nonlinear. In general, the increases in sales tend to decrease as more salespeople are added. A point (A) is reached when the sales from adding a salesperson are not sufficient to cover the additional costs.

salespeople increases sales considerably more than the selling costs. However, as salespeople continue to be added, sales increases tend to decline until a point is reached when the costs to add a salesperson are more than the revenues that salesperson can generate. In fact, the profit maximization point is when the marginal costs of adding a salesperson are equal to the marginal profits generated by that salesperson. It typically becomes more difficult to maintain high sales productivity levels at larger salesforce sizes. This makes it imperative that management consider the relationship between sales and costs when making decisions on salesforce size.

Turnover

Salesforce turnover is extremely costly. Because some turnover is going to occur for all firms, it should always be considered when determining salesforce size. Once the appropriate salesforce size is determined—that is, one sufficient for salespeople to call on all the firm's accounts and prospects in a productive manner—this figure should be adjusted to reflect expected turnover. If an increase or maintenance of current salesforce size is desired, excess salespeople should be in the recruiting-selecting-training pipeline. If a decrease is desired, turnover might be all that is necessary to accomplish it. For example, a grocery products marketer that found that its salesforce should be reduced from 34 to 32 salespeople achieved the two-salesperson reduction through scheduled retirements in the near future instead of firing two salespeople.

Organizational Strategy

Salesforce size decisions must also be consistent with the firm's organizational strategy. Companies that focus on serving current customers and achieving limited growth during slow economic times might reduce salesforce size as a way to lower costs. In contrast, companies trying to gain market share, capture new customers, and take advantage of market opportunities are likely to increase salesforce size. In fact, increasing salesforce size at the right time can provide a firm with a competitive advantage. For example, when Rilston Electrical Components sensed that economic conditions were improving, it added three salespeople to its salesforce of eight. Because it responded to opportunities before its competitors did, the company was able to increase market share and grow sales by 25 percent.[19]

The pharmaceutical industry provides an interesting example. Most pharmaceutical companies find sales calls to doctors a more effective way to increase prescriptions than consumer advertising. Thus, the number of pharmaceutical salespeople tripled to over 90,000 in the past decade. Merck is typical. It added 1,500 salespeople, bringing its salesforce to about 7,000. The increased number of salespeople increased drug sales, but there are problems. Sales organization costs are up significantly. Many doctors feel bombarded by pharmaceutical salespeople and have refused to see them or have severely limited their access. This has lowered sales productivity as the number of meetings with a doctor for an average pharmaceutical salesperson has dropped from 808 per year to around 529 per year.[20]

Pharmaceutical companies are responding to pressure from doctors, consumer groups, and government regulators by reducing the size of their salesforces. The 100,000 pharmaceutical salespeople in the United States is expected to decrease by about 20 percent in the next few years. Pfizer cut 2,200 salespeople in the United States and is decreasing its European salesforce by 20 percent. Other pharmaceutical companies are doing the same.[21]

Analytical Tools

The need to consider sales, costs, productivity, and turnover makes salesforce size a difficult decision. Fortunately, some analytical tools are available to help management process relevant information and evaluate salesforce size alternatives more fully. Before describing these analytical tools, we want to make it clear that there are several types of salesforce size decisions (see Figure 4.16). The most straightforward situation is when a firm has one generalized salesforce. However, as discussed earlier, many firms employ multiple specialized salesforces, in which case both the total number of salespeople employed by the firm and the size of each individual salesforce are important. Both generalized and specialized salesforces are normally organized into geographic districts, zones, regions, and so on. The number of salespeople to assign to each district, zone, region, and so on is a type of salesforce size decision.

These decisions are similar conceptually and can be addressed by the same analytical tools, provided that the type of salesforce size decision being addressed is specified. Unless stated otherwise, you can assume the situation of one generalized salesforce in the following discussion.

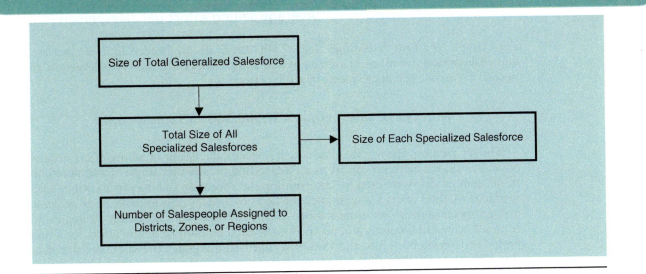

Salesforce Size Decisions   **FIGURE 4.16**

Depending on the sales organization structure of a firm, sales managers may be faced with several different types of salesforce size decisions. Each requires the same basic concepts and analytical methods.

Breakdown Approach

A relatively simple approach for calculating salesforce size, the **breakdown approach**, assumes that an accurate sales forecast is available. This forecast is then "broken down" to determine the number of salespeople needed to generate the forecasted level of sales. The basic formula is

$$\text{Salesforce size} = \text{Forecasted sales/Average sales per salesperson}$$

Assume that a firm forecasts sales of $50 million for next year. If salespeople generate an average of $2 million in annual sales, then the firm needs 25 salespeople to achieve the $50 million sales forecast:

$$\text{Salesforce size} = \$50{,}000{,}000/\$2{,}000{,}000 = 25 \text{ salespeople}$$

The basic advantage of the breakdown method is its ease of development. The approach is straightforward, and the mathematical calculations are simple. However, the approach is conceptually weak. The concept underlying the calculations is that sales determine the number of salespeople needed. This puts the cart before the horse, because the number of salespeople employed by a firm is an important determinant of firm sales. A sales forecast should be based on a given salesforce size. The addition of salespeople should increase the forecast, and the elimination of salespeople should decrease it.

Despite this weakness, the breakdown method is probably the one most often used for determining salesforce size. It is best suited for relatively stable selling environments in which sales change in slow and predictable ways, and no major strategic changes are planned, and for organizations that use commission compensation plans and keep their fixed costs low. However, in many selling situations the costs of having too many or too few salespeople are high. More rigorous analytical tools are recommended for calculating salesforce size in these situations.

Workload Approach

The first step in the **workload approach** is to determine how much selling effort is needed to cover the firm's market adequately. Then the number of salespeople required to provide this amount of selling effort is calculated. The basic formula is

$$\text{Number of salespeople} = \frac{\text{Total selling effort needed}}{\text{Average selling effort per salesperson}}$$

For example, if a firm determines that 37,500 sales calls are needed in its market area and a salesperson can make an average of 500 annual sales calls, then 75 salespeople are needed to provide the desired level of selling effort:

$$\text{Number of salespeople} = 37{,}500/500 = 75 \text{ salespeople}$$

The key factor in the workload approach is the total amount of selling effort needed. Several workload methods can be used, depending on whether single factor, portfolio, or decision models were used for determining the allocation of effort to accounts. Each workload method offers a way to calculate how many sales calls to make to all accounts and prospects during any time period. When the sales call allocation strategies are summed across all accounts and prospects, the total amount of selling effort for a time period is determined. Thus, the workload approach integrates the salesforce size decision with account effort allocation strategies.

The workload approach is also relatively simple, although its simplicity depends on the specific method used to determine total selling effort needs. The approach is conceptually sound, because salesforce size is based on selling effort needs established by account effort allocation decisions. Note, however, that we have presented the workload approach in a simplified manner here by considering only selling effort. A more realistic presentation would incorporate nonselling time considerations (e.g., travel time, planning time) in the analysis. Although incorporating these considerations does not change the basic workload concept, it does make the calculations more complex and cumbersome.

The workload approach is suited for all types of selling situations. Sales organizations can adapt the basic approach to their specific situation through the method used to calculate total selling effort. The most sophisticated firms can use decision models for this purpose, whereas other firms might use portfolio models or single factor approaches.

Incremental Approach

The most rigorous approach for calculating salesforce size is the **incremental approach**. Its basic concept is to compare the marginal profit contribution with the marginal selling costs for each incremental salesperson. An example of these calculations is provided in Exhibit 4.4. At 100 salespeople, marginal profits exceed marginal costs by $10,000. This relationship continues until salesforce size reaches 102. At 102 salespeople, the marginal profit equals marginal cost, and total profits are maximized. If the firm added one more salesperson, total profits would be reduced, because marginal costs would exceed marginal profits by $5,000. Thus, the optimal salesforce size for this example is 102. The major advantage of the incremental approach is that it quantifies the important relationships between salesforce size, sales, and costs, making it possible to assess the potential sales and profit impacts of different salesforce sizes. It forces management to view the salesforce size decision as one that affects both the level of sales that can be generated and the costs associated with producing each sales level.

The incremental method is, however, somewhat difficult to develop. Relatively complex response functions must be formulated to predict sales at different salesforce sizes (sales=f[salesforce size]). Developing these response functions requires either historical data or management judgment. Thus, the incremental approach cannot be used for new salesforces where historical data and accurate judgments are not possible.

Turnover

All the analytical tools incorporate various elements of sales and costs in their calculations. Therefore, they directly address productivity issues but do not directly consider turnover in the salesforce size calculations. When turnover considerations are important, management should adjust the recommended salesforce size produced by any of the analytical methods to reflect expected turnover rates. For example, if an analytical tool recommended a salesforce size of 100 for a firm that experiences 20 percent annual turnover, the effective salesforce size should be adjusted to 120. Recruiting, selecting, and training plans should be based on the 120 salesforce size.

SALES MANAGEMENT IN THE 21ST CENTURY

Designing Sales Territories

Tom Simpson, Vice President of Sales and COO for Elite Printing, discusses the important factors in designing effective sales territories.

Designing effective sales territories is a challenging but important task. Each of our salespeople is responsible for a sales territory that includes existing clients and key target prospects. Territories may overlap geographic areas based on different vertical markets and product lines. Our goal is to *ensure that each territory receives optimal coverage of accounts and provides each sales representative with an equitable chance for success. This is a tough balancing act. We consider a number of different factors when establishing sales territories. These include number of accounts, geography, account size, sales potential, and experience of each sales representative. We integrate our analysis of these factors and use them to generate sales territories most likely to meet our overall goals and keep our staff motivated.*

EXHIBIT 4.4	Incremental Approach	
Number of Salespeople	**Marginal Salesperson Profit Contribution**	**Marginal Salesperson Cost**
100	$85,000	$75,000
101	$80,000	$75,000
102	$75,000	$75,000
103	$70,000	$75,000

Failure to incorporate anticipated salesforce turnover into salesforce size calculations can be costly. Evidence suggests that many firms may lose as much as 10 percent in sales productivity due to the loss in sales from vacant territories or low initial sales when a new salesperson is assigned to a territory. Thus, the sooner that sales managers can replace salespeople and get them productive in their territories, the less loss in sales within the territory.

Outsourcing the Salesforce

The salesforce size decisions we have been discussing apply directly to an ongoing company salesforce. However, there may be situations where a company needs salespeople quickly, for short periods of time, for smaller customers, or for other reasons, but does not want to hire additional salespeople. An attractive option is to outsource the salesforce. A growing number of companies can provide salespeople to a firm on a contract basis. These salespeople only represent the firm and customers are typically not aware that these are contracted salespeople. Contracts can vary as to length, customer assignment, and other relevant factors. This gives the client firm a great deal of flexibility.

The situation at GE Medical Systems is illustrative. Salespeople at GE Medical Systems called on hospitals with 100 or more beds in major metropolitan areas. This left the market for smaller hospitals in rural areas to competitors. GE decided it needed to pursue these smaller markets, but did not want to hire additional salespeople or to have existing salespeople take time away from their large customers. So, GE contracted with a firm to provide seven salespeople experienced in capital equipment sales to serve the smaller markets. The salespeople were hired, trained on GE products, and in the field within three months. These contracted reps grew annual GE sales in the smaller markets to $260 million within five years. The results were so spectacular that GE has renewed the outsourcing contract and continues to use the contracted salespeople.[22]

Designing Territories

As discussed earlier, the size of a salesforce determines the total amount of selling effort that a firm has available to generate sales from accounts and prospects. The effective use of this selling effort often requires that sales **territories** be developed and each salesperson be assigned to a specific territory. A territory consists of whatever specific accounts are assigned to a specific salesperson. The overall objective is to ensure that all accounts are assigned salesperson responsibility and that each salesperson can adequately cover the assigned accounts. Although territories are often defined by geographic area (e.g., the Oklahoma territory, the Tennessee territory), the key components of a territory are the accounts within the specified geographic area.

The territory can be viewed as the work unit for a salesperson. The salesperson is largely responsible for the selling activities performed and the performance achieved in a territory. Salesperson compensation and success are normally a direct function of territory performance; thus, the design of territories is extremely important to the individual salespeople of a firm as well as to management. An example of trying to balance company and salesperson needs is presented in "Sales Management in the 21st Century: Designing Sales Territories."

Territory Considerations

The critical territory considerations are illustrated in Exhibit 4.5.[23] In this example, Andy and Sally are salespeople for a consumer durable goods manufacturer. They have each been assigned a geographic territory consisting of several trading areas. The exhibit compares the percentage of their time currently spent in each trading area with the percentages recommended from a decision model analysis. A review of the information provided in the exhibit highlights territory design problems from the perspective of the firm and of each salesperson.

The current territory design does not provide proper selling coverage of the trading areas. The decision model analysis suggests that the trading areas in Andy's territory should require only 36 percent of his time, yet he is spending all his time there. Clearly, the firm is wasting expensive selling effort in Andy's territory. The situation in Sally's territory is just the opposite. Proper coverage of Sally's trading areas should require more than two salespeople, yet Sally has sole responsibility for these trading areas. In this situation the firm is losing sales opportunities because of a lack of selling attention.

From the firm's perspective, the design of Andy's and Sally's territories limits sales and profit performance. Sales performance in Sally's territory is much lower than it might be if more selling attention were given to her trading areas. Profit performance is low in Andy's territory because too much selling effort is being expended in his trading areas. The firm is not achieving the level of sales and profits that might be achieved if the territories were designed to provide more productive market coverage. Thus, one key consideration in territory design is the productive deployment of selling effort within each territory.

From the perspective of Andy and Sally, the poor territory design affects their level of motivation. Andy is frustrated. He spends much of his time making sales calls in trading areas where little potential exists for generating additional sales. Andy's motivational level is low, and he may consider resigning from the company. By contrast, Sally's territory has so much sales potential that she can limit her sales calls to the largest accounts or the easiest sales. She is not motivated to develop the potential of her territory but can merely "skim the cream" from the best accounts. The situations facing Andy and Sally illustrate how territory design might affect salesperson motivation,

Territory Design Example   EXHIBIT 4.5

	Trading Area[a]	Present Effort (%)[b]	Recommended Effort (%)[b]
Andy	1	10	4
	2	60	20
	3	15	7
	4	5	2
	5	10	3
Total		100	36
Sally	6	18	81
	7	7	21
	8	5	11
	9	35	35
	10	5	11
	11	30	77
Total		100	236

[a]Each territory is made of up several trading areas.
[b]The percentage of salesperson time spent in the trading area (100% = 1 salesperson). Thus, the deployment analysis suggests that Andy's territory requires only 0.36 salespeople, whereas Sally's territory needs 2.36 salespeople for proper coverage.

morale, and even turnover. These potential effects are important considerations when designing territories.

Recent research results support the example. Studies of sales managers in several countries found positive relationships between satisfaction with territory design and salesperson performance. These results are confirmed in a study of salespeople. The study concluded that salespeople who are satisfied with the design of their sales territory worked harder, performed better, and were more satisfied with their job. This research provides strong evidence for the impact of sales territory design on the attitudes, behavior, and performance of salespeople.[24]

Procedure for Designing Territories

A general procedure for designing territories is presented in Figure 4.17. Each step in the procedure can be performed manually or by using computer models. The procedure is illustrated manually by using Andy's and Sally's territories as an example application. The basic problem is to organize the 11 trading areas into three territories that provide proper market coverage of accounts in each territory and fair performance opportunities for each salesperson. Three territories are developed because the decision model results presented in Exhibit 4.5 indicate that two salespeople cannot adequately cover these trading areas. The data needed to design the sales territories are presented in Exhibit 4.6.

Select Planning and Control Unit

The first step in territory design is to select the **planning and control unit** that will be used in the analysis—that is, some entity that is smaller than a territory. The total market area served by a firm is divided into these planning and control units, then they are analyzed and grouped together to form territories.

Examples of potential planning and control units are illustrated in Figure 4.18. In general, management should use the smallest unit feasible. However, data are often not available for small planning and control units, and the computational task becomes more complex as more units are included in the analysis. The selection of the appropriate planning and control unit therefore represents a trade-off between what is desired and what is possible under the given data or computational conditions. In our example, trading areas have been selected as the planning and control unit.

Analyze Opportunity of Planning and Control Unit

First, determine the amount of opportunity available from each planning and control unit. Specific methods for performing these calculations will be covered in the appendix to Chapter 4. However, the most often used measure of opportunity is *market potential*. The market potentials for the 11 trading areas in our example are provided in Exhibit 4.6. Everything else being equal, the higher the market potential, the more opportunity is available.

FIGURE 4.17   Territory Design Procedure

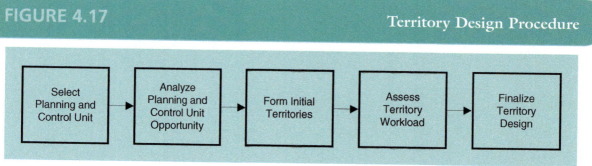

Designing territories requires a multiple-stage approach. Although most territory design approaches follow the stages presented in this figure, the methods used at each stage differ considerably, depending on the analytical tools used.

Trading Area	Market Potential	Number of Sales Calls
	Territory Design Data EXHIBIT 4.6	
1	$250,000	25
2	$700,000	100
3	$350,000	35
4	$150,000	15
5	$200,000	20
6	$2,000,000	175
7	$750,000	65
8	$500,000	50
9	$1,000,000	100
10	$500,000	50
11	$1,750,000	175

Potential Planning and Control Units   FIGURE 4.18

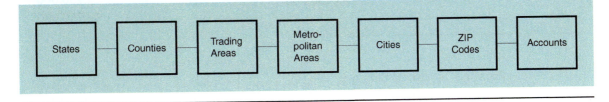

Planning and control units represent the unit of analysis for territory design. Accounts are the preferred planning and control unit. However, often it is not possible to use them as such, in which case a more aggregate type of planning and control unit is used.

Form Initial Territories

Once planning and control units have been selected and opportunity evaluated, initial territories can be designed. The objective is to group the planning and control units into territories that are as equitable as possible in opportunity. This step may take several iterations, as there are probably a number of feasible territory designs. It is also unlikely that any design will achieve complete equality of opportunity. The best approach is to design several territory arrangements and evaluate each alternative. Each alternative must be feasible in that planning and control units grouped together are contiguous. This can be a cumbersome task when done manually, but is much more efficient when computer modeling approaches are used.

Two alternative territory designs for our example are presented and evaluated in Exhibit 4.7. Although the first design is feasible, the territories are markedly unfair in opportunity. However, a few adjustments produce reasonably equal territories.

Assess Territory Workloads

The preceding step produces territories of nearly equal opportunity. It may, however, take more work to realize this opportunity in some territories than in others. Therefore, the workload of each territory should be evaluated by (1) the number of sales calls required to cover the accounts in the territory, (2) the amount of travel time in the territory, (3) the total number of accounts, and (4) any other factors that measure the amount of work required by a salesperson assigned to the territory. In our example, workload for each trading area and territory is evaluated by the number of sales calls required. This information is presented in Exhibit 4.8.

EXHIBIT 4.7   Initial Territory Design

	Alternative 1		Alternative 2	
	Trading Area	**Market Potential**	**Trading Area**	**Market Potential**
Territory 1	1	$250,000	1	$250,000
	2	700,000	2	700,000
	3	350,000	5	200,000
	4	150,000	8	500,000
	5	200,000	9	1,000,000
		$1,650,000		$2,650,000
Territory 2	6	$2,000,000	6	$2,000,000
	7	750,000	7	750,000
	8	500,000		$2,750,000
		$3,250,000		
Territory 3	9	$1,000,000	3	$350,000
	10	500,000	4	150,000
	11	1,750,000	10	500,000
		$3,250,000	11	1,750,000
				$2,750,000

Finalize Territory Design

The final step is to adjust the initial territories to achieve equal workloads for each sales-person. The objective is to achieve the best possible balance between opportunity and workload for each territory. Typically, both of these objectives cannot be completely achieved, so management must decide on the best trade-offs for its situation. Any inequalities in the final territories can be addressed when quotas are established, as discussed in Chapter 10.

Achieving workload and opportunity balance for our example is illustrated in Exhibit 4.9. The equal opportunity territories resulted in somewhat unequal workloads (see

EXHIBIT 4.8   Workload Evaluations

	Trading Area	**Sales Calls**
Territory 1	1	25
	2	100
	5	20
	8	50
	9	100
		295
Territory 2	6	175
	7	65
		240
Territory 3	3	35
	4	15
	10	50
	11	175
		275

	Trading Area	Market Potential	Sales Calls
		Final Territory Design EXHIBIT 4.9	
Territory 1	1	$250,000	25
	5	200,000	20
	7	750,000	65
	8	500,000	50
	9	1,000,000	100
		$2,700,000	260
Territory 2	2	$700,000	100
	6	2,000,000	175
		$2,700,000	275
Territory 3	3	$350,000	35
	4	150,000	15
	10	500,000	50
	11	1,750,000	175
		$2,750,000	275

Exhibit 4.8). The final territory design moved trading area 7 to territory 1 and trading area 2 to territory 2. This produces territories that are reasonably equal in both opportunity and workload.

Performing territory design analyses manually is difficult and time-consuming. Fortunately, advances in computer hardware and software make it possible to consider multiple factors and rapidly evaluate many alternatives when designing territories.

Assigning Salespeople to Territories

Once territories have been designed, salespeople must be assigned to them. Salespeople are not equal in abilities and will perform differently with different types of accounts or prospects. Some sales managers consider their salespeople to be either farmers or hunters. *Farmers* are effective with existing accounts but do not perform well in establishing business with new accounts. *Hunters* excel in establishing new accounts but do not fully develop existing accounts. Based on these categories, farmers should be assigned to territories that contain many ongoing account relationships, and hunters should be assigned to territories in new or less-developed market areas.

Using Technology

We have taken you through the territory design process manually so that you understand what is involved in each step. Many sales organizations still perform this process manually using maps, grease pencils, and calculators. There are, however, several software programs that automate the process. Most of these programs make it easy to design potential territories, print maps, and compare opportunity and workload. Then, changes can be made easily and new maps and comparisons produced quickly. This allows sales managers to evaluate many possible territory designs and to assess the impact of territory design changes easily. Examples of available software include Sales Territory Configurator (www.rochestergroup.com), Tactician® (www.tactician.com), and TerrAlign (www.terralign.com).

"PEOPLE" CONSIDERATIONS

Our discussion of salesforce deployment decisions has, to this point, focused entirely on analytical approaches. This analytical orientation emphasizes objective sales and cost considerations in evaluating different allocations of sales calls to accounts, different salesforce sizes, different territory designs, and different assignments of salespeople to territories. Although such analytical approaches are valuable and should be used by sales managers, final deployment decisions should also be based on "people" considerations. These "people" considerations can produce some problems as presented in "An Ethical Dilemma." Statistics are numbers, whereas sales managers, salespeople, and customers are people. Analysis of statistical data provides useful but incomplete information for deployment decisions. Models are only representations of reality, and no matter how complex, no model can incorporate all the people factors that are important in any salesforce deployment decision. Accordingly, while using the appropriate analytical approaches, sales managers should temper the analytical results with people considerations before making final deployment decisions.

What are the important people considerations in salesforce deployment? The most important ones concern relationships between salespeople and customers and between salespeople and the sales organization. Consider the allocation of selling effort to accounts. The analytical approaches for making this decision produce a recommended number of sales calls to each account based on some assessment of expected sales and costs for different sales call levels. Although these approaches may incorporate a number of factors in developing the recommended sales call levels, there is no way that any analytical approach can use the detailed knowledge that a salesperson has about the unique needs of individual accounts. Therefore, an analytical approach may suggest that sales calls should be increased or decreased to a specific account, whereas the salesperson serving this account may know that the account will react adversely to any changes in sales call coverage. In this situation, a sales manager would be wise to ignore the analytical recommendation and not change sales call coverage to the account because of the existing relationship between the salesperson and customer.

Salesforce size decisions also require consideration of people issues. A decision to reduce the size of a salesforce means that some salespeople will have to be removed from the salesforce. How this reduction is accomplished can affect the relationship between salespeople and the sales organization. Achieving this reduction through attrition or offering salespeople other positions is typically a better approach than merely firing salespeople.

Increasing salesforce size means that the new salespeople must be assigned to territories. Consequently, some accounts will find themselves being served by new salespeople. These changes in assignment can have a devastating effect on the existing customer-salesperson relationship. Not only should that relationship be considered,

AN ETHICAL DILEMMA

Business is booming at ACM office supplies in Orlando, Florida. Central Florida University is now the largest university in Florida and the Orlando metro area is the fastest-growing area in the southeast. Forty new schools have opened in the metro area. The ACM salesforce had a record-breaking year. The commission checks they receive are now more than their generous base salary. The school systems and universities in the areas have purchased record orders on: pads of paper, pencils, pens, chalk, erasers, you name the school supply; it is being purchased in record volume. The management team at ACM has a dilemma, every one of their sales representatives is making more per year than they are. Cindy Clark, National Sales Manager, has proposed that territories be reduced and some of the major customers become house accounts handled by the management team. Cindy justifies this by stating, "The management team has been out of the field for a while and they could all use a little customer contact." What should Cindy do?

a. Tell the sales reps to stop complaining, get out in their territory and sell.
b. Cindy should reconsider since this could demotivate her salesforce.
c. Cindy should work with her sales team to create a win-win for management and the sales team.

but also the issue of fairness in taking accounts from one salesperson and assigning them to another. The situation can be a delicate one, requiring careful judgment as to how these people considerations should be balanced against analytical results.

In sum, sales managers should integrate the results from salesforce deployment analysis with people considerations before implementing changes in sales call allocation, salesforce size, or territory design. A good rule of thumb is to make salesforce deployment changes that are likely to have the least disruptive effect on existing relationships.

SUMMARY

1. **Define the concepts of specialization, centralization, span of control versus management levels, and line versus staff positions.** *Specialization* refers to the division of labor such that salespeople or sales managers concentrate on performing certain activities to the exclusion of others. *Centralization* refers to where in the organization decision-making responsibility exists. Centralized organizations locate decision-making responsibility at higher organizational levels than decentralized organizations. Any sales organization structure can be evaluated in terms of the types and degrees of specialization and centralization afforded by the structure. Sales management organization design also requires decisions concerning the number of management levels, spans of control, and line versus staff positions. In general, more *management levels* result in smaller *spans of control*, and more *staff positions* result in more sales management specialization.

2. **Describe the ways salesforces might be specialized.** A critical decision in designing the sales organization is determining whether the salesforce should be specialized and, if so, the appropriate type of specialization. The basic types of salesforce specialization are geographic, product, market (including major account organization), and functional. The appropriate type of specialization depends on the characteristics of the selling situation. Important selling situation characteristics include the similarity of customer needs, the complexity of the firm's product offering, the market environment, and the professionalism of the salesforce. Specific criteria of importance are affordability and payout, credibility and coverage, and flexibility. The use of different types and levels of specialization typically requires the establishment of separate salesforces.

3. **Evaluate the advantages and disadvantages of sales organization structures.** Because each type of sales organization structure has certain advantages and disadvantages, many firms use hybrid structures that combine the features of several types. Usually, the strengths of one structure are weaknesses in other structures.

4. **Name the important considerations in organizing strategic account management programs.** Identifying strategic accounts (which should be both large and complex) and organizing for coverage of them are the important considerations in strategic account management.

5. **Explain how to determine the appropriate sales organization structure for a given selling situation.** There is no one best way to structure a sales organization. The appropriate way to organize a salesforce and sales management depends on certain characteristics of a particular selling situation. Also, because the sales organization structure decision is dynamic, it must be adapted to changes in a firm's selling situation that occur over time.

6. **Discuss salesforce deployment.** Salesforce deployment decisions entail allocating selling effort, determining salesforce size, and designing territories. These decisions

are highly interrelated and should be addressed in an integrated, sequential manner. Improvements in salesforce deployment can produce substantial increases in sales and profits.

7. **Explain three analytical approaches for determining allocation of selling effort.** Single factor, portfolio, and decision models can be used as analytical tools to determine appropriate selling effort allocations. The approaches differ in terms of analytical rigor and ease of development and use. Sales organizations should use the approach that best fits their particular selling situation.

8. **Describe three methods for calculating salesforce size.** The breakdown method for calculating salesforce size is the easiest to use but the weakest conceptually. It uses the expected level of sales to determine the number of salespeople. The workload approach is sounder conceptually, because it bases the salesforce size decision on the amount of selling effort needed to cover the market appropriately. The incremental method is the best approach, although it is often difficult to develop. It examines the marginal sales and costs associated with different salesforce sizes.

9. **Explain the importance of sales territories from the perspective of the sales organization and from the perspective of the salespeople, and list the steps in the territory design process.** Territories are assignments of accounts to salespeople. Each becomes the work unit for a salesperson, who is largely responsible for the performance of the assigned territory. Poorly designed territories can have adverse effects on the motivation of salespeople. From the perspective of the firm, territory design decisions should ensure that the firm's market area is adequately covered in a productive manner. The first step in the territory design process is to identify planning and control units. Next, the opportunity available from each planning and control unit is determined, initial territories are formed, and the workloads of each potential territory are assessed. The final territory design represents management's judgment concerning the best balance between opportunity and workload.

10. **Discuss the important "people" considerations in salesforce deployment.** Although analytical approaches provide useful input for salesforce deployment decisions, they do not address people considerations adequately. Sales managers should always consider existing relationships between salespeople and customers, and between salespeople and the sales organization, before making salesforce deployment changes. Many of these people considerations have ethical consequences.

UNDERSTANDING SALES MANAGEMENT TERMS

specialization
centralization
span of control
management levels
line sales management
staff sales management
geographic specialization
product specialization
market specialization
functional specialization
strategic account
strategic account organization
national account management (NAM)

global account management (GAM)
hybrid sales organization
salesforce deployment
single factor models
portfolio models
decision models
sales productivity
breakdown approach
workload approach
incremental approach
territory
planning and control unit

DEVELOPING SALES MANAGEMENT KNOWLEDGE

1. Discuss the situational factors that suggest the need for specialization and centralization. Provide a specific example of each factor discussed.

2. Why do you think there is a trend toward more salesforce specialization?

3. What are the advantages and disadvantages of structuring a sales organization for strategic account management?

4. What are some problems that a firm might face when undertaking a major restructuring of its sales organization?

5. What are the important relationships between span of control, management levels, line positions, staff positions, specialization, and centralization?

6. How are salesforce deployment decisions related to decisions on sales organization structure?

7. How can the incremental method be used to determine the number of salespeople to assign to a sales district?

8. How are salesforce size decisions different for firms with one generalized salesforce versus firms with several specialized salesforces?

9. How can computer modeling assist sales managers in designing territories?

10. Should firms always try to design equal territories? Why or why not?

BUILDING SALES MANAGEMENT SKILLS

1. Assume that you are the national sales manager for Replica Inc., a manufacturer and marketer of photocopy equipment and supplies. The firm's products are sold both nationally and internationally by a salesforce of 5,000. Replica sells to accounts of various sizes across several industries. Prepare a proposal that illustrates your recommended sales organization structure. Be sure to justify your recommended structure.

2. As an organization, your university has a specified structure. Identify this structure (draw it or obtain a copy of it). How specialized is this structure? What is its degree of centralization? What does the span of control look like and how appropriate is it? How many levels of management exist? Is this enough or too much? What are the relationships between line and staff positions? Are they appropriate? Assuming you would like the university to run as efficiently and effectively as possible, what changes would you recommend making to this structure and why? If no changes are recommended, why not?

3. Give an example of why a firm might want to organize around a geographic, product, market, or a functional specialization.

4. Using the following information, calculate the total salesforce size necessary by using each of the following approaches: breakdown, workload, and incremental. (Your answers may vary because each piece of information does not apply to the same company.) Be sure to show your work. Also, explain the advantages and disadvantages of each approach. Which approach would you recommend using to determine salesforce size? Why?

   - Sales of $80 million are forecast for next year.
   - Fifteen thousand calls are needed in the market area to be covered.
   - Salespeople generate an average of $2 million in annual sales.
   - A salesperson can make an average of 500 annual sales calls.
   - Marginal salesperson cost is $65,000. With 88 salespeople, the marginal salesper-

son profit contribution is $75,000. This profit contribution decreases by $5,000 with each additional salesperson added to the base of 88 salespeople. Marginal salesperson cost remains constant.

- Turnover is 10 percent annually.

ROLE PLAY

5. **Role Play**

Situation: Read An Ethical Dilemma on p. 79.

Characters: Two sales managers: LA and GA account managers.

Scene: *Location*—Headquarters' conference room.
Action—Role-play a meeting between the sales managers concerning the sales teams competing against each other.

MAKING SALES MANAGEMENT DECISIONS

CASE 4.1 INNOVATIVE PACKAGING, INC.
Background

Innovative Packaging, Inc. (IPI) is a national manufacturer of a wide variety of polyethylene and polystyrene packaging products, including food and ice bags; Styrofoam egg cartons, meat trays, and food service products; laundry and dry-cleaning packaging; trash bags, and construction film and plastic shipping pallets. IPI is a strong competitor in all of its product lines. Not an innovative company, IPI leverages its large manufacturing capacity to drive its costs down, which allows the company to sell its products at highly attractive price levels.

IPI operates five regional offices: Charlotte, Boston, Minneapolis, Denver, and San Francisco. These offices are located at manufacturing plants that serve each region. IPI is organized by product line, with each product line run by a regional product manager and a regional sales manager. Eight to 10 sales representatives report to each of the five regional sales managers. The product managers and sales managers in each region report to a regional marketing manager. The key products and customers for each product line are shown in Exhibit 4.10.

Current Situation

Jackie Settles, Western Region marketing manager, has called her four sales managers and four product managers to San Francisco to discuss alternative approaches to organizing the IPI salesforce. Thirty days earlier, Settles and her managers had hosted a key customer roundtable at the annual meeting of the Plastics Packaging Manufacturers' Association. Settles was troubled by several themes that emerged from the roundtable. Some of the most influential paper and plastic distributors are disturbed by the fact that IPI sells to grocery chains, garment manufacturers, egg packers/processors, and uniform rental companies on a direct basis. This is puzzling to Settles, since IPI has always sold through distributors when feasible. Further, distributors are informed before stocking IPI products that if end users meet certain sales volume requirements and request that they be sold on a direct basis, IPI will sell direct rather than risk losing the business.

Settles is also concerned that many of the grocery chain buyers and paper and plastic distributors complained about the amount of time it takes for them to see several IPI salespeople. These customers wanted to deal with a single IPI

Product Line	Key Products	Key Customer Types
Food Packaging	Produce bags	Grocery chains Food coops Paper and plastic distributors
	Foam meat trays	Grocery chains Meat and poultry processors Food coops Paper and plastic distributors
Institutional	Trash bags	Paper and plastic distributors Restaurant wholesalers Janitorial wholesalers
	Food service (plastic plates, bowls)	Restaurant wholesalers Grocery store delis Institutional food wholesalers Paper and plastic distributors
Agricultural	Egg cartons	Grocery chains Egg packers/processors
Garment	Poly bags	Laundries and dry cleaners Uniform rental companies Garment manufacturers Paper and plastic distributors

PPI Product Lines and Key Customer Types   EXHIBIT 4.10

representative, not one from each product line. An additional concern was that IPI did not allow aggregation of products across product lines to make it easier for these buyers to achieve the maximum quantity discounts.

To prepare for the meeting, Jackie Settles asked each product manager/sales manager team to come ready to discuss these issues:

1. Is it time for IPI to reconsider its salesforce organization by product line?

2. What are the advantages and disadvantages of organizing the IPI salesforce by product line?

3. What are the advantages and disadvantages of developing a new sales organization for the Western Region that would organize according to these customer types: (a) grocery chains and food coops; (b) distributors, including paper and plastic distributors, restaurant wholesalers, institutional food wholesalers, and janitorial wholesalers; and (c) end users, including meat and poultry processors, grocery store delis, egg packers/processors, laundries and dry cleaners, uniform rental companies, and garment manufacturers?

Assume you are the sales manager for the food packaging product line. Address the preceding questions as if you will attend the upcoming meeting. In addition, outline your thoughts on other alternatives for organizing the salesforce.

Role Play

ROLE PLAY

Situation: Read Case 4.1.

Characters: Jackie Settles, Western Region marketing manager; sales manager for food packing product line; one or more other product/sales managers.

Scene 1:   *Location*—Settles' office. *Action*—Role-play between Settles and sales manager for food packing product line, discussing the advantages and disadvantages of a salesforce organized by product line.

Scene 2:   *Location*—Meeting room. *Action*—Role-play meeting with Settles and all product/sales managers, discussing the advantages and disadvantages of different alternatives for organizing IPI's salesforce and arriving at a decision.

CASE 4.2: APPLEGATE INSURANCE COMPANY
Background
Applegate Insurance Company (AIC) is a 30-year-old company that specializes in providing small businesses with supplemental insurance benefits that aren't covered with normal insurance plans. AIC focuses on small businesses with 20 or fewer employees such as machine shops, law firms, account firms, and small restaurants. AIC has three sales representatives serving the Cincinnati, Ohio metropolitan market.

Darnell Smith, AIC's founder and current president, was the company's first salesperson. When the company grew to the point that Smith had a hard time serving all of his accounts, he added Terrell Johnson as a sales representative. Smith gave Johnson 15 of his existing accounts and instructed him to go after potential customers not yet in contact with AIC. A few years later, Julie Burton was hired as a sales representative and added in much the same fashion. Burton was not quite as experienced as Johnson, so Smith and Johnson turned over 20 accounts to Burton, 10 each. She also was instructed to add new customers not already doing business with AIC. Both Julie Burton and Terrell Johnson report directly to Darnell Smith. Of AIC's total sales volume, Darnell Smith accounted for approximately 60 percent. The remaining 40 percent was split evenly between Burton and Johnson. Burton and Johnson are paid a percentage of AIC's billings to their clients.

Current Situation
Smith is planning to retire in another year as a sales producer. In this so-called semi-retirement Smith plans to continue as sales manager and president. Smith has decided to bring in his son Vince as his replacement. Vince has no prior sales experience, so he will learn the business over the next three months, then step full-time into a sales role. Darnell Smith is gathering information that will help him decide how to design AIC's territories after he gives up his sales responsibilities. He is not comfortable turning over all of his accounts to his son, Vince. Although he is hard working, Vince is inexperienced in the insurance consulting industry. A recent graduate of Xavier University in Cincinnati and a double major in Finance and Accounting, Vince has a goal of becoming president of AIC, then expanding company operations into other markets.

Smith has been evaluating the sales performance of Burton and Johnson. Both had been solid, dependable performers over the years, but Johnson had recently slowed down a bit. While his sales volume compared favorably to Burton's, Foster was selling in a higher potential sales territory. Further, he had a five-year head start on Burton in developing new accounts, yet Burton had brought in almost as much new business as Johnson during the past year. Smith had talked to Johnson about the lack of sales growth in his territory but only heard excuses about why his sales had leveled off (i.e., slow economy). Johnson promised to try harder to bring in new business. Smith suspected that Johnson was comfortable with his earnings and simply did not want to work much harder, even if he could make more money.

After several weeks of analysis, Darnell Smith finally had a rough draft of a new territory design policy that would go into effect at the start of the next new quarter. The key points of the new policy are:

1. Half of Darnell Smith's accounts will be split between Terrell Johnson and Julie Burton. Darnell Smith's remaining accounts will be assigned to Vince Smith.

2. After one year, sales territories will be redesigned so that the three territories will be comparable in terms of workload and sales potential.

3. For the current year, AIC salespeople will continue to earn a commission based on AIC billings to their clients.

4. After the sales territories are redesigned in a year, the commission rate for existing clients will be reduced, and a higher commission rate will be implemented for new accounts added within the past year.

Darnell Smith distributed the draft plan to Julie, Terrell, and Tony. Both Julie and Terrell questioned the idea of assigning half of Darnell's accounts to Vince. Terrell came right to the point, saying, "Look, Darnell, he's your son and he will do just fine with some seasoning. But I think he ought to start with a smaller group of accounts. He'll learn the business a lot faster if he has to build it by adding his own accounts."

Julie and Terrell were also concerned that they would have some of Darnell's former accounts for a year, and then lose them to Vince. Vince remained neutral on these issues, and voiced neither support nor opposition to the draft plan.

Questions

1. What are the implications for Julie Burton and Terrell Johnson if the draft plan is implemented?

2. What are the implications for AIC's customers if the draft plan is implemented?

3. What are the pros and cons of Smith's draft plan?

4. What changes and additions would you make to the draft plan?

ROLE PLAY

Role Play

Situation: Read Case 4.2.

Characters: Darnell Smith, president; Vince Smith, son and salesperson; Terrell Johnson, company's first salesperson; Julie Burton, company's second salesperson.

Scene 1:   *Location*—Meeting room. *Action*—Role-play discussion among Darnell Smith, Vince Smith, Terrell Johnson, and Julie Burton about the draft territory design plan.

Scene 2:   *Location*—Meeting room. *Action*—Role-play discussion among Darnell Smith, Vince Smith, Terrell Johnson, and Julie Burton about alternatives to the draft territory design plan and a final territory design decision.

DEVELOPING FORECASTS

A meteorologist used all the latest technology to predict a bright and sunny day in the mid-80s. It rained most of the day and never got warmer than 70 degrees. The weather forecast missed the mark on this particular occasion, but the meteorologist will continue to make weather forecasts and to work on improving weather forecasting procedures.

Sales managers face a situation similar to that of the meteorologist. The business environment is complex and dynamic, there are a number of forecasting methods available, and often forecasts are incorrect. Nevertheless, sales managers must continue to forecast and to work on improving their forecasting procedures.

Why is forecasting so important to sales managers? In one sense, all sales management decisions are based on some type of forecast. The sales manager decides on a certain action because he or she thinks that it will produce a certain result. This expected result is a **forecast,** even though the sales manager may not have quantified it or may not have used a mathematical forecasting procedure. More specifically, forecasts provide the basis for the following sales management decisions:

1. Determining salesforce size

2. Designing territories

3. Establishing sales quotas and setting budgets

4. Determining sales compensation levels

5. Evaluating salesperson performance

6. Evaluating prospective accounts

FORECASTING BY SALES MANAGERS

Although top management levels are most concerned with total firm forecasts, sales managers are typically interested in developing and using forecasts for specific areas, such as accounts, territories, districts, regions, and/or zones. For example, a district sales manager would be concerned with the district forecast as well as forecasts for individual territories and accounts within the district. There are, however, different types of forecasts that sales managers might use in different ways, and different approaches and methods might be used to develop these forecasts.

Types of Forecasts

The term *forecast* is ordinarily used to refer to a prediction for a future period. Although this usage is technically correct, it is too general for managerial value. As illustrated in Figure 4A.1, at least three factors must be defined when referring to a forecast: the product level, the geographic area, and the time period. The figure presents 90 different forecasts that might be made, depending on these factors. Thus, when using the term *forecast*, sales managers should be specific in defining exactly what is being forecast, what geographic area is being targeted, and what period is being forecast.

FIGURE 4A.1   **Defining the Forecast**

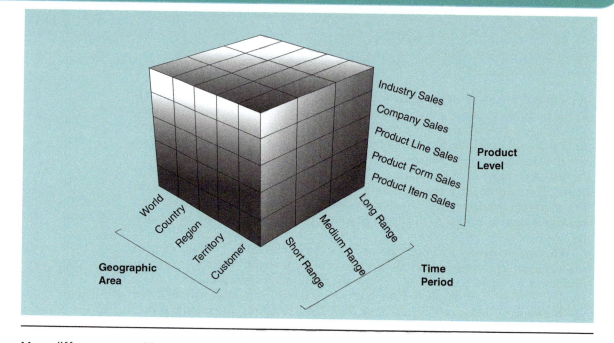

Many different types of forecasts are possible. Every forecast should be defined in terms of geographic area, product level, and time period.

A useful way for viewing what is being forecast is presented in Exhibit 4A.1. This exhibit suggests that it is important to differentiate between industry and firm levels and to determine whether the prediction is for the best possible results or for the expected results given a specific strategy. Four different types of forecasts emerge from this classification scheme:

1. *Market potential*—the best possible level of industry sales in a given geographic area for a specific period.

2. *Market forecast*—the expected level of industry sales given a specific industry strategy in a given geographic area for a specific period.

3. *Sales potential*—the best possible level of firm sales in a given geographic area for a specific period.

4. *Sales forecast*—the expected level of firm sales given a specific strategy in a given geographic area for a specific period.

Notice that the geographic area and period are defined for each of these terms and that a true *sales forecast* must include the consideration of a specific strategy. If a firm changes this strategy, the sales forecast should change also.

As an example, assume that you are the district sales manager for a firm that markets personal computers (PCs) to organizational buyers. Your district includes Missouri, Kansas, Iowa, and Nebraska. You are preparing forecasts for 2016. You might first try to assess market potential. This market potential forecast would be an estimate of the highest level of PC sales by all brands in your district for 2016. Then, you might try to develop a market forecast, which would be the expected level of industry PC sales in your district for 2016. This forecast would be based on an assumption of the strategies that would be used by all PC firms operating in your district. If you think that new firms are going to enter the industry or that existing firms are going to leave it or change their

Types of Forecast EXHIBIT 4A.1

	Best Possible Results	Expected Results for Given Strategy
Industry Level	**Market Potential**	**Market Forecast**
Firm Level	**Sales Potential**	**Sales Forecast**

Four different types of forecasts are typically important to sales managers depending upon whether a forecast is needed for the industry or firm, and whether the best possible or expected results are forecast.

strategies, your industry forecast will change. Another type of forecast might be a determination of the best possible level of 2016 sales for your firm's PCs in the district. This would be a sales potential forecast. Finally, you would probably want to predict a specific level of district sales of your firm's PCs given your firm's expected strategy. This would result in a sales forecast that would have to be revised whenever strategic changes were made.

Uses of Forecasts

Because different types of forecasts convey different information, sales managers use certain types for specific sales management decisions. Forecasts of market potential and sales potential are most often used to identify opportunities and to guide the allocation of selling efforts. Market potential provides an assessment of overall demand opportunity available to all firms in an industry. Sales potential adjusts market potential to reflect industry competition and thus represents a better assessment of demand opportunity for an individual firm. Both of these forecasts of potential can be used by sales managers to determine where selling effort is needed and how selling effort should be distributed. For example, as discussed earlier, designing territories requires an assessment of market potential for all planning and control units. Specific territories are then designed by grouping planning and control units together and evaluating the equality of market potential across the territories.

Market forecasts and sales forecasts are used to predict the expected results from various sales management decisions. For example, once territories are designed, sales managers typically want to forecast expected industry and company sales for each specific sales territory. These forecasts are then used to set sales quotas and selling budgets for specific planning periods. Thus, it is important to develop accurate forecasts. Furthermore, inaccurate forecasts may result in detrimental effects such as increased inventory costs due to over-forecasting or lost sales and profits resulting from under-forecasting.[1]

Top-Down and Bottom-Up Forecasting Approaches

Forecasting methods can be classified in a variety of ways.[2] Specific examples of two basic approaches are presented in Figure 4A.2. **Top-down approaches** typically consist of different methods for developing company forecasts at the business unit level. Sales managers then break down these company forecasts into zone, region, district, territory, and account forecasts. **Bottom-up approaches**, by contrast, consist of different methods

Forecasting Approaches

FIGURE 4A.2

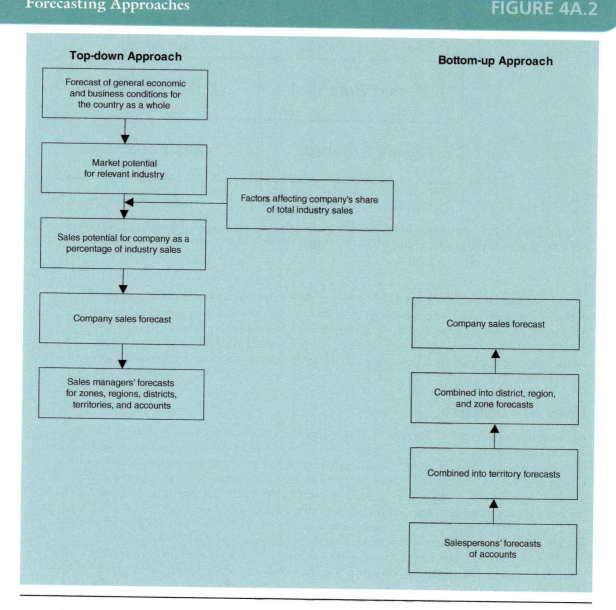

In top-down approaches, company personnel provide aggregate company forecasts that sales managers must break down into zone, region, district, territory, and account forecasts. In bottom-up approaches, account forecasts are combined into territory, district, region, zone, and company forecasts.

for developing sales forecasts for individual accounts. Sales managers then combine the account forecasts into territory, district, region, zone, and company forecasts. The top-down and bottom-up approaches represent entirely different perspectives for developing forecasts, although some forecasting methods can be used in either approach. However, the focus is on the most popular forecasting methods for each approach.

Top-Down Approach

Implementing the top-down approach requires the development of company forecasts and their breakdown into zone, region, district, territory, and account levels. Different methods are used to develop company forecasts and break them down to the desired levels.

Company Forecasting Methods

Although a variety of methods is available for developing company forecasts, this discussion is limited to three popular time series methods: moving averages, exponential smoothing, and decomposition methods.

Moving averages is a relatively simple method that develops a company forecast by calculating the average company sales for previous years. Thus, the company sales forecast for next year is the average of actual company sales for the past three years, past six years, or some other number of years. An example of calculating a moving averages company sales forecast for two- and four-year time frames is presented in Exhibit 4A.2. This exhibit shows that the forecast predicted for 2014 was derived by adding actual sales in 2012 of $8,400,000 to actual sales in 2013 of $8,820,000 and then dividing by two ([$8,400,000 + $8,820,000]/2 = $8,610,000). This was repeated to get the projected forecast for each successive year. To get the forecast for 2020, actual sales for 2018 and 2019 were added together and divided by two ([$9,674,000 + $10,060,000]/2 = $9,867,000). The same procedure is used to calculate the four-year moving average, but rather than using two years of actual sales and dividing by two, four years are summated and then divided by four (e.g., sales forecast for 2020 is [$8,622,000 + $9,484,000 + $9,674,000 + $10,060,000]/4 = $9,460,000).

As illustrated in this example, the moving averages method is straightforward and requires simple calculations. Management must, however, determine the appropriate number of years to include in the calculations. In addition, this method weights actual company sales for previous years equally in generating the forecast for the next year. This equal weighting may not be appropriate if company sales vary substantially from year to year or if there are major differences in the business environment between the most recent and past years.

Exponential smoothing is a type of moving averages method, except that company sales in the most recent year are weighted differently from company sales in past years.[3] An example of the exponential smoothing method is provided in Exhibit 4A.3. This exhibit shows that the sales forecast predicted for 2020 using an alpha of 0.2 was derived by multiplying actual sales in 2019 by 0.2 and adding it to 0.8 times the forecasted sales in 2019 ([.2 × $10,060,000 + .8 × $8,884,000] = $9,119,000). Each of the previous years' forecasts was derived in the same manner.

A critical aspect of this method involves determining the appropriate weight (α) for this year's company sales. This is typically accomplished by examining different weights for historical sales data to determine which weight would have generated the most accurate

Moving Averages Example   EXHIBIT 4A.2

Moving Averages Forecast

Year	Actual Sales	Two-Year	Four-Year
2012	$8,400,000		
2013	8,820,000		
2014	8,644,000	$8,610,000	
2015	8,212,000	8,732,000	
2016	8,622,000	8,428,000	$8,520,000
2017	9,484,000	8,418,000	8,574,000
2018	9,674,000	9,054,000	8,740,000
2019	10,060,000	9,579,000	8,998,000
2020	?	9,867,000	9,460,000

where

$$\text{Sales forecast for next year} = \frac{\text{Actual sales for past two or four years}}{\text{Number of years (two or four years)}}$$

EXHIBIT 4A.3 Exponential Smoothing Example

Year	Actual Sales	Sales Forecast for Next Year		
		$\alpha = 0.2$	$\alpha = 0.5$	$\alpha = 0.8$
2012	$8,400,000			
2013	8,820,000	$8,400,000	$8,400,000	$8,400,000
2014	8,644,000	8,484,000	8,610,000	8,736,000
2015	8,212,000	8,516,000	8,627,000	8,662,000
2016	8,622,000	8,455,000	8,420,000	8,302,000
2017	9,484,000	8,488,000	8,521,000	8,558,000
2018	9,674,000	8,687,000	9,003,000	9,299,000
2019	10,060,000	8,884,000	9,339,000	9,599,000
2020	?	9,119,000	9,700,000	9,968,000

where

Sales forecast for next year $= (\alpha)$(actual sales this year) $+ (1 - \alpha)$(this year's sales forecast)

sales forecasts in the past. Based on the analysis in Exhibit 4A.3, management should probably use a weight of 0.8 for this year's company sales.

Decomposition methods involve different procedures that break down previous company sales data into four major components: trend, cycle, seasonal, and erratic events. These components are then reincorporated to produce the sales forecast. An example of a decomposition method is presented in Exhibit 4A.4. Notice that the trend, cycle, and erratic events components are incorporated into the annual forecast but that the seasonal component is used only when forecasting sales for periods of less than a year, such as months or quarters. Decomposition methods are sound conceptually but often require complex statistical approaches for breaking down the company sales data into the trend components. Once this decomposition has been completed, it is relatively easy to reincorporate the components into the development of a company forecast.

EXHIBIT 4A.4 Decomposition Method Example

Assume that various analyses have decomposed previous sales data into the following components:

A 5% growth in sales is predicted due to basic developments in population, capital formation, and technology (trend component). A 10% decrease in sales is expected due to a business recession (cycle component). Increased tensions in the Middle East are expected to reduce sales by an additional 5% (erratic events component). Sales results are reasonably consistent throughout the year except for the fourth quarter, where sales are expected to be 25% higher than the other quarters (seasonal component).

A marketer of consumer products might recombine the different components in the following manner to forecast sales for 2020:

Sales in 2019 were $10,060,000. The trend component suggests that 2020 sales will be $10,563,000 ($10,060,000 × 1.05). However, incorporating the expected business recession represented in the cycle component changes the sales forecast to $9,506,700 ($10,563,000 × 0.90). The annual sales forecast is reduced to $9,031,365 when the erratic events component is introduced ($9,056,700 × 0.95). Quarterly sales forecasts would initially be calculated as $2,257,841 ($9,031,365 ÷ 4). However, incorporating the seasonal component suggests fourth-quarter sales of $2,822,302 ($2,257,841 × 1.25) and sales for the other three quarters of $2,069,688 ($9,031,365 − $2,822,302 ÷ 3).

Breakdown Methods

Once sales managers receive a company forecast, they can use different market factor methods to break it down to the desired levels. **Market factor methods** typically involve identifying one or more factors that are related to sales at the zone, region, district, territory, or account levels and using these factors to break down the overall company forecast into forecasts at these levels.

One approach is for a firm to develop a buying power index for its specific situation. For example, a general aviation aircraft marketer developed a buying power index for its products in each county in the United States. The basic formula was

$$\text{Index} = (5I + 3AR + 2P) \div 10$$

where

I = Percentage of U.S. disposable income in county

AR = Percentage of U.S. aircraft registrations in county

P = Percentage of U.S. registered pilots in county

These calculations produced an index for each county. The index calculated for each county can then be multiplied by the total company sales forecast to break it into a forecast for each county. The firm could take U.S. forecasts provided by the industry trade association and convert them to market and sales forecasts for each county by using their calculated indices and market shares.

The use of market factor methods is widespread in the sales management area. Indices developed by specific firms and other market factor methods can be extremely valuable forecasting tools for sales managers. These indices and market factors should be continually evaluated and improved. They can be assessed by comparing actual sales in an area to the market factor value for the area. For example, the general aviation aircraft marketer found high correlations between actual aircraft sales in a county and the county indices. This finding provided support for the use of the calculated index as an indirect forecasting tool.

Bottom-Up Approach

Implementing the bottom-up approach requires various methods to forecast sales to individual accounts and the combination of these account forecasts into territory, district, region, zone, and company forecasts. This section focuses on the survey of buyer intentions, jury of executive opinion, Delphi, and salesforce composite methods as used in a bottom-up approach.

The **survey of buyer intentions method** is any procedure that asks individual accounts about their purchasing plans for a future period and translates these responses into account forecasts. The intended purchases by accounts might be obtained through mail surveys, telephone surveys, personal interviews, or other approaches. For example, companies such as Dow Chemical and Hewlett-Packard have asked their business customers for feedback regarding intended future needs. At times, forecasts based on customer intentions may be distorted due to buyers' unwillingness to put much effort into predicting future needs. Moreover, buyers are often unwilling to reveal plans for selling a vendor's product out of fear competitors may retaliate if they find out.[4]

The **jury of executive opinion method** involves any approach in which executives of the firm use their expert knowledge to forecast sales to individual accounts. Separate forecasts might be obtained from managers in different functional areas. These forecasts are then averaged or discussed by the managers until a consensus forecast for each account is reached. Team-based approaches such as this are believed to result in more accurate long-range industry-level forecasts than individually based approaches.[5]

The **Delphi method** is a structured type of jury of executive opinion method. The basic procedure involves selection of a panel of managers from within the firm. Each member of the panel submits anonymous forecasts for each account. These forecasts are

FIGURE 4A.3   Quarterly Forecasting Form for Salespeople

Account	Projected Sales by Product Group for Quarter Beginning 7/5/2015								Totals
	364-60	364-80	28B	460	28				
Ace	1,250	960	1,400	2,100	160				5,870
Sentry	950	1,250	1,930	470	968				5,568
Cutter	—	2,110	—	960	1,750				4,820
Grossman	—	—	—	—	364				364
Paycass	400	1,800	—	—	720				2,920
American	—	—	—	—	1,230				1,230
Pro	—	—	—	—	—				700
Totals	2,600	6,820	3,330	3,530	5,192				21,472

This is an example of a form used by a firm to get salespeople to forecast sales for each account and product group.

summarized into a report that is sent to each panel member. The report presents descriptive statistics concerning the submitted forecasts with reasons for the lowest and highest forecasts. Panel members review this information and then again submit anonymous individual forecasts. The same procedure is repeated until the forecasts for individual accounts converge into a consensus. Because this procedure involves written rather than verbal communication, such negatives as domination, undue conservatism, and argument are eliminated, while team members benefit from one another's input.[6]

The salesforce composite method involves various procedures by which salespeople provide forecasts for their assigned accounts, typically on specially designed forms (see Figure 4A.3), electronically via computer, or through the company's CRM system. At Cisco Systems, reps submit data electronically to a company database that provides information about their pipelines, including opportunity size, customer technology requirements, and competitors. Managers then use this data to develop weekly, monthly, and quarterly forecasts.[7] Research results suggest that salesperson forecasts can be improved by developing detailed instructions about the forecasting procedures and providing salespeople with detailed information about their accounts and feedback concerning the accuracy of previous forecasts.[8]

Forecasting with Regression Analysis

Regression analysis is a statistical technique that can be used to develop sales forecasts at all organizational levels, as well as company wide.[9]

A market response framework to guide this type of approach is presented in Figure 4A.4.[10] Depending on the planning and control unit of interest (territory, district, region, or zone), different determinants of market response (e.g., sales, market share) might be important. However, these determinants can be classified as either environmental, organizational, or salesperson factors. Once the determinant and market response factors are identified, their values for each planning and control unit in the previous period must be measured.

Statistical packages such as SPSS can then be used to estimate the parameters of the regression equation. For example, if you are a district sales manager interested in forecasting territory sales, you would identify and measure specific environmental, organizational, and salesperson factors, as well as sales for each territory in the previous year. You could then develop a regression model of the following form:

$$\text{Territory sales} = a + (b1)(\text{environmental factor}) + (b2)(\text{organizational factor}) + (b3)(\text{salesperson factor})$$

The a, $b1$, $b2$, and $b3$ values are the model parameters supplied by the regression procedure to define the relationship between the determinant factors and territory sales.

Although this type of model might be useful, it suffers from two basic weaknesses. First, it incorporates only the independent effects of the determinant variables, yet these variables are highly interrelated. Second, this type of equation is linear, yet the determinant variable relationships are probably nonlinear. These weaknesses can be addressed by performing the linear regression on the logarithms of the actual data, producing a multiplicative power function of the following form:

$$\text{Territory sales} = (a)(\text{environmental factor}^{b1})(\text{organizational factor}^{b2}) (\text{salesperson factor}^{b3})$$

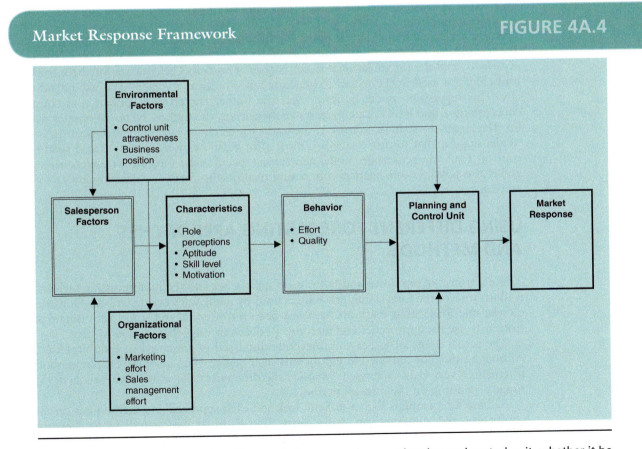

Market Response Framework   FIGURE 4A.4

These are the types of factors that affect market response for any planning and control unit, whether it be accounts, territories, districts, regions, or zones. Market response might be profits, market share, or some other response, but sales is usually the market response variable of interest to sales managers.

EXHIBIT 4A.5   Regression Model Examples

Territory sales $= (800.82)(\text{potential}^{.53})(\text{concentration}^{.03})(\text{experience}^{.08})$
$(\text{span of control}^{-.55})$

	Territory 1	Territory 2	Territory 3
Potential (number of persons employed by firms in customer industry located in territory)	114,000	125,000	87,000
Concentration (number of persons employed by the large plants in customer industry located in territory)	94,000	52,000	12,000
Experience (months salesperson has been with company)	30	10	20
Span of control (number of salespeople supervised by sales manager)	5	8	10
Territory sales forecast	$586,000	$238,400	$173,200

This function is nonlinear and incorporates interactions through the multiplication of determinant variables.

A specific example illustrating this type of function is presented in Exhibit 4A.5.[11] The environmental factors are *potential* and *concentration,* the salesperson factor is *experience,* and the organizational factor is *span of control.* The data are for three territories and are used in the model to generate sales forecasts for each territory individually. This regression model indicates that the higher the territory potential, account concentration, and level of salesperson experience are, the higher the territory sales will be. The larger the span of control is, the lower the territory sales. The exponents in the model suggest that territory sales are most affected by territory potential and span of control. Thus, the regression model generates a specific sales forecast for each territory, and it also provides information concerning relationships between determinant factors and sales.

USING DIFFERENT FORECASTING APPROACHES AND METHODS

This discussion of top-down and bottom-up approaches and several forecasting methods is illustrative of the forecasting procedures used by many sales organizations. However, all available forecasting methods have not been introduced, and some sales organizations may use the approaches and methods in different ways than discussed here.

The actual usage of forecasting methods discussed is presented in Exhibit 4A.6.[12] Although this study did not ask respondents their degree of usage of the Delphi method, it remains a very viable approach.[13] Notice the differences that exist in the frequency of usage depending on the forecast period.

Because forecasting is such a difficult task and each approach and method has certain advantages and disadvantages, most firms use multiple forecasting approaches and methods. Then, various approaches are used to combine the results from each method into a final forecast.[14] If different approaches and methods produce similar sales forecasts, sales managers can be more confident in the validity of the forecast. If extremely divergent

	Percentage of Firms Using Method by Forecast Period		
Forecasting Method	**Less than 3 months**	**3 months to 2 years**	**More than 2 years**
Top-Down			
Moving average	9	45	11
Exponential smoothing	8	92	16
Decomposition	2	40	10
Bottom-Up			
Survey of buyer intentions	5	38	15
Jury of executive opinion	4	77	55
Salesforce composite	5	38	15
Regression Analysis	4	69	30

EXHIBIT 4A.6 Usage of Forecasting Methods

forecasts are generated from the different approaches and methods, additional analysis is required to determine the reasons for the large differences and to make the adjustments necessary to produce an accurate sales forecast. Some firms even take advantage of available sales forecasting software, such as ForecastPro (www.forecastpro.com), to help them in the forecasting process. Microsoft provides a premade sales forecasting template (http://office.microsoft.com/en-us/templates/TC011347871033.aspx?pid=Ct101441951033) that can help streamline the forecasting process.

Even though firms use multiple forecasting methods, research evidence indicates that several criteria are used to select specific forecasting methods.[15] The most important criterion identified in this study was the accuracy of the forecasting method. Other criteria that were considered in decreasing importance were ease of use, data requirements, cost, and familiarity with methods. These results suggest that the selection of forecasting methods often represents a trade-off between the accuracy of the method and the ease with which it can be implemented. Some of the more accurate forecasting methods are difficult to use and have substantial data requirements. Thus, firms may have to sacrifice some accuracy by selecting methods that they are able to readily implement. This situation is illustrated in Exhibit 4A.6, where some of the more accurate methods (e.g., decomposition) are not used by many firms. Strengths and weaknesses of each forecasting method are found in Exhibit 4A.7.

EXHIBIT 4A.7   Strengths and Weaknesses of Forecasting Methods

Technique	Strengths	Weaknesses
Moving averages	Well suited to situations in which sales forecasts are needed for a large number of products Good for products with fairly stable sales Smoothes out small random fluctuations Can compensate to some degree for trend if double moving average model is used	Requires a large amount of historical data Adjusts slowly to changes in sales Assigns equal weight to each period, ignoring the fact that more recent periods usually have more impact on future sales Results cannot be tested statistically
Exponential smoothing	Fairly simple to understand and use Provides more weight to recent data points Requires little data storage Generally accessible software packages are available Fairly good accuracy for short-term forecasts	Much searching may be needed to find appropriate weight Poor for medium- and long-term forecasts Erroneous forecasts can result due to large random fluctuations in recent data Requires a large amount of past data
Decomposition method	Simple to understand Included in most computer packages Acknowledges three key factors affecting sales—trend, seasonal, cycles Breaks past sales into component parts, making it easier to understand the sales pattern	Does not lend itself to longer-range forecasts Does not lend itself to statistical analysis of forecast values (no confidence limits or tests of significance)
Survey of buyer intentions	Forecasts are based on customers' buying plans Contacts with customers can also provide feedback about possible problems with the firm's products Relatively inexpensive if only a few key customers need to be contacted	Intentions frequently do not culminate in actual purchases Some firms may not be willing to disclose buying intentions, especially if they are not regular customers
Jury of executive opinion	Provides input from the firm's key functional areas Executives usually have a solid understanding of broad-based factors and how they affect sales Can provide fairly quick forecasts	May require excessive amounts of executives' time Executives removed from the marketplace may not understand the firm's sales situation Not well suited to firms with a large number of products One or two influential people may dominate the process

Strengths and Weaknesses of Forecasting Methods—*continued*   **EXHIBIT 4A.7**

Technique	Strengths	Weaknesses
Delphi method	Eliminates the need for committee or group meetings Eliminates group decision-making pitfalls, such as specious persuasion or a bandwagon effect Participants receive input from other "experts" in an isolated environment Allows for voicing of unusual opinions and anonymous mind changing Proper facilities (email) enable rapid exchange of ideas	Participants are often selected more on their willingness to participate and their accessibility than on their real knowledge or representativeness Can take a great deal of time to arrive at a consensus Process may suffer because of high dropout rate of participants
Salesforce composite	Uses input from persons closest to actual markets Provides reasonably detailed forecasts (by product, customer, or territory) May enhance salesforce morale by letting their input guide decisions	Salespeople may underestimate sales when their forecasts are being used to set sales quotas Can take excessive amounts of salespeople's time if done too often Salespeople often lack the knowledge to evaluate the economic situation and how it might affect future sales
Regression analysis	Identifies unknown factors affecting market response Provides an objective forecasting method Develops sales forecasts that explicitly consider the characteristics of a control unit, making them easy to translate into sales quotas	Requires a large amount of data to produce a reliable model Requires some technical skill and expertise to use Factors affecting market response must be accurately identified Does not consider effects of seasonal variations

Developing the Salesforce

The two chapters in Part 3 concentrate on the development of a productive salesforce. In Chapter 5, we review the process of acquiring sales talent through recruitment and selection. Standard recruitment and selection tools such as advertising, job interviews, and tests are discussed. Legal and ethical issues are also raised, and the topic of salesforce socialization is introduced.

Chapter 6 focuses on the continual development of salespeople through sales training. A model of the sales training process provides a framework for discussing needs assessment; training objectives; alternatives for training; and the design, performance, and evaluation of sales training.

OBJECTIVES

After completing this chapter, you should be able to

1. Explain the critical role of recruitment and selection in building and maintaining a productive salesforce.

2. Describe how recruitment and selection affect salesforce socialization and performance.

3. Identify the key activities in planning and executing a program for salesforce recruitment and selection.

4. Discuss the legal and ethical considerations in salesforce recruitment and selection.

ACQUIRING SALES TALENT AT MARLIN BUSINESS SERVICES

Marlin Business Services Corporation® finances commercial equipment and provides working capital loans to small businesses across the U.S. They are committed to providing excellent service to equipment dealers, manufacturers, resellers, and distributors through their financing and lease programs.

Following an economic downturn, in which many competitors left the market, Marlin found itself in a position to grow rapidly. They wanted to hire 60–70 sales reps in a short period of time and were able to ramp up to 80 sales representatives in the next few years. However, over the next year they lost approximately half of them due to both voluntary and involuntary turnover. According to Ed Siciliano, Chief Sales Officer at the time, being at a desk making 70 calls each day is not the easiest job. "Still," he confessed, "the turnover rate was alarming."

The Marlin executive team recognized that to reach its sales goals and company objectives it needed to dramatically cut its turnover of sales representatives and increase their productivity. Ed began investigating all the company's talent acquisition and turnover data. "We are a very data-centric company," he described. "I track many, many, business drivers. When it comes to turnover, I track why people leave which sales teams, and where the hires came from. For example, how many were employee referrals versus job postings or job fairs, how many came from college recruiting versus outside recruiting or previous employment, and so on." Ed decided that he needed to reconsider how Marlin went about acquiring and retaining talent.

Ed's first step was to convene his four vice presidents and ten managers responsible for most of the hiring for a brainstorming session. Besides examining where they source potential employees, they solicited Caliper, an employee assessment and talent development solutions provider, to determine the personality profile of an effective Marlin salesperson. "I took my top fifteen employees and put them through the Caliper Profile assessment," said Ed. "Then, we took the amalgamation of those results to determine what a Marlin top sales representative looks like. That gave us the blueprint for the type of salesperson we should be looking for." Marlin job applicants now take the Caliper profile assessment. Those whose scores fail to meet established standards are considered a poor fit and unlikely to succeed with the firm over the long term.

The new hiring process appears to be a success. According to Ed, "Caliper helped me determine what a Marlin top sales rep looks like, and since we began hiring from that model, our turnover has dropped from nearly 50% to 16%." Hiring the right people has enabled Marlin to reduce turnover, increase productivity, reduce the cost of sales and increase company profit. And, their proven hiring model will allow them to successfully grow into the future.

Source: Success Stories: Marlin Leasing, Caliper, www.calipercorp.com/component/stories/successsstory/marlin-leasing (accessed May 15, 2018).

As illustrated in the opening vignette, the recruitment and selection process can be tricky. However, investing the necessary resources to hire the right sales talent is essential. Recruiting and selecting those best qualified for a position can make the difference between a firm's long-run ultimate success and failure. Although many factors influence sales performance, sales managers cannot survive without doing a competent job in recruiting and selecting salespeople. The vital and complex nature of the job is summarized by Munson and Spivey:

> The process is complicated by various conflicting factors—the need to select applicants with characteristics related to job success, the difficulty of determining these characteristics, inadequacies inherent in the various selection techniques themselves, and the need to simultaneously insure that the selection process satisfies existing governmental regulations pertaining to discrimination in hiring practices.[1]

Today, the recruitment and selection process must be adjusted to the demographics of a younger salesforce with a higher proportion of women and minorities than in the past.[2] Sales managers also face challenges associated with acquiring talent for an international salesforce, as well as with recruiting and selecting for team selling. Proper staffing of the salesforce is critical given the strong impact of the recruiting process on a firm's performance and profits.[3] Today's sales manager's role in recruitment and selection is explored in this chapter. Before examining a basic model of the process, let's discuss further the importance of recruitment and selection.

IMPORTANCE OF RECRUITMENT AND SELECTION

In most sales organizations, sales managers with direct supervisory responsibilities for salespeople have the primary responsibility for recruitment and selection. They may have the support of top management or coordinate their efforts with human resource personnel or other managers within the firm, but it is the sales manager who generally retains primary recruitment and selection responsibilities. To emphasize the importance of recruitment and selection, consider a few of the problems associated with inadequate implementation:

1. Inadequate sales coverage and lack of customer follow-up

2. Increased training costs to overcome deficiencies

3. More supervisory problems

4. Higher turnover rates

5. Difficulty in establishing enduring relationships with customers

6. Suboptimal total salesforce performance

Clearly, salesforce performance will suffer if recruitment and selection are poorly executed. Other sales management functions become more burdensome when the sales manager is handicapped by a multitude of "bad hires." The full costs of unsuccessful recruitment and selection are probably impossible to estimate. In addition to sales trainee salaries, advertising fees; screening, interviewing, and assessment costs; and employment agency fees, among others, there are hidden costs associated with salesforce turnover, such as the loss of the relationships that salespeople build with their customers over time, negative impact on employee morale, and increased managerial problems that defy calculation. (For a more detailed look at the costs of a bad hire, go to www.salestestonline.com/sales-test-the-cost-of-failure-calculator-what-does-it-cost-to-hire-the-wrong-sales-person). Estimates suggest that it costs a firm anywhere from one third to five times a worker's annual salary to replace a bad hire.[4] Federated Insurance estimates it invests nearly $225,000 in each new marketing development trainee before the trainee is assigned to his/her own marketing representative territory.[5] For a bad hire, such an investment represents sunk costs that may be nonrecoverable. And in view of studies that tell us that a significant number of salespeople should not be in sales for one reason or another,[6] it is apparent that recruitment and selection are among the most challenging and important responsibilities of sales management.

INTRODUCTION TO SALESFORCE SOCIALIZATION

Salesforce socialization (sometimes referred to as *onboarding*) refers to the process by which salespeople acquire the knowledge, skills, and values essential to perform their jobs. The process begins when the sales recruit is first exposed to the organization and may extend for several years. A model of salesforce socialization is shown in Figure 5.1. This model suggests that important job outcomes such as job satisfaction, job

Proposed Model of Salesforce Socialization   FIGURE 5.1

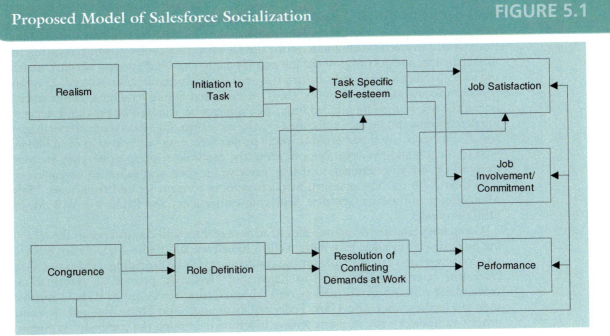

Sales organizations must present accurate portrayals of the sales job (achieving realism) to sales recruits, who must possess skills and needs compatible with the needs and offerings of the organization (achieving congruence). If these objectives of recruiting and selection are met, salesforce socialization is enhanced, and ultimately, salesforce performance, job satisfaction, and job involvement and commitment are improved.

SALES MANAGEMENT IN THE 21ST CENTURY

Achieving Congruence and Realism at W.B. Mason Office Products

Marty Zucker, Regional Office Coffee Services Manager for W.B. Mason Office Products, comments on achieving congruence and realism.

W.B. Mason Office Products is the nation's largest independent office supply company. Operating out of 13 New England States and an additional 40 breakpoints throughout the USA and competing against the nation's largest publicly held office supply companies, requires a highly talented salesforce to be successful. This requires hiring salespeople who are a good fit with our organization. As a 120-year-old company, we have a track record that attracts candidates with a desire to sell for a company with a long history and great reputation in the industry. New college recruits must have a

4-year degree with extra-curricular activities. We are looking for those young men and women that show the desire to excel. We prefer that the candidate is involved with sports, music or business clubs. These people are accustomed to being inspired and motivated in order to excel. They are willing to put forth the extra effort and work well in a team environment. However, we will not exclude anybody from the interview or hiring process just because they do not have these specific extra-curricular activities, but they must have a desire to excel. Prior to a formal offer, however, the candidate must do a one-day drive along with one of our sales trainers. This is the reality check! This is the first time our candidates will see first-hand what is expected of them. If this preview does not match the candidate's job expectations, we are not likely to have a good fit.

involvement and commitment, and performance are directly and indirectly affected by recruitment and selection procedures.

The socialization process is discussed again in subsequent chapters. For now, accept the idea that socialization affects salesforce performance and that recruitment and selection procedures play a major role in the socialization process. The two stages of socialization relevant to recruitment and selection are (1) **achieving realism**, which is giving the recruit an accurate portrayal of the job and (2) **achieving congruence**, which is matching the capabilities of the recruit with the needs of the organization. According to one study of executives, more than one third believed that failing to achieve congruence is one of the top reasons for a failed hire.[7] Realism can be achieved by providing accurate job descriptions and perhaps offering a **job preview** through a field visit with a salesperson. Congruence can be achieved through proper screening and selection of candidates who fit the job and the organization. From the candidates' perspective, they are more likely to choose an organization if they perceive its goals and values to be congruent with theirs.[8] To see how one firm works to achieve congruence and realism see "Sales Management in the 21st Century: Achieving Congruence and Realism at W.B. Mason Office Products."

Companies take several approaches to achieve realism and congruence in the recruiting process. For instance, to achieve realism some companies give students an opportunity to view what a career in sales at the company entails by providing a video to college placement centers. Others, such as Xerox and Hershey's, provide an informational video, along with other information, on a job applicant gateway on the Web. Companies such as Hershey Chocolate USA, Federated Insurance, and Hertz Equipment Rental provide candidates with a comprehensive brochure describing the company, its philosophy, and its products. Some companies provide informational sessions on college campuses for recruits, while others offer a ride-along on a sales call. Congruence is achieved through various selection tools, such as interviewing and testing, which will be discussed later in this chapter.

RECRUITMENT AND SELECTION PROCESS

Figure 5.2 illustrates the steps in the recruitment and selection process. The first step involves **planning activities**: conducting a job analysis, establishing job qualifications, completing a written job description, setting recruitment and selection objectives, and developing a recruitment and selection strategy. These planning activities are conducted within the overall planning framework of the organization to ensure consistency with the objectives, strategies, resources, and constraints of the organization.

The second step is **recruitment**, which, simply put, is the procedure of locating a sufficient number of prospective job applicants. A number of internal (within the company) and external (outside the company) sources may be used to develop this pool of candidates.

The next step in the model is **selection**, the process of choosing which candidates will be offered the job. Many screening and evaluation methods, including evaluation of resumes and job application forms, interviews, tests, assessment centers, background investigations, and physical exams, are used in this step. A more detailed discussion of each step in the recruitment and selection process follows.

Planning for Recruitment and Selection

Given the critical nature of recruitment and selection, it would be difficult to overstate the case for careful planning as part of the process. Sales managers are concerned with the current staffing needs of their organizations; but perhaps more important, they are also concerned with future staffing needs, which is what makes planning so essential.

Proper planning provides more time for locating the best recruits. Upper management can be alerted in advance to probable future needs, rather than having to be convinced quickly when the need becomes imminent. Also, training can be planned more effectively when the flow of new trainees into the organization is known. Overall, the main benefit of adequate planning for the recruitment and selection process is that it helps prevent the kind of poor decisions that often prove so expensive both emotionally and financially. About fifty percent of new hires turn out to be a bad choice.[9] Proper planning could help reduce this number. The key tasks in planning for recruitment and selection are the following:

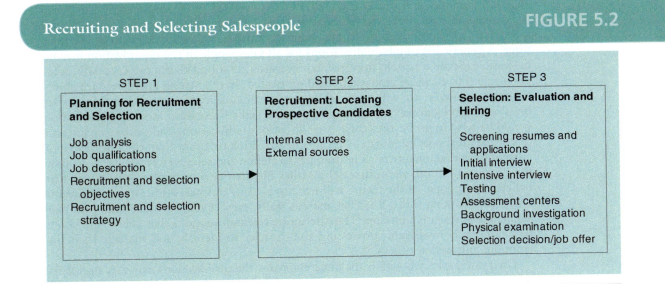

Recruiting and Selecting Salespeople   **FIGURE 5.2**

STEP 1	STEP 2	STEP 3
Planning for Recruitment and Selection	**Recruitment: Locating Prospective Candidates**	**Selection: Evaluation and Hiring**
Job analysis Job qualifications Job description Recruitment and selection objectives Recruitment and selection strategy	Internal sources External sources	Screening resumes and applications Initial interview Intensive interview Testing Assessment centers Background investigation Physical examination Selection decision/job offer

Three main steps are involved in recruiting and selecting salespeople: planning, recruiting, and selection.

Job Analysis

To effectively recruit and select salespeople, sales managers must have a complete understanding of the job for which candidates are sought. Because most sales managers have served as salespeople in their companies before entering management, it is reasonable to think that they would have a good understanding of the sales jobs for which they are recruiting. However, some have lost touch with changing conditions in the field and thus have an obsolete view of the current sales task to be accomplished.

To ensure an understanding of the sales job, the sales manager may need to conduct, confirm, or update a **job analysis**, which entails an investigation of the tasks, duties, and responsibilities of the job. For example, will the selling tasks include responsibilities for opening new accounts as well as maintaining existing accounts? Will the salesperson be responsible for collecting account receivables or completing administrative reports? The job analysis defines the expected behavior of salespeople, indicating which areas of performance will be crucial for success. In most larger companies, the job analysis is completed by human resource managers or other corporate managers, but even then, the sales manager may have input into the job analysis.

Job Qualifications

The job analysis indicates what salespeople are supposed to do on the job, whereas **job qualifications** refer to the aptitude, skills, knowledge, personal traits, and willingness to accept occupational conditions necessary to perform the job. For example, when hiring a sales associate, Fastenal looks for candidates who are 18 years of age or over, have a valid driver's license, possess or are working towards a degree in business/marketing or have equivalent industry experience and knowledge of the local market, have excellent written and oral communication skills, have strong computer skills and math aptitude, have a strong aptitude for sales and desire to earn commission after the training period, are highly motivated, self-directed, and customer service oriented, demonstrate ambition, innovation, integrity and teamwork, have the ability to lift, slide and lower packages that typically weigh 25–50lbs, and have the ability to pass the required drug screening.[10]

Common sales job qualifications address sales experience, educational level, willingness to travel, willingness to relocate, interpersonal skills, communication skills, problem-solving skills, relationship management skills, organizational skills, ability to overcome objections, tenacity, competitiveness, self-discipline, persistence, time management skills, follow-up skills, adaptability, attitude, enthusiasm, work ethic, empathy, ego drive, ego strength, integrity, self-motivation, and ability to work independently. In addition, today's salesperson is expected to analyze data, think strategically and learn the business.[11]

Consistent with our earlier discussion of the diversity of personal selling jobs, there is a corresponding variance in job qualifications for different sales jobs. Therefore, each sales manager should record the pertinent job qualifications for each job in the salesforce. A generic list of job qualifications for all salespeople in the organization may not be feasible. Some research, however, has consistently found that more successful salespeople tend to be more empathetic and motivated, have a strong ego drive, are able to build trust quickly, are willing to ask for commitments, and in some sales roles possess more acute problem-solving and organizational skills.[12] Forward-looking organizations would be wise to go beyond their current list of qualifications and outline characteristics of the ideal sales candidate. This profile may look different than the one describing current salesforce members as it attempts to define the salesperson necessary to move the organization into the future. The Miller Heiman Group, a sales consultancy firm, believes salespeople of the future will need to possess business and commercial insight, analytical thinking skills, financial analysis skills, project management skills and management and systems thinking.[13] Furthermore, research suggests that salespeople should be emotionally intelligent, possessing the capacity to identify and manage their own emotions and well as others'.[14]

For a given sales job within the same company, the qualifications may vary in different selling situations. For example, a multinational company whose salespeople sell the same products to the same types of customers may require different qualifications in different countries. Qualifications considered unimportant, and even discriminatory, in hiring salespeople in the United States, such as social class and religious and ethnic background, are important in hiring overseas.[15] In general, when sending salespeople on international assignments, it is helpful if they are mature, emotionally stable, culturally empathetic, energetic, patient, flexible, confident, persistent, motivated, and tolerant of new ways of doing things; have a desire to work abroad; enjoy travel; possess a breadth of knowledge and a positive outlook, and have a sense of humor.[16]

Job Description

Based on the job analysis and job qualifications, a written summary of the job, the **job description**, is completed by the sales manager or, in many cases, the human resource manager. Job descriptions for salespeople could contain any or all of the following elements:

1. Job title (e.g., sales trainee, senior sales representative)

2. Duties, tasks, and responsibilities of the salesperson

3. Administrative relationships indicating to whom the salesperson reports

4. Types of products to be sold

5. Customer types

6. Significant job-related demands, such as mental stress, physical strength or stamina requirements, travel requirements, or environmental pressures to be encountered

Job descriptions are an essential document in sales management. Their use in recruitment and selection is only one of their multiple functions. They are used to clarify duties and thereby reduce role ambiguity in the salesforce, to familiarize potential employees with the sales job, to set objectives for salespeople, and eventually, to aid in evaluating performance by setting performance standards. A typical job description for a sales representative is shown in Exhibit 5.1.[17]

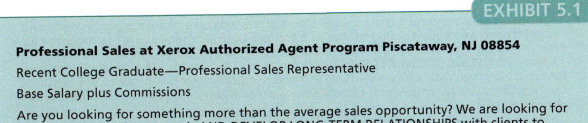

EXHIBIT 5.1

Professional Sales at Xerox Authorized Agent Program Piscataway, NJ 08854

Recent College Graduate—Professional Sales Representative

Base Salary plus Commissions

Are you looking for something more than the average sales opportunity? We are looking for SALES Professionals to consult AND DEVELOP LONG-TERM RELATIONSHIPS with clients to create long term solutions for THEIR BUSINESS ISSUES. Are you passionate about technology and enjoy educating your clients on tools to make their business more efficient? If so then you should be working for COMPLETE DOCUMENT SOLUTIONS as a professional sales representative.

Working for a locally owned independent Xerox Authorized Sales Agency you'll be backed by the world-class resources, products, and solutions of Xerox Corporation. As an Account Executive you will have the support and stability of the Xerox name along with the freedom and personalized attention of a small company. You will have state of the art technology; including your database in hand at all times on your company provided iPad. No other competitive dealer has the ability to enable you to effectively market your territory, schedule your day, and follow-up with clients so conveniently, professionally, and effectively.

What will you be doing?

- Planning and implementing strategies to market Xerox products and services.
- Maintain a large database of qualified prospects through cold calling, personal visits, and networking.
- Identify qualified prospective clients and develop customer relationships.
- Deliver an established number of Xerox proposals to clients on a monthly basis.

EXHIBIT 5.1 *continued*

- Demonstrate Xerox products and software advantages and benefits.
- Close business and provide after-sales reports.
- Grow year-over-year sales results.

What do you need to do the job?.

- Excellent verbal and written communication skills.
- Ability to create a positive buying experience; strong closing skills.
- Ability to detect individual customer needs and clearly present key benefits of doing business with CDS-Xerox.
- Self-motivation, strong work ethic, commission driven, career oriented.
- Drive, persistence, and the ability to meet and exceed sales targets/goals.
- Ability to function independently in a team environment with little supervision.
- Professional appearance and stable work history.
- Excellent organizational skills.
- Proficient computer skills.
- Prior sales experience is a plus, but not necessary.
- College degree mandatory.

What do you get in this opportunity?

- Base salary paid weekly and commissions paid monthly.
- Extensive professional training, sales skills development and coaching.
- Continued career growth.
- Bonuses.
- Medical, Dental, Vision.
- Company Paid Life Insurance.
- Paid Time Off.
- Compensation for Training.
- iPad, Tolls, Car usage and Travel Expenses Paid.

About the company:

COMPLETE DOCUMENT SOLUTIONS, a Xerox Authorized Sales Agent and one of Xerox's largest business partners, boasts a unique blend of the structure of a large corporation with the agility and excitement similar to that of a venture capital organization, our exceptional, entrepreneurial environment will facilitate rapid personal and income growth. For over 10 years, COMPLETE DOCUMENT SOLUTIONS has helped thousands of companies across the East coast improve their office workflow, increase productivity and improve their overall business practice. Our employees' success is our success and we are committed to taking that journey with you.

Ready to take your next steps toward your new journey!

Recruitment and Selection Objectives

To be fully operational, recruitment and selection objectives should be specifically stated for a given period. The following general objectives of recruitment and selection could be converted to specific operational objectives in a given firm:

- Determine present and future needs in terms of numbers and types of salespeople (as discussed in Chapter 4).
- Meet the company's legal and social responsibilities regarding composition of the salesforce.
- Reduce the number of underqualified or overqualified applicants.
- Increase the number of qualified applicants at a specified cost.
- Evaluate the effectiveness of recruiting sources and evaluation techniques.

By setting specific objectives for recruitment and selection, sales managers can channel resources into priority areas and improve organizational and salesforce effectiveness.

Recruitment and Selection Strategy

After objectives have been set, a **recruitment and selection strategy** can be developed. Formulating this strategy requires the sales manager to consider the scope and timing of recruitment and selection activities as follows:

- When will the recruitment and selection be done?
- How will the job be portrayed?
- How will efforts with intermediaries, such as employment agencies and college placement centers, be optimized?
- What are the most likely sources for qualified applicants?
- What type of salespeople will be hired when developing an international salesforce?
- How much time will be allowed for a candidate to accept or reject an offer?

Recruitment and selection are perpetual activities in some sales organizations but in others are conducted only when a vacancy occurs. Some recruit seasonally. For example, large companies often concentrate their efforts to coincide with spring graduation dates on college campuses. However, most sales organizations could benefit by ongoing recruitment to facilitate selection when the need arises.

A strategic decision must be made in terms of how the job will be portrayed, particularly in advertisements. Initial descriptions of the job in the media are necessarily limited. Should earnings potential be featured, or perhaps the opportunity for advancement? Or is this job correctly portrayed as ideal for the career salesperson? Consider how the advertisement in Exhibit 5.2[18] portrays the salesperson's job at Heartland Payment Systems.

Strategy also involves coordinating recruiting needs and activities with employment agencies and college placement centers. For instance, dates and times for interviewing on campus must be arranged. If an employment agency is to be used, it will need a job description and job qualifications for the position to be filled.

When developing an international salesforce, the sales manager must consider the type of salesperson best suited for selling outside the home country. Options include hiring expatriates, who are salespeople from the firm's home country, hiring host-country nationals, or hiring third-country nationals. Advantages and disadvantages of hiring each type of salesperson are shown in Exhibit 5.3.[19]

Another strategic decision is the length of time a candidate will be given to accept an offer. This time element is important, because other recruitment and selection activities may be temporarily suspended until the decision is made. Strategy also involves identifying the sources that look most promising for recruitment. This subject is discussed in detail in the following section.

Recruitment: Locating Prospective Candidates

As Figure 5.2 showed, the next step in recruitment and selection is to locate a pool of prospective job candidates. This step, the actual recruiting, may use a variety of internal and external sources.

Internal Sources

One of the most popular methods of locating quality sales recruits is through **employee referral programs**. These programs can be both efficient and effective. Compared with other means of recruiting, employee referrals have the highest applicant to hire conversion rate (while only seven percent apply, 40% are hired), generally begin their position more quickly, have greater job satisfaction and longer tenure, are hired more quickly and less expensively, and are socialized into the organization more quickly.[20] An employee who furnishes a referral may be paid a "finder's fee." For example, Federated Insurance provides its current Marketing Representatives with a $2,400 referral bonus when a referred candidate is hired and an additional $1,600 bonus when the referred candidate completes his or her first 12 months in the field.[21] Existing salespeople are

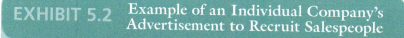

EXHIBIT 5.2 Example of an Individual Company's Advertisement to Recruit Salespeople

~ INTRODUCING THE SALES PROFESSIONAL BILL OF RIGHTS ~

Declare your independence from an unfulfilling career.

The Sales Professional Bill of Rights was established to empower you to know exactly what you should expect from your employer.

1. The right to an employer who tells the truth and is transparent.

2. The right to a consistent employee compensation model.

3. The right to the opportunity to earn and own a portion of the recurring revenues added to the employer's income statement.

4. The right to earn comprehensive benefits including medical insurance, dental insurance and 401(k) contributions.

5. The right to effective training and support from a direct manager.

6. The right to earn monthly income that builds uncapped wealth.

7. The right to a proven sales model that encourages and allows successful sales professionals freedom to establish their work schedule in conjunction with the company's goals.

8. The right to be paid timely on closed and installed sales.

9. The right to work efficiently with innovative sales tools.

10. The right to earn recognition and awards and to be considered for career advancement based on proven skills and demonstrated merit.

Visit SPBOR.com for more information.

Heartland
PAYMENT SYSTEMS

EXHIBIT 5.3 Advantages and Disadvantages of Salesperson Types for International Salesforce Development

Salesperson Type	Advantages	Disadvantages
Expatriates	High product knowledge Good follow-up service Good training for promotion Greater home-country control	Highest maintenance costs High turnover rates High training costs
Host-Country Nationals	Easy and inexpensive to hire Significant market knowledge Speak the native language Cultural understanding Quickly penetrate market	Need extensive product training Sales often considered low-esteem position Difficult to instill organization's culture Hard to ensure organizational loyalty
Third-Country Nationals	Possible cultural understanding and language skills if from similar region Economical labor force Allows regional sales coverage May allow sales to country in conflict with home country	Nationality unrelated to organization or place of work Low promotion potential Need extensive product and company training Sales often considered low-esteem position Potential difficulty of adapting to new environments Difficult to instill organization's culture Hard to ensure organizational loyalty

obviously good sources for referral programs because they have a good understanding of the type of person sought for a sales position. Purchasing agents within the company may also be helpful in identifying prospective sales candidates. Employee referral programs can be enhanced by publicly recognizing successful referrals, by regularly providing incentives and promptly rewarding successful referrals, by offering a proactive program that encourages employee participation, and by quickly providing feedback concerning the status of referrals to those making them.[22] Be sure, however, not to rely solely on an employee referral program when recruiting, as doing so could be discriminatory according to the Civil Rights Act of 1964.[23]

Other internal methods include announcing sales job openings through newsletters, on the company's intranet, in meetings, or on the bulletin board. Internal transfers or promotions may result from announcing an opening on the salesforce. One study found that employees of the firm who transfer to sales positions can be expected to yield more long-run profits than salespeople from any other source.[24]

External Sources

Although it is a good idea to include internal sources as part of a recruitment and selection program, there may not be enough qualified persons inside the organization to meet the human resource needs of the salesforce. The search then must be expanded to external sources. Marty Zucker, Regional Office Coffee Services Manager for W.B. Mason Office Products, comments on its sources for sales candidates in "Sales Management in the 21st Century: Locating Sales Candidates at W.B. Mason Office Products."

Locating Sales Candidates at W.B. Mason Office Products

Marty Zucker, Regional Office Coffee Services Manager for W.B. Mason Office Products, comments on its sources for sales candidates.

Staying in business for 120 years as an independent office supply company requires an effective recruitment and selection strategy. The W.B. Mason model calls for constant sales recruitment at every one of its locations. The recruiting process teams our human resource managers and our sales managers in a never-ending quest to hire the best people available. We heavily recruit college students but look for industry veterans as well. W.B. Mason's recruiting teams attend numerous college job fairs every month. In addition, we host several open houses. It is not unusual to make offers to college seniors in their first semester and hold the position open until graduation. When looking at industry veterans, we look for those who have a following of loyal customers. This provides them with a lot of potential customers when joining W.B. Mason.

Online

The Internet provides an effective and relatively inexpensive way to recruit. Companies can list job openings on bulletin boards or in job boards such as monster.com, indeed.com or careerbuilder.com, as well as several sales-specific job sites such as salesjobs.com and repphunter.com, where candidates seeking a position can reply to an ad online. Employers also might consider advertising on a site such as Glassdoor.com, an employee-generated site that job seekers use to investigate the work culture of prospective employers. Most newspapers have added Web versions of their classified sections. Furthermore, many companies are using their Web site to advertise job openings and allow candidates to apply online. A company Web site should provide ample information about the position and the company, make it easy to apply, and give the candidate a favorable impression overall.[25] Companies can even create a Web page specifically for their job listings under the ".jobs" domain. It may be useful to follow guidelines such as those found in Exhibit 5.4[26] when writing for online recruitment. Since Web recruiting can produce a tremendous number of resumes, it may be helpful to use an automated applicant tracking system, such as that provided by iCIMS Recruit (www.icims.com), to identify the applicants who are most appropriate for the position.

Independent recruiting services are also widely available. For example, Wonderlic, Inc. offers sales managers an automated application service that allows them to screen applicants before taking a phone call or handling a resume or application. Applicants respond to questions related to the position for which the firm is hiring and are assessed on their cognitive ability, motivation and personality. A score is calculated, and applicants can be assessed against one another based on their scores. The hiring firm can then decide which job candidates it would like to pursue further. Jobs in Pods (www.jobsinpods.com) will develop an audio/video podcast interview of a company's employees answering typically asked questions by job candidates (e.g., What's it like to work here?), and publish it on its site. Another approach is offered by a company such as Entelo, Inc. (www.entelo.com), which searches out job candidates by scouring the Web for public information on individuals, and then provides an ap that recruiters can use to search for candidates based on various criteria.

Recruiting software, such as that provided by Oracle (www.oracle.com) and PCRecruiter (www.PCRecruiter.net), are available to help manage the recruitment process. This application allows for automating much of the recruiting process from posting the position online, to screening and contacting candidates, to scheduling interviews and assigning in-house interviewing responsibilities such as prescreening.

Increasingly, social networking sites such as LinkedIn, Facebook and Twitter are being used to recruit job candidates. More than 84 percent of companies use social

| Writing for Online Recruitment | EXHIBIT 5.4 |

Writing for the online medium is a different art than writing for print.

Job summary. Online job boards show a position summary before the potential applicant sees the full ad. Be sure to present the job opportunity in terms of the outcomes the position will produce for the prospective applicant.

Keep it brief. It is much harder to read on screen than paper, and experts say you should cut the number of words by 50 percent compared to print.

Key words. Include key words and phrases you believe candidates would use to search for your position.

Job titles. Job titles commonly used in the industry tend to be picked up more readily by search engines than company-specific job titles.

Job skills. The relevance of your ad in search results can be increased by including all important job skills.

Job description. Provide brief but clear company and job descriptions.

Access points. Draw one's attention to different parts of the ad by using crossheadings and bullet points.

Mind your language. Minimize ambiguity by avoiding long sentences, using plain English, and being consistent in tone and style throughout.

Link up—but sparingly. Word count may be minimized by providing a link to a corporate career site for additional information.

How to apply. Provide contact details and be specific about how applicants should apply.

media to recruit. They not only use it to both actively and passively recruit, but to build employer brand recognition. Forty-three percent use social media or public search engines to screen job candidates to provide information about work-related performance.[27] In one survey of human resource managers, respondents (73 percent) considered LinkedIn the most effective social media site for recruiting, followed by Facebook (66 percent) and Twitter (53 percent).[28] LinkedIn, for instance, allows millions of professionals to post career profiles and find prospective employees globally online via company placed recruiting ads. Furthermore, companies can participate in industry-specific group discussion forums provided by LinkedIn in order to attract talent. When Bob Greenberg, regional sales manager for Agilent Technologies vacuum products division, put the word out on LinkedIn that he was hiring, he received responses from higher-quality candidates than those he typically received from his human resources department and ended up hiring a candidate he had previously met from a competing firm.[29] Jobcast.net offers a recruiting app that allows companies to build a fully branded career page in Facebook that can be used to post jobs and embed YouTube videos in order to attract passive job candidates.

Some companies are acquiring talent by "tweeting" (text broadcasting) position openings via Twitter. Approximately two-thirds of those seeking jobs use Twitter in their job search, with most using it to view company profiles and to follow companies/recruiters. Besides posting job openings on Twitter, recruiters can track certain words or phrases relevant to the position they are posting for proactive outreach on hot leads. Moreover, by highlighting individual employees, companies can stand out. For instance, using the #LifeAtATT hashtag, AT&T employees explained their job responsibilities, recommended qualities that candidates need to be successful and described why they like working at AT&T. When tweeting, be sure to use a hashtag with either a general job-related term (e.g., #hiring), the location of a job (e.g., #Kansas City) or the type of job being highlighted (e.g., #sales).[30] Related, online career communities, such as Sales Gravy (www.salesgravy.com), allow recruiters to reach professionals who use such sites to learn more about their career or industry, read white papers, blog, connect, and look for jobs.

Recruiting online offers several benefits. For one, it has the potential for fast turn-around. While a week may pass by the time an ad appears in the Sunday paper and the first applications are received, an opening can be posted online and applications received as early as the same day. There is also a cost saving, as ads posted on national job Web sites tend to run significantly less than similar offline classified ads. Finally, given the large number of job seekers who use the Internet, having a presence there appears critical. Nevertheless, this method should not be used exclusively since portions of the population may be excluded. Not all demographics use the Internet on an equally proportional basis. As such, strictly relying on online sources to recruit may result in violating antidiscrimination laws.[31]

Print Advertisements

Although less extensively used, print advertisements may be used to attract qualified applicants in the form of classified or display ads. Classified ads are often found in print and online, and require a relatively short lead time for ad placement. Advertisements in trade publications can attract those already in a specified field. In the case of trade magazines, lead time to place an advertisement in the next issue is longer than with newspapers—typically six to eight weeks. Other specialty publications provide nationally distributed employment listings, such as those published by the *Wall Street Journal.*

Research suggests that printed advertising material should provide important information regarding the job, otherwise applicants view the organization as being less concerned about their needs. Furthermore, the ads must be distinctive and stand out from others through physical representation or the presentation of unusual information (e.g., promise uncommon benefits such as pet insurance). By focusing on job candidates' needs and interests and emphasizing unique aspects of the job, print ads are likely to garner greater attention.[32]

Private Employment Agencies

A commonly used source when recruiting is the **private employment agency**. The fee charged by the agency may be paid by the employer or the job seeker, as established by contract before the agency begins work for either party. Fees vary, but typically amount to 15 to 35 percent (generally around 25 percent) of the first-year earnings of the person hired through the agency. The higher the caliber of salesperson being sought, the greater the probability the employer will pay the fee.

Many agencies, such as the Porter Group, Inc. (www.portergroup.com), and Sales Talent Inc. (www.salestalentinc.com), specialize in the placement of salespeople. Such agencies can be extremely useful in national searches, particularly if the sales manager is seeking high-quality, experienced salespeople. This is true because high-performing salespeople are usually employed but may contact an agency just to see if a better opportunity has arisen.

Employment agencies usually work from a job description furnished by the sales manager and can be instructed to screen candidates based on specific job qualifications. The professionalism of private employment agencies varies widely, but there are enough good agencies that a sales manager should not tolerate an agency that cannot refer qualified candidates.

Employment agencies that specialize in part-timers are sometimes used when a need arises to hire part-time salespeople to support or supplant the full-time salesforce. In most cases, part-time salespeople are not eligible for fringe benefits, so the cost of sales coverage can be reduced by using them.

Colleges and Universities

A popular source for sales recruits, especially for large companies with extensive training programs, are colleges and universities. College students usually can be hired at lower salaries than experienced salespeople, yet they have already demonstrated their learning abilities. Some universities even provide professional selling programs designed to specifically train students for a career in sales. Companies seeking future managers often look here for sales recruits.

Campus placement centers can be helpful in providing resumes of applicants, arranging interviews, and providing facilities for screening interviews. Some campus placement centers offer videoconferencing systems that allow corporate recruiters to interview students from the home office. Some universities allow employers to post job vacancies directly to their career services Web site, which is accessible by all students. College campuses are also common sites for career conferences in which multiple companies participate in trade show fashion to familiarize students with sales job opportunities. Most placement centers also provide access to alumni in addition to the current student body. In some instances, contacts with faculty members may provide sales recruits. Fastenal, Inc., for instance, works closely with university faculty to identify strong sales candidates. Sometimes companies are even able to get into the classroom to discuss career opportunities with students.

Another campus recruiting method is to offer sales internships, which allow both the company and the student an opportunity to see whether a match exists. The internship as a recruiting vehicle is gaining popularity. Northwestern Mutual Financial Network's internship program is designed to develop college students personally and professionally. Likewise, Vector Marketing, Xerox, and AFLAC all offer sales internships in hopes of developing future reps for the company. To facilitate their university recruiting efforts, State Farm, Inc. has even gone as far as sponsoring a university sales competition and offering sales scholarships as a mechanism for getting closer to students.

On the international scene, college campuses are gaining in popularity as a source of sales recruits. College students in foreign countries are beginning to see United States–based firms as viable alternatives to home-country firms.

Career Fairs

Several employers are brought together in one location for recruiting purposes by career fairs. Candidates visit the booths of employers they are interested in, or companies request a meeting with a candidate based on a favorable reaction to the candidate's resume. Career fairs are best conducted in the evening hours so that currently employed salespeople can attend. However, virtual career fairs on the Internet circumvent this problem. Companies can participate in online career fairs hosted by companies such as vFairs (www.vfairs.com). The company provides a virtual medium for keynote speakers and presentations where applicants can gather information about career choices and possible employers. Hosted career fairs offer employers the opportunity to interact with job seekers in real time or on demand, provide collateral, presentations and videos, list job openings and position descriptions and participate in Q&A sessions.

Professional Organizations

Another worthwhile source of sales recruits is professional organizations. A primary reason sales executives join professional organizations is to establish a network of colleagues who have common interests. Organizations such as Sales and Marketing Executives International or the National Association of Sales Professionals meet regularly and provide the opportunity to establish contacts with professional sales executives, who may provide the names of prospective salespeople. Some professional organizations publish newsletters or operate a placement service, which could also be used in recruiting.

Selection: Evaluation and Hiring

The third step in the recruitment and selection model shown in Figure 5.2 is selection. As part of the selection process, various tools are used to evaluate the job candidate in terms of job qualifications and to provide a relative ranking compared with other candidates. Keep in mind that the characteristics of the ideal sales candidate may vary by position and by company. In this section, commonly used evaluation tools are presented and some of the key issues in salesforce selection are discussed.

Screening Resumes and Applications

The pool of prospective salespeople generated in the recruiting phase often must be drastically reduced before engaging in time-consuming, expensive evaluation procedures such as personal interviews. Initially, sales recruits may be screened based on a review of a resume or an application form.

In analyzing resumes, sales managers check job qualifications (e.g., education or sales experience requirements), the degree of career progress by the applicant, and the frequency of job change. Depending on the format and extensiveness of the resume, it may be possible to examine salary history and requirements, travel or relocation restrictions, and reasons for past job changes. Also, valuable clues about the recruit may be gathered from the appearance and completeness of the resume. Recruiters, however, should be cautious to inadvertently infer the candidate's personality based on his or her resume. Research indicates that such inferences tend to be unreliable and invalid, leading to poor assessments of applicants' employability.[33]

Technology makes it possible to screen resumes electronically. Screening software helps select the best applicants by screening for certain words or phrases, thus eliminating the need to examine every single resume received.[34] In addition, companies such as Oracle and PeopleFluent offer advanced search and artificial intelligence to locate top candidates and even communicate with them. Caution, however, should be exercised when using screening software. If the screening criteria are not carefully chosen, groups of people from various protected categories may be eliminated.[35] Companies are increasingly exploring personal Web sites, blogs, message boards, and social networking sites through the use of artificial intelligence to determine if a candidate is a good fit.

A **job application form** can be designed to gather all pertinent information and exclude unnecessary information. There are three additional advantages of application forms as a selection tool. First, the application form can be designed to meet antidiscriminatory legal requirements, whereas resumes often contain such information. For example, if some applicants note age, sex, race, color, religion, or national origin on their resumes and others do not, a legal question as to whether this information was used in the selection process might arise. A second advantage of application forms is that the comparison of multiple candidates is facilitated because the information on each candidate is presented in the same sequence. This is not the case with personalized resumes. Finally, job applications may be filled out in handwriting, so the sales manager can observe the attention to detail and neatness of the candidate. In some sales jobs, these factors may be important for success. Despite its usefulness, some companies are replacing the traditional application form with chatbots that communicate in one-on-one, instant messaging conversations on platforms like Facebook Messenger and text messages to gather information required in an application form. Unlike a static application form, this method has the advantage of actively reminding candidates to finish answering the questions and collecting incomplete information.[36]

Interviews

Interviews of assorted types are an integral part of the selection process. Because interpersonal communications and relationships are a fundamental part of sales jobs, it is only natural for sales managers to weigh interview results heavily in the selection process.

Although sales managers agree that interviews are important in selecting salespeople, there is less agreement on how structured the interviews should be and how they should be conducted. For example, some sales managers favor unstructured interviews, which encourage the candidates to speak freely about themselves. Others favor a more structured approach in which particular answers are sought, in a particular sequence, from each candidate. Research suggests, however, that interviews are improved as a selection tool when using a structured approach.[37]

Initial Interviews

Interviews are usually designed to get an in-depth look at the candidate. In some cases, however, they merely serve as a screening mechanism to support or replace a review of resumes or application forms. These **initial interviews** are typified by the on-campus interviews conducted by most sales recruiters. They are brief, lasting less than an hour. The recruiter clarifies questions about job qualifications and makes a preliminary judgment about whether a match exists between the applicant and the company. Such interviews may also be conducted one-on-one over the telephone or through teleconferencing or video-conferencing if there is a need to involve multiple parties.

A promising time-saving technique for initially interviewing candidates involves them responding to a series of questions on the Internet or over the telephone. Companies such as Interview Connect (www.interviewconnect.com) provide a means for companies who are recruiting to record interview questions, each as a separate digital clip. These questions are then presented via the Web to candidates anywhere throughout the world who respond to the digital clips and have their answers automatically recorded using a digital camera. The results are then forwarded to the hiring company. These interviews alleviate some of the costs involved in conducting a personal interview, as unqualified applicants are omitted prior to the personal interview. Some companies, such as HireVue, go as far as using facial and speech recognition software to analyze a candidate's body language, the tone of their voice, their stress level and more to provide greater insight to improve hiring decisions.[38]

During this phase of selection, sales managers should be careful to give the candidate an accurate picture of the job and not oversell it. Candidates who are totally "sold" on the job during the first interview only to be rejected later suffer unnecessary trauma.

Intensive Interviews

One or more **intensive interviews** may be conducted to get an in-depth look at the candidate. Often, this involves multiple sequential interviews by several executives or several managers at the company's facilities. The interview process at Federated Insurance for Marketing Representative candidates, for example, includes six to eight interviews, two days of field observations with current Federated Marketing Representatives, and a one-day field observation with a District Marketing Manager.[39] Another variation on the theme, used less often, is to interview several job candidates simultaneously in a group setting.

When a candidate is to be interviewed in succession by several managers, planning and coordination are required to achieve more depth and to avoid redundancy. Otherwise, each interviewer might concentrate on the more interesting dimensions of a candidate and some important areas may be neglected. An interviewing guide such as the one in Exhibit 5.5[40] could be used with multiple interviewers, each of whom would

---

AN ETHICAL DILEMMA

John Smith, sales manager for Rockline Industries, a manufacturer and marketer of heavy-duty industrial construction equipment, has just finished evaluating several different sales candidates for a vacant position. He has narrowed the list to two candidates that stand out. Both Brad and Beth meet the job qualifications. In fact, on paper Beth appears to be a stronger candidate, having nearly twice as much industry-related sales experience as Brad. John, however, believes that the construction industry is a man's world. He fears that many of Rockline's customers (and even its own employees) may not respect a woman salesperson. Thus, even though Beth appears to be the most qualified for the position, John is leaning toward hiring Brad. What should John do? Why?

a. Hire Brad because Beth will likely not fit in with the current salesforce nor be respected by customers and would soon quit the job.

b. Hire Beth because she is the most qualified candidate for the job.

c. Tell Beth that you don't think she will be accepted by Rockline's customers and hope that she withdraws her name for the position.

EXHIBIT 5.5 Interview Guide

Meeting the Candidate

At the outset, act friendly but avoid prolonged small talk—interviewing time costs money.
- Introduce yourself by using your name and title.
- Mention casually that you will make notes. ("You don't mind if I make notes, do you?")
- Assure the candidate that all information will be treated in confidence.

Questions
- Ask questions in a conversational tone. Make them both concise and clear.
- Avoid loaded and negative questions. Ask open-ended questions that will force complete answers: "Why do you say that?" (Who, what, where, when, how?)
- Don't ask direct questions that can be answered "yes" or "no."

Analyzing
- Attempt to determine the candidate's goals. Try to draw the candidate out, but let him or her do most of the talking. Don't sell—interview.
- Try to avoid snap judgments.

Interviewer Instructions

You will find two columns of questions on the following pages. The left-hand column contains questions to ask yourself about the candidate. The right-hand column suggests questions to ask the candidate. During the interview it is suggested that you continually ask yourself, "What is this person telling me about himself or herself?" What kind of person is he or she? In other parts of the interview, you can cover education, previous experience, and other matters relating to specific qualifications.

Ask Yourself	**Ask the Candidate**
I. Attitude	
• Can compete without irritation?	1. Ever lose in competition? Feelings?
• Can bounce back easily?	2. Ever uncertain about providing for your family?
• Can balance interest of both company and self?	3. How can the American way of business be improved?
• What is important to him or her?	4. Do you think that you've made a success of life to date?
• Is he or she loyal?	5. Who was your best boss? Describe the person.
• Takes pride in doing a good job?	6. How do you handle customer complaints?
• Is he or she a cooperative team player?	
II. Motivation	
• Is settled in choice of work?	1. How does your spouse (or other) feel about a selling career?
• Works from necessity, or choice?	2. When and how did you first develop an interest in selling?
• Makes day-to-day and long-range plans?	3. What mortgages, debts, etc., press you now?
• Uses some leisure for self-improvement?	4. How will this job help you get what you want?
• Is willing to work for what he or she wants in face of opposition?	5. What obstacles are most likely to trip you up?
III. Initiative	
• Is he or she a self-starter?	1. How (or why) did you get (or want to get) into sales?
• Completes own tasks?	2. Do you prefer to work alone or with others?
• Follows through on assigned tasks?	3. What do you like most and like least about selling?
• Works in assigned manner without leaving own trademark?	4. Which supervisors let you work alone? How did you feel about this?
• Can work independently?	

Interview Guide *continued*   **EXHIBIT 5.5**

Ask Yourself	**Ask the Candidate**
	5. When have you felt like giving up on a task? Tell me about it.

IV. Stability

- Is he or she excitable or even-tempered?
- Impatient or understanding?
- Uses words that show strong feelings?
- Is candidate poised or impulsive; controlled or erratic?
- Will he or she broaden or flatten under pressure?
- Is candidate enthusiastic about job?

1. What things disturb you most?
2. How do you get along with customers (people) you dislike?
3. What buyers' actions irritate you?
4. What were your most unpleasant sales (work) experiences?
5. Most pleasant sales (work) experiences?
6. What do you most admire about your friends?
7. What things do some customers do that are irritating to other people?

V. Planning

- Ability to plan and follow through? Or will depend on supervisor for planning?
- Ability to coordinate work of others?
- Ability to think of ways of improving methods?
- Ability to fit into company methods?
- Will he or she see the whole job or get caught up in details?

1. What part of your work (selling) do you like best? Like least?
2. What part is the most difficult for you?
3. Give me an idea of how you spend a typical day.
4. Where do you want to be five years from today?
5. If you were manager, how would you run your present job?
6. What are the differences between planned and unplanned work?

VI. Insight

- Realistic in appraising self?
- Desire for self-improvement?
- Interested in problems of others?
- Interested in reaction of others to self?
- Will he or she take constructive action on weaknesses?
- How does he or she take criticism?

1. Tell me about your strengths and weaknesses.
2. Are your weaknesses important enough to do something about them? Why or why not?
3. How do you feel about those weaknesses?
4. How would you size up your last employer?
5. Most useful criticism received? From whom? Tell me about it. Most useless?
6. How do you handle fault-finders?

VII. Social Skills

- Is he or she a leader or follower?
- Interested in new ways of dealing with people?
- Can get along best with what types of people?
- Will wear well over the long term?
- Can make friends easily?

1. What do you like to do in your spare time?
2. Have you ever organized a group? Tell me about it.
3. What methods are effective in dealing with people? What methods are ineffective?
4. What kind of customers (people) do you get along with best?
5. Do you prefer making new friends or keeping old ones? Why?
6. How would you go about making a friend? Developing a customer?
7. What must a person do to be liked by others?

delve into one or more of the seven categories of information about the candidate. When developing questions, one might consider the different types of questions to ask as outlined in Exhibit 5.6.[41]

Given the emphasis placed today on developing enduring customer relationships, it is important to hire salespeople who value honesty and integrity, characteristics necessary for developing such relationships. Exhibit 5.7[42] outlines some sample questions geared toward gathering information that illustrate whether a candidate's ethical values are compatible with those of the organization. Most interview situations would require using only two or three such questions. The "rightness" or "wrongness" of the answers is up to the interviewer's judgment. As such it's important to train interviewers to follow up with more questions to pin down behavior and the thinking behind the behavior as well as to ask for additional examples. Interviewers then meet so that multiple interpretations of the answers can be obtained and discussed. The interviewers would then agree on a rating for the candidate's level of integrity.

Interviews, like any other single selection tool, may fail to predict adequately applicants' future success on the job. **Interviewer bias**, or allowing personal opinions, attitudes, and beliefs to influence judgments about a candidate, can be a particularly acute problem with some interviewers. Sales managers, like other human beings, tend to have preferences in candidates' appearances and personalities—and any number

---

EXHIBIT 5.6   Types of Interview Questions

Competency-Based Questions	Ask the candidate to explain previous experiences that relate to job-specific competencies. "Describe a situation in which you . . ."
Open-Ended Questions	Provide an opportunity for the applicant to discuss something. "What do you do when a customer complains?"
Hypothetical Questions	Are phrased in the form of a job-related problem and presented to the applicant for a solution. "What would you do if . . ."
Probing Questions	Follow-up questions to dig deeper for information. "Why? "How often?"
Closed-Ended Questions	Generally answered with a single word, such as yes or no. "What was your major in college?"

EXHIBIT 5.7   Interviewing for Integrity

1. Please describe a time when you maintained confidentiality, even when pressured by others to release private information.
2. How have you handled situations in the past where you were asked to put your integrity aside or look the other way?
3. What do you consider to be examples of ethical and unethical behavior in the workplace?
4. What do you consider to be your most ethical qualities?
5. Have you experienced any kind of loss for following something right and just?
6. Tell me about the time when you spoke up within a situation that was unfavorable to you.
7. How does being an ethical individual differ from being an ethical corporation?
8. Would you ever lie for me?
9. What's your idea of an ethical organization?
10. Have you ever suffered in your career for doing what was right? Do you have any regrets?
11. Were you ever aware of a co-worker who violated a company's ethics policy? What did you do?
12. Have you read our company's ethics policy? What do you think?

of other subjective feelings that may be irrelevant for a given interview situation.

Research confirms the subjective nature of interviewing, concluding that different interviewers will rate the same applicant differently unless there is a commonly accepted stereotype of the ideal applicant.[43] For instance, research suggests that race bias is a potential concern.[44] Bias related to attractiveness and gender also is a common problem.[45] Sales managers must not let bias interfere with the hiring decision. To see how bias may influence one's decision, see "An Ethical Dilemma" on p. 147.

Testing

To overcome the pitfalls of subjectivity and a potential lack of critical analysis of job candidates, many firms use tests as part of the selection process. Selection tests may be designed to measure intelligence, aptitudes, personality, and other interpersonal factors.

Historically, the use of such tests has been controversial. In the late 1960s, it appeared that testing would slowly disappear from the employment scene under legal and social pressure related to the lack of validity and possible discriminatory nature of some testing procedures. Instead, selection tests have changed, and perhaps managers have learned more about how to use them as a legitimate part of the selection process. Therefore, they are frequently used today.

Those who have had success with tests suggest they are useful for identifying candidates' strengths and weaknesses, as well as for revealing candidates who possess key personality traits associated with successful salespeople.[46] For example, the traits "conscientiousness," "learned optimism," and "playfulness" appear to be valid predictors of sales performance,[47] as does the need for cognition (i.e., the desire to engage in effortful thinking) and self-monitoring (i.e., the degree to which one engages in impression management and ambiversion (having characteristics of both extroverts and introverts).[48] The Caliper Profile employee assessment tool, for instance, measures 25 personality traits that influence salesperson performance. It can be taken online or on paper and its results offer objective information on a sales candidate's limitations, strengths, motivation and potential performance in a specific sales role.[49] Sales Success Profile (www.salessuccessprofile.com), a 50-question, multiple-choice test, measures salespeople's strengths and weaknesses in 13 critical areas, including the ability to approach, involve, and build rapport; the ability to identify a buyer's needs and motivations; skill at overcoming objections; and time management. An Internet-based test offered by ANOVA Communications Group called Profile Sales Indicator measures sales performance and attempts to predict behavior by benchmarking a company's successful salespeople and then identifying candidates whose answers to the test approximate those of successful performers. Intelligence tests are likewise useful, as they tend to predict cognitive ability, which has been found to predict future salesperson performance.[50] Valid tests measuring certain personality traits, sales skills, strengths, or cognitive ability may be used to supplement other salesforce selection tools. They can often be completed online at relatively little expense.

Those who remain reluctant to use tests ask three questions: (1) Can selection tests really predict future job performance? (2) Can tests give an accurate, job-related profile of the candidate? (3) What are the legal liabilities arising from testing? In addressing the first question, one must admit it is sometimes difficult to correlate performance on a test at a given point in time with job performance at a later date. For example, how can sales managers account for performance variations caused primarily by changes in the uncontrollable environment, as might be the case in an unpredictable economic setting?

Question 2 really is concerned with whether the tests measure the appropriate factors in an accurate fashion. The precise measurement of complex behavioral variables such as motivation is difficult at best, so it is likely that some tests do not really measure what they purport to measure.

Answers to question 3 depend largely on the complete answers to questions 1 and 2. The capsule response to the third question is that, unless test results can be validated as a meaningful indicator of performance, there is a strong possibility that the sales manager is in a legally precarious position.

Suggestions to sales managers to improve the usefulness of tests as selection tools include:[51]

1. Do not attempt to construct tests for the purpose of selecting salespeople. Leave this job to the testing experts and human resource specialists.

2. If psychological tests are used, be sure the standards of the American Psychological Association have been met.

3. Use tests that have been based on a job analysis for the particular job in question.

4. Select a test that minimizes the applicant's ability to anticipate desired responses.

5. Use tests as part of the selection process, but do not base the hiring decision solely on test results.

Tests can be useful selection tools if these suggestions are followed. In particular, tests can identify areas worthy of further scrutiny if they are administered and interpreted before a final round of intensive interviewing. For example, Federated Insurance requires applicants to take a written personality test as part of the application process.

Sales managers may use commercial testing services in selecting salespeople. For example, Wonderlic, Inc. (www.wonderlic.com) offers a computer-scored test called the Comprehensive Personality Profile that assesses personality from a job compatibility perspective. This extensively validated test can be used to analyze candidates' strengths and weaknesses related to a position in sales. Companies such as Cardinal Health, for instance, test job candidates' sales skills utilizing online assessment and testing services provided by the HR Chally Group (www.chally.com).[52] Chally works with companies to determine specific job requirements and then tailors an assessment to determine candidates who meet these requirements.

Tests may prove useful for selecting among local candidates when operating in a foreign country. Tests such as the Occupational Personality Questionnaire (OPQ), which measures 32 factors, including sociability and the ability to persuade others, can be created on a country-by-country basis.[53] One must be careful when testing globally, however, as tests do not always translate well into other languages and cultures.

Assessment Centers

An **assessment center** offers a set of well-defined procedures for using techniques such as group discussion, business game simulations, presentations, and role-playing exercises for the purpose of employee selection or development. The participant's performance is evaluated by a group of assessors, usually members of management within the firm. Although somewhat expensive because of the high cost of managerial time to conduct the assessments, such centers are being used more often in the selection of salespeople. Research finds that assessment center ratings correlate with general intelligence, achievement motivation, social competence, and self-competence, all desirable salesperson characteristics.[54]

An interesting report on the use of an assessment center to select salespeople comes from the life insurance industry, well known for its continual need for new salespeople. Traditional selection methods used in this industry apparently leave something to be desired because turnover rates are among the highest for salespeople. An assessment-center approach was used by one life insurance firm to select salespeople based on exercises simulating various sales skills, such as prospecting, time management, and sales presentation skills. Results of the study indicated that this program was superior to traditional methods of selecting salespeople in the insurance industry in terms of predicting which salespeople would survive and which would drop out within six months of being hired.[55] Some companies are even using sales simulation software to assess candidates' selling skills. Sales reps from a large U.S. transportation firm who scored highly on AlignMark's sales simulator, AccuVision, reached 130 percent of their sales quota, as opposed to 90 percent for low scorers one year after being hired.[56] Moving forward, technology appears to be in place that will allow for virtual assessment centers, greatly expanding the number of participants and evaluators that can be involved.[57]

Background Investigation

Job candidates who have favorably emerged from resume and application screening, interviewing, testing, and perhaps an assessment center may next become the subject of a **background investigation**. This may be as perfunctory as a reference check or comprehensive if the situation warrants it. For instance, Federated Insurance reviews each Marketing Representative applicant's motor vehicle and credit reports, conducts a criminal background check, and conducts at least 10 reference checks.[58] In conducting background investigations, it is advisable to request job-related information only and to obtain a written release from the candidate before proceeding with the investigation.

If a reference check is conducted, two points should be kept in mind. First, persons listed as references are biased in favor of the job applicant. As one sales manager puts it, "Even the losers have three good references—so I don't bother checking them." Second, persons serving as references may not be candid or may not provide the desired information. This reluctance may stem from a personal concern (i.e., Will I lose a friend or be sued if I tell the truth?) or from a company policy limiting the discussion of past employees. One suggestion for conducting a reference check is to ask your finalists to provide 10 references. Call the references when they will not be available and leave a voice mail indicating that your company is hiring for an important position and that they should only call back if the candidate is really outstanding.[59] Another option involves using an automated system such as ChequedReference, offered by Chequed com. This automated system sends emails to references from candidates asking them to complete a short online survey about their experience together. This approach has improved reference response rate from 30 to more than 80 percent.[60]

Despite these and other limitations, a reference check can help verify the true identity of a person and possibly confirm his or her education and employment history. Learning that an applicant or employee lied on the application form can also be used as a defense in a hiring or firing discrimination suit.[61] With personal misrepresentation and resume fraud being very real possibilities (one study showed 85 percent of employers caught applicants lying on their resumes or applications), a reference check is recommended.[62] Furthermore, a valid reference check may be useful in helping a company prevent a lawsuit resulting from a negligent hire.[63] Exhibit 5.8[64] provides techniques for getting valid information in a background check. When questioning references, be sure to avoid any questions that could be discriminatory, such as those referencing age, race, color, religion, marital status, sexual orientation and other protected classifications. Also, avoid questions concerning arrests, financial disclosure matters, family and medical history, as well as those questions as to whether the applicant filed any lawsuits or claims against the employer.[65]

Physical Examination

Requiring the job candidate to pass a physical examination is often a formal condition of employment. In many instances, the insurance carrier of the employing firm requires a physical examination of all incoming employees. The objective is to discover any physical problem that may inhibit job performance.

Drug testing also may be required as a condition for employment. When instituting a drug testing program as part of the hiring process, the company should first develop a written policy stating when and how the testing will be performed, the types of drugs for which testing will be performed, and what will happen to an applicant who tests positive for drug use (e.g., reject or require employer-sponsored drug counseling as a condition for employment).[66] The need for the drug testing should be reasonably related to potential job functions and all applicants should be required to be tested. Furthermore, applicants should be informed of the test before taking it and the results should be kept confidential.[67]

Selection Decision and Job Offer

When making the selection decision, the sales manager must evaluate candidates' qualifications relative to characteristics considered most important for the job. It may be

EXHIBIT 5.8   How to Get Valid Information in a Background Check

The HR Chally Group's experience shows that many employers never really check references, or else they do it hastily and it becomes little more than a rubber stamp. Here are 10 techniques to make the background check a useful and productive tool in aiding the selection process. While it is often difficult to get references to cooperate because of cautious internal policies or other legal concerns, many will comment orally or off the record, but not in writing.

1. **Be wary of first-party references.**
   Good sales candidates are not going to name references who will describe them negatively. Such first-party references are not as valuable as the candidate's past customers, who will probably be more candid. These references can indicate how loyal and satisfied the customers were with the candidate, which is a good indication of a prospective employee's past performance.

2. **Radial search referrals might be used.**
   The radial search for referrals is a method of reference checking that requires getting additional references from the first-party references. Such "second generation" references will not be carefully selected to present only a positive impression.
   Remember: Ask references to help you out; don't ask them just to criticize. Ask them to highlight strengths and let them build up the salesperson, and see how high they are willing to go.

3. **Use an interview background check.**
   This will show whether or not the salesperson is likely to change in terms of work performance. In other words, what degree of reliability do the references suggest? What "odds" do they give for the person's future success?

4. **Use the critical incident technique.**
   Determine the one trait or incident for which the candidate is best remembered. Could this be described as primarily good, bad, or neutral? Does it indicate an individual who is results-oriented or service-oriented?

5. **Pick out problem areas.**
   Determine the candidate's customers who were the most difficult to handle, and those problems that were the toughest to solve. Even first-party references may reveal difficulties that can be indicative of future sales performance. Find out if the candidate eventually overcame the difficulties.

6. **Obtain a numerical scale reference rating.**
   Keep in mind that 70 points on a 100-point scale is "passing" to most people; 50 points would be "failing." Reference rating scales are often easier for people to deal with. For example, references generally do not like to say negative things, but they may be willing to call a person an "85" instead of flatly saying "average."

7. **Identify an individual's best job.**
   Notice whether or not the reference needs to think excessively about identifying an individual's best job. This may suggest that the individual's behavior was consistent, but not necessarily exceptional.

8. **Check for idiosyncrasies.**
   Did the candidate have any outstanding idiosyncrasies? If so, did they help or hinder job performance?

9. **Check financial and personal habits.**
   Credit difficulties and any indication of alcoholism or gambling are clearly negative indicators for future success. A strong interest in betting, even associated with a measure of success, is frequently associated with long-term problems in sales.

10. **Get customer opinion.**
    Has the candidate kept regular customers? How loyal are customers to the candidate personally, as opposed to the product or the company? Why? Was the candidate seen as efficient, dependable, and genuinely interested in the customers?

Selection Tool	Profile Characteristic (Behavioral Indicator)	Rating 0–10
Application Form	Attention to detail; completeness	——
Interviews with Sales Associates	Fit with organizational culture	——
	Fit with sales culture	——
	Listening skills	——
	Verbal communication skills	——
Testing		——
Assessment Center	Verbal communication skills	——
	Overcoming objections	——
	Time management skills	——
Background Investigation		——
Overall Score		——

Example: Selection Rating Sheet **EXHIBIT 5.9**

helpful to design a form similar to the one shown in Exhibit 5.9 to track each sales candidate through the selection process.[68] A decision must be made about whether a candidate's strength in one characteristic can compensate for a weakness in another characteristic, whether a characteristic is so important that a weakness in it cannot be tolerated, or whether the candidate must meet certain minimum levels to be successful.[69] At times, the sales manager may face a dilemma similar to that found in "An Ethical Dilemma" on p. 155.

After evaluating the available candidates, the sales manager may be ready to offer a job to one or more candidates. Some candidates may be "put on hold" until the top candidates have made their decisions. Another possibility is that the sales manager may decide to extend the search and begin the recruitment and selection process all over again.

In communicating with those offered jobs, it is now appropriate for the sales manager to "sell" the prospective salesperson on joining the firm. In reality, top salespeople are hard to find, and the competition for them is intense. Therefore, a sales manager should

AN ETHICAL DILEMMA

You are the district sales manager for an electronics manufacturing company and are responsible for all the recruitment and selection decisions in your district. The company's national sales manager has asked you to interview his daughter for a sales position that has just opened up in your district. Coincidentally, he mentions that a regional sales manager position (which you desire very much) is about to open up. On interviewing the national sales manager's daughter, along with several other candidates, you find that she is not the best qualified for the position. What would you do?

a. Select the most qualified candidate.
b. Select the most qualified candidate and recommend that the national sales manager's daughter apply in another of the company's districts.
c. Hire the national sales manager's daughter to protect my job.

enthusiastically pursue the candidate once the offer is extended. As always, an accurate portrayal of the job is a must. In addition to standard enticements, such as salary, performance bonuses, company car, and fringe benefits, certain extra incentives are sometimes offered to prospective salespeople. Candidates may be offered relocation assistance and reimbursement for other expenses. Another incentive is the **market bonus** paid on hiring to salespeople having highly sought-after skills and qualifications. This one-time payment recognizes an existing imbalance in supply and demand in a given labor market. Using a market bonus could be a reasonable alternative if the supply-demand imbalance is thought to be temporary, because the bonus is a one-time payment and not a permanent addition to base compensation.

The offer of employment should be written, but can be initially extended in verbal form. Any final contingencies, such as passing a physical examination, should be detailed in the offer letter. Candidates not receiving a job offer should be notified in a prompt, courteous manner. A specific reason for not hiring a candidate need not be given. A simple statement that an individual who better suits the needs of the company has been hired is sufficient.

LEGAL AND ETHICAL CONSIDERATIONS IN RECRUITMENT AND SELECTION

Key Legislation

The possibility of illegal discrimination permeates the recruitment and selection process, and a basic understanding of pertinent legislation can be beneficial to the sales manager. Some of the most important legislation is summarized in Exhibit 5.10.[70] The legislative acts featured in Exhibit 5.10 are federal laws applicable to all firms engaged in interstate commerce. Companies not engaging in interstate commerce are often subject to state and local laws that are similar to these federal laws.

Guidelines for Sales Managers

The legislation reviewed in Exhibit 5.10 is supported by various executive orders and guidelines that make it clear that sales managers, along with other hiring officials in a firm, have legal responsibilities of grave importance in the recruitment and selection process. In step 1 of the process, planning for recruitment and selection, sales managers must take care to analyze the job to be filled in an open-minded way, attempting to overcome any personal mental biases.

Job descriptions and job qualifications should be accurate and based on a thoughtful job analysis. The planning stage may also require that the sales manager consider fair employment legislation and affirmative action requirements before setting recruitment and selection objectives.

In step 2 of the process, recruitment, the sources that serve as intermediaries in the search for prospective candidates should be informed of the firm's legal position. The firm must be careful to avoid sources that limit its hiring from protected classes.[71] It is also crucial that advertising and other communications be devoid of potentially discriminatory content. For example, companies that advertise for "young, self-motivated salesmen" may be inviting an inquiry from the Equal Employment Opportunity Commission on the basis of age and gender discrimination.

Finally, all applicants should be treated equally. A variety of selection tools related to job performance should be used and generally must be applied to all applicants.[72] When interviewing, one must be careful not to violate the law. Exhibit 5.11[73] provides some basic rules for legally interviewing job applicants. Munson and Spivey summarize legal advice for selection by stating, "At each step in the selection process, it would be advisable to be as objective, quantitative, and consistent as possible, especially because present federal guidelines are concerned with all procedures suggesting employment discrimination."[74]

Legislation Affecting Recruitment and Selection   EXHIBIT 5.10

Legislative Act	Purpose
Fifth and Fourteenth Amendments to the U.S. Constitution	Provide equal protection standards to prevent irrational or unreasonable selection methods.
Equal Pay Act (1963)	Requires that men and women be paid the same amount for performing similar job duties.
Civil Rights Act (1964)	Prohibits discrimination based on age, race, color, religion, sex, or national origin.
Age Discrimination in Employment Act (1967; amended 1987)	Prohibits discrimination against people of ages 40 and older.
Fair Employment Opportunity Act (1972)	Founded the Equal Employment Opportunity Commission to ensure compliance with the Civil Rights Act.
Rehabilitation Act (1973)	Requires affirmative action to hire and promote handicapped persons if the firm employs 50 or more employees and is seeking a federal contract in excess of $50,000.
Vietnam Veterans Readjustment Act (1974)	Requires affirmative action to hire Vietnam veterans and disabled veterans of any war. Applicable to firms holding federal contracts in excess of $10,000.
Pregnancy Discrimination Act (1978)	Prohibits discrimination based on pregnancy or pregnancy-related conditions.
Immigration and Reform Control Act (IRCA) of 1986	Prohibits the employment of illegal aliens.
Americans with Disabilities Act (1990)	Prohibits discrimination against qualified disabled people in all areas of employment. Prohibits the use of employment tests, qualification standards, and selection criteria that tend to screen out individuals with disabilities unless the standard is job related or consistent with business necessity.
Civil Rights Act (1991)	Prohibits employers from adjusting scores of, using different cutoff scores for, or otherwise altering the results of employment-related tests on the basis of race, color, religion, sex, or national origin.
Amendment to Fair Credit Reporting Act (1997)	When seeking background information from a reporting service company, employers must inform job applicants or employees in writing that a report on them will be procured and must obtain their signature authorizing the move.
Genetic Information Nondiscrimination Act of 2008	Makes it illegal to discriminate against employees or applicants because of genetic information.

When recruiting salespeople, employers must be careful not to request certain information from candidates in either job applications or interviews or they may be open to charges of discrimination. Applicants must not be asked to provide their age, date of birth, length of time at present address, height, weight, marital status, ages of children, occupation of spouse, relatives already employed by the firm, person to notify in case of an emergency, or type of military discharge. Additionally, employers should avoid requesting a photograph of the applicant, a birth certificate, or a copy of military discharge papers. Further questions to avoid are those concerning the original name of the

---

EXHIBIT 5.11   Basic Rules of the Job Interview

Rule 1—Questions should focus on job-related topics, such as job requirements and applicant qualifications and credentials.

Rule 2—Properly phrase questions. Good questions are based on the job description and advertised position requirements; relate to genuine job qualifications; go beyond a yes/no response; and are understandable and succinct.

Rule 3—You do not have to ask every applicant the same questions.

Rule 4—With regards to religion and disability, reasonable accommodations must be made to the interviewee, even at the pre-employment stage. For example, if a candidate could not interview on a certain day, due to religious observance, the interview must be rescheduled, unless doing so would cause an "undue hardship."

---

applicant, race or color, religion (including holidays observed), nationality or birthplace of the applicant, arrests, home ownership, bankruptcy or garnishments, disabilities, handicaps and health problems, and memberships in organizations that may suggest race, religion, color, or ancestral origin of the applicant.[75]

Ethical Issues

Two ethical issues of particular importance are (1) how the job to be filled is represented and (2) how interviews are conducted. Misrepresentation of the job does not always extend into the legal domain. For example, earnings potential may be stated in terms of what the top producer earns, not expected first-year earnings of the average salesperson. Or perhaps the opportunities for promotion are somewhat overstated but no completely false statements are used. As simple as it may sound, the best policy is a truthful policy if the sales manager wants to match the applicant to the job and avoid later problems from those recruited under false pretenses.

Some ethical issues also arise in interviewing, especially regarding the stress interview. This technique is designed to put job candidates under extreme, unexpected, psychological duress for the purpose of seeing how they react. A common tactic for stress interviewing in the sales field is to demand an impromptu sales presentation for a convenient item such as a ballpoint pen. Such requests may seem unreasonable to a professional salesperson who is accustomed to planning a presentation before delivering it. Another stress interviewing tactic is to ridicule the responses of the job candidates or to repeatedly interrupt the candidates' responses to questions before they have an adequate opportunity to provide a complete response.

Sales managers who use stress interviewing justify its use by pointing out that salespeople must be able to think on their feet and react quickly to unanticipated questions from customers. Although this is true, there would seem to be better ways of assessing a candidate's skills. The stress interview may create an unfavorable image of the company, and it may alienate some of the better candidates causing them to decline a job offer.[76] It appears to be a risky, and ethically questionable, approach.

SUMMARY

1. **Explain the critical role of recruitment and selection in building and maintaining a productive salesforce.** Recruitment and selection of salespeople can be an expensive process, characterized by uncertainty and complicated by legal considerations. If the procedures are not properly conducted, a multitude of managerial problems can arise, the worst of which being that salesforce performance is suboptimal. The sales manager is the key person in the recruitment and selection process, although other managers in the hiring firm may share responsibilities for staffing the salesforce.

2. **Describe how recruitment and selection affect salesforce socialization and performance.** Socialization, the process by which salespeople adjust to their jobs, begins when the recruit is first contacted by the hiring firm. Two stages of socialization should be accomplished during recruitment and selection: achieving realism and achieving congruence. Realism means giving the recruit an accurate portrayal of the job. Congruence refers to the matching process that should occur between the needs of the organization and the capabilities of the recruit. If realism and congruence can be accomplished, future job satisfaction, involvement, commitment, and performance should be improved. These relationships are shown in a model of the socialization process in Figure 5.1.

3. **Identify the key activities in planning and executing a program for salesforce recruitment and selection.** Figure 5.2 depicts a model of the recruitment and selection process. There are three steps in the process: planning, recruitment, and selection. *Planning* consists of conducting a job analysis, determining job qualifications, writing a job description, setting objectives, and formulating a strategy. *Recruitment* involves locating prospective job candidates from one or more sources within or outside the hiring firm. The third step, *selection,* entails an evaluation of the candidates culminating in a hiring decision. Major methods of evaluating candidates include resume and job-application analysis, interviews, tests, assessment centers, background investigations, and physical examinations.

4. **Discuss the legal and ethical considerations in salesforce recruitment and selection.** Every step of the recruitment and selection process has the potential to discriminate illegally against some job candidates. Federal laws and guidelines provide the basic antidiscriminatory framework, and state and local statutes may also be applicable. The most important legislation that applies are the Civil Rights Act and the Fair Employment Opportunity Act. Two primary ethical concerns are (1) misrepresentation of the job to be filled and (2) using stress interviews in the selection stage.

UNDERSTANDING SALES MANAGEMENT TERMS

salesforce socialization
achieving realism
achieving congruence
job preview
planning activities
recruitment
selection
job analysis
job qualifications
job description
recruitment and selection strategy
employee referral programs

private employment agency
career fairs
professional organizations
job application form
initial interviews
intensive interviews
interviewer bias
assessment center
background investigation
market bonus
misrepresentation
stress interview

DEVELOPING SALES MANAGEMENT KNOWLEDGE

1. What are some of the problems associated with improperly executed recruitment and selection activities?

2. To enhance salesforce socialization, recruitment and selection should ensure realism and congruence. How can this be accomplished?

3. Refer to p. 134 to "Sales Management in the 21st Century: Achieving Congruence and Realism at W.B. Mason Office Products." What does W.B. Mason Office Products do to help it achieve congruence and realism in its salesforce?

4. Describe the relationship between conducting a job analysis, determining job qualifications, and completing a written job description.

5. What are the advantages of using employee referral programs to recruit salespeople? Can you identify some disadvantages?

6. Refer to p. 142 to "Sales Management in the 21st Century: Locating Sales Candidates at W.B. Mason Office Products." Where does W.B. Mason Office Products find its sales candidates?

7. How can private employment agencies assist in the recruitment and selection of salespeople? Who pays the fee charged by such agencies: the hiring company or the job candidate?

8. Briefly describe the commonly used evaluation tools in the selection process.

9. Summarize the primary legislation designed to prohibit illegal discrimination in the recruitment and selection process.

10. What is stress interviewing? How do some sales managers justify using stress interviews?

BUILDING SALES MANAGEMENT SKILLS

1. Access HR-Guide.com at https://hr-guide.com. Click on "2000 interview questions" and (found under the "selection/staffing" tab) then go to the section (bottom of the page) that has these organized by topics. Put together a list of 25 questions (five for each category) that could be used to assess a sales candidate's creativity, analytical thinking, organization, achievement, and flexibility in a job interview. Be sure to consider questions that would be most appropriate to ask a sales candidate. Please label the category for each set of five questions.

2. Find job qualifications and a position description for a sales position at a company of your choice. Design a series of questions that you could use as a guide to interview a candidate for this position. Now, find a classmate who also has found job qualifications and a position description for a sales position, and swap information. Using your interview guide, take turns interviewing each other. (The information you swapped with your classmate serves as a guide for the interviewee.) Make an audio or video recording of your interview. Finally, listen to or view your recording and write a critique of your interview, explaining what went well and what did not.

3. The Web is filled with many sites that could be beneficial in the recruitment and selection process. Using an Internet search engine, type in a key word from this chapter such as "recruitment." This should provide you with several sites that could be useful in the recruitment and selection process. Explore some of these sites, and then choose three that you believe would be helpful to a sales manager involved in recruitment and selection. First, provide each site address. Second, provide a description of each site. Finally, explain how each site or the information it contains could be useful in the recruitment and selection process.

4. Access the following video on YouTube (www.youtube.com/watch?v=4rs0NaybFFk) that provides direction for interviewing sales candidates: Selling Power, "How to Interview Sales Candidates." Watch the video and answer the following questions:

   a. When interviewing a salesperson, why should a sales manager focus on past experiences rather than hypotheticals?

   b. Why is it important to probe into a person's responses when interviewing him or her?

   c. Why should testing be used at the beginning of the interview process?

   d. What are the three elements of sales drive?

5. The Sinclair Corporation's main competitor, Lexington Company, just filed for bankruptcy, presenting a potential opportunity for an increase in customers and revenue at Sinclair. As a result, several of Lexington's salespeople have contacted Todd White, Sinclair's vice president of sales, inquiring about employment with Sinclair. Currently White has no openings on his 10-person salesforce. However, he does not want to dismiss the Lexington reps, some of whom are top performers that might be able to enhance Sinclair's revenue stream that has been falling for the past year.

   After speaking to his CEO about adding a position to his salesforce, White was given permission to do so as long as the new salesperson made more of his salary in commissions than base salary. White, however, would like to add three of Lexington's salespeople. Currently there are four salespeople on White's staff that outperform the other six, who are approximately equal in talent. Yet, White is hard-pressed to identify a clear laggard whom he would dismiss in favor of the competition's salespeople. White is also concerned that he could disrupt the team chemistry he has worked hard to build the past two years by firing some of his current salespeople and hiring those from Lexington. However, he does not know if he can pass up this opportunity to upgrade his salesforce.

   How should White approach this dilemma? Should he hire the new reps and deal with the ramifications of letting two of his people go, or can he afford to pass on the new reps altogether?[75]

ROLE PLAY

6. This exercise consists of a series of different role plays involving two characters: a sales manager and a candidate seeking a sales position. Find another classmate to assume one of the roles. Role-play the following situations:

   1. The sales manager misrepresents the job in an interview.

   2. The sales manager employs a stress interview.

   3. The sales manager opens him/herself up to charges of discrimination during an interview.

   On completion of the role plays, address the following questions:

   1. What are the dangers of misrepresenting the position during an interview?

   2. What are the pros and cons of using a stress interview?

   3. How can you avoid possible discrimination charges as a result of interviewing?

ROLE PLAY

7. **Role Play**

   Situation: Read An Ethical Dilemma on p. 155.

   Characters: District sales manager; national sales manager.

   Scene: *Location*—National sales manager's office. *Action*—Having completed the interview process, the district sales manager explains to the national sales manager who will be hired and why.

8. Search the Web for an online testing service. Print the home page of this site. Analyze the pros and cons of using this testing service as a selection tool in the hunt for sales talent. Would you recommend using this service? Why or why not? Attach a copy of the home page you printed to your analysis.

9. Find three advertisements for sales positions (one from a newspaper, one from a trade magazine, and one from the Internet). After examining each ad, list the job qualifications for the position being advertised. Then, develop a job description based on the ad's contents. Finally, provide your suggestions for improving each ad. Please attach your ads to your write-up.

MAKING SALES MANAGEMENT DECISIONS

CASE 5.1: IN NEED OF A SALES REP
Background

Frank Slade, sales manager for StopFast, a regional manufacturer of automotive brakes based out of Des Moines, Iowa, has been experiencing a difficult time filling an open sales rep position that was vacated by a rep who quickly left the company due to his spouse's job transfer. As the weeks and months passed, Frank began to feel significant pressure and was becoming anxious about filling this position. Reps in his district were complaining that helping to service customers in the open territory was taking a toll on relationships with their existing customers. Consequently, Frank was concerned with the level of service current customers in the vacated territory were receiving. Moreover, no prospecting had been conducted in the territory since it was vacated, making it difficult to increase sales volume. To compound matters, Frank has been helping to cover the vacated territory and it was starting to detrimentally affect his ability to properly manage his salesforce. Frank realized that the longer the position was left vacant, the greater the chances for damaged customer relationships and the larger the lost sales opportunity. Frank's boss, Sal Lavon, was a tolerant individual, but his patience was wearing thin. Frank knew that if he did not fill the position soon, not only would his personal income be hurt, but he risked receiving a poor performance appraisal. Given that his last appraisal was less than stellar he wanted to avoid this at all costs.

Frank has been undertaking an extensive search to fill the vacant position. He placed a classified ad in the local newspaper, the *Des Moines Register*. Additionally, he contacted the career placement offices of local colleges and universities to see whether they had any leads on potential candidates. This attracted a limited pool of candidates, several of whom were interviewed for the position. However, Frank was having a difficult time finding a proper fit. Some candidates were simply unqualified for the position. The qualified candidates seemed to lose interest upon learning more about what the position entailed.

The vacant position is demanding. It requires extensive overnight travel and some weekend travel. The job is also physically demanding, requiring lifting heavy product, assembling displays and spending grueling hours on the road driving from account to account. The salary is primarily commission-based, with the average salesperson earning about $45,000 his or her first year. Within five years, the average salesperson with the company makes about $90,000 a year. However, the earnings potential is great for star performers, with some earning $180,000 annually. Although there was money to be made as a salesperson, the company's size limited the opportunities for promotion. The company offers little formal training. Salespeople are provided a training manual and most of the training occurs on the job.

Salespeople at StopFast are required to be very customer-oriented. In addition, they need good prospecting skills since the company is constantly trying to acquire new customers given its relatively high customer turnover rate. Furthermore, the person who fills this position must have outstanding planning and organizing skills, leadership skills, be persuasive, show initiative, and possess strong communication skills, including the ability to write, speak and listen.

Current Situation

Frank believes that his inability to fill the vacant position stems from not making the position look attractive enough to potential candidates. Thus, to increase the attractiveness of the position, he decided to rewrite his newspaper ad, neglecting to mention some of the responsibilities of the job. In particular, he downplayed the travel associated with the position and emphasized the high earnings potential. In doing so, he noticed an increase in job applications. Frank reasoned that if he could make the job sound attractive enough he could persuade someone to take it, who surely later would find it a rewarding opportunity.

What follows are some excerpts from a recent interview with Vince Pram, a candidate attracted by the new round of advertising. Vince recently graduated with a degree in marketing from a well-respected university in the area. Although he has limited sales experience, he otherwise appears to be qualified for the position.

Frank: Vince, you'll be responsible for selling various lines of brakes to retailers throughout the Midwest. You'll service existing accounts in your territory as well as prospect for new accounts. We participate in four trade shows a year, which should provide you with good opportunities to prospect.

Vince: Does the position entail overnight stay?

Frank: Yes, there's some overnight travel involved, depending upon where your customers are located. However, we pay for all your travel expenses, including your lodging and meals. I haven't heard many complaints from our salesforce regarding travel requirements.

Vince: Do you have a training program?

Frank: We have a fine training program. Our current salespeople have been through our training program and each one is performing quite well right now. Our training manual is particularly helpful for learning new product knowledge. Once you get into the field, you will find the product practically sells itself.

Vince: Are there ample opportunities for promotion?

Frank: We try to promote from within as much as possible. There is no reason why a hardworking ambitious person should not be able to get promoted in this company. In fact, I began my career as a delivery person for StopFast, was promoted to sales, and from there moved into sales management.

Vince: I understand the job pays a salary plus commission.

Frank: That's correct. Our starting base salary is $25,000. However, with commission, you could earn as much as $180,000! With little effort you should have no problem making about $50,000–$60,000 your first year.

After interviewing two candidates for the position resulting from his new approach, Frank decided he would forgo any more interviews and make a job offer to Vince, given his apparent interest, and Frank's strong desire to quickly fill the position. Vince was very excited about the offer Frank extended to him. Two days ago he interviewed for a sales position at another company that also extended him an offer. Although this company was reputable, and the offer sounded like a solid opportunity, it did not sound as appealing as the opportunity at StopFast. He is leaning toward accepting the offer from StopFast, but he wants to talk it over with his wife. He likes the fact that there is not much overnight travel. He and his wife recently had a baby son and Vince does not want to be away from his new family too much. The fact that the company provides training also appeals to him. Although he took a sales class in college, he believes he can be more successful with additional company training. The other company Vince interviewed with offered a one-week training program, which he thought might not be enough. The compensation is particularly appealing. The offer from the other company included a higher base salary, but first-year earnings were expected to be only about $45,000 and there was no mention of earning $180,000. With student loans to pay off, Vince is interested in earning as much as he can as quickly as possible. Although Vince is eager to sell, he wants to land a job with a company that provides ample opportunity for promotion. Based on his conversation with Frank, Vince sensed such opportunity existed at StopFast.

Questions

1. Assess Frank's interview with Vince.

2. How are the key concepts of socialization related to this situation? Explain.

3. What do you think might happen to Vince should he accept the position?

4. What responsibility does Vince have when interviewing for a position such as this?

5. How do you think that Frank could improve his recruitment and selection process?

Role Play

Situation: Read Case 5.1.

Characters: Frank Slade, sales manager; Sal Lavon, Frank's boss; Vince Pram, sales candidate.

Scene 1: *Location*—Sal's office. *Action*—Frank meets with Sal to discuss the actions that have been taken to date to fill the vacant sales position. Sal provides Frank with advice on how to improve his recruitment and selection strategy.

Scene 2: *Location*—Frank's office. *Action*—Frank interviews Vince for the position. This time he is careful to avoid misrepresentation and takes actions to achieve realism and congruence.

CASE 5.2: OLD HABITS DIE HARD
Background

Farming Industries manufactures and markets tractors and combines throughout the United States. Last year, Farming did more than $1.5 billion in sales and appeared to be in an upward growth trend. The company has grown considerably since its inception in 1972. Founder and CEO Andy Braut is proud of the progress the company has achieved over the years, despite considerable aggressive competition. He attributes much of Farming's success to his management team, most of whom have been with him since the company's founding.

Don Brown had been vice president of sales and marketing at Farming since 1998. Two months ago, he retired and was replaced by James Mone. James had been in product design and engineering at Farming since 2000. Well-educated, articulate, and likable, James was believed to be the best candidate for the position.

James, a very methodical individual, set as his first task an assessment of the marketing program. One of the main things concerning him was the composition of the salesforce. In particular, he was concerned about two items. First, the salesforce was aging, with the average age being 51. Several salespeople were nearing retirement. Only a small percentage were in their twenties or thirties. Second, he noticed that the salesforce did not include any minorities or women. James scheduled a meeting to discuss these issues with Farming's national sales manager, Tim Ash.

Tim loves his job. He has been with Farming for nearly 25 years. He began as a salesperson and worked his way up to national sales manager. Surprisingly, many of his salespeople have been with the company for 20 years or more. Tim takes pride in the accomplishments of his salesforce. He believes they have been instrumental in Farming's growth over the years.

Current Situation

At their scheduled meeting, James explained to Tim his ideas concerning the composition of the salesforce. The following are excerpts from their meeting:

Tim: I realize we will have several salespeople soon retiring, but could you explain why it is necessary to hire women and minorities to replace these individuals?

James: Many of the companies we sell equipment to are now being closely monitored and regulated by federal and state governments. Several companies in our industry have recently come under attack from the Equal Employment Opportunity Commission. The Commission is putting pressure on these companies to hire women and minorities. It is only a matter of time before they take aim at us. We need to get women and minorities into the salesforce so that they can eventually work their way up into management positions.

Tim: I can't imagine a woman going into the field trying to sell a tractor or combine. How seriously do you think a woman will be taken in this business? Not very, I can assure you. Our customers want to speak to someone who really understands how this equipment operates.

James: Women can learn to sell our equipment. Just because they may not operate it doesn't mean they can't understand how it works. As a matter of fact, a few months ago a woman was involved in selling us a piece of manufacturing equipment for our operations. She did an outstanding job.

Tim: Maybe so. However, when we hire a replacement, we try to find the best person for the job. As a result, I believe we currently have some of the best salespeople in the business.

James: Unfortunately, that person always seems to be a white male. There are plenty of intelligent and

motivated women and minorities graduating from business schools today who are capable of performing the job. Regardless of governmental threats, it is still the right thing to do, and the profitable one. I would like to see us take a leadership role in this area in our industry and begin to make an effort to hire women and minorities.

Tim was not convinced. He was very concerned that minorities, and women in particular, would not be positively accepted by buyers. The farming equipment industry is largely male-dominated. This, in turn, could have a negative impact on sales. Moreover, given that much of his salesforce was composed of "old-timers," he was concerned about how hiring these groups might affect salesforce morale.

Turnover in the salesforce was relatively low. Thus, specific hiring procedures were not well developed. Tim decided he would recruit women and minorities to appease James but would develop an entrance test that would be difficult for women and minorities to pass. This way he could actively recruit women and minorities but tell James they did not qualify because they did not pass the entrance test. Tim was only a few years from retirement and was unwilling to change his current practices at this juncture, particularly in light of the success his salesforce had experienced over the years.

Questions

1. Should James be concerned about the present composition of the salesforce? Explain.

2. How do you evaluate Tim's method for dealing with the salesforce composition issue?

3. What steps could be taken to effectively bring about a salesforce comprised of more women and minorities?

ROLE PLAY

Role Play

Situation: Read Case 5.2.

Characters: James Mone, vice president of sales and marketing; Tim Ash, national sales manager.

Scene 1:   *Location*—James's office. *Action*—Role-play the meeting between Tim and James.

Scene 2:   *Location*—Tim's office. *Action*—James gets a copy of the selection test, figures out what Tim is up to, and decides to confront him.

CONTINUAL DEVELOPMENT OF THE SALESFORCE: SALES TRAINING

OBJECTIVES

After completing this chapter, you should be able to

1. Understand the role of sales training in salesforce socialization.

2. Explain the importance of sales training and the sales manager's role in sales training.

3. Describe the sales training process as a series of six interrelated steps.

4. Discuss six methods for assessing sales training needs and identify typical sales training needs.

5. Name some typical objectives of sales training programs, and explain how setting objectives for sales training is beneficial to sales managers.

6. Identify the key issues in evaluating sales training alternatives.

7. Identify key ethical and legal issues in sales training.

SALES TRAINING: COMPANIES TAKE DIFFERENT PATHS TO SUCCESS

As evidenced by the following companies listed on *Training* magazine's top 125 training companies for their employer-sponsored workforce training and development, sales training is delivered by a variety of methods and media and can produce positive results.

Faced with introducing a new value-based selling model to its salesforce, Janssen Pharmaceuticals, a company of Johnson & Johnson, determined that a new way to transfer learning was required. The goal was to improve salespeople's field skills and ability, while providing dependable, impactful message delivery across the United States. Using the Rehearsal video platform, representatives were given a video scenario from their manager. Reps received training and then were asked to respond to the scenario by recording their response. Reps could produce multiple "takes" until each produced one he/she was ready to share back with the manager. The manager then provided feedback on the role-play to the trainee. Janssen credits this training with improving market share by more than 26 percent.

Salespeople at Dow AgroSciences LLC (U.S. Operations) work in an environment characterized by innovation, taxing customers and escalating competition. To prepare them for this environment, the company offers a phased sales training program during the salesperson's first year. The program involves real-world selling scenarios, role-plays, peer and facilitator feedback, and learning resources. Trainees work on projects for an average of 8.5 months before they are assigned a sales territory. The company estimated an annualized return on investment of 323% for this training during 2017.

At Alamo Pharma Services, training programs are offered throughout the year that are developed to engage and motivate salespeople to build on behaviors and skills they need in the field. Partnering with Skillsoft, Alamo offers courses two times each month that focus on core skills, and provide both product refresher and mobile intelligence training. Regional sales trainers survey sales managers and reps to determine which topics to offer. Participants use the company's learning management system to register, view and complete courses. The company utilizes blended learning and courses combine polling, breakout sessions, video and chat rooms.

Smith & Nephew developed a training program they refer to as the electronic plan of action (ePOA) to develop their salespeople's selling skills and improve their product knowledge. The program is delivered via a learning app specifically designed for this. Salespeople accessed the ePOA content almost 19,000 times during a three-month period in 2017, averaging 42 access points per seller. Salespeople who completed all of the ePOA assets increased sales at a 13 percent rate compared to an increase of only five percent for those who did not complete all the learning modules.

Source: "Training TOP 125," *Training*, Vol. 55 (January–February, 2018): 55–85.

As the opening vignette illustrates, companies often may take different approaches to training the salesforce, and training can be used to achieve a number of objectives and fulfill various needs. Today's salespeople must be prepared to meet the demands of value-conscious customers. Salespeople must do their part by providing solutions to problems, acting as strategic advisors, adding value, and meeting service requirements expected to satisfy customer needs. Proper training can prepare salespeople to meet these challenges.

In this chapter several training issues and methods are discussed. First, the role of sales training in salesforce socialization is examined. Then the importance of sales training is considered and management of the sales training process is discussed.

ROLE OF SALES TRAINING IN SALESFORCE SOCIALIZATION

Recall from Chapter 5 that salesforce *socialization* refers to the process by which salespeople acquire the knowledge, skills, and values essential to perform their jobs. Training plays a key role in this process. Newly hired salespeople usually receive a company orientation designed to familiarize them with company history, policies, facilities, procedures, and key people with whom salespeople interact. Some firms go well beyond a perfunctory company orientation in an effort to enhance salesforce socialization. By referring to Figure 5.1 in Chapter 5, you can see how sales training can affect salesforce socialization. During initial sales training, it is hoped that each salesforce member will experience a positive **initiation to task**—the degree to which a sales trainee feels competent and accepted as a working partner—and satisfactory **role definition**—an understanding of what tasks are to be performed, what the priorities of the tasks are, and how time should be allocated among the tasks.[1]

The need for socialization as part of the training process is supported by expected indirect linkages between socialization and beneficial job outcomes. As suggested in Figure 5.1, trainees who have been properly recruited and trained tend to be more confident on the job and have fewer problems with job conflicts, leading to higher job satisfaction, involvement, commitment, and performance.

The positive relationships between salespeople's job-related attitudes and perceptions and their commitment to their companies have been supported in empirical studies. For example, a study of salespeople in the food industry found that "among approaches within a company's control, programs aimed at minimizing new salespeople's role ambiguity and improving their satisfaction are most likely to be most effective in building commitment to the company."[2] Another study of manufacturers' salespeople found a positive relationship between job satisfaction and salespeople's commitment to the organization.[3] In addition, a study of industrial salespeople found that when salespeople believe the company is taking certain actions to support the salesforce and reduce the difficulties associated with a sales position, they are more committed to and satisfied with the job.[4] These studies reinforce the importance of sales managers taking an active role in socializing their salespeople to maximize overall salesforce productivity.

Newly hired salespeople should be extremely interested in learning about their jobs, peers, and supervisors. A basic orientation may be insufficient to provide all the information they desire, so more extensive socialization may be indicated. At Federated Insurance, newly hired Marketing Representatives participate in a three phase eight-month training program. In phase one, trainees learn company products, prime markets, corporate history, the mission statement and the company's Business Plan. Phase two involves more product training, sales skills training, learning how to audit competitors' policies, and gaining a better understanding of the underwriting, field services and claims functions. Finally, in phase three, trainees move into the field where they focus on serving clients, sharpening their communication skills and developing effective time management skills.[5]

The need for salesforce socialization is especially likely to extend past the initial training period. This is particularly true if salesforce members have limited personal contact with peers, managers, and other company personnel.

SALES TRAINING AS A CRUCIAL INVESTMENT

A comprehensive review of sales management research concludes that whom one recruits is important, but it is probably not as important in determining salesforce performance as what sales managers do with the recruits—and to the recruits—after they have been hired.[6] Perhaps that is why 69 percent of sales organizations in one study indicated that salesperson training is the top service offering provided by companies to enable their sales organization's success.[7]

Sales training is a crucial investment necessary for maintaining and/or improving the performance of the salesforce. Training can help to improve the effectiveness of salespeople, which is critical. A survey of 70,000 business decision makers found that 39 percent of purchasing decisions depend on the effectiveness of the sales rep, a larger portion than any other aspect, including price, product or service.[8] Not only is training important in developing effective salespeople, but also in keeping them. One comprehensive study of salesforce effectiveness found inadequate sales training to be a driving force in turnover.[9]

Most organizations need sales training of some type, perhaps because of inadequacies of current training programs and/or because new salespeople have joined the organization. Sales organizations consider decreasing the time it takes to bring new sales hires to full productivity to be one of their most important productivity goals.[10] It should be stressed that the need for sales training is continual, if for no other reason than that the sales environment is constantly changing. Not surprisingly, a study of world class sales practices found organizational cultural support for the continuous development of salespeople to be one of the top ten world-class sales practices.[11] Thus, an ongoing need exists to conduct sales training to improve salesforce performance.

Companies view training as an important means for protecting their investments in their salesforces. Consequently, they spend a lot of time and money training salespeople. Seventy-one percent of companies take six months or longer to onboard new salespeople, while a third of all companies spend nine months initially training their sales representatives.[12] While the amount of money spent on sales training will vary by factors such as company size and industry, according to a study conducted by the Association for Talent Development, organizations spend an average of $954,070 on sales training every year, or $1,459 per salesperson.[13] As research shows, this training generally pays off in terms of improvement in salesforce productivity, quality and financial results.[14] Moreover, salespeople who are effectively trained produce at even higher levels.[15]

One aspect of the investment in sales training is the amount of time required of the sales manager. Usually, sales managers are involved not only in the "big picture" of planning, but also in the time-consuming details of implementing training, such as the following:

- Arranging for salespeople to work with key personnel in various departments in the firm to familiarize them with the functions of those departments
- Selecting literature, sales aids, software, and materials for study
- Enrolling salespeople in professional workshops or training programs
- Accompanying salespeople in the field to critique their sales behavior and reinforce other training
- Conducting periodic training meetings and professional training conferences

Sales training is indeed expensive, and sales managers should take special care to see that time and money are wisely spent. With these thoughts in mind, let's examine a model for the judicious analysis, planning, and implementation of a sales training program.

MANAGING THE SALES TRAINING PROCESS

The sales training process is depicted as six interrelated steps in Figure 6.1: assess training needs, set training objectives, evaluate training alternatives, design the sales training program, perform sales training, and conduct follow-up and evaluation.

Assess Training Needs

The purpose of sales training **needs assessment** is to compare the specific performance-related skills, attitudes, perceptions, and behaviors required for salesforce success with the state of readiness of the salesforce. Such an assessment usually reveals a need for changing or reinforcing one or more determinants of salesforce performance. When assessing training needs, it is important to consider the knowledge, skills and abilities salespeople must have to fulfill both organizational level and salesforce level goals and objectives.[16]

All too often, the need for sales training becomes apparent only after a decline in salesforce performance is revealed by decreasing sales volume, rising expenses, or perhaps low morale. Sales training for correcting such problems is sometimes necessary, but the preferred role of sales training is to prevent problems and improve salesforce productivity on a proactive, not reactive, basis.

Needs assessment requires that sales managers consider the training appropriate for both *sales trainees* and experienced salespeople. A sales trainee is an entry-level sales-person who is learning the company's products, services, and policies in preparation

FIGURE 6.1

Sales Training Process

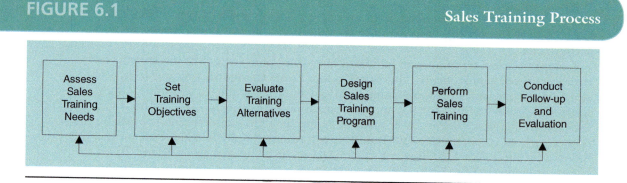

The sales training process is performed in six steps, beginning with an assessment of training needs. The follow-up and evaluation step provides feedback that may alter future sales training.

for a regular sales assignment. Entry-level salespeople may need basic training in sales techniques, whereas experienced salespeople could benefit from training in advanced sales techniques. At Fastenal, each store sales rep has a distinct, time-phased training plan that offers suggested training for that position. Given that top salespeople are often much more productive than many in the salesforce, it is important to continue to invest training dollars in them. In addition, the training needs of selling teams must be considered.

Methods of Needs Assessment

Proactive approaches to determining sales training needs include a salesforce audit, performance testing, observation, a salesforce survey, a customer survey, and a job analysis. Needs assessment can be conducted in-house or by companies such as Richardson (www.richardson.com).

Salesforce Audit

A **salesforce audit** is "a systematic, diagnostic, prescriptive tool which can be employed on a periodic basis to identify and address sales department problems and to prevent or reduce the impact of future problems."[17] The salesforce audit (discussed fully in Chapter 9) includes an appraisal of all salesforce activities and the environment in which the salesforce operates. In the sales training area, the audit examines such questions as these:

- Is the training program adequate in light of objectives and resources?
- Does the training program need revision?
- Is an ongoing training program available for senior salespeople?
- Does the training program positively contribute to the socialization of sales trainees?

To be effective, a salesforce audit should be conducted annually. More frequent audits may be warranted in some situations, but the comprehensive nature of an audit requires a considerable time and money investment. As a result, other periodic assessments of sales training are suggested.

Performance Testing

Some firms use **performance testing** to help determine training needs. This method specifies the evaluation of particular tasks or skills of the salesforce. For example, salespeople may be given periodic examinations on product knowledge to check retention rates and uncover areas for retraining. Salespeople may be asked to exhibit particular sales techniques, such as demonstrating the product or using the telephone to set up sales appointments while the sales trainer evaluates their performance. Sales managers may even want to administer a scientifically developed measure of selling skills; this measure assesses salespeople's interpersonal, salesmanship, and technical skills.[18]

Observation

First-level sales managers spend a considerable amount of time in the field working with salespeople. They also may have direct responsibility for some accounts, acting as a salesperson or as a member of a sales team. Through **observation** of these field selling activities, sales managers often identify the need for particular sales training. In some instances, the training need is addressed instantaneously by critiquing the salesperson's performance after the sales call has been completed and offering constructive feedback. In other situations, frequent observation of particularly deficient or outstanding sales behavior may suggest future training topics.

Salesforce Survey

The salesforce may be surveyed in an attempt to isolate sales training needs. The **salesforce survey** may be completed as an independent activity or combined with other sales management activities, such as field visits or even included as part of the routine salesforce reporting procedures. The weekly reports submitted by many salespeople to their sales managers often have sections dealing with problems to be solved and areas in which managerial assistance is requested. For example, a faltering new product introduction may signal the need for more product training, additional sales technique sharpening, or perhaps training needs specific to an individual salesperson.

By surveying the salesforce, the task of assessing training needs may become more complex than if sales management alone determines training needs. To ignore the salesforce in this step of the training process, however, could be a serious sin of omission. For example, when implementing a CRM strategy, a company might find resistance from its salesforce. By surveying the salesforce, the company could determine its salespeople's computer capabilities and deficiencies, and design a training program that fits its salespeople's needs. If sales managers and their salespeople should disagree on training needs, it is far better to discover this disagreement and resolve it before designing and delivering specific sales training programs.

Customer Survey

Intended to define customer expectations, a **customer survey** helps determine how competitive the salesforce is compared with other salesforces in the industry. If personal selling is prominent in the firm's marketing strategy, some sort of customer survey to help determine sales training needs is highly recommended. For example, upon surveying its customers, Paxar, a supplier of labels to retailers and apparel manufacturers, learned that its salespeople were miscommunicating with customers and were failing to understand their market needs.[19] Online services such as QuestionPro.com (http://questionpro.com) or SurveyMonkey (www.surveymonkey.com) make it easy to design, deliver, and analyze Web-based customer surveys.

Job Analysis

The **job analysis,** defined in Chapter 5, is an investigation of the task, duties, and responsibilities of the sales job. In a well-run sales organization, a job analysis will be part of the recruitment and selection process and then will continue to be used in sales training and other managerial functions. Because the job analysis defines expected behavior for salespeople, it is a logical tool to be used in assessing training needs. Since sales jobs may vary within the same salesforce, job analyses may also help in determining individualized sales training needs or the needs of different groups of salespeople.

Typical Sales Training Needs

As the preceding discussion implies, the need for sales training varies over time and across organizations. However, the need for salesforce training on certain topics is widespread. A discussion of some of the more popular sales training topics follows.

Sales Techniques

There is a universal, ongoing need for training on "how to sell." One important topic in sales training is teaching salespeople **sales techniques.** Common mistakes salespeople make in this area include the following:

- Ineffective listening and questioning
- Failure to build rapport and trust
- Poor job of prospecting for new accounts
- Lack of preplanning for sales calls
- Reluctance to make cold calls (without an appointment)
- Lack of sales strategies for different accounts
- Failure to match call frequency with account potential
- Spending too much time with long-standing customers
- Overcontrolling the sales call
- Failure to respond to customers' needs with related benefits
- Giving benefits before clarifying customers' needs
- Ineffective handling of negative attitudes
- Failure to effectively confirm the sale

This rather lengthy list of common shortcomings is remarkable in that proper training could erase these problems entirely. In fact, most formal sales training programs spend considerable time on sales techniques.

As mentioned previously, the basic nature of sales techniques training is changing, and more emphasis is being placed on developing trusting, enduring relationships with customers. Salespeople are receiving more training on listening and questioning skills so that they may be more effective in learning the customer's needs. Limited research supports the idea that effective listening skills are positively associated with sales performance and work satisfaction.[20] Salespeople also must work on developing their soft skills. Some research indicates that strong soft skills account for 85% of job success.[21] Salespeople need to be able to read the situation around them and respond to customers empathetically. This calls for the development of salespeople's emotional intelligence, whereby they can effectively express their emotions and understand and manage others' emotions as well. Furthermore, high-pressure sales techniques are declining in popularity and are being replaced with sales techniques based on need satisfaction, problem solving, and partnership-forming with the customer's best interests as the focus. According to one study, both salespeople and sales managers believe that learning how to craft customer solutions is extremely important.[22] This makes sense in light of research showing that buyers want salespeople who help them achieve their needs, are available when needed, understand their preferences, and act as a trusted advisor.[23] IBM's consultative training program teaches salespeople to work with customers as consultants to jointly solve problems and build close relationships.[24] Research by the HR Chally Group outlined in Exhibit 6.1[25] highlights relationship-building characteristics at which salespeople must excel to best serve business-to-business customers and achieve sales excellence.

Product Knowledge

Salespeople must have thorough **product knowledge,** including its benefits, applications, competitive strengths, and limitations. Product knowledge may need updating in the event of new product development, product modification, product deletions, or the development of new applications for the product. For example, in an effort to constantly provide its distributors with the most current product knowledge available, Blue Hawk, a purchasing cooperative whose members distribute a range of HVACR-related products, such as heating, air conditioning and refrigeration units, and tools for construction markets, provides numerous online product training courses, with new ones added weekly.

Generally speaking, product knowledge is one of the most commonly covered topics in sales training programs. In fact, in one study salespeople ranked it as the most important training topic.[26] As expected, the more complex the product or service, the higher the likelihood that detailed knowledge about the offering will be stressed in the training program.

Although it is an essential requirement, adequate product knowledge will not necessarily lead to sales success. Studies have shown that product knowledge levels of high-performing salespeople are not significantly different from those of moderate performers.[27] Having product knowledge is not enough—the salesperson must know the customer and have the necessary sales skills to apply the knowledge of the product to the customer's situation. To learn the importance of training in both product and customer knowledge at World Protective Products, see "Sales Management in the 21st Century: Tactical Sales Training at World Protective Products."

Customer Knowledge

Sales training may include information relating to customers' needs, buying motives, buying procedures, and personalities (i.e., **customer knowledge**). Faced with situational and individual differences among customers, some firms use classification methods to categorize buyers according to personality and the buying situation. An

---

EXHIBIT 6.1   Relationship Building Characteristics Required of Salespeople

The HR Chally Group spent 14 years interviewing 80,000 business customers and collecting data on 300,000 sales professionals representing 7,200 salesforces from over 15 major industries. They found that customers want salespeople who:

1. personally manage the customer's desired results.
2. fully understand the customer's business.
3. act as a customer advocate.
4. are knowledgeable of product applications.
5. are easily accessible.
6. solve the customer's problems.
7. provide innovative responses to customer needs.

SALES MANAGEMENT IN THE 21ST CENTURY

Tactical Sales Training at Worldwide Protective Products

Troy Secchio, Sr. Business Development Manager with Worldwide Protective Products, comments on product and customer tactical sales training:

At Worldwide Protective Products, we take our brand image seriously, thus we go through an extensive sales tactical training process in order to uphold a clear and concise message as to our worth to the marketplace. Worldwide Protective Products is a manufacturer of high performance hand, arm and body protection that sells through distribution, which in turn, sells to the end user. The end user is defined as industrial manufacturers who produce product in such verticals as food, oil & gas, construction, and automotive, just to name a few.

The key focus of our tactical sales training is based on the impact our products bring to the end users' application. An example of impacting an end user's application would be manufacturing a cut and slip resistant glove specific to workers handling sharp edged cans in a food processing plant. This focus goes along with our value statement "we do not simply manufacture product; we produce products that impact specific plant application". In order to truly impact an end user's application, we first must structure sales into what we term verticals, meaning Worldwide Protective Products has a representative or group of representatives who focus on a specific industry (i.e., food, oil & gas, construction, automotive . . .).

This investment of learning becomes critical, where representatives are being trained on all aspects of our product within their focused vertical. The representative is trained on all value points of product and engages in a product excellence process. Representatives first learn why a product was developed and how it is positioned relative to competitive brands. After a series of training modules within this process, the representative begins to study their focused vertical, which includes studying industry publications, riding with seasoned representatives to see the product working at plant locations, and afterward, sitting down with product management to discuss and reengage product to end user application. Once completed, the representative shifts to a product excellence process in which he or she keys in on specific product attributes and addresses detailed improvements needed to enhance value within their focused vertical. Not only does this help enhance the sales representative's learning curve and command for end user application, but it also provides valuable product improvements toward impacting Worldwide's marketplace image.

Tactical sales training is an intense time consuming investment. Depending upon the skill set of the employee, the initial baseline learning process can take up to 6–9 months. Worldwide's learning and discovery investment is a continual training process due to the dynamic changes that occur within the industrial markets. Simply put, it is critical to train and manage our salesforce, along with any action put forth by the company, in order to protect and enhance Worldwide's brand image in the marketplace.

Kind of Buyer	Sales Training Topic
Sales Training for Different Types of Buyers　EXHIBIT 6.2	
1. Hard Bargainer (a difficult person to deal with)	1. Teach psychologically oriented sales strategies (e.g., transactional analysis). 2. Teach sales *negotiation* strategies (e.g., the use of different bases of power). 3. Teach listening skills and the benefits of listening to the prospect. 4. Emphasize how to handle objections. 5. Emphasize *competitive* product knowledge.
2. Sales Job Facilitator (attempts to make the sales transaction go smoothly)	1. Teach importance of a *quid pro quo*. 2. Communicate advantages of having a satisfied customer base. 3. Show how customers can assist salespeople (e.g., by pooling orders, providing leads).
3. Straight Shooter (behaves with integrity and propriety)	1. Teach importance of selling the "substance" of the product offering and not just the "sizzle." 2. Teach straightforward techniques for handling objections (e.g., a direct denial approach).
4. Socializer (enjoys personal interaction with salespeople)	1. Communicate company policy information about giving gifts and entertaining and socializing with customers. 2. Discuss ethical and legal implications of transacting business. 3. Emphasize importance of salespeople maintaining an appropriate balance between socializing with customers and performing job responsibilities.
5. Persuader (attempts to "market" his or her company)	1. Communicate importance of qualifying prospects. 2. Teach techniques for qualifying customers.
6. Considerate (shows compassion for salesperson)	1. Communicate importance of obtaining market information from customers. 2. Teach importance of a *quid pro quo*.

example of different types of buyers and suggested sales training topics is presented in Exhibit 6.2.[28]

As minority populations increase and companies expand their global selling efforts, training programs must address multicultural differences and business protocol in subcultures and foreign countries. For instance, female Hispanic business owners generally take longer to make decisions.[29] Such information can be useful in determining the selling cycle. Gift-giving, for example, is a sensitive area internationally because well-intentioned expressions of goodwill can backfire and instead become personal insults to a prospective customer. It is important that salespeople are trained in intercultural communication to improve their chances of developing international buyer-seller relationships.[30] The U.S. government provides a series of country commercial guides (www.export.gov/ccg) that provide information that may be useful in preparing salespeople to sell abroad. Some insights for understanding foreign customers are provided in Exhibit 6.3.[31]

Competitive Knowledge

Salespeople must know competitive offerings in terms of strengths and weaknesses to plan sales strategy and sales presentations effectively and to be able to respond effectively to customer questions and objections. This area is extremely important for

EXHIBIT 6.3   Understanding Foreign Customers

Many selling skills that are successful in the United States will also work in other countries. However, one must be aware of cultural variations that can make the difference between closing a deal and losing a customer. Here is a sampling of advice for conducting business in certain countries around the world.

Argentia

- Argentineans sense of personal space is much closer than that of U.S. citizens. Do not be surprised when they stand close to you to converse.

Brazil

- Ever optimistic, Brazilians always think that there is a solution to a problem. Beware of the term "jeito," which infers rule-breaking or their idea that nothing is set in stone.

China

- Chinese names are typically written with last names first. Be sure to use their last name and title when greeting your Chinese colleague. For instance, Wong Chi would be addressed as Mr. Wong.

Dubai

- Do not schedule a meeting or conference on a Friday, a day of prayer and rest for Muslims. Also, no eating or drinking in public from sunrise to sundown during the month of Ramadan.

France

- To gain the respect of a Frenchman, show constraint. Being overly friendly may come across as disingenuous.

Greece

- Be careful with "yes" and "no" in Greece. Greeks will raise their eyebrows and click their tongue to mean "no." A downward tilted head slightly to one side indicates "yes." In Greek, the word for yes is "nai," which sounds a lot like "no."

India

- Indians consider the foot unclean. Touching another's foot or using your foot to nudge someone is a serious insult. Apologize immediately. If invited by a host to dinner, expect to check your shoes at the door.

Japan

- Japanese business dress is conservative; women should never wear pants. There are no casual Fridays. Also, one should not blow their nose in public, but rather head to a rest-room for this.

Russia

- Do not refuse a drink (usually vodka) at a dinner meeting as it will be viewed as an insult to their hospitality. Socializing generally occurs prior to business discussions.

Saudi Arabia

- Because devout male Muslims avoid touching members of the opposite sex who are not relatives, women should wait for the male businessman in Saudi Arabia to initiate a hand shake.

salespeople who are new to the industry because the competitor's salespeople may have years of experience and be quite knowledgeable. Furthermore, customers may exploit a salesperson's lack of **competitive knowledge** to negotiate terms of sale that may be costly to the selling firm. For example, salespeople who are not familiar with a competitor's price structure may unnecessarily reduce their own price to make a sale, thereby sacrificing more revenue and profits than they should have. Besides researching the competition, salespeople should be trained to ask customers probing questions about the competition.

Time and Territory Management

The quest for an optimal balance between salesforce output and salesforce expenditures is a perennial objective for most sales managers. Therefore, training in **time and territory management (TTM)** is often included in formal sales training programs. Essentially, the purpose of TTM training is to teach salespeople how to use time and efforts for maximum work efficiency.

TTM training is important for all sales organizations but especially for those in declining, stagnant, or highly competitive industries. In such situations, salespeople are often overworked, and there comes a point when working harder to improve results is not realistic. Such circumstances call for "working smarter, not harder."[32]

Efforts to make more efficient use of time and increase salesperson productivity have been bolstered by salesforce automation. Salesforce automation (e.g., cellular phones, tablets, faxes, laptops, databases, artificial intelligence, the Internet, personal digital assistants, CRM, and electronic data interchange) can boost productivity. To do so, salespeople often need training in computer and software applications. As part of this training, attention should be given to improving salespeople's use of social media technologies (e.g., Facebook, Twitter, LinkedIn), as these methods of communicating are changing the means by which salespeople interact with prospects and customers. Furthermore, as artificial intelligence becomes more prominent, the need for technological literacy and data analysis skills in the salesforce will increase. Studies indicate that proper training in salesforce automation is necessary for it to be effective.[33]

Perhaps time and territory management could be improved by training salespeople in **self-management**. Self-management refers to an individual's effort to control certain aspects of his or her decision making and behavior, and as such employs strategies that assist individuals in structuring the environment and facilitating behaviors necessary to achieve performance standards. This might include improving salespeople's (1) self-assessment, whereby the salesperson identifies areas that need improvement; (2) self-direction, whereby strategies for achieving desired change are identified by the salesperson; (3) self-monitoring, whereby the salesperson assesses advancement toward completing desired changes; and (4) self-reinforcement, whereby the salesperson develops strategies for reinforcement or punishment to sustain the desired changes.[34] Research suggests that salespeople trained in self-management increase both short- and long-term performance.[35]

Set Training Objectives

Having assessed the needs for sales training, the sales manager moves to the next step in the sales training process shown in Figure 6.1: setting specific, measurable, and obtainable **sales training objectives**. Because training needs vary from one sales organization to the next, so do the objectives. In general, however, one or more of the following general objectives are included.

1. Increase sales or profits.

2. Create positive attitudes and improve salesforce morale.

3. Assist in salesforce socialization.

4. Reduce role conflict and role ambiguity.

5. Introduce new products, markets, and promotional programs.

6. Develop salespeople for future management positions.

SALES MANAGEMENT IN THE 21ST CENTURY

Fulfilling Company Objectives Through Strategic Training at Worldwide Protective Products

Troy Secchio, Sr. Business Development Manager with Worldwide Protective Products, comments on strategic training at Worldwide Protective Products designed to meet an important ongoing company objective:

In today's complex business environment and with the chatter of all the various types of "real time" electronic communication, staying on point with what a company represents to the marketplace is more critical than ever before. An important objective at Worldwide is to ensure that every one of the company's marketplace touch points are strategically aligned to support and reinforce the company's value proposition. Marketplace touch points include any action taken by a company that reaches, and more importantly impacts, outside the organization. These touch points include, but are not limited to, the outside salesforce, inside sales, marketing, customer service, social media, warehouse, shipping, and all administration functions.

Marketplace touch points have many influencers that can misguide the company's message such as individuals from different backgrounds, personalities, age groups, and departmental functions with locations positioned throughout the country and abroad. As you can see, strategic training is a serious task to passionately embrace. In order to rein in all the chaos, companies must put forth strategic training, keeping in mind every marketplace touch point, to ensure the company's message is on point each and every time.

For Worldwide, in order to stay consistent with its brand image, strategic training is an important process. Strategic training is a cross functional overview of how each department and action contributes to its brand image and value proposition. Tactical training is specific to the role within each department and reinforces the department's functions; this is done in order to align with Worldwide's brand image. Although strategic training is above and beyond tactical training, it is important that both training objectives blend together. Strategic training gives relevance to departmental tactical training.

7. Ensure awareness of ethical and legal responsibilities.

8. Teach administrative procedures (e.g., expense accounts, call reports).

9. Ensure competence in the use of sales and sales support tools, such as CRM technology.

10. Minimize salesforce turnover rate.

11. Prepare new salespeople for assignment to a sales territory.

12. Improve teamwork and cooperative efforts.

These objectives are interrelated. For example, if salespeople gain competence in the use of a new sales tool, sales and profit may improve, salesforce morale may be positively affected, and other beneficial outcomes may occur. By setting objectives for sales training, the manager avoids the wasteful practice of training simply for training's sake. Furthermore, objectives force the sales manager to define the reasonable expectations of sales training rather than to view training as a quick-fix panacea for all the problems faced by the salesforce. By defining expectations up-front, it is possible to later determine if objectives have been met and more reasonably calculate a return on training investment.[36] As seen in "Sales Management in the 21st Century: Fulfilling Company Objectives Through Strategic Training at Worldwide Protective Products," companies use different types of training to fulfill company objectives. Additional benefits of setting objectives for sales training are as follows:

• Written objectives become a good communications vehicle to inform the salesforce and other interested parties about upcoming training.

- Top management is responsive to well-written, specific objectives and may be more willing to provide budget support for the training.
- Specific training objectives provide a standard for measuring the effectiveness of training.
- By setting objectives, the sales manager finds it easier to prioritize various training needs, and the proper sequence of training becomes more apparent.

Evaluate Training Alternatives

In the third step of the sales training process, the sales manager considers various approaches for accomplishing the objectives of training. Certainly, many more alternatives exist today than in the past, thanks to such technologies as computer-assisted instruction, video conferencing, and the Internet. There are an abundant number of sales training professionals for hire. There are also numerous book titles related to building sales skills, along with audio and video recordings on the subject. Some associations are even offering training courses to help improve the skills of salespeople in their industry.

Critiquing all these alternatives is a monumental job, so it is recommended that fairly stringent criteria, including cost, location of the training, flexibility of prepackaged materials, opportunity for reinforcement training, and time required to implement an alternative be established for preliminary screening.

The evaluation of alternatives for training inevitably leads to three key questions. First, who will conduct the training? An answer to this question will require the consideration of internal (within the company) and external (outside the company) trainers. The second question deals with location for the training. Sales training may be conducted in the field, in the office, at a central training location, virtually, at hotels and conference centers, or at other locations. The third question is which method (or methods) and media are best suited for conducting the training?

Selecting Sales Trainers

In general, companies rely most heavily on their own personnel to conduct sales training. In this endeavor, the sales manager is the most important **sales trainer**. In larger companies, a full-time sales trainer is often available. Senior salespeople may also be involved as trainers. For example, Hitachi Data Systems has salespeople from each of its global locations deliver local training. Hitachi claims their salespeople love to learn through examples and war stories and tend to trust fellow salespeople more than a trainer who is not a salesperson.[37]

Why are internal sources used so often in sales training? First, and perhaps most important, company personnel are intimately aware of job requirements and can communicate in very specific terms to the sales trainee. However, outside consultants may be only superficially informed about a specific sales job and often offer generic sales training packages. Second, sales managers are the logical source for training to be conducted in the field, where valuable learning can occur with each sales call. It is extremely difficult to turn field training over to external trainers. Finally, using internal trainers simplifies control and coordination tasks. It is easier to control the content of the program, coordinate training for maximum impact, and provide continuity for the program when it is the sales manager who does the training or who designates other company personnel to do the training.

At some point, a sales manager's effectiveness may be improved by using external trainers. Internal resources, including time, expertise, facilities, and personnel, may be insufficient to accomplish the objectives of the sales training program. Also, outside trainers might be looked to for new ideas and methods. Large training firms such as, Sales Performance International (www.SPISales.com), Miller Heiman Group (www.millerheimangroup.com) and The Brooks Group (www.brooksgroup.com) often customize their generic programs for use within specific companies. Others, such as Wilson Learning Corporation, deliver training programs via the Web that include interactive stories, tutorials, interactive questions, online exercises, role plays, games,

---

EXHIBIT 6.4   Questions to Consider when Choosing an Outside Training Program

- Is the training company willing to invest time in learning about your business?
- Does the content of the training program align with your training priorities or can it be customized for your business?
- Is the training program focused on skills application?
- Will the training program fit into your schedule?
- How flexible is the delivery of the training (e.g., virtual, in-person)?
- What is the reputation of the company and character of the trainer?
- Who will actually manage the training and do the work?
- How experienced is the sales trainer?
- How responsive and professional is the training company?
- Does the training program include reinforcement components, as well as pre- and post-training assessments?
- Can the training company provide you with references?
- What is the length of the training program contract?
- How much does the training program cost? (Consider your ROI.)

---

summaries, and post-tests. Exhibit 6.4[38] outlines questions to consider when shopping for an outside training program.

Selecting Sales Training Locations

Most sales training is conducted in home, regional, or field offices of the sales organization. Manufacturing plants are also popular training sites, and some firms use non-company sites such as hotels or conference centers to conduct training. Having the training on-site, however, saves costs on transportation, lodging, and meeting-room rental. Central training facilities are another possibility, used by companies such as Federated Insurance, Edward Jones, and General Electric, among others.

As video broadcasting, teleconferencing and webcasting become more prevalent, many firms are enjoying some of the benefits of a centralized training facility without incurring the travel costs and lost time to transport the salesforce to and from training. Field offices arrange for video hook-up, either in-house or at video-equipped conference hotels, and trainees across the country share simultaneously in training emanating from a central location.

Selecting Sales Training Methods

A variety of methods can be selected to fit the training situation. Indeed, the use of multiple methods and media for blended learning is encouraged over the course of a training program to help maintain trainee attention and enhance learning. For instance, according to one study, millennials (the largest generation in the U.S. workforce) prefer hands-on learning as opposed to classroom instruction and believe that role-play with manager feedback is 33 percent more important than the average salesperson perceives it.[39] There are four categories of training methods: classroom/conference, on-the-job, behavioral simulations, and absorption.

Classroom/Conference Training

The **classroom** or **conference** setting features lectures, demonstrations, and group discussion with expert trainers serving as instructors. This method is often used for training on basic product knowledge, new product introductions, administrative procedures, and legal and ethical issues in personal selling. At Fastenal, for instance, trainees spend time in the classroom learning about the company's sales process, among other things. The format often resembles a college classroom, with regularly scheduled examinations and overnight homework assignments. When appropriate, classroom sessions may be recorded and used at a later date for refresher training. In addition to using internal facilities and personnel, some companies send their salespeople to seminars sponsored by organizations such as the American Management Association, American Marketing Association, Sales and Marketing Executives International, and local colleges and universities. These organizations offer training on practically any phase of selling and sales management.

On-the-Job Training

In the final analysis, salespeople can be taught only so much about selling without actually experiencing it. Consequently, **on-the-job training (OJT)** is extremely important and is a very prevalent method of training salespeople. OJT puts the trainee into actual work circumstances under the observant (it is hoped) eye of a supportive **mentor** or sales manager. Other OJT methods approximate a "sink or swim" philosophy and often produce disastrous results when the trainee is overwhelmed with unfamiliar job requirements.

Mentors have different objectives from company to company, but they usually strive to make the new hires feel at home in their jobs, relay information about the corporate culture, and be available for discussion and advice on topics of concern to the trainee. A good mentor represents the organization's values and norms, is a good communicator, and demonstrates attitudes and behaviors the mentee can successfully adopt.[40] Mentoring tends to work best when the protégé makes clear to the mentor what he or she expects from the relationship and the mentor "shows" rather than "tells" the protégé how to do something.[41] Coworker mentoring is popular among salesforces, and in some companies, the sales manager serves as the mentor. For instance, Lotta Laitinen, a manager at If, a Scandinavian insurance broker, decided to take more time to mentor her salespeople by listening in on client calls, observing her top salespeople and coaching them one-on-one. This resulted in a 5 percent increase in sales over a three-week period, with the largest gains coming from below average performers.[42] Helpshift.com has found that pairing trainees with experienced salespeople has worked best for bringing trainees on board quickly.[43] Research indicates that salespeople with mentors have higher performance and less intent to leave than those with no mentors, and that manager mentors inside the organization are superior to peer mentors or those outside of the organization.[44] The mentoring concept is yet another way that companies are striving to improve salesforce socialization, especially the role definition and initiation-to-task steps explained earlier in this chapter. However, mentoring programs are not without challenges, as seen in "An Ethical Dilemma."

Other than working with a senior salesperson or a mentor, common OJT assignments include the trainee's filling in for a vacationing salesperson, working with a sales manager who acts as a "coach," and job rotation. The sales manager's role as coach is discussed in Chapter 7, on supervision and leadership of the salesforce. When senior salespeople act as mentors, they too are undergoing continual training as their ideas and methods are reassessed, and sometimes refined, with each trainee. **Job rotation**, the exposure of the sales trainee to different jobs, may involve stints as a customer service representative, a distribution clerk, or perhaps in other sales positions. Job rotation is often used to groom salespeople for management positions.

Behavioral Simulations

Methods that focus on behavioral learning by means of business games and simulations, case studies, and role playing—where trainees portray a specified role in a staged situation—are called **behavioral simulations**. They focus on defining desirable behavior or in correcting behavioral mistakes, in part by allowing salespeople to experience the consequences of their actions. This is a popular method of training, as one study found that 84 percent of top-performing sales organizations use simulations.[45]

Games can increase engagement and enjoyment for learners and come in a variety of forms. For instance, companies such as Oracle have utilized a board game called Apples and Oranges to help its sales reps better understand how executive-level decision makers think by having them run a mock manufacturing company over a simulated three-year period. During a five- to six-hour training session, reps are divided into teams of three

AN ETHICAL DILEMMA

As a senior sales rep at the ABC Company, Clint is always more than willing to help out. Clint is a hard-working, high-performing salesperson who is both well liked and well respected by his colleagues. So, when sales manager Tim asked Clint to mentor a new trainee, Rachel, as part of the company's new sales mentorship program, he gladly stepped up to the challenge. Clint was asked to take Rachel, a recent college grad embarking on her first sales position, under his wings and show her the ropes. In doing so, Clint became very attracted to Rachel and wanted more than simply a "working" relationship. Rachel felt Clint was a nice guy, but she was not interested in a relationship. She began to feel uncomfortable with Clint's advances but was afraid to complain, feeling that it might jeopardize her job. Moreover, Rachel felt that her sales manager Tim, being a male, would likely brush it off as Clint just being friendly.

Rachel finally got up enough nerve to approach Tim with her concern. Upon hearing this, Tim was dismayed. Having knowing Clint for five years he believed this conduct to be completely out of character for Clint. In fact, he had his doubts about the truthfulness of Rachel's accusation.

What should Tim do?

a. Tell Rachel that he will look into it but never do so, fearing it could upset Clint and possibly lead to him leaving.

b. Visit with Clint to get his feedback on how the mentorship is going. If Tim determines that Clint is making unwanted advances toward Rachel he should fire him for sexual harassment.

c. He should immediately assign Rachel a different mentor.

or four. As players progress along the board, they must make decisions regarding productivity changes, resource allocation, and cash flow management. The game helps salespeople learn what customers to pursue to help build a profitable customer base.[46] International Paper credits a board game called Zodiak with helping its salesforce bring value to its customers and add profits to its bottom line. This game teaches sellers how to think like their customers by having them simulate ownership and operation of a company.[47] There is even a book available called the *The Big Book of Sales Games* that provides 50 games that reinforce selling techniques.

There are a variety of sales simulations available on the market or a company may choose to develop its own. An interesting example of a behavioral simulation to teach product knowledge comes from B. Braun Medical Inc., a manufacturer of infusion therapy and pain management products. When they found that their salespeople did not feel that they had the clinical expertise necessary to establish credibility with their customers or correctly set expectations for use of its IV catheter, they developed a simulation to improve their reps' product understanding. To enable salespeople to understand what clinicians experienced when they used the product, salespeople were trained how to place the IV catheter through scenario-based simulation training in which they practiced inserting the catheter into a "demo arm" with blood pressure and fake blood. The company credits the simulation with improving participants' knowledge and skills by 25 percent.[48]

Virtual reality provides another opportunity to use behavioral simulation. United Rentals, Inc. is using virtual-reality to train its salespeople. In a virtual simulation, salespeople are led to the edge of a construction site where they are given two minutes to observe and determine what equipment is necessary before an avatar of a construction boss approaches and they have to start their sales presentation. The company anticipates such training will halve the time of their current week-long training program.[49] Such simulations provide the advantage of reaching large populations at once via the Internet, company intranet, or CD-ROM.

Along with OJT, **role playing** is extremely popular for teaching sales techniques. Typically, one trainee plays the role of the salesperson and another trainee acts as the buyer. The role playing is video-recorded or performed live for a group of observers who then critique the performance. This can be an extremely effective means of teaching personal selling, without the risk of a poor performance in the presence of a real customer. It is most effective when promptly critiqued with emphasis on the positive points of the performance as well as suggestions for improvement. A good way to maximize the benefits of the critique is to have the person who has played the role of the salesperson offer opinions first and then solicit opinions from observers. After role playing, the "salesperson" is usually modest about his or her performance, and the comments from observers may bolster this individual's self-confidence. In turn, future performance may be improved.[50] While role playing offers the opportunity for a positive learning experience, this may not always be the case, as seen in "An Ethical Dilemma" below.

Absorption Training
As the name implies, **absorption training** involves furnishing trainees or salespeople with materials that they peruse (or "absorb") without opportunity for immediate feedback and questioning. Product manuals, direction-laden memoranda, audio and video recordings and sales bulletins are used in absorption training. Federated Insurance, for example, maintains a substantial library of audio and video recordings, books, workbooks, and self-study material for employees to use.[51] One time-effective method of absorption training involves furnishing the salesforce with CDs so that driving time can be used as training time. At Newell Rubbermaid, salespeople are provided audiocasts so that they can listen to training material on the move.[52]

Companies such as Astellas, a pharmaceutical company, are using podcasts, audio recordings that can be downloaded from the Internet to an MP3 player or mobile phone, to disseminate training material.[53] Some sales training firms are now offering 15-minute podcasts on a variety of topics from "competitive smarts" to "winning sales proposals" that can be downloaded to a computer or a portable media player.[54] Companies are increasingly using technology to offer learning portals, where salespeople can log into a portal and access sales training materials, company and industry news, white papers, case studies, press releases, and current communication from top executives.[55] It should be noted that absorption training is most useful as a supplement to update salesforce knowledge, reinforce previous training, or introduce basic materials to be covered in more detail at a later date.

AN ETHICAL DILEMMA

During a recent training session, national sales manager Kyle was not happy with trainee Sarah's performance in a role-playing exercise. Upon conclusion of the exercise, Kyle began to mock Sarah's role-playing behavior in front of the other trainees to illustrate how inadequate her performance was. Kyle believed that his gesture would leave a lasting impression on the trainees and help make his point stick. Furthermore, he informed Sarah and the others that if they performed like that on a sales call, they would be looking for a new job very soon.

How do you think that Kyle should have handled this situation?

a. Kyle should have asked another trainee to perform the role-play to show everyone the proper way to perform.

b. Kyle should have asked Sarah to self-critique and then provided her with constructive criticism for how to improve her performance.

c. Kyle should have asked the trainees to provide feedback to Sarah.

Selecting Sales Training Media

Communications and computer technology have expanded the range of **sales training media** dramatically. Sales trainers warn against the tendency to be overly impressed with the glamorous aspects of such training media, but they agree that it is advisable to evaluate new media continually to see whether they should be incorporated into the sales training program. Among other things, electronic media typically allow trainees to learn at their own pace in a risk-free environment. The most promising new media are found at the communications/computer technology interface and are often referred to as e-learning or virtual media. This type of learning can be delivered synchronously, whereby trainees congregate simultaneously in an online classroom and training is delivered live, or asynchronously, in which participants partake in self-paced training modules comprised of instructional content, videos, and presentations that have been prepared to consume at the trainee's convenience. Some companies are using asynchronous e-learning modules ahead of classroom training to teach trainees concepts that are then practiced and discussed during classroom meetings.[56]

The Internet offers opportunities to cost-effectively train the salesforce across different times and locations without taking salespeople out of the field. Cisco Systems, for example, has moved heavily into virtual media and conducts training sessions through the Web on a variety of topics, including understanding profit-and-loss statements, how to understand customers' business, and how to conduct an executive dialogue, among others.[57] The Web also offers an opportunity to provide video-on-demand content, whereby salespeople can review training videos at their convenience. AT&T, for instance, provides videos to trainees of top-performing sales coaches explaining how top salespeople implement key techniques. One study reports that 83 percent of top-performing sales organizations use video-based content for training.[58] Research indicates that more than 80 percent of learning occurs visually.[59] At Baxter Healthcare, e-learning is used for teaching basic knowledge, but it still conducts instructor-led training by webinar, video conferencing, or in the classroom for competitive information and selling skills practice.[60] Companies such as WebEx (www.webex.com) and GoToMeeting (www.gotomeeting.com) provide Web, video, and telephone conferencing services. Using the Web, trainers can display slides, whiteboard visual concepts, introduce real-time interaction, share desktop applications, and lead a Web tour.

Several media are particularly useful for delivering content that can be viewed or heard by salespeople on the move. Dell, for instance, produces training videos through DellTV that employees can access from any desktop or mobile device, whenever and wherever they are. They have produced content that includes key messages and technical deep-dives from their engineers for their salespeople to view to be able to more clearly explain to customers how their products function.[61] Sales associates at RE/MAX can access training materials on demand anywhere, from their computer, their iPhone, TV, or office training center.[62] Learning material can be sent by email to personal digital assistants and mobile phones. Some companies, such as Eli Lilly and Daimler-Chrysler AG, have even used video email for sales training.[63] When Sprint added GPS software to its phones, it made five-minute training videos available so that its reps could dial in and view the videos while sitting in a lobby or their car.[64] Exhibit 6.5 provides tips for designing mobile learning content.[65]

Another technology, personal computer videoconferencing, allows sales managers and salespeople to see each other and trade information via their personal computers. For example, Cadence Design Systems, an electronic design tool organization, developed a program to train its global salesforce on new products and features, selling strategies, and handling competition, among other things, that was delivered through video, in-person, and online.[66] Similarly, audiographics connects the instructor simultaneously with several sites via computer displays and audio link. Or sales managers may want to set up an online chatroom to train salespeople interactively at remote locations. Baltimore Aircoil, a cooling and refrigeration equipment manufacturer for the industrial market, has had success training salespeople by setting up a chat room for its 250 independent salespeople to trade success stories.[67] These technologies can be used to simultaneously train salespeople dispersed in several remote locations.

1. Limit content to two minutes.
2. Use animation, even for serious content.
3. Offer customized content in a conversational style.
4. Offer information to make the user better, smarter or faster.
5. Focus on areas of work that are done incorrectly or lack compliance.
6. Invite users to help design content to encourage participation.
7. Encourage users to look for the content, rather than push it on them.
8. Encourage users to diagnose their own training needs.
9. Make the content readily available so that users can access it when and where they need it.
10. Make the content interactive.
11. Incorporate images and videos.
12. Provide clear instructions for how to navigate the content.

E-learning or virtual media provide several benefits. First, costs of delivery and travel can be reduced. Cisco Systems claims to save more than 85 percent on each training session's delivery cost and 100 percent on travel costs through virtual media. Second, by allowing trainees to take in smaller chunks of information at once, trainees avoid fatigue, more quickly absorb the material, and retention and comprehension are improved. Third, gains in productivity can be realized, as less time is spent out of the field or office. Fourth, it is flexible, providing salespeople with access to training in a place and time suitable to them. Fifth, customized solutions tailored to specific learners can be developed. Sixth, trainees can easily revisit learning materials. Finally, adoption is often enhanced as electronically communicated information can be quickly put to use.[68] For tips on successfully using virtual media to train see Exhibit 6.6.[69] Although companies utilize various methods and media for training, as seen in Exhibit 6.7[70] classroom training is still predominantly used. Interestingly, while it is considered an effective means for training, it is not considered as effective as the lesser used coaching/mentoring.

Tips for Successfully Using Virtual Media to Train   EXHIBIT 6.6

- Provide the training in short, manageable segments over a shorter time period. Consider two-hour sessions over multiple days.
- Plan material so that it fits into the time you allotted for any synchronous virtual session, and then keep training participants on schedule.
- At the beginning of each virtual training session, teach participants how to use the technology (e.g., how to use the icon to raise one's hand, use the chat window, participate in breakout sessions, or contribute to whiteboard sessions). Ask learners to turn off phones and email, and to limit other distractions.
- After reviewing the technology, discuss the training's purpose and the skills participants are expected to learn.
- Allow time for participants to virtually socialize and get to know one another in order to build stronger teamwork.
- Use virtual breakout rooms to group participants together to work on assignments.
- Be creative and keep participants engaged. Use graphics and color and keep something moving on the screen (even if it is just a pointer) to keep participants involved. Test attentiveness by using periodic polls or asking questions where each participant must respond. Use virtual quizzes.
- Have senior management reinforce the importance and value of virtual training to solicit participant buy-in. After a training session, send out a transcript of questions and answers as well as providing a link to a recording of the session.

EXHIBIT 6.7   Training Modalities: Use vs Effectiveness

Average Score on a 5-point scale (with 5 being the highest)

Modality	Use	Effectiveness
In-person, instructor-led classroom	3.40	3.79
eLearning modules	2.78	3.23
Informal peer-to-peer learning	2.59	3.56
On-the-job exercies	2.58	3.71
Coaching/mentoring	2.48	3.88
Paper-based performance support	2.43	2.85
Online performance support	2.33	3.23
Conference calls	2.28	2.53
Video learning	2.17	2.95
Virtual synchronous classrooms	2.13	3.00
Industry conferences/events	2.07	2.82
Pre-recorded instructor led training	2.03	2.56
Recorded webinars	2.01	2.51
Published books or research	1.83	2.37
Social/collaboration tools	1.83	2.98
Mobile learning delivery	1.70	2.86
On-line academic institutions	1.69	2.70
In-person academic institutions	1.68	2.95
Games/simulations (in-person)	1.52	3.00
Games/simulations (online)	1.48	2.83
Podcasts	1.45	2.39

Source: 2016 Brandon Hall Group Training Benchmarking.

Design the Sales Training Program

The fourth step in the sales training process is a culmination of, and condensation of, the first three steps shown in Figure 6.1. Working toward selected objectives based on needs assessment and having evaluated training alternatives, the sales manager now commits resources to the training to be accomplished. At this point in the process, sales managers may have to seek budget approval from upper management.

In this step of designing the training program, the necessary responses to *what*, *when*, *where*, and *how* questions are finalized. Training is scheduled, travel arrangements are made, media is selected, speakers are hired, and countless other details are arranged. Keep in mind that training may take a blended approach in which a variety of methods and media are used. Moreover, given that 91 percent of respondents from one study indicated that learning from their peers helps them to succeed, determining how to use trainees to assist in the training process may prove beneficial.[71] Certainly designing the training program can be the most tedious part of the sales training process, but attention to detail is necessary to ensure successful implementation of the process.

When selling globally, an additional challenge involves determining the extent to which the training program will be standardized globally. Hitachi Data Systems, a global storage solutions company, plans globally, yet acts locally, with regards to its approach to worldwide sales training. The company's global headquarters team generally develops all training with an enterprise reach, such as global sales methodology training and global product launch training. Each geographical location, however, is given the opportunity to adapt the training to the culture and selling style of a particular geographical location. For global instructor-led training, the company first trains local trainers, who in turn localize the program for their geographical location.[72] Some research, however, indicates that multinational companies differ significantly between the sales training provided domestically and abroad.[73]

Perform Sales Training

The fifth step in the process, actually performing the training, may take only a fraction of the time required by the previous steps. This is particularly true in better sales training programs. As the training is being conducted, the sales manager's primary responsibility is to monitor the progress of the trainees and to ensure adequate presentation of the training topics. In particular, sales managers should assess the clarity of training materials. It is also recommended that some assessment of the trainees' continuing motivation to learn be made. Motivation to learn can be increased by making sure that salespeople understand how they will benefit from the training prior to conducting it. In addition, some companies are turning to gamification to increase motivation, engagement and enjoyment for learners. This could involve activities such as awarding points, achievement badges, and levels; giving quizzes and assessments; displaying leaderboards or progress; or giving feedback or rewards throughout the training process.[74] Also feedback from the trainees might be solicited on everything from the effectiveness of external trainers to the adequacy of the physical training site.

An alternative to using trainers and a specified training program is to incorporate a self-directed training program. With this program, salespeople are responsible for diagnosing their individual training needs, formulating learning goals, identifying, choosing, and implementing learning strategies, and assessing learning outcomes, all within guidelines set by supervisors.[75] Self-directed training programs may be induced, whereby management determines the training content, and evaluation of learning outcomes is measured by others; synergistic, which is essentially the same, but participation is considered optional; voluntary, in which salespeople choose their personal learning goal, as well as learning material; and scanning, in which the salesperson monitors current trends to keep up to date and remain relevant in the field.[76]

Microtraining might work well as part of a self-directed training program. Offering microtraining, in which bite-sized, quick, and easily digestible bits of information are provided that can be conveniently accessed and processed in three to seven minutes, offers an alternative to longer training sessions. Such learning matches working memory capacity and creates 50 percent more engagement, allowing learners to retain more information.[77]

Conduct Follow-Up and Evaluation

It is always difficult to measure the effectiveness of sales training. In a study of 1,400 executives worldwide, respondents indicated that measuring the effectiveness of sales training is one of their greatest challenges.[78] This is a long-standing problem, due in some cases to a lack of clearly stated sales training objectives. Even with clearly stated objectives, however, it is hard to determine which future performance variations are a result of sales training. Other factors, such as motivation, role perceptions, and environmental factors, may affect performance more or less than training in different situations. Nevertheless, given that poor training not only wastes time and money, but negatively impacts sales team morale and discourages salespeople from participating in future training, follow-up and evaluation should be conducted.[79]

Although scientific precision cannot be hoped for, a reasonable attempt must nevertheless be made to assess whether current training expenditures are worthwhile and whether future modification is warranted. Evaluations can be made before, during, and after the training occurs.[80] However, one commonly used model for evaluating training and development programs involves four steps.[81] Figure 6.2 outlines these steps.

Step one involves determining how well the trainees liked the training program. This involves assessing their satisfaction with the different elements (e.g., trainer, content, delivery, facilities, etc.) of the training program, which might be assessed via a short survey that could be created and implemented online by using a company such as SurveyMonkey (www.surveymonkey.com) at the conclusion of the training. Trainee reactions are important given research indicating that trainees who are satisfied with their training are more likely to retain and use what they learned, resulting in greater selling effectiveness, improved customer relations, and a stronger commitment to the organization.[82]

The second step includes determining the principles, techniques and facts that were learned. Was there a transfer of knowledge and skills? To determine this, pretraining evaluation should first be conducted. This might include an examination of sales trainees to assess their level of knowledge, corroborate or deny the need for training and further define the objectives of the training. While adjustments might be made during the sales training, follow-up is essential to determine what was learned. This might include "final exams" or retention exams at later dates to compare them to pretests. At Cisco, trainees are monitored throughout its training program by a series of assessments including role-playing activities and virtual and written tests focused on behavior, technical skills, and product knowledge. In addition, by examining results of tests, instructors identify and reinforce content that was not clearly understood.[83]

Step three entails assessing the changes in job behavior resulting from the sales training program. During this step it is determined if salespeople put into action what was learned. This might be assessed by having sales managers observe salespeople in the field as they work or by soliciting customer feedback.

Finally, step four involves determining the results of the training program in terms of factors such as new customer acquisition, increases in sales, quota achievement, or customer satisfaction. The impact of sales training on both organizational level and salesforce level goals and objectives must be determined.[84] At Motorola, Inc., the effectiveness of sales training has been determined by measuring customer satisfaction, along with measuring salespeople's ability to affect customer value.[85] Dell has measured the strength of its customer relationships as a means of assessing its sales training, as has Dr Pepper/7 UP, which also gauged volume, distribution, and display.[86]

During step four, it is also useful to determine the return on investment (ROI) from the sales training.[87] This can be difficult because many factors (e.g., closing of a competitor) can affect anticipated outcomes (e.g., sales increases) from sales training besides the training itself. Determining ROI requires measuring changes in metrics (e.g., sales, customer acquisition, customer satisfaction, sales cycle time, etc.) expected to be affected by the sales training relative to the cost of the training. One useful way to do this is to look at these changes across low, medium, and high sales performers, since high performers may not be expected to increase as much. A company may even want to go so far as to have one part of the salesforce not initially participate in the sales training and then compare changes in outcome metrics between the two groups.[88] Paetec, a communications technology solutions provider, performs a full ROI analysis that includes factors such as cost of the trainer's time, time of the employees being out

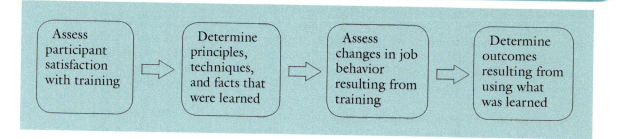

FIGURE 6.2 **Evaluating Training and Development Programs**

of the field, travel costs, and opportunity costs, on 15 to 20 percent of all its training.[89]

It is also important to reinforce the training in subsequent weeks. The Ebbinghaus forgetting curve suggests that an individual loses as much as 60% of information learned within a few days. Yet, one study indicates that post-training reinforcement is provided by less than half of companies, despite those offering it seeing 34 percent more of their first-year sales reps achieving quota.[90] Post-training implementation and reinforcement are critical to enhanced behavior change. Reinforcement should be integrated with the sales organization's daily work. Some companies, for instance, reinforce their training through frequent informal coaching sessions with their salespeople. The Fort Hill Company of Wilmington Delaware connects training to priority work upon trainees' return to work. This includes three months of post-course, structured, Web-based follow-through.[91] Exhibit 6.8[92] provides tips for reinforcing sales training.

A reasonable approach to sales training is to ensure that it is not prohibitively expensive by carefully assessing training needs, setting objectives, and evaluating training alternatives before designing the training program and performing the training. Furthermore, the sales training process is incomplete without evaluation and follow-up.

ETHICAL AND LEGAL ISSUES

Ethical and legal issues are being included in sales training programs more often than in the past. One catalyst for this change has been product liability litigation that has awarded multimillion-dollar judgments to plaintiffs who have suffered as a result of unsafe products. Another is to lessen liability due to criminal violations of the Federal Sentencing Guidelines. Firms who train employees on compliance and ethics can lessen fines due to violations by up to 95 percent.[93] Research has found that salespeople face a number of ethical and legal dilemmas on the job and that salespeople want more direction from their managers on how to handle such dilemmas.[94] Companies may benefit by training salespeople how to handle the situations or practices identified in a study by buyers as being unethical, as listed in Exhibit 6.9.[95]

Training in the legal area is extremely difficult because laws are sometimes confusing and subject to multiple interpretations. Training salespeople in ethics is even more difficult because ethical issues are often gray, not black or white. Companies that address ethics and legal issues in their sales training programs usually rely on straightforward guidelines that avoid complexity. Salespeople should be provided with the company's code of ethics and informed of the organization's policies concerning ethical behavior. Furthermore, by providing salespeople with potentially troubling ethical scenarios, having them respond, and then explaining how a similar situation could be handled, it may be possible to lessen salespeople's concerns about such situations.[96] Salespeople are given basic training on applicable legal dimensions and advised simply to tell the truth and seek management assistance should problems arise. Owens Corning, for instance, has used a lawyer to speak to its salespeople about legal and ethical issues.[97] Another possibility includes role playing, in which trainees learn to develop consistently legal interactive scripts.[98] These guidelines may sound simplistic, but such training can greatly reduce a salesperson's ethical conflict on the job, teach salesperson behaviors that help facilitate development of profitable long-term relationships with customers, and reduce the liability of the salesperson and the organization. There is even evidence that suggests that training in sales ethics leads salespeople to experience higher levels of satisfaction with supervisors and coworkers.[99]

The legal framework for personal selling is extensive. Some of the key components of this framework are antitrust legislation, contract law, local ordinances governing sales practices, and guidelines issued by the Federal Trade Commission dealing with unfair trade practices. A partial listing of important legal reminders that should be included in a sales training program is shown in Exhibit 6.10. Salespeople must be made aware of changes in the legal environment as soon as they occur.

EXHIBIT 6.8   Tips for Reinforcing Sales Training

- Include refresher training throughout the year. Facilitated reinforcement sessions should occur at 30/60/90 day intervals following the initial training.

- Provide short (five minutes or less) learning modules that are easily accessible. Try to integrate these into the customer relationship management program.

- Provide coaching and mentoring to reinforce what was learned.

- Use gamification to motivate and reinforce learned information. Periodic quizzes and games can help reinforce material.

- Review learner progress periodically to determine if material is sticking.

EXHIBIT 6.9   Sales Practices Viewed as Unethical by Buyers

1. The salesperson exaggerates how quickly orders will be delivered to get a sale.

2. The salesperson hints if order is placed, the price might be lower on the next order, when it is not so.

3. The salesperson grants price concessions to purchasing agents of a company they own stock in.

4. The salesperson gives a potential customer a gift worth $50 or more at Christmas or other occasion.

5. The salesperson seeks confidential information about competitors by questioning suppliers.

6. The salesperson attempts to get the buyer to divulge competitors' bid in low-bid buying situation.

7. The salesperson gives the purchaser who was one of the best customers a gift worth $50 or more at Christmas or other occasion.

8. The salesperson seeks information from the purchaser on competitors' quotations for the purpose of submitting another quotation.

9. The salesperson in a shortage situation allocates product shipments to purchasing agents the seller personally likes.

10. In reciprocal buying situation, salesperson hints unless order is forthcoming, prospect's sales to firm might suffer.

11. The salesperson stresses only positive aspects of the product, omitting possible problems the purchasing firm might have with it.

12. The salesperson attempts to sell product to a purchasing agent that has little or no value to the buyer's company.

13. The salesperson has less competitive prices or other terms for buyers who depend on the firm as the sole source of supply.

14. The salesperson lets it be known that they have information about a competitor if purchasing agent is interested.

15. The salesperson intends to use economic power of their firm to obtain concessions from the buyer.

Note: Ranked from most to least unethical in a survey of buyers.

> **Legal Reminders for Salespeople**   EXHIBIT 6.10
>
> 1. Use factual data rather than general statements of praise during the sales presentation. Avoid misrepresentation.
>
> 2. Thoroughly educate customers before the sale on the product's specifications, capabilities, and limitations. Remind customers to read all warnings.
>
> 3. Do not overstep authority because the salesperson's actions can be binding to the selling firm.
>
> 4. Avoid discussing these topics with competitors: prices, profit margins, discounts, terms of sale, bids or intent to bid, sales territories or markets to be served, and rejection or termination of customers.
>
> 5. Do not use one product as bait for selling another product.
>
> 6. Do not try to force the customer to buy only from your organization.
>
> 7. Offer the same price and support to all buyers who purchase under the same set of circumstances.
>
> 8. Do not tamper with a competitor's product.
>
> 9. Do not disparage a competitor's product, business conduct, or financial condition without specific evidence of your contentions.
>
> 10. Avoid promises that will be difficult or impossible to honor.

SUMMARY

1. **Understand the role of sales training in salesforce socialization.** Newly hired salespeople usually receive a company orientation designed to familiarize them with company history, policies, facilities, procedures, and key individuals with whom they will interact. During initial sales training, it is hoped that each salesforce member will experience a positive initiation to task and satisfactory role definition.

2. **Explain the importance of sales training and the sales manager's role in sales training.** Most organizations have a continual need for sales training as a result of changing business conditions, the influx of new salespeople into the organization, and the need to reinforce previous training. Sizable investments in training are likely in larger companies. The sales manager has the overall responsibility for training the salesforce, although other people may also conduct sales training.

3. **Describe the sales training process as a series of six interrelated steps.** Figure 6.1 presents the sales training process in six steps: assess sales training needs, set training objectives, evaluate training alternatives, design the sales training program, perform sales training, and conduct follow-up and evaluation. The time spent to perform sales training may be only a fraction of the time spent to complete the other steps in the process, especially in well-run sales organizations.

4. **Discuss six methods for assessing sales training needs and identify typical sales training needs.** Sales managers may assess needs through a salesforce audit, performance testing, observation, a salesforce survey, a customer survey, or a job analysis. It is recommended that salesforce training needs be assessed in a proactive fashion; that is, needs should be assessed before performance problems occur rather than after problems occur. Typical sales training needs include product, customer, and competitive knowledge; sales techniques; and time and territory management.

5. **Name some typical objectives of sales training programs, and explain how setting objectives for sales training is beneficial to sales managers.** The objectives of sales training vary over time and across organizations, but they often include preparing sales trainees for assignment to a sales territory, improving a particular dimension of performance, aiding in the socialization process, or improving salesforce morale and motivation. By setting objectives, the sales manager can prioritize training, allocate resources consistent with priorities, communicate the purpose of the training to interested parties, and perhaps gain top management support for sales training.

6. **Identify the key issues in evaluating sales training alternatives.** Evaluation of alternatives is a search for an optimal balance between cost and effectiveness. One key issue is the selection of trainers, whether from outside the company (external) or inside the company (internal). Another is the potential location or locations for training. Still another important factor is the method or methods to use for various topics. Sales training methods include classroom/conference training, on-the-job training, behavioral simulations, and absorption training. The sales manager must also consider whether to use various sales training media, such as printed material, audio- and video-recordings, and computer-assisted instruction.

7. **Identify key ethical and legal issues in sales training.** Because of increasing product liability litigation, legal and ethical issues are being incorporated into salesforce training. Exhibits 6.9 and 6.10 point out several issues that should be covered in sales training. Lectures and role playing provide useful means for training in this area.

UNDERSTANDING SALES MANAGEMENT TERMS

initiation to task	time and territory management (TTM)
role definition	self-management
needs assessment	sales training objectives
salesforce audit	sales trainer
performance testing	classroom/conference training
observation	on-the-job training (OJT)
salesforce survey	mentor
customer survey	job rotation
job analysis	behavioral simulations
sales techniques	role playing
product knowledge	absorption training
customer knowledge	sales training media
competitive knowledge	

DEVELOPING SALES MANAGEMENT KNOWLEDGE

1. How is sales training related to recruiting and selecting salespeople? How can sales training contribute to salesforce socialization?

2. Why is it important to invest in sales training?

3. What are six methods of assessing sales training needs? Can each of these methods be used in either a proactive or reactive approach to determining training needs?

4. Refer to "Sales Management in the 21st Century: Tactical Sales Training at Worldwide Protective Products" on p. 172. What is involved in sales tactical training at Worldwide Protective Products and why is it done?

5. How is the process of setting objectives for sales training beneficial to sales managers?

6. Refer to "Sales Management in the 21st Century: Fulfilling Company Objectives Through Strategic Training at Worldwide Protective Products" on p. 176. What important objective does strategic training help Worldwide Protective Products fulfill? What does strategic training at Worldwide Protective Products involve?

7. When the sales manager is evaluating sales training alternatives, what four areas should he or she consider?

8. Discuss four methods for delivering sales training.

9. What is the purpose of the follow-up and evaluation step in the sales training process? When should evaluation take place?

10. What are some of the important ethical and legal considerations that might be included in a sales training program?

BUILDING SALES MANAGEMENT SKILLS

1. Go to www.webex.com. What is WebEx? What are the advantages and disadvantages of using a company such as WebEx to assist a company with its sales training? What types of sales training do you believe would work best with this media and why? What types of sales training might not be as appropriate with this media and why?

2. As a sales manager, you have decided it would be a good idea to survey your customers to determine how well their needs are being met by your 50-person salesforce. Develop a series of questions that could be used to determine this and explain how your customer survey will be implemented.

3. There is a universal ongoing need for training on "how to sell." For instance, knowing how to listen effectively is an extremely important skill that contributes to the success of salespeople. Find several articles on listening. Use this information to design a training program to improve salespeople's listening skills. Assume that you will conduct the training session. Determine what you will teach, along with the methods and media you will use. Also, decide how you will assess whether the training was successful. If possible, conduct your training program on a small group such as your fraternity, sorority, student American Marketing Association chapter, or any other student group.

ROLE PLAY

4. As the sales manager for ABC company, you have decided that as part of your training program you would like to use role playing to achieve three objectives: (1) teach salespeople how to set appointments with prospects properly via the phone, (2) teach salespeople how to approach prospects and build rapport, and (3) teach salespeople how to question prospects effectively. Design three role plays (one for each objective) to achieve these goals. Then, have a classmate play the salesperson and you play the buyer and act out each role play. On completing each role play, critique the salesperson's performance, being sure to emphasize the positive points and to make suggestions for improvements. Consider soliciting self-assessment feedback from the salesperson before making your own critique.

5. Access Rapid Learning Institute (https://rapidlearninginstitute.com) and click on the "sales training" tab at the top and then scroll down to the library. Address the following questions:

   a. What types of sales skill training needs does this company address with its online training?

   b. What are some potentially important training needs that are not addressed?

   c. What are the advantages and disadvantages of using this type of online training?

6. The Web contains various sales training Web sites. Search the Web to find a company that offers sales training. Briefly explain the types of training the company offers, the methods and media they use to deliver the training, and the pros and cons of using the company to train the salesforce.

7. As a sales manager, you would like to teach your salespeople how to handle different buyer types. Using Exhibit 6.2 on p. 173 as a guide, explain the methods and media you would use to prepare your salespeople to deal with each buyer type.

8. **Role Play**

   ROLE PLAY

   Situation: Read An Ethical Dilemma on p. 181.

   Characters: Kyle, national sales manager; Sarah, sales trainee.

   Scene: *Location*—Company training room. *Action*—Kyle acts out an alternative method for handling Sarah's poor role-play performance.

9. You would like to develop a game to help train your salesforce. Choose a specific sales training learning objective and develop a game to be administered to salespeople to achieve the objective. Explain the format of the game, including its object, how it is played, who is involved, its rules, and any props necessary to implement the game.

MAKING SALES MANAGEMENT DECISIONS

CASE 6.1 DEVELOPING A TRAINING PROGRAM AT SOFT GLOW CANDLES

Background

Soft Glow Candles is a small independently owned candle manufacturer located in the Southern United States. The company has held its own in the highly fragmented candle manufacturing market having steadily increased sales each year of its existence. Although the company has only been in existence for about nine years, it has likewise steadily grown its salesforce to 18 members. Each salesperson brings his or her own unique set of skills and talents to the company, as it has never before offered any formal sales training, that is, until now.

Current Situation

It was a Friday afternoon when Chad Flame, VP of sales at Soft Glow, met with company owner Candice Wax to discuss plans for taking the salesforce to the next level. Candice had been pressuring Chad to improve sales significantly this year. Chad felt confident that his salespeople were doing all they could. In his opinion, members of his sales team appeared highly motivated and hard working. Perhaps, he thought, they could hire a couple more salespeople. However, when he had mentioned this to Candice a few weeks earlier she seemed lukewarm to the idea. Thus, Chad decided he would propose to Candice the idea of conducting formal salesforce training. He believed this could help make his sales team stronger and ultimately increase company sales. Candice was excited about the idea. Prior to starting Soft Glow she had worked in sales at Xerox and had undergone extensive sales training. She felt it was instrumental in helping her develop as a salesperson. Moreover, after leaving Xerox she had developed some sales training programs herself when she served as VP of sales at a small office supply company. Therefore, Candice accepted Chad's proposal to develop sales training and sent him on his way.

Chad was excited. Training the salesforce would surely help his team take the next step. The question was, what exactly should he teach his salespeople? Given Candice's push to increase sales, Chad decided that if he could improve the prospecting skills of his salesforce, they could obtain more customers, and thus increase sales. Since the market is very competitive, Chad felt that it may be useful to increase the competitive knowledge of his salesforce. In addition, Chad felt that if his salespeople better understood their customers they surely would do a better job of selling. Chad also thought that his salespeople should be very customer-

oriented and treat customers fairly. In doing so, it was important that salespeople closely adhered to the company's code of ethics. Therefore Chad decided that he also would conduct training in sales ethics. Finally, Chad was a big believer in being organized, as he felt this helped one to work more efficiently and effectively. Thus, he surmised that his salespeople could use training in time and territory management.

Having determined the areas in which he wanted to train the salesforce, Chad set some goals he hoped to achieve by implementing his training: (1) find more customers; (2) increase sales and profits; (3) improve teamwork and cooperative efforts; (4) improve salespeople's customer orientation; and (5) develop a smarter salesforce. If my training can accomplish these goals, Chad thought, then sales will increase and Candice will get off my back.

Next, some details concerning the training needed to be worked out. Who would do the training? Chad considered hiring an external trainer but decided to do it himself. He felt that his intimate knowledge of the industry, his company and his sales team put him in the best position to serve as trainer. Another question involved how to conduct the training. Chad had been doing a lot of reading lately on the benefits of virtual training. He felt this would be a good way to train his busy salesforce, as it could save both time and money. He could host an interactive synchronous webinar that his salesforce could attend via a computer and an Internet connection. He was familiar with a company called WebEx that provides services for conducting virtual meetings. Having participated as an attendee in a webinar a few years ago that used WebEx he decided to go with them. Since Chad had several topics to cover, he determined that he would host a series of webinars, one on each topic for the next five Tuesdays from 10:00 to 11:30 a.m. Having hammered out these details, Chad went about designing the material that would be covered in each session.

Once the training finally got underway, Chad began to experience some problems. He found some salespeople joining the sessions late or others not at all. Many of his salespeople were not familiar with the technology, having never participated in a webinar. Several of them had no idea how to "raise their hand" to ask a question, participate in polls, or use the online whiteboard. As a result, they became confused, found it difficult to keep up, and failed to learn. Some of the sessions involved no interaction on the part of salespeople. In these sessions, some salespeople had a difficult time focusing and became disengaged. Many felt as though they simply could have read the material on their own time.

Upon concluding the training sessions, Chad wondered whether the training would pay off. Having heard some comments from his salespeople, he realized that there were some difficulties. But that's not uncommon in training, he thought. As he reflected on the training, he was just sure that his salespeople received some value. But only time would tell, he concluded. Chad then began to prepare his report that detailed the training program and its impact on the salesforce for his meeting with Candice later in the week.

Questions

1. If you were in charge of the training for this salesforce, explain how you would have gone about designing a training program.

2. Do you believe that the training program outlined in this case will achieve its objectives? Explain.

3. What kind of reactions might Chad expect from his salespeople after implementing this training program?

ROLE PLAY

Role Play

Situation: Read Case 6.1.

Characters: Chad Flame, VP of sales; Candice Wax, owner of Soft Glow Candles.

Scene: *Location*—Candice's office. *Action*— Chad meets with Candice to discuss the sales training program. Chad overviews what he did and why, and then gives his assessment of how well the training went. Candice interacts with Chad and provides feedback on how to improve sales training in the future.

CASE 6.2: A SALES CALL GONE WRONG: A NEED FOR TRAINING?

Background

Eve Perplexed joined American Payment Register, 18 months ago. She was interested in working for a progressive company with growth potential. American Payment Register, appeared to be such a company. The company sold a variety of business computing systems. Eve was assigned to sell computerized cash register systems.

The salesforce was taught to practice adaptive selling in which salespeople learned how to probe for customer needs and respond to customer wants. This method of selling has proven to be very successful for the company. In fact, the company credits its move in market position from number five to number three in the last three years to its implementation of adaptive selling and its salesforce's ability to build strong customer relationships.

Current Situation

Eve was running behind as usual. She had a major presentation scheduled with a well-qualified prospect that could bring a substantial payoff to both her and her company. As a result, she had to cancel her first scheduled appointment of the day so that she could finish preparing her presentation for this prospect. This was not the first time she had to cancel an appointment. Just last week she canceled an appointment because she realized she would be unable to make it to the client's firm before it closed. She had failed to budget enough time into her schedule to allow her to travel from one appointment to the next.

Eve arrived at Handyman Hardware five minutes late. Luckily for Eve the owner of Handyman, Brian Wrench, had been on an important conference call that ran a little longer than anticipated. Brian was hoping to purchase a new cash register system that could track his inventory. He was concerned about inventory loss, particularly in terms of pilferage and the possibility of employees inaccurately (both on purpose and otherwise) ringing up sales. Moreover, he hoped to implement a system that would allow him to track sales better, while at the same time expedite the checkout process. Currently, he is using antiquated equipment that does not provide him with the ability to scan merchandise or systematically track inventory and sales.

After introducing herself and her company, Eve got right down to business. She went into a 30-minute presentation explaining the CR2000, a cash register system she believed would be appropriate for Brian's store. What follows are excerpts from her meeting with Brian:

Eve: Although we sell several systems, Mr. Wrench, I believe the CR2000 cash registers would be good for you. They are relatively inexpensive, provide a more rapid system for checking out customers, and are superior to what you now have.

Brian: As I mentioned earlier, I want a system that provides me with the ability to track inventory and total sales. Does this system do that?

Eve: No, it doesn't. We sell systems that can monitor inventory, but they are more expensive. You presently have some type of system for tracking inventory, don't you?

Brian: Yes, but it is time-consuming and I have always been concerned about its accuracy.

Eve: We could provide you with an inventory tracking system. But, in your case, it may not be worth the extra cost.

Brian: I'd really be interested in a system that is quicker than my present system and can track sales and inventory. I would also like to begin using bar codes, rather than individually pricing each item.

Eve: We carry the CR2500. This system would provide you with the ability to do these things. However, this system runs quite a bit more.

Brian: Will this system allow me to monitor sales hourly?

Eve: I believe it will. This is a fairly new system. It's an update of an earlier model. Some changes were made, and I'm not sure exactly what has been changed.

Brian: Can the system break out sales by department?

Eve: The older version of this system could. I am sure the new version can also. If you would like, Mr. Wrench, I can write you a proposal for installing the CR2500. When I finish the proposal we can meet again to further discuss the CR2500.

Questions

1. With regard to Eve, what sales training needs can you identify?

2. If you were Eve's sales manager and you discovered that several of your salespeople had training needs similar to those of Eve, what methods would you suggest for training the salesforce to improve in deficient areas?

3. What are the effects of sales training on salesforce motivation and morale?

ROLE PLAY

Role Play

Situation: Read Case 6.2.

Characters: Eve Perplexed, sales rep; Brian Wrench, store owner; Tammy Dun, Eve's sales manager.

Scene 1:   (optional) *Location*—Handyman Hardware. *Action*—Eve is making her presentation to Brian Wrench as her sales manager Tammy Dun observes.

Scene 2:   *Location*—Outside Handyman Hardware following Eve's meeting with Brian Wrench. *Action*—Tammy coaches Eve regarding her sales presentation (for more detail on coaching, see Chapter 7).

Directing the Salesforce

This part contains two chapters dealing with the direction of the activities of the salesforce. Chapter 7 presents a model of sales leadership. Contemporary views of sales leadership are discussed, along with important leadership functions such as coaching. The critical role of ethics in leadership is emphasized.

Chapter 8 deals with motivating the salesforce to work hard on the right activities over a sustained period of time. Reward systems, with an emphasis on financial and nonfinancial compensation, are discussed. Special issues related to team compensation and compensating a global salesforce are presented. Guidelines for motivating and rewarding salespeople are offered.

SALES LEADERSHIP, MANAGEMENT, AND SUPERVISION

OBJECTIVES

After completing this chapter, you should be able to

1. Distinguish between salesforce leadership, management, and supervision.

2. Discuss the importance of situational factors in determining the most effective sales leadership approaches.

3. Explain how leadership style approaches contribute to contemporary sales leadership.

4. Discuss five bases of power that affect sales leadership.

5. Explain five influence strategies used in sales leadership.

6. Discuss issues related to coaching salespeople, conducting sales meetings, and promoting ethical behavior.

SALES LEADERSHIP: BUILDING A CHAMPIONSHIP SALES TEAM AT THE PHLIADELPHIA 76ers

Building a winning sales organization for a losing team is no easy task. Yet, as the Philadelphia Seventy Sixers' win–loss record sank to a dismal 37–199 over a three-year period, the sales organization tripled new season ticket sales, culminating in the highest level of new ticket sales in the NBA from February 2016 to January 2017. During the same period, the team's season ticket renewal rate reached over 90 percent and they increased group sales by 30 percent. How was such a feat accomplished? Through effective sales leadership.

Jake Reynolds, senior VP, ticket sales and service and Christopher Heck, chief sales and marketing officer joined the Sixers' organization in mid-2013. Facing an uphill battle, the two decided that even though the team was not winning, they needed to build a winning sales culture built on people, learning, and fun. Although they could not control on the court activity, they knew they could control ticket sales.

It started with hiring the right people. According to Reynolds, sales hires need to possess intellectual curiosity, have a desire to learn and grow, be willing to listen, be open to feedback, and have a desire to compete and work hard. The two were able to build a winning team with a strong retention rate (82 percent) despite lacking a formal testing procedure for identifying these characteristics among sales candidates (they are currently developing a personality test to help identify these characteristics).

It generally takes nine weeks for the Sixers to recoup its investment in new salespeople. At the end of year two, salespeople are expected to sell two and one-half times the revenue they sold in their first year. To accomplish these goals, Reynolds and Heck push, challenge, and invest in their salespeople.

To achieve success, Heck and Reynolds went about creating a highly competitive but collaborate environment with the goal of being the top season ticket seller in the NBA. In doing so, they pinned their hopes on millennials, which drives much of their leadership decisions. Ninety-nine percent of their 115-person sales team are millennials. Understanding their millennial sales team's need for recognition, reward, and feedback, the Sixers' sales management team presents over 15 employee recognition awards each week. Conducted like press conferences with a backdrop and podium, each winner is announced by explaining the qualities and achievements that led to the award. Each winner is given a chance to give a speech, and there are photo ops with jerseys, and sometimes even a fog machine. Parents of winners are often invited to join the celebration. Reynolds says that salespeople claim that these award ceremonies rank near the top of the moments for which they are the proudest.

Heck and Reynolds know how hard salespeople work so they like to keep it fun. Besides the conspicuous recognition ceremonies, salespeople enjoy bonuses such as fully-stocked kitchens, team-building paintball games, and weekly employees-only basketball games in which Harris Blitzer Sports & Entertainment CEO Scott O'Neil participates. To encourage salespeople to share insights with leadership, sales leadership hosts an executive speaker series, lunch and learn programs with executives, breakfast with the CEO, and other events.

Even though he's now team president, Heck still takes time to visit with salespeople in order to keep up with what is happening at the front line of sales. This relentless pursuit of developing a winning sales culture around people, learning, and fun has led to a championship sales organization at the Philadelphia 76ers.

Source: Heather Baldwin, "Net Profit: How the Philadelphia 76ers Slam Dunked Their Way to Sales Success Despite on Court Losses," *Selling Power* online, (November 7, 2017), www.sellingpower.com/2017/11/07/13192/net-profit (accessed June 15, 2018).

The opening vignette highlights the leadership activities of senior sales leaders in developing a winning sales team at the Philadelphia 76ers. Sales managers in different positions and salespeople at many firms are involved in a variety of leadership, management, and supervisory activities. Exhibit 7.1 presents a description of typical leadership, management, and supervisory responsibilities for senior sales leaders, field sales managers, and salespeople.[1]

EXHIBIT 7.1   Sales Organization Positions and Activities

	Leadership	Management	Supervision
Senior Sales Leaders	Influencing the entire sales organization or a large subunit by creating a vision, values, culture, direction, alignment, and change, and by energizing action	Planning, implementation, and control of sales management process for entire sales organization or large subunit	Working with sales administrative personnel on day-to-day basis
Field Sales Managers	Influencing assigned salespeople by creating a climate that inspires salespeople	Planning, implementation, and control of sales management process within assigned sales unit	Working with salespeople on day-to-day basis
Salespeople	Influencing customers, sales team members, others in the company, and channel partners	Planning, implementation, and control of sales activities within assigned territory	Working with sales assistants on day-to-day basis

Senior sales leaders include all positions within a sales organization that have direct responsibility for other sales executives or field sales managers. Typical senior sales leader titles are chief sales executive, national sales manager, or regional sales manager. Field sales managers have direct responsibility for an assigned group of salespeople and normally include titles like district sales manager or sales manager. The major distinguishing characteristic between senior sales leader and field sales managers is that salespeople report directly to field sales managers but not to senior sales leaders. Notice that Exhibit 7.1 also includes salespeople. Salespeople are often involved in leadership, management, and sometimes supervisory activities.

Although the terms *leadership, management,* and *supervision* are often used interchangeably, we think it is important to differentiate among them. **Sales leadership** includes activities that influence others to achieve common goals for the collective good of the sales organization and the company. The leadership activities of senior sales leaders are directed at the entire sales organization or large subunits, and focus on creating the appropriate direction, environment, and alignment within the sales organization. Field sales manager leadership activities emphasize creating the right climate to inspire their assigned salespeople to achieve high levels of performance. Salespeople, in contrast, are engaged in self-leadership and sometimes play a leadership role with customers, others in the sales organization and company, and with channel partners.

Sales management activities are those related to the planning, implementation, and control of the sales management process, as presented in Exhibit 7.1. Senior sales leaders address the broader aspects of the sales management process, while field sales managers are more involved in implementing the process with their assigned salespeople. For example, senior sales leaders typically establish the recruiting and selection process for the sales organization, while field sales managers implement the process by actually recruiting, interviewing, evaluating, and often hiring salespeople. The management activities of salespeople are more focused on the planning, implementation, and control of sales activities within their assigned territory.

Sales supervision refers to working with subordinates on a day-to-day basis. Senior sales leadership and salespeople are normally not as involved with supervision as field sales managers. Sales supervision is an extremely important component of the field sales manager position, because field sales managers spend a great deal of time working with assigned salespeople on a day-to-day basis.

This chapter focuses primarily on sales leadership by sales managers, because sales leadership activities are becoming increasingly important for sales management positions at all levels in a sales organization. However, sales management and supervision are also addressed. Sales leadership, management, and supervision are interrelated and sales managers are involved in all three areas.

SITUATIONAL SALES LEADERSHIP PERSPECTIVES

Sales researchers have examined leadership from a variety of perspectives. Each perspective offers insight from a different vantage point and can help improve the leadership activities of sales managers throughout a sales organization.[2]

Many studies have tried to uncover what makes an effective leader. One popular category of this research is called the **trait approach**, which attempts to determine the personality traits of an effective leader. To date, trait research, however, has not been enlightening. The **behavior approach**, which seeks to catalog behaviors associated with effective leadership, has likewise failed to identify what makes an effective leader. As the behavior and trait studies continue to be inconclusive, it has become increasingly apparent that the situation could have a strong impact on leadership. A **contingency approach** to leadership recognizes the importance of the interaction between situational factors and other factors. Examples of situational contingency factors include the firm's market orientation; sales organization culture; company policies and procedures; the importance of the issue requiring attention; the time available to react; and the power, resources, and interdependencies of the parties involved. When time is at a premium, crisis management is called for, which requires totally different leadership behaviors than usual.

Sales Leadership Styles

A **leadership style** is the general orientation toward leadership activities. Two basic leadership styles have been examined by sales researchers: transactional and transformational. A **transactional leadership style** is characterized as a contingent reward or contingent punishment orientation. Sales leaders exhibiting a transactional leadership style focus on getting subordinates to perform desired behaviors and achieve high performance levels by providing rewards and punishments. A **transformational leadership style,** in contrast, is represented by an orientation toward inspiring subordinates to engage in desired behaviors and perform at high levels. Specific aspects of a transformational leadership style include articulating a vision, providing an appropriate model, fostering the acceptance of group goals, having high performance expectations, giving individual support, and providing intellectual stimulation.[3]

Although transactional and transformational are the two basic leadership styles, there are individual styles within each category. For example, visionary, coaching, affiliative, democratic and servant are viewed as transformational styles, and pace setting and commanding as transactional approaches. Effective leaders employ multiple leadership styles, depending on the situation. For instance, research suggests that transactional leadership can be used to reduce the role stress of highly self-efficacious salespeople operating in demanding markets with complex customers.[4] Other research suggests that by using servant leadership, which focuses on serving others first, leaders can improve the positive outcomes of transformational leadership by incrementally increasing salesperson job satisfaction, sales performance, extra-role behaviors toward coworkers and customers, and attitudes toward helping communities and society.[5] Thus, sales managers might have a general transactional or transformational leadership style, but adapt to each salesperson and situation by using the most appropriate leadership style.[6] This is particularly important when implementing leadership styles internationally given that a country's cultural values can impact the effectiveness of different leadership styles.[7]

SALES MANAGEMENT IN THE 21ST CENTURY

#1 Attribute for Sales Leadership at Abstrakt Marketing Group

John Schwepker, Vice President of Sales at Abstrakt Marketing Group in St. Louis, MO discusses the most important attribute for leading a sales team:

First and foremost, I think that leadership is based on trust. Your sales directors, sales managers and salespeople must all trust the person leading the sales division. Once you've established that, it's a matter of putting the correct action plans in place that will lead to success for the individual salespeople as well as the managers in terms of financial rewards, self-fulfillment and recognition within the organization. This goes for your customers as well. To have a successful sales department, the prospects must trust the salespeople that they are meeting with. At Abstrakt, we spend a great deal of time talking about what it takes to build trust on a sales pitch. Since we are a sales organization that primarily sells over the phone we need to establish trust with our prospects immediately to grow our organization. Trust comes from the actions you take as the leader, making sure that you follow through on the promises that you make and helping people to grow within their positions and into other positions within the organization, and by leading them to where they want to go. You must lead your team through your actions. If people trust you they will follow you. To be a great leader for your team, you must show them that you are willing to get in the trenches with them and they must believe that you are capable and willing to do what you are asking them to do. I feel that as a sales leader it's my job to make sure that my managers are delivering the day to day tactical responsibilities and that I am not interfering in those. Further, it is my job to engage with all the individual reps and managers and to identify things that they are doing right so that I can acknowledge and motivate them.

Sales Leadership Relationships

In addition to general leadership styles, sales researchers have examined the development of relationships between sales managers and salespeople. The **Leader-Member Exchange (LMX) model** focuses on the relationships in each salesperson–sales manager dyad. LMX proposes that sales managers interact uniquely with individual salespeople rather than employing a specific leadership style for each situation. Studies have shown that reciprocal trust between sales managers and salespeople has a positive effect on the salesperson–sales manager relationship. This research indicates a positive relationship between trust and job satisfaction, satisfaction with the manager, a positive psychological climate, a willingness to change, goal commitment, performance, and a negative relationship with role conflict.[8] Importantly, as sales organizations turn towards delivering customer value through customer-oriented ethical salesforces, research finds that a positive LMX relationship between sales manager and salespeople can influence salespeople's commitment to providing superior customer value, increase their workgroup socialization, decrease their ethical ambiguity and diminish their intent to behave unethically.[9]

One appealing aspect of the LMX model is that many sales organizations are reorienting their sales processes toward more long-term, trust-based relationships with customers. Salespeople and sales managers in these companies are learning the benefits of building trust in customer relationships and are likely to be motivated to engage in trust-building in the salesperson–sales manager dyad. By developing quality working relationships with salespeople, sales managers may be able to foster more adaptive selling behaviors by salespeople as a way to develop customer relationships.

The need for salespeople to play more of a sales leadership role than in the past has led sales researchers to view the development of relationships between sales managers and salespeople from vertical exchange theory perspective. This means that the relationship is based upon the exchange of information between a sales manager and salesperson. Sometimes the sales manager provides the information, but other times the salesperson is the focal point. For example, a sales manager might provide a salesperson with information about goals, strategies, and new ideas. Information from the salesperson to the sales manager could include what strategies are working or not, customer developments, and action plans. These social interactions between the sales manager and salesperson are the basis for their dyadic relationship. Thus, both the sales manager and salesperson are responsible for the sales leadership activities required to develop an effective relationship.[10]

Effective sales leadership requires many skills. Sales leaders must employ the appropriate leadership style for each salesperson and situation, as well as developing unique relationships with each salesperson. John Schwepker, Vice President of Sales at Abstrakt Marketing Group, discusses his approach to sales leadership in "Sales Management in the 21st Century: #1 Attribute for Sales Leadership at Abstrakt Marketing Group."

Power and Sales Leadership

In most job-related interpersonal situations, sales managers and the parties with whom they interact hold power in some form or another. The possession and use of this power will have a major impact on the quality of leadership achieved by a sales manager. To simplify discussion, the sales manager–salesperson relationship is emphasized, but keep in mind that sales managers must use their leadership skills in dealing with other personnel in the firm, as well as outside parties such as employment agencies, external trainers, customers, and suppliers.

The power held by an individual in an interpersonal relationship can be of one or more of the following five types.[11] For each type, a sample comment from a salesperson recognizing the sales manager's power is shown in parentheses.

1. **Expert power**—based on the belief that a person has valuable knowledge or skills in a given area. ("I respect her knowledge and good judgment because she is well-trained and experienced.")

2. **Referent power**—based on the attractiveness of one party to another. It may arise from friendship, role modeling, or perceived similarity of personal background or viewpoints. ("I like him personally and regard him as a friend.")

3. **Legitimate power**—associated with the right to be a leader, usually as a result of designated organizational roles. ("She has a legitimate right, considering her position as sales manager, to expect that her suggestions will be followed.")

4. **Reward power**—stems from the ability of one party to reward the other party for a designated action. ("He is in a good position to recommend promotions or permit special privileges for me.")

5. **Coercive power**—based on a belief that one party can remove rewards and provide punishment to affect behavior. ("She can apply pressure to enforce her suggestions if they are not carried out fully and properly.")

It should be stressed that it is the various individuals' perceptions of power, rather than a necessarily objective assessment of where the power lies, that will determine the effects of power in interpersonal relationships. For example, a newly appointed district sales manager may perceive her expert power to be extremely high, whereas more experienced salespeople may not share this perception. Such differences in perceptions regarding the nature and balance of power are often at the root of the problems that challenge sales managers.

Many sales managers have been accused of relying too much on reward and coercive power. This is disturbing for three reasons. First, coercive actions are likely to create strife in the salesforce and may encourage turnover among high-performing salespeople who have other employment opportunities. Second, as salespeople move through the career cycle, they tend to self-regulate the reward system. Senior salespeople are often seeking rewards that cannot be dispensed and controlled by sales managers, such as a sense of accomplishment on the job. As a result, rewards lose some of their impact. Third, salespeople are typically more satisfied with their sales manager, if the relationship is based on expert and referent power. Thus, it is recommended that sales managers who wish to become effective leaders develop referent and expert power bases.

At times, salespeople have more power in a situation than the sales manager. For example, senior salespeople may be extremely knowledgeable and therefore have dominant expert power over a relatively inexperienced sales manager. Or a sales manager with strong self-esteem needs may be intent on winning a popularity contest with the salesforce, which could give salespeople a strong referent power base. When a sales manager senses that the salesperson is more powerful in one of these dimensions, there is a strong tendency to rely on legitimate, coercive, or reward power to gain control of the situation. Again, it is suggested that these three power bases be used sparingly, however, and that the sales manager work instead toward developing more expert and referent power.

This recommendation is getting results in progressive sales organizations. For example, Marty Reist, National Sales Manager for MPRS Sales, has used expert and referent power to bring about double-digit sales increases. One of his salespeople at MPRS explains, "He doesn't direct his team from a throne, he gets down in the trenches with you."[12]

The concepts of teamwork and employee participation in management decision making are often used and are largely incompatible with the heavy-handed use of coercive and legitimate power. Sales managers interested in developing an effective power base might consider the advice given in Exhibit 7.2.[13]

One additional point on sales managers' use of power is that a combination of power bases may be used in a given situation. For example, it might be a sales manager's referent and expert power that allows him or her to conduct a highly effective leadership function, such as an annual sales meeting. The use of combinations of power bases more accurately reflects reality than does the exclusive use of one power base for all situations.

How Sales Managers Can Develop Power	EXHIBIT 7.2

Suggestions for sales managers in developing their power bases:

- Decide on overall objectives.
- Listen to your sales team's wants, needs, and dreams.
- Align the sales team with the firm's corporate culture.
- Be versatile and adapt to different situations.
- Discover how your behavior differs when you are busy and avoid any of these behaviors that are negative.
- Learn what invigorates other people and adapt how you work with them to influence that energy.
- Develop strong relationships with important people in your organization.
- Demonstrate empathy towards others.
- Exhibit energy and enthusiasm.
- Meet key customers and industry leaders.
- Make appearances at image-enhancing events.
- Secure support of upper management for sales management programs and activities.
- Use one-on-one meetings to motivate salespeople.
- Develop an information management system to minimize the flow of irrelevant information.

Sales Leadership Influence Strategies

Because sales managers have power from different sources to use in dealing with salespeople, peers, and superiors, they have the opportunity to devise different **influence strategies** according to situational demands. Influence strategies can be based on threats, promises, persuasion, relationships, and manipulation.[14] All are appropriate at some time with some salespeople but not necessarily with superiors or peers.

1. Threats. In a strategy based on **threats,** a manager might specify a desired behavior and the punishment that will follow if the behavior is not achieved. "If you do not call on your accounts at least once a week, you will lose your job," is an example. Threats should be viewed as a last resort, but they should not be eliminated as a viable influence strategy.

2. Promises. Sales managers can use reward power as a basis for developing influence strategies based on **promises**. Promises typically produce better compliance than threats. This would seem to be especially true for well-educated mobile employees, which many professional salespeople are. Furthermore, influence strategies based on promises as opposed to threats help foster positive feelings among salespeople and boost salesforce morale.

3. Persuasion. An influence strategy based on **persuasion** can work without the use of reward or coercive power. Because persuasive messages must be rational and reasonable, however, expert and referent power bases are necessary to make them effective. Persuasion implies that the target of influence must first change his or her attitudes and intentions to produce a subsequent change in behavior. For example, a sales manager might persuade the salesforce to submit weekly activity reports by first convincing them of the importance of the reports in the company's marketing information system. Generally speaking, persuasion is preferred to threats and promises, but it does require more time and skill.

4. Relationships. Two types of **relationships** can affect influence processes. The first type is based on referent power. It builds on personal friendships, or feelings of trust, admiration, or respect. In short, one party is willing to do what the other party desires, simply because the former likes the latter. In a salesforce setting, these kinds of relationships are consistent with the notion of the salesforce as a cooperative team.

In the second type of relationship, one party has legitimate power over the other party by virtue of position in the organizational hierarchy. Sales managers have legitimate power in dealing with salespeople. As a result, they can influence salespeople in many situations without the use of threats, promises, or persuasion.

You are a field sales manager with 10 salespeople on your team. All of your salespeople are performing well, except for one. You have tried different leadership styles, relationship approaches, and influence strategies, but this problem salesperson has not responded to any of your leadership approaches. Feeling desperate, you are thinking about telling this problem salesperson that you are going to have to terminate one salesperson from your team, because your firm wants to reduce the size of its salesforce. The top candidates for termination are the problem salesperson and another salesperson who is currently performing better than the problem salesperson. Although none of this is true, you think it might motivate the problem salesperson to work harder and perform better. What would you do?

a. Tell the problem salesperson that you need to terminate one salesperson and that he/she is one of the top two candidates who will be let go unless there is an improvement in his/her performance.
b. Tell the problem salesperson that you will give him/her a bonus if his/her performance improves over the next 30 days.
c. Ask the salesperson how you can help him/her improve his/her sales performance.

5. *Manipulation.* Unlike the other influence strategies, **manipulation** does not involve direct communications with the target of influence. Rather, circumstances are controlled to influence behavior. For example, a salesperson lacking self-confidence might be assigned to work on a temporary assignment with a confident senior salesperson. In team selling, the sales manager might control the group dynamics within teams by carefully selecting compatible personality types to compose the teams. Manipulation might also involve "office politics" and the use of third parties to influence others. For example, a sales manager might use the backing of his or her superior in dealing with peers on the job. Sometimes manipulation influence strategies can pose moral questions as presented in "An Ethical Dilemma."

Sales Leadership Communications

Clear, consistent, and effective communication is an important sales leadership skill. Senior sales leaders must continuously communicate to the entire sales organization, especially during times of change. For example, SunGard, a software and technology services firm, was able to successfully transform its sales organization to meet its goals by using effective communication from the beginning and throughout the entire process. This included communicating the need for the transformation to top corporate executives and then to the entire sales organization, getting input from salespeople about changes that would help them improve, presenting a new vision and plan, and updating progress on a regular basis.[15] Research suggests that at least 15 percent of a senior sales leader's time should be spent communicating a clear course for establishing and accomplishing the current sales plan.[16]

Field sales managers need to focus on communicating effectively to members of their sales team on a regular basis. In addition to coaching and sales meetings, discussed later in this chapter, field sales managers should create a communication plan that meets the needs of the sales team and the sales organization situation. Two examples illustrate different approaches:

- Mike Nelson leads a team of salespeople from ON24. The salespeople are located across the country. He communicates with them on a daily basis using a mixture of phone calls, instant messages, and emails. Sales meetings are held when needed.[17]

- Lawson Products uses several means to communicate with its widely dispersed mobile salesforce. For one, members of senior management spend a day each month riding along with salespeople calling on customers to listen to their ideas, concerns and challenges. Every few years the company holds a North American sales meeting, that involves an internal tradeshow, networking, teambuilding opportunities, and learning workshops. Information is provided throughout the year to salespeople via district meetings, webinars, and conference calls. Lawson developed a mobile app that allows salespeople to check orders and access real-time product pricing and inventory status via their cell phones. The company provides 24/7 online access to knowledge sharing and problem-solving communities. In addition, each quarter customized sales townhall meetings are held via conference call to update salespeople on important company information and to answer any questions they may have.[18]

A critical part of using communication in leadership processes is knowing how to use appropriate communication tools effectively. In today's productivity-driven environment, sales managers are using every conceivable device to improve the efficiency of their communication with the salesforce. Cell phones, Web conferencing, voice mail, email, Internet, company intranet, Twitter, CRM systems, satellite, and companywide video networks are some of the more popular tools being used to speed communication to salesforces in far-flung locations. The key is to use the communication mechanisms most appropriate to the sales organization.

All communication with the salesforce must be carefully planned to ensure accuracy and clarity. The latest technological developments offer some valuable communication advantages. For example, NBC Universal uses Salesforce.com's Chatter to share information throughout the sales organization. Everyone gets automatic updates when something changes. So, if something happens with a customer, all sales managers and salespeople get the latest information. Even though this type of technology can communicate information throughout the sales organization efficiently, the personal communication between a sales manager and a salesperson is still of prime importance in sales leadership.[19] In fact, research suggests that more frequent and informal communication between a sales manager and salespeople is likely to result in better job performance and greater job satisfaction.[20] Exhibit 7.3[21] provides tips for more effective communication.

Tips for More Effective Communication   EXHIBIT 7.3

- Begin with a story (especially about people) and use statistics and visuals to support it. Stories are processed intellectually, emotionally and visually.
- Build suspense in your communication.
- Use alliteration, repetition, and rhythm to add interest when speaking.
- Apply powerful quotes to help effectively convey your message.
- Break down complicated ideas into small parts.
- Where appropriate, use "we" rather than "I" and "you" to promote inclusion.
- Be honest in conveying your message and work toward developing trust. Do not try to hide negative or bad news.
- Take a helpful approach when communicating by asking the receiver how you can help him or her.
- Be consistent in your tone across your communications.
- Be authentic in your communication.
- Be an attentive listener.

IMPORTANT SALES LEADERSHIP FUNCTIONS

This section examines three leadership functions that are particularly relevant to sales managers: coaching salespeople, conducting sales meetings, and promoting ethical behavior.

Coaching Salespeople

One of the most critical tasks for sales managers, especially field sales managers, is coaching. In fact, in one study, 74 percent of leading companies indicated that front-line sales managers' most important role is coaching. Salespeople likewise believe coaching is valuable as 46 percent believe it is one of the best ways to reinforce sales training, and 60 percent are more likely to leave their job if their manager is a poor coach. By using coaching to reinforce sales training, companies may see up to four times their return on investment from the training.[22] Given that 94 percent of salespeople who receive exceptional coaching achieve quota, the power of coaching should not be underestimated.[23] Coaching includes working directly with salespeople to help them develop professionally, plan and execute sales strategies for specific customers, and improve all aspects of the sales process. A formalized approach to coaching that covers areas such as those listed in Exhibit 7.4[24] has been found to lead to the greatest improvements in salespeople's win rates and quota achievement. Sales managers at high performing sales organizations often spend 20 percent of their time coaching.[25] The importance of coaching has been recognized for many years:

- Comcast engaged in a sales transformation to improve the ability of its inside salespeople to create more value for customers and to increase the productivity of the entire sales organization. Salespeople received training to improve the quality of its conversations with customers. Sales managers reinforced the sales training by focusing on coaching. A study of sales managers found a direct correlation between coaching time and salesperson performance. The sales managers that spent the most time coaching had the highest-performing sales teams.[26]

- A sales manager was assigned to a sales team that was consistently ranked in the bottom quartile of the 100 sales teams at the company. This team had never received coaching from a sales manager. The new manager began an intensive coaching approach and used every interaction with a salesperson as a coaching opportunity. Within 18 months, this sales team had improved to the top 10 percent of the company's sales teams.[27]

EXHIBIT 7.4   Coaching Areas of Focus

Lead and Opportunity Coaching
Coaching focuses on understanding the customer, their business challenges and goals, your company's value proposition, the customer's buying center members, and planned sales call objectives.

Funnel or Pipeline Coaching
Coaching focuses on forecasting opportunities, moving opportunities through the pipeline, looking at the number of opportunities and their time horizons, and prioritizing opportunities.

Skills and Behaviors Coaching
Coaching focuses on aligning the sales conversation with the customer's path, uncovering customer needs, communicating and demonstrating value to the customer, and sales call skills such as rapport building, communication, use of visuals, closing, etc.

Account Coaching
Coaching focuses on understanding of accounts (e.g., their customers and markets) through research and analysis, threats and opportunities facing current accounts, and developing strategic opportunities within accounts.

Territory Coaching
Coaching focuses on identifying appropriate industries, verticals and customer segments, identifying important buyer roles within these, and planning how to improve and evaluate presence in these industries, verticals, and segments.

Sales managers have many opportunities to coach salespeople. Sales managers can take advantage of every interaction with a salesperson as an opportunity to develop salespeople through coaching. Sometimes, coaching can occur during short meetings of the entire sales team. For example, sales managers at Comcast have a daily "huddle" with their sales team to discuss challenges, present best practices, and recognize salesperson accomplishments.[28] Finally, the most typical coaching approach is to have one-to-one scheduled meetings with salespeople to discuss various issues and review progress concerning commitments from previous meetings. Today, artificial intelligence software can even help managers prepare for coaching sessions. The software records salespeople's calls to customers, analyzes the components of the sales call, and provides notes to the sales manager who can use this data to provide feedback to salespeople for improving.[29]

Many sales organizations have sales managers spend time with salespeople in the field and conduct sales calls together. At the end of a field visit and after the completion of a sales call, the sales manager typically conducts a coaching session designed to help improve the salesperson's performance in the future. A typical approach is to have sales managers accompany salespeople in the field once a month. After every field ride, sales managers provide salespeople with a coaching guide that analyzes their performance in categories such as work ethic, technical knowledge, and sales skills. Managers provide suggestions for improvement along with positive feedback. By ensuring a close link between the coaching session and the appropriate event (e.g., a field visit or sales call), the sales manager is using the principle of *recency* to assist the developmental, or learning, process. Essentially this principle holds that learning is facilitated when it is immediately applied. By making a practice of holding coaching sessions after each sales call, sales managers are also using *repetition*, another powerful learning tool.

In addition to using repetition and recency to facilitate learning, sales managers should consider the type of feedback they offer to salespeople during coaching sessions. Feedback can be described as either outcome feedback or as cognitive feedback. **Outcome feedback** is information about whether a desired outcome is achieved. By contrast, **cognitive feedback** is information about how and why the desired outcome is achieved. The importance of outcome and cognitive feedback is evident in the coaching suggestions presented in Exhibit 7.5.[30]

Coaching Suggestions   EXHIBIT 7.5

1. Take a "we" approach instead of a "you" approach. Instead of telling the salesperson, "You should do it this way next time," say, "On the next call, we can do it this way."
2. Address only one or two problems at a time. Prioritize problems to be attacked, and deal with the most important ones first.
3. Instead of criticizing salespeople during coaching, help them improve by giving how-to advice. Repeatedly tell them what you like about their performance.
4. Ask questions to maximize the salesperson's active involvement in the coaching process. Have salespeople make suggestions for improving.
5. Recognize differences in salespeople and coach accordingly. Although salespeople should work together as a team, direct some efforts toward meeting individual needs.
6. Coordinate coaching with more formal sales training. Coaching is valuable, but it cannot replace formal sales training. Train regularly to enhance skills, then reinforce with coaching.
7. Encourage continual growth and improvement of salespeople. Use team or one-on-one sessions to evaluate progress and celebrate accomplishments.
8. Insist that salespeople evaluate themselves. Self-evaluation helps develop salespeople into critical thinkers regarding their work habits and performance.
9. Reach concrete agreements about what corrective action is to be taken after each coaching session. Failure to agree on corrective action may lead to the salesperson's withdrawal from the developmental aspects of coaching.
10. Keep records of coaching sessions specifying corrective action to be taken, objectives of the coaching session, and a timetable for accomplishing the objective. Follow up to ensure objectives are accomplished.

SALES MANAGEMENT IN THE 21ST CENTURY

Coaching vs. Managing at Abstrakt Marketing Group

John Schwepker, Vice President of Sales at Abstrakt Marketing Group in St. Louis, MO, discusses the difference between coaching and managing sales reps:

There is a major difference between coaching and managing sales reps. At Abstrakt we feel that you need to do both. We establish metrics that are required by our sales reps on a daily, weekly, monthly, and annual basis. These are managed daily and are the building blocks that will lead to success. These metrics allow our managers to coach individual reps to help them achieve the highest level of individual success. We use a method called MAPs (Major Activities/Projects and Potential Issues). This involves a weekly coaching session between the sales rep and their immediate manager. This gives the manager a chance to personally tell each rep how he or she is doing by measuring their performance weekly through objective, quantifiable results. The rep and manager determine the 5 most important activities that will lead to the rep's success and then discuss the outcomes in their weekly coaching session.

Successful coaching occurs in an environment of trust and respect between the sales manager and salesperson. By demonstrating honesty, reliability, and competency and by listening to salespeople's needs, sales managers can earn the trust and respect of salespeople and enhance their own chances of being a successful coach. As coaches, sales managers must be role models that set positive examples through their behavior. This is crucial because salespeople will emulate the work habits, positive attitudes, and goals of their managers. John Schwepker, Vice President of Sales at Abstrakt Marketing Group, discusses the difference between coaching and managing sales reps in "Sales Management in the 21st Century: Coaching vs. Managing at Abstrakt Marketing Group."

Coaching is a position that carries tremendous power and responsibilities. Sales coaching should be an individualized development process designed to change a salesperson's behavior to better meet an organization's goal for customer happiness and financial performance. Through coaching, salespeople should benefit from ongoing observation, analysis, feedback, and encouragement. Basic principles for coaching are summarized in Exhibit 7.6.[31]

EXHIBIT 7.6   Basic Principles of Coaching

- First determine what might be causing a problem. With your salesperson, brainstorm possible solutions. Then focus on what you want to achieve (e.g., a behavior change) from a coaching session.
- Develop an atmosphere of open communication and mutual respect in order to develop trust. Practice active listening. This will enable you to ask effective questions.
- Get buy-in from the salesperson that there is a performance issue, clarify what is possible if action is taken, and explain the consequences of failing to make a change.
- Recognize differences in individual learning and communication styles among salespeople, be flexible, and respond appropriately.
- Provide clear expectations regarding behavior change. Later, provide feedback regarding goal progress.
- Align your coaching with your company's core values.
- Coaching conversations should be interactive. Don't do all the talking.
- Hold salespeople accountable for agreed upon suggestions for improving.
- Be positive and inspiring.

Conducting Sales Meetings

One of the best ways for sales managers to demonstrate leadership is to conduct a **sales meeting.** Sales meetings are usually held on a regular basis and intended for salespeople and sales managers, but sometimes other business functions are included. The meetings typically have multiple purposes and include a variety of activities, such as sales training, strategic planning, motivational programs, recognition events, as well as recreation and entertainment. For example, Fusion Learning holds weekly sales meetings each with a variety of activities. These might include trivia games, telling funny stories, sharing weekly sales highlights, or commenting on upcoming monthly goals.[32]

The success of sales meetings requires careful planning and execution. Salespeople and sales managers do not like to be taken out of the field for a meeting, unless the meeting is enjoyable and valuable to them. Therefore, the needs of salespeople should be taken into consideration when planning a sales meeting.

Planning and conducting a sales meeting involves creative, sometimes glamorous, activities, such as selecting a theme for the meeting, arranging for the appearance of professional entertainers, or even assisting in the production of special films and other audiovisual materials. For example, Latitude Communications, an online conferencing provider, developed the theme "Fire Up" for its national sales meeting. The meeting began with a volcano erupting with smoke and sound effects and a performance from a fire dancer, and included, among other things, the vice president of marketing performing a rap song about company sales. To foster teamwork and keep with the meeting's theme, salespeople were taken offsite to participate in exercises used to train firefighters, such as a simulated rescue from a five-story tower, a fire-victim carrying race, the passing of water buckets, and extinguishing a fire with authentic firefighting equipment.[33] However, the ultimate success of all meetings depends on the planning and execution of rather detailed activities, such as communicating with all parties before the meeting, checking site arrangements, preparing materials for the meeting, arranging for audiovisual support, and ensuring that all supplies are on hand when the meeting begins. To increase the effectiveness of a major meeting, sales managers would be well served to heed the advice given in Exhibit 7.7.[34]

Tips for Conducting an Effective Sales Meeting   EXHIBIT 7.7

- Clearly establish the objective(s) of the meeting and its agenda. Give plenty of notice to salespeople prior to the meeting and share with them the agenda. Be sure to "sell" salespeople on the value of the meeting.
- Keep the meeting as short as necessary to achieve the meeting's objective(s). Avoid covering too many issues in any one meeting. For weekly meetings, 30 minutes to an hour should suffice.
- Start and end the meeting on time.
- If holding weekly meetings, be consistent on the time from week to week to create a routine and boost attendance.
- If possible, consider sending some of the material that will be covered during the meeting to salespeople to review in advance.
- Be positive and forward-looking. Build salespeople's morale rather than diminish it.
- Recognize and praise performance. Salespeople love recognition.
- Do not spend a lot of time dealing with one person. Follow up with this person after the meeting.
- Allow time for salespeople to provide input and discuss issues. Provide an interactive element to maintain focus and create cohesiveness.
- Do not waste time on updates that could be provided by other means.
- Implement activities that motivate and reward.
- Provide an educational component to help improve salesperson skills.
- Consider integrating other departments, such as marketing, into your meeting.
- Provide "next steps" for anything decided upon at the meeting.

EXHIBIT 7.8   Steps for Facilitating a Sales Meeting

Before your meeting
1. Distribute meeting notice/agenda.
2. Plan and prepare the meeting content, both text and visuals, in terms of the needs of your audience.
3. Rehearse.
4. Check out room and equipment.

At the start of the meeting
1. Review the agenda.
2. Review meeting objectives.
3. Explain what role the participants will have in the meeting.

During the meeting (encouraging participation)
1. Ask open-ended questions ... that is, questions that can't be answered with "yes" or "no."
2. Ask one or two participants to bring specific relevant information to share at the meeting.
3. Reinforce statements that are on target with meeting objectives.
4. When questions are asked of you, redirect them to the group or to the questioner.
5. Use examples from your own personal experience to encourage the group to think along similar lines.

During the meeting (maintaining control)
1. Ignore off-target remarks. Do not reinforce.
2. Ask questions specifically related to the task at hand.
3. Restate relevant points of the agenda when the discussion veers from objectives.
4. When one person is dominating the discussion, tactfully, but firmly, ask him or her to allow others to speak.
5. Ask the group's opinion about whether a certain subject is on target or not with the agenda.

At the end of the meeting
1. Summarize.
2. State conclusions and relate to original meeting objectives.
3. Outline actions to be taken as a result of the meeting (who is expected to do what and by when).

Cautions
1. Encourage, don't resent, questions.
2. Be a facilitator and not a monopolizer of discussion.
3. A little humor is welcome at most any meeting, but don't attempt to be a constant comic.
4. Don't put anybody down in public. If you have a problem participant, take him or her aside at a break and ask for cooperation.
5. Coming unprepared is worse than not coming.

Increasingly, communication technology allows off-site meeting participants to join in meetings. This is often an attractive option for salesforces that are geographically dispersed. Computer networks, groupwork software, Web meetings, and videoconferencing can replace some face-to-face meetings without any loss in meeting effectiveness. The cost is often lower, as well. For instance, Web conferencing allows participants to talk while sharing information on the Web, provides online facilities that enable participants to ask questions, and includes tools that can be used to poll attendees. Nonetheless, face-to-face meetings remain a crucial sales leadership activity. Exhibit 7.8[35] outlines steps for facilitating a sales meeting.

Promoting Ethical Behavior

The development of trust-based, long-term relationships between buyers and sellers requires ethical behavior by salespeople and others in the sales organization and throughout the company. Research results suggest positive relationships between salesperson ethical behavior and buyer trust and relationship commitment.[36] The importance of ethical behavior is stressed in every chapter in this book by highlighting specific ethical dilemmas faced by sales managers and salespeople. A general framework for different approaches to management ethics is presented in Exhibit 7.9.[37]

AN ETHICAL DILEMMA

You are a district sales manager for a rapidly growing technology firm. There are eight salespeople in your district. Your company has set an aggressive district quota for this year. But, if your district exceeds this quota, you will receive a nice bonus, which is what you need to make the down payment on a house that you and your wife want to purchase. As you review the performance of your district, it looks like you have a good chance of exceeding your district quota. Most of your sales reps are on track, but your star salesperson is 10 percent over quota already. It looks like this salesperson will ensure that your district quota is achieved, so you want to make sure you support this salesperson as much as you can throughout the remainder of the year. However, as you are reviewing recent expense reports, it becomes obvious to you that this star salesperson has been "padding" his expense report by claiming reimbursement for personal expenses. If true, this is a violation of your sales organization's code of ethics and could warrant termination of the salesperson. What would you do?

a. Ignore the expense account padding. My star salesperson deserves a little extra for all he does for our organization.

b. Discuss this finding with my star salesperson to confirm that it is a violation. Tell him to stop expensing personal items or he will be reprimanded.

c. Discuss this finding with my star salesperson to confirm that it is a violation. Tell him that expensing personal items is against company policy and terminate him.

Approaches to Management Ethics   EXHIBIT 7.9

Organizational Characteristics	Immoral Management	Amoral Management	Moral Management
Ethical Norms	Management decisions, actions, and behavior imply a positive and active opposition to what is moral (ethical). Decisions are discordant with accepted ethical principles. An active negation of what is moral is implied.	Management is neither moral nor immoral, but decisions lie outside the sphere to which moral judgments apply. Management activity is outside or beyond the moral order of a particular code. May imply a lack of ethical perception and moral awareness.	Management activity conforms to a standard of ethical, or right, behavior. Management activity conforms to accepted professional standards of conduct. Ethical leadership is common on the part of management.
Motives	Selfish. Management cares only about its or the company's gains.	Well-intentioned but selfish in the sense that impact on others is not considered.	Good. Management wants to succeed but only within the confines of sound ethical precepts (fairness, justice, due process).

(continued)

EXHIBIT 7.9   Approaches to Management Ethics—*continued*

Organizational Characteristics	Immoral Management	Amoral Management	Moral Management
Goals	Profitability and organizational success at any price.	Profitability. Other goals are not considered.	Profitability within the confines of legal obedience and ethical standards.
Orientation toward Law	Legal standards are barriers that management must overcome to accomplish what it wants.	Law is the ethical guide, preferably the letter of the law. The central question is what we can do legally.	Obedience toward letter and spirit of the law. Law is a minimal ethical behavior. Prefer to operate well above what law mandates.
Strategy	Exploit opportunities for corporate gain. Cut corners when it appears useful.	Give managers free rein. Personal ethics may apply but only if managers choose. Respond to legal mandates if caught and required to do so.	Live by sound ethical standards. Assume leadership position when ethical dilemmas arise. Enlightened self-interest.

The **immoral management** and **amoral management** approaches either disregard or do not consider the morality or ethical implications of management decisions and behavior. These approaches are likely to lead to some of the troubling unethical situations presented in the business or popular press in recent years.

Moral management, in contrast, actively incorporates moral considerations into all aspects of management and takes proactive measures to promote ethical behavior throughout the firm and sales organization. Many sales organizations have created a **code of ethics** to communicate the values and expected behaviors of salespeople and sales managers. Professional associations often have codes of ethics and require members to adhere to these standards of ethical behavior. An example of a code of ethics for professional salespeople is one provided by Sales & Marketing Executives International presented in Exhibit 7.10.[38]

Although ethical codes can have a positive impact, sales managers have an important role to play in promoting ethical behavior. Sales managers face a number of situations with ethical implications as they interact with salespeople, customers, and others in their firm. Some of the most difficult situations are those related to a conflict of interest. One example of this type of situation is presented in "An Ethical Dilemma" on page 213.

Sales leadership activities are also very important in promoting ethical behavior in a sales organization. The ethical situations faced by salespeople and sales managers are often complex. As a result, the ethical decision-making process is based on a number of individual and organizational factors.[39] Sales managers need to reinforce the importance of ethical behavior in all of their leadership activities. Employing transformational leadership style, building trust-based relationships with salespeople, creating an ethical climate, addressing ethics during the socialization process, and incorporating an ethical perspective into the overall approach for managing salespeople are leadership activities related to ethical behavior in a sales organization.[40]

Recently **ethical leadership** has been advocated as a style of leadership that may be implemented to promote ethical behavior in the salesforce. Ethical leaders communicate an ethics and values message, role model acceptable ethical behavior, listen to employees, and consider their best interests in making fair and balanced decisions, develop employee trust, judge success by how results are obtained, and punish unethical behavior.[41] By

> **Sales & Marketing Creed: The International Code of EXHIBIT 7.10 Ethics for Sales & Marketing**
>
> *Your pledge of high standards in serving your company, its customers, and free enterprise*
>
> 1. I hereby acknowledge my accountability to the organization for which I work and to society as a whole to improve sales knowledge and practice and to adhere to the highest professional standards in my work and personal relationships.
> 2. My concept of selling includes as its basic principle the sovereignty of all consumers in the marketplace and the necessity for mutual benefit to both buyer and seller in all transactions.
> 3. I shall personally maintain the highest standards of ethical and professional conduct in all my business relationships with customers, suppliers, colleagues, competitors, governmental agencies, and the public.
> 4. I pledge to protect, support, and promote the principles of consumer choice, competition, and innovation enterprise, consistent with relevant legislative public policy standards.
> 5. I shall not knowingly participate in actions, agreements, or marketing policies or practices which may be detrimental to customers, competitors, or established community social or economic policies or standards.
> 6. I shall strive to ensure that products and services are distributed through such channels and by such methods as will tend to optimize the distributive process by offering maximum customer value and service at minimum cost while providing fair and equitable compensation for all parties.
> 7. I shall support efforts to increase productivity or reduce costs of production or marketing through standardization or other methods, provided these methods do not stifle innovation or creativity.
> 8. I believe prices should reflect true value in use of the product or service to the customer, including the pricing of goods and services transferred among operating organizations worldwide.
> 9. I acknowledge that providing the best economic and social product value consistent with cost also includes: (a) recognizing the customer's right to expect safe products with clear instructions for their proper use and maintenance; (b) providing easily accessible channels for customer complaints; (c) investigating any customer dissatisfaction objectively and taking prompt and appropriate remedial action; (d) recognizing and supporting proven public policy objectives such as conserving energy and protecting the environment.
> 10. I pledge my efforts to assure that all marketing research, advertising, and presentations of products, services, or concepts are done clearly, truthfully, and in good taste so as not to mislead or offend customers. I further pledge to assure that all these activities are conducted in accordance with the highest standards of each profession and generally accepted principles of fair competition.
> 11. I pledge to cooperate fully in furthering the efforts of all institutions, media, professional associations, and other organizations to publicize this creed as widely as possible throughout the world.
>
> © Sales & Marketing Executives International, Inc. All rights reserved.
> Source: www.smei.org.

practicing ethical leadership, sales managers can positively influence salespeople's customer orientation, commitment to providing superior customer value and sales performance.[42] Sales managers must orient and coordinate all aspects of their sales leadership and management activities toward promoting ethical behavior.

SUMMARY

1. **Distinguish between salesforce leadership, management, and supervision.** As noted in Exhibit 7.1, senior sales leaders, field sales managers, and salespeople can all be involved in leadership, management, and supervision activities. **Sales leadership**

includes all activities performed by those in a sales organization to influence others to achieve common goals for the collective good of the sales organization and company. The leadership activities of senior sales leaders are directed at the entire sales organization or large subunits, while field sales manager leadership activities emphasize creating the right climate to inspire their assigned salespeople. Salespeople, in contrast, are engaged in self-leadership and sometimes play a leadership role with customers, others in the sales organization and company, and with channel partners. **Sales management** activities are those related to the planning, implementation, and control of the sales management process. Senior sales leaders address the broader aspects of the sales management process, while field sales managers are more involved in implementing the process with their assigned salespeople. The management activities of salespeople are more focused on the planning, implementation, and control of sales activities within their assigned territory. **Sales supervision** refers to working with subordinates on a day-to-day basis. Senior sales leadership and salespeople are normally not as involved with supervision activities as are field sales managers.

2. **Discuss the importance of situational factors in determining the most effective sales leadership approaches.** Research indicates that the best sales leadership approaches depend upon the situation facing a sales manager. Different situations require the use of different sales leadership styles, relationship strategies, power bases, influence strategies, and communication approaches.

3. **Explain how leadership style approaches contribute to contemporary sales leadership.** Transformational leadership recognizes the necessity and importance of change in most sales organizations by inspiring salespeople to engage in the desired behaviors and perform at high levels. A transactional leadership style, in contrast, emphasizes rewards and punishments to get salespeople to improve performance. These leadership styles may be complemented by various other leadership styles.

4. **Discuss five bases of power that affect sales leadership.** The five power bases are coercive, reward, legitimate, referent, and expert. Coercive power is associated with punishment and is the opposite of reward power. Legitimate power stems from the individual's position in the organizational hierarchy. Referent power is held by one person when another person wants to maintain a relationship with that person. Expert power is attributed to the possession of information. A sales manager and those with whom he or she interacts may use one or more power bases in a given situation.

5. **Explain five influence strategies used in sales leadership.** Influence strategies used by sales managers could be based on threats, promises, persuasion, relationships, or manipulation. Unlike the other four strategies, manipulation does not involve face-to-face interactions with the target of influence. Threats use coercive power, whereas promises stem from the reward power base. Persuasion uses expert and referent power. Legitimate and referent power are used when the influence strategy is based on interpersonal relationships.

6. **Discuss issues related to coaching salespeople, conducting sales meetings, and promoting ethical behavior.** Coaching involves the continual development of the salesforce. A most critical part of coaching is one-on-one sessions with a salesperson. Coaching relies on the learning principles of recency and repetition and is often conducted in the field before and after sales calls. Integrative meetings accomplish multiple sales management functions. Sales managers are involved in creative aspects of planning integrative meetings, but paying attention to detail is the key to successful meetings. Meeting ethical responsibilities is not necessarily easy but is essential to long-term success in a sales career.

UNDERSTANDING SALES MANAGEMENT TERMS

sales leadership
sales management
sales supervision
trait approach
behavior approach
contingency approach
leadership style
transactional leadership style
transformational leadership
Leader–Member Exchange (LMX)
   model
expert power
referent power
legitimate power
reward power

coercive power
influence strategies
threats
promises
persuasion
relationships
manipulation
coaching
outcome feedback
cognitive feedback
sales meeting
immoral management
amoral management
moral management
code of ethics
ethical leadership

DEVELOPING SALES MANAGEMENT KNOWLEDGE

1. Explain why the following views of leadership are relevant for sales organizations: transactional leadership and transformational leadership.

2. What do you think are the most important situational factors a field sales manager should consider when determining the most effective sales leadership approaches?

3. Describe five types of power that affect leadership. What are the problems associated with overreliance on reward and coercive power?

4. How does the contingency approach to leadership differ from the trait approach and the behavior approach?

5. How can new technologies be used most effectively in sales leadership communication?

6. Describe five influence strategies, including the power bases related to each strategy.

7. What is the difference between outcome feedback and cognitive feedback? Which is most important in coaching?

8. Sales managers may learn a lot about their organizations and salespeople simply by spending time observing activities in the office or in the field and talking with the people involved. To maximize their own learning while simultaneously providing leadership, which power bases would be especially important?

9. Refer to "Sales Management in the 21st Century: #1 Attribute for Sales Leadership at Abstrakt Marketing Group" on page 202. Why is developing trust a critical aspect of sales leadership?

10. Refer to "Sales Management in the 21st Century: Coaching vs. Managing at Abstrakt Marketing Group" on page 210. Discuss the key aspects of John Schwepker's strategy for coaching salespeople.

BUILDING SALES MANAGEMENT SKILLS

1. Austin has been a steady contributor as an automotive parts representative with Premier Auto Parts for the past five years. Conscientious and hard-working, he has always been willing to pull his weight and then some. Customers and coworkers find

that his cheerful and pleasant demeanor make him a joy to be around. Over the past month, his sales manager, Warren, has noticed a significant change in Austin's behavior. Austin appears to be worn down, less than enthusiastic, and reluctant to make as many sales calls as he has in the past. His positive, upbeat demeanor seems to have been replaced with a more pessimistic attitude about things. His generally steady sales results have been on the decline. If you were Austin's sales manager, what would you do? Explain.

2. Choose an individual who is considered to be (or to have been) a great leader. Use library resources, the Internet, and so on, to examine this individual to determine what makes (or made) this person such a good leader. In your analysis, explain this leader's traits or characteristics and the leadership skills that contributed to his or her success. Also, attempt to identify and explain the sources of power generally used by this leader. Finally, explain what you learned about this leader that you could use to help you become a more successful leader.

3. Google "sales leadership." Select three articles from the results of this search. Read each article and discuss how it applies to one or more topics covered in this chapter.

ROLE PLAY

4. **Role Play**

     Situation: Sales manager Jillian is accompanying sales rep Kiley on a sales call to a local grocery store, Price Chopper. Kiley is attempting to gain shelf space for a new flavor of Lipton bottled tea.

     Characters: Jillian, sales manager; Kiley, sales representative; James, store manager.

     Scene 1:   *Location*—Price Chopper grocery store. *Action*—Kiley attempts to convince James to give her shelf space for a new flavor of Lipton bottled tea. She is very unenthusiastic. Furthermore, she is having trouble overcoming objections, particularly James' concern about the need for a new flavor and the space desired. Jillian observes the sales call.

     Scene 2:   *Location*—In Kiley's car on the way to their next sales call. *Action*—Jillian coaches Kiley regarding her visit with James.

ROLE PLAY

5. **Role Play**

     Situation: Read "An Ethical Dilemma" on p. 206.

     Characters: Yourself as field sales manager; the problem salesperson.

     Scene: *Location*—Field sales manager's office.
Action—You are meeting with the problem salesperson again to motivate him/her to work harder and perform better. The exact discussion in this meeting will depend on whether or not you decide to use the manipulation influence strategy.

ROLE PLAY

6. **Role Play**

     Situation: Read "An Ethical Dilemma" on p. 213.

     Characters: Yourself as district sales manager; the star salesperson.

     Scene: *Location*—District sales manager's office.

       Action—You are meeting with the star salesperson to address issues related to performance and the possibility of "expense padding." The exact discussion in this meeting will depend on your decision about how to handle the possible "expense padding" situation.

7. Access the Center for Creative Leadership at www.ccl.org. Examine the contents of the Web site. What types of resources are available to sales managers to help them become better leaders (explain at least two of these). Be sure to explain how the resources could be utilized by sales managers.

MAKING SALES MANAGEMENT DECISIONS

CASE 7.1: THE GOOD REST COMPANY

Background

The Good Rest Company has been very successful at selling a sleep aid product to small- and medium-sized retailers throughout the Midwest. It has built its reputation on a quality product, strong service, honesty, and integrity. The company credits much of its success to its salespeople, who provide the main link between it and its customers. The ability of Good Rest's salespeople to build strong customer relationships has helped keep the company profitable despite increasing competition.

Current Situation

Good Rest district sales manager Jane Devine recently received the following letter from one of the company's biggest customers.

February 22, 2020
3242 Grand Avenue
St. Louis, MO 63441

Ms. Jane Devine
District Sales Manager
The Good Rest Company
1675 Main
St. Charles, MO 63301

Dear Jane:

We have always been pleased with your company's products and service. The sales rep who calls on us, Noah Sand, has gone out of his way to ensure our satisfaction. Lately, however, I have noticed some changes in Noah's behavior. Normally I would not complain, but the treatment we have been getting recently is dramatically different from that to which we are accustomed, and I am concerned about Noah.

Over the past couple of months, I have noticed a dramatic shift in Noah's behavior. Usually steady and dependable, his behavior has become erratic. He has been late, or not shown up at all, for some of his scheduled appointments. Noah also has failed to follow through on several occasions. Sometimes he visits us and he is so enthusiastic it is almost unbearable, whereas on other visits he appears very tired and worn down. I think he might be having some personal problems.

As I said earlier, over the years we have been happy with your products and service. However, if this type of behavior persists, we will be forced to look for another supplier. We simply cannot afford to jeopardize our business.

Sincerely,

Kathy Moore

Kathy Moore

Purchasing Agent, Spellman Groceries, Inc.

Jane was perplexed. Noah is one of her top performers. He has worked for the company for four years and has been salesperson of the year the past two years. She had not noticed a change in Noah. Then again, she has not had much direct contact with Noah lately because she has been concentrating her efforts on three newly hired sales reps. She wonders if she should confront Noah or simply ignore it. He is making the company a lot of money, and she has not heard any other complaints. If she confronts him, he might quit. Perhaps Kathy is simply exaggerating and is really upset about something else. Maybe Kathy needs to be confronted. Ignoring her may result in the loss of a big customer.

Questions

1. Should Jane confront Noah? If not, why? If so, how should she handle the situation?

2. Should Jane speak to Kathy? Why or why not? If so, what should she say to her?

3. If Noah has personal problems, what do you recommend that Jane do? How can she prevent problems like this in the future?

Role Play

Situation: Read Case 7.1.

Characters: Jane Devine, district sales manager; Kathy Moore, purchasing agent; Noah Sand, sales representative

Scene 1:   *Location*—Jane's office. *Action*—Jane has called a meeting with Noah to confront him regarding the issue brought to her attention by Kathy Moore.

Scene 2:   *Location*—Kathy Moore's office at Spellman Groceries, Inc.. *Action*—After speaking to Noah, Jane decides to visit Kathy to discuss the situation with her.

CASE 7.2: UNIVERSAL VENTURES, LLC
Background

Guy Steel was a drill sergeant in the U.S. Marine Corps for five years before joining Universal Ventures seven years ago as a sales representative. In the Corps, he had been through some tough times and was always willing to face a challenge. A disciplined man, he rapidly became one of the company's best salespeople. However, his goal was to move into sales management. Because of his strong determination and hard work, he was eventually promoted to district sales manager, replacing Sandy Bright, who recently retired.

Sandy had done an outstanding job with the district. Her district's sales figures were consistently among the top in the company. She was well liked and respected by her salespeople. Sandy practiced good management skills and was adept at planning, organizing, controlling, and leading. Although she always took the ultimate responsibility for planning, she often consulted salespeople when she thought their ideas might be helpful. When it came to organizing, her goal was to motivate her salespeople to work as a team. As a result, she was able to get salespeople to help each other when the needs arose. She had control over her salespeople, but it was primarily through self-control. By setting realistic and individual-specific goals, she was able to motivate her salespeople not only to commit to those goals but also to supervise their own efforts effectively. Finally, Sandy had a real knack for leadership. She had the ability to get salespeople to realize their true potential and then help them achieve it. It was her contention that a leader should develop people, and she did. In fact, over the years, her salespeople were consistently promoted into management positions.

Guy took a different approach to managing, primarily as a result of his military background. He was a hard-working individual who demanded respect from those around him. He wanted to make sure those he supervised knew he was the boss. His attitude toward planning was that he made the plans and others carried them out. He did not need or seek input from others. He ran a tight organization, calling all the shots. When it came to control, he liked to scrutinize his salespeople closely, making sure they were doing what they were supposed to do.

Current Situation

On Monday afternoon, Guy completed a sales call with Tara Blaze, a three-year veteran at Universal Ventures. Although not the most outstanding salesperson in the district, Tara was a good performer. She credited much of her success to Sandy, who had helped bring her along. It was Tara's opinion that Sandy could have easily let her go after her rocky start but instead invested the time in coaching her to become a better salesperson. After the call, Guy indicated that he would like to meet with Tara on Friday to discuss the sales call. He had some other business he had to attend to right away, so they could not meet that afternoon. She agreed and an appointment was scheduled for Friday afternoon.

After finishing her appointments Friday morning, Tara met with Guy as scheduled. Following are excerpts from their meeting:

Guy: I was disappointed with your sales call on Monday. It surprised me to see a veteran such as yourself perform so sloppily. You should be ashamed.

Tara: I realize I didn't make the sale. But for the first visit, I felt I made progress in beginning to establish trust and build a relationship.

Guy: You spent too much time attempting to build rapport. You wasted valuable time that could be spent calling on other prospects or servicing current customers.

Tara: I always spend a little more time building rapport. I think it pays off in the long run.

Guy: Your handling of objections was poor. Your response to the question on pricing was totally inadequate. Your response to the question on delivery time was likewise inept. You need to work on handling objections.

Tara: My responses may not have been perfect, but I did not sense the prospect was unsure about what I was saying or had a problem with my responses.

Guy: And where did you learn to close? You need to drive the sale home. You played it a little too soft. I expect to see some real improvement on our next outing. If you can't do any better than this, maybe I'll have to find someone who can.

That evening after work Tara met with a few of her colleagues for some drinks and dinner. The following conversation ensued:

Tara: I'm sick of Guy bossing us around like we are a bunch of his soldiers. This isn't the army. We deserve to be treated with a little more respect.

Isaac: I hear you. The other day Guy went with me on a sales call. All I heard was what a horrible job I was doing. It was as if nothing I did on my call was right.

Kay: Guy always has something to say, and it's usually negative. He doesn't have any problem telling me what's wrong, but he never offers any advice on how to improve.

Tom: Come on, you guys. Give the guy a break. He's just doing what he thinks is right. He's trying to impress upper management by showing them he has everything under control down here. Once he sees this hard-guy stuff doesn't work, he'll loosen up.

Isaac: Yeah, if half the salesforce doesn't quit first. I don't like working for a guy like him. Why should I bust my tail to make him look good? I won't put up with it for long. I've heard some of the others [salespeople] talking and they aren't happy, either. Morale really seems to be down.

Kay: Maybe Tom's right. Perhaps, soon, Guy will loosen up a bit.

Tara: I don't know, Kay. It's been eight months now. Once a sergeant, always a sergeant.

Questions

1. How would you characterize Guy's leadership style? How would you assess his sales management performance thus far?

2. What suggestions can you provide to Guy regarding coaching?

3. What would you recommend Guy do differently?

ROLE PLAY

Role Play

Situation: Read Case 7.2.

Characters: Guy Steel, district sales manager; Tara Blaze, sales rep; Isaac, sales rep; Kay, sales rep; Tom, sales rep.

Scene 1:   *Location*—Guy's office. *Action*—Role-play the meeting between Guy and Tara.

Scene 2:   *Location*—A local bar and grill. *Action*—Role play the conversation between Tara, Isaac, Kay, and Tom.

Scene 3:   *Location*—Guy's office on Monday morning. *Action*—Tara, Isaac, Kay, and Tom decide to confront Guy about his leadership style, letting him know their concerns about his leadership approach.

MOTIVATION AND REWARD SYSTEM MANAGEMENT

OBJECTIVES

After completing this chapter, you should be able to

1. Explain the key components of motivation: intensity, persistence, and direction.

2. Explain the difference between compensation rewards and noncompensation rewards.

3. Describe the primary financial and nonfinancial compensation rewards available to salespeople.

4. Describe salary, commission, and combination pay plans in terms of their advantages and disadvantages.

5. Explain how to determine an appropriate financial compensation level.

6. Explain the fundamental concepts in sales-expense reimbursement.

7. Discuss issues associated with sales contests, equal pay for equal work, team compensation, global compensation, and changing a reward system.

8. List the guidelines for motivating and rewarding salespeople.

MONEY MAY TALK, BUT SALESPEOPLE EVENTUALLY STOP LISTENING

You have defined sales goals to reach, and you need your salespeople to reach their individual goals to get you there. But recent studies show 40 to 70 percent of salespeople will fall short of their sales goals. You have to get your reps in line to produce results—you have to get them to change their behaviors. But there is a universal fact working against you: it is impossible to *force* another person to do anything. You can encourage them; you can compensate them for specific activities; you can threaten them with the loss of their job—but in the end, people must *choose* to do what you are asking.

Just as most people want to personally succeed—they also want their company to succeed. Your challenge as a sales manager is how to create conditions that align their behavioral choices with the actions needed to succeed. Your salespeople want to do the right things, but need your help in making the right choices as an engaged member of the team. Engaged team members are emotionally committed to their work and successful performance. And while compensation is certainly important, it is more complex than just compensation. You cannot buy engagement—but you can fail to buy it.

What will improve sales rep engagement and generate gains in sales performance? Notable companies including DreamWorks Animation, Microsoft, and Boeing have built success on responding to that challenge through fair and equitable compensation plus coaching for and communication of the goals to be achieved, the expected sales behaviors aligned with goal achievement, clear feedback on progress, and the individual payoff for success—what's in it for me? Successful sales performance is dependent upon effective compensation and incentive plans integrated with sales coaching which addresses each of these performance motivation factors:

- **What is it you want me to do and why is it important?** Understanding the desired outcomes we are working to achieve gives the salesperson a vision of success and a roadmap for how to get there.

- **How do I do it and how do I know when I've done it?** Make sure salespeople have the right knowledge and skills and receive regular feedback and progress reporting to keep them engaged moving forward.

- **What's in it for me?** Demonstrate why it is important to them individually to undertake the expected behaviors. Understanding how success will pay off for them individually is critical—whether it's bonus compensation, opportunities for advancement, or winning the big prize. Having a personal stake in the outcome generates and enhances engagement and sales performance.

Sales compensation and incentive programs which effectively answer each of these questions help salespeople align their sales goals and behaviors with those of the organization and provide the understanding and motivation to drive successful performance in the field.

Sources: Paul Nolen, "The High Cost of a Disengaged Work Force," *Sales & Marketing Management* (January 27, 2017), https://salesandmarketing.com/node/6813, accessed August 29, 2018; and Mike Donnelly, "5 Questions to Climb to New Sales Heights," *Sales & Marketing Management* (June 6, 2018), https://salesandmarketing.com/content/5-questions-climb-new-sales-heights, accessed September 2, 2018.

The opening vignette introduces several important points regarding salesforce motivation and reward systems management, including the importance of integrating sales compensation into a systemic process of sales coaching that communicates the goals to be achieved, the expected sales behaviors and activities aligned with sales success, iterative feedback on progress, and the individual payoff for achieving sales goals. A cross section of successful organizations including DreamWorks Animation, Microsoft, and Boeing have discovered the positive impact on sales performance resulting from pairing fair compensation packages with coaching and communication that effectively aligns the salesperson's behavior with goals to be achieved and the motivational incentive of the personal payoff for sales success.

A salesforce reward system, because of its impact on motivation and job satisfaction, is one of the most important determinants of short- and long-term sales performance. This chapter examines the sales manager's role in motivating the salesforce through the use of reward systems. We first define motivation and explain some key concepts in reward system management. In the next section of this chapter, the characteristics of an effective reward system, along with the reward preferences of salespeople in general, are discussed. The following section concentrates on financial rewards, such as salaries, commissions, and bonuses. As seen in Exhibit 8.1,[1]

EXHIBIT 8.1	Financial Compensation for Sales Managers, Sales Supervisors, and Salespeople

Job Title	Average Annual Financial Compensation
Sales managers (nonretail)	$123,150
First-line sales supervisors (nonretail)	$82,890
Financial services salespeople	$102,510
Sales engineers	$101,790
Wholesale and manufacturing representatives (technical products)	$85,610
Wholesale and manufacturing representatives (nontechnical products)	$65,000
Insurance sales agents	$63,610
Advertising sales agents	$57,000

expenditures for financial rewards are quite substantial, often being the largest component of the sales organization's budget.

Nonfinancial rewards, such as opportunities for growth, recognition, and promotion, are reviewed. Expense reimbursement is also covered. Current issues in reward system management, such as the use of sales contests, equal pay for equal work, team compensation, global compensation, and changing reward systems, are presented. This chapter concludes with summary guidelines for managing salesforce reward systems.

MOTIVATION AND REWARD SYSTEMS

An important part of sales management is motivating salespeople to accomplish organizational goals. Many factors, including job design, interactions with others on the job, personal goals and preferences of employees, and work-related rewards can impact salespeople's motivation.[2] In this chapter, we will focus on the role of reward systems as a key sales management motivational tool. Definitions of **motivation** often include three dimensions: intensity, direction, and persistence.[3] **Intensity** refers to the amount of mental and physical effort put forth by the salesperson. **Direction** implies that salespeople choose where their efforts will be spent among various job activities. **Persistence** describes the salesperson's choice to expend effort over time, especially when faced with adverse conditions.

Because salespeople are often faced with a diverse set of selling and nonselling job responsibilities, their choice of which activities warrant action is just as important as how hard they work or how well they persist in their efforts. The motivation task is incomplete unless salespeople's efforts are channeled in directions consistent with the overall strategic role of the salesforce within the firm.[4]

Motivation is an unobservable phenomenon, and the terms *intensity, persistence,* and *direction* are concepts that help managers explain what they expect from their salespeople. It is important to note that, although sales managers can observe salespeople's behavior, they can only infer their motivation. Indeed, it is the personal, unobservable nature of motivation that makes it such a difficult area to study.

Motivation can also be viewed as intrinsic or extrinsic. If salespeople find their job to be inherently rewarding, they are **intrinsically motivated.** If they are motivated by the rewards provided by others, such as pay and formal recognition, they are **extrinsically motivated.** Although a salesperson's overall motivation could be a function of both intrinsic and extrinsic motivation, some will have strong preferences for extrinsic rewards, such as pay and formal recognition awards, whereas others will seek intrinsic rewards, such as interesting, challenging work.

Reward system management involves the selection and use of organizational rewards to direct salespeople's behavior toward the attainment of organizational objectives. An organizational reward could be anything from a $5,000 pay raise to a compliment for a job well done.

Organizational rewards can be classified as compensation and noncompensation rewards. **Compensation rewards** are those that are given in return for acceptable performance or effort. Compensation rewards can include nonfinancial compensation, such as recognition and opportunities for growth and promotion.

Noncompensation rewards include factors related to the work situation and well-being of each salesperson. Sales jobs that are interesting and challenging can increase salespeople's motivation, as can allowing salespeople some control over their own activities. Sales managers can also improve salesforce motivation by providing performance-enhancing feedback to salespeople. Other examples of noncompensation rewards are (1) providing adequate resources so that salespeople can accomplish their jobs and (2) practicing a supportive sales management leadership style. In this chapter, the focus is on compensation rewards, including financial and nonfinancial compensation.

OPTIMAL SALESFORCE REWARD SYSTEM

The optimal reward system balances the needs of the organization, its salespeople, and its customers against one another. From the organization's perspective, the reward system should help accomplish the following results:

1. Provide an acceptable ratio of costs and salesforce output in volume, profit, or other objectives. The salesforce must deliver value equal to or greater than the costs of doing so.

2. Encourage specific activities consistent with the firm's overall, marketing, and salesforce objectives and strategies. For example, the firm may use the reward system to encourage the selling of particular products or to promote teamwork in the salesforce.

3. Attract and retain competent salespeople, thereby enhancing long-term customer relationships.

4. Reward salesperson performance based on measurable criteria that are easy to comprehend.

5. Allow the kind of adjustments that facilitate administration of the reward system. A clearly stated, reasonably flexible plan assists in the administration of the plan.

From the perspective of the salesperson, reward systems are expected to meet a somewhat different set of criteria than from the sales manager's perspective. As indicated in the previous chapter, salespeople expect to be treated equitably, with rewards comparable to those of others in the organization doing a similar job—and to the rewards of competitors' salespeople. Most salespeople prefer some stability in the reward system, but they simultaneously want incentive rewards for superior performance. Because the most productive salespeople have the best opportunities to leave the firm for more attractive work situations, the preferences of the salesforce regarding compensation must be given due consideration. While the most commonly used sales incentive is cash, there is considerable research showing non-cash incentives to be more effective in motivating higher sales performance and also having more residual and positive influence on sales performance after the incentive has been awarded.[5]

In recent years, the needs of the customer have become more important than the needs of the salesforce in determining the structure of reward systems in sales organizations. Companies such as IBM, General Motors, and Xerox tie compensation to customer satisfaction. A majority of technology companies tie compensation to customer satisfaction and loyalty. Some automobile dealers have tried to reduce customer dissatisfaction stemming from high-pressure sales techniques by paying their salespeople a salary instead of a commission based on sales volume. Others adjust the salesperson's commission based on customer satisfaction with the salesperson's handling of the sale.

Meeting the needs of customers, salespeople, and the sales organization simultaneously is indeed a challenging task. As you might suspect, compromise between sometimes divergent interests becomes essential for managing most salesforce reward systems. As noted by Greenberg and Greenberg, "A salesforce is comprised of individual human beings with broadly varying needs, points of view, and psychological characteristics who cannot be infallibly categorized, measured, and punched out to formula."[6]

TYPES OF SALESFORCE REWARDS

For discussion purposes, the countless number of specific rewards available to salespeople are classified into five categories: pay, promotion, sense of accomplishment, personal growth opportunities, and recognition. Each of these reward categories is discussed in the next two sections of this chapter. As we discuss salesforce rewards in the following sections, keep in mind that the motivational power of various rewards is dependent on a multitude of factors, including individual salesperson preferences, cultural variations around the world, and workplace differences between sales organizations. Even so, it is possible to generalize by saying that, for most salespeople, pay is the most sought-after reward and that all of the other rewards discussed in this chapter are important to a significant number of salespeople across a wide variety of workplaces.

FINANCIAL COMPENSATION

In many sales organizations, financial compensation is composed of current spendable income, deferred income or retirement pay, and various insurance plans that may provide income when needed. The discussion here is limited to the current spendable income because it is the most controllable, and arguably most important, dimension of a salesforce reward system. The other components of financial compensation tend to be dictated more by overall company policy rather than by sales managers.

Current spendable income includes money provided in the short term (weekly, monthly, and annually) that allows salespeople to pay for desired goods and services. It includes salaries, commissions, and bonuses. Bonus compensation may include noncash income equivalents, such as merchandise and free-travel awards. The three basic types of salesforce financial compensation plans are straight salary, straight commission, and a salary plus incentive, with the incentive being a commission and/or a bonus. A discussion of each type follows (summarized in Exhibit 8.2).

Straight Salary

Paying salespeople a straight salary (exclusively by a salary) is uncommon. Such plans are well suited for paying sales support personnel and sales trainees.

	Summary of Financial Compensation Plans		EXHIBIT 8.2
Type of Plan	**Advantages**	**Disadvantages**	**Common Uses**
Salary	Simple to administer; planned earnings facilitates budgeting and recruiting; customer loyalty enhanced; more control of nonselling activities	No financial incentive to improve performance; pay often based on seniority, not merit; salaries may be a burden to new firms or to those in declining industries	Sales trainees; sales support
Commission	Income linked to results; strong financial incentive to improve results; costs reduced during slow sales periods; less operating capital required	Difficult to build loyalty of salesforce to company; less control of nonselling activities	Real estate; insurance; wholesaling; securities; automobiles
Combination	Flexibility allows frequent reward of desired behavior; may attract high-potential but unproven recruits	Complex to administer; may encourage crisis-oriented objectives	Widely used— most popular type of financial pay plan

Sales support personnel, including missionaries and detailers, are involved in situations in which it is difficult to determine who really makes the sale. Because missionaries and detailers are concerned primarily with dissemination of information rather than direct solicitation of orders, a salary can equitably compensate for effort. Compensation based on sales results might not be fair.

Salaries are also appropriate for sales trainees, who are involved in learning about the job rather than producing on the job. In most cases, a firm cannot recruit sales trainees on a college campus without the lure of a salary to be paid at least until training is completed.

Advantages of Salary Plans

One advantage of using salary plans is that they are the simplest ones to administer, with adjustments usually occurring only once a year. Because salaries are fixed costs, **planned earnings** for the salesforce are easy to project, which facilitates the salesforce budgeting process. The fixed nature of planned earnings with salary plans may also facilitate recruitment and selection. For example, some recruits may be more likely to join the sales organization when their first-year earnings can be articulated clearly in salary terms rather than less certain commission terms.

Salaries can provide control over salespeople's activities, and reassigning salespeople and changing sales territories is less of a problem with salary plans than with other financial compensation plans. There is general agreement that salesforce loyalty to the company may be greater with salary plans and that there is less chance that high-pressure, non-customer-oriented sales techniques will be used. Salary plans also make it easier to encourage teamwork and customer service.

Salaries are also used when substantial developmental work is required to open a new sales territory or introduce new products to the marketplace. Presumably, the income stability guaranteed by a salary allows the salesperson to concentrate on job activities rather than worry about how much the next paycheck will be. In general, salary plans allow more control over salesforce activities, especially nonselling activities.

Disadvantages of Salary Plans

The most serious shortcoming of straight-salary plans is that they offer little financial incentive to perform past a merely acceptable level. As a result, the least productive members of the salesforce are, in effect, the most rewarded salespeople. Conversely, the most productive salespeople are likely to think salary plans are inequitable. As such, it may be difficult to attract high-performing salespeople.

Differences in salary levels among salespeople are often a function of seniority on the job instead of true merit. Even so, the constraints under which many salary plans operate may cause **salary compression,** or a narrow range of salaries in the salesforce. Thus sales trainees may be earning close to what experienced salespeople earn, which could cause perceptions of inequity among experienced salespeople, leading to diminished motivation.

Salaries represent fixed overhead in a sales operation. If the market is declining or stagnating, the financial burden of the firm is greater with salary plans than with a variable expense such as commissions based on sales.

Straight Commission

Unlike straight-salary plans, commission-only plans (or **straight commission**) offer strong financial incentives to maximize performance. However, they also limit control of the salesforce. Some industries—real estate, insurance, automobiles, and securities— traditionally have paid salespeople by straight commission. In these industries, the primary responsibility of salespeople is simply to close sales; nonselling activities are less important to the employer than in some other industries.

Manufacturers' representatives, who represent multiple manufacturers, are also paid by commission. Wholesalers, many of whom founded their businesses with limited working capital, also traditionally pay their salesforce by commission.

The huge direct-sales industry, including such companies as Mary Kay Cosmetics, Tupperware, and Avon, also pays by straight commission. The large number of salespeople working for these organizations makes salary payments impractical from an overhead and administrative standpoint.

Commission Plan Variations

There are several factors to be considered in developing a commission-only plan:

1. **Commission base**—volume or profitability

2. **Commission rate**—constant, progressive, regressive, or a combination

3. **Commission splits**—between two or more salespeople or between salespeople and the employer

4. **Commission payout event**—when the order is confirmed, shipped, billed, paid for, or some combination of these events

Commissions may be paid according to sales volume or some measure of profitability, such as gross margin, contribution margin, or, in rare cases, net income. Recently, there has been more experimentation with profitability-oriented commission plans in an effort to improve salesforce productivity. Despite the gradual adoption of profitability-based commission plans by various companies, the most popular commission base appears to be sales volume.[7]

Commission rates vary widely, and determining the appropriate rate is a weighty managerial task. The commission rate, or percentage paid to the salesperson, may be a **constant rate** over the pay period, which is an easy plan for the salespeople to understand and provides incentive for them to produce more sales or profits (because pay is linked directly to performance). A **progressive rate** increases as salespeople reach prespecified targets. This provides an even stronger incentive to the salesperson, but it may result in overselling and higher selling costs. A **regressive rate** declines at some predetermined point. Regressive rates might be appropriate when the first order is hard to secure but reorders are virtually automatic. Such is the case for many manufacturer salespeople who sell to distributors and retailers.

Some circumstances might warrant a combination of a constant rate with either a progressive or regressive rate. For example, assume that a manufacturer has limited production capacity. The manufacturer wants to use capacity fully (i.e., sell out) but not oversell, because service problems would hamper future marketing plans. In such a case, the commission rate might be fixed, or perhaps progressive up to the point at which capacity is almost fully used, then regressive to the point of full use.

When salespeople are paid on straight commission, the question of splitting commissions is of primary concern. To illustrate this point, consider a company with centralized purchasing, such as Delta Airlines. Delta may buy from a sales representative in Atlanta, where its headquarters are located, and have the product shipped to various hubs across the country. The salespeople in the hub cities are expected to provide local follow-up and be sure the product is performing satisfactorily. Which salespeople will receive how much commission? Procedures for splitting commissions are best established before such a question is asked.

No general rules exist for splitting commissions; rather, company-specific rules must be spelled out to avoid serious disputes. A company selling to Delta Airlines in the situation just described might decide to pay the salesperson who calls on the Atlanta headquarters 50 percent of the total commission and split the remaining 50 percent among the salespeople who serve the hub cities. The details of how commissions are split depend entirely on each company's situation.

Another issue in structuring straight-commission plans is when to pay the commission. The actual payment may be at any time interval, although monthly and quarterly payments are most common. The question of when the commission is earned is probably just as important as when it is paid. Many companies operating on the basis of sales-volume commissions declare the commission earned at the time the customer is billed for the order, rather than when the order is confirmed, shipped, or paid for.

Salesforce automation has made it easier to track complicated commission systems. For instance, CORE Commissions (www.corecommissions.com) offers a multi-tiered commission tracking application that enables organizations to rapidly design, process, and communicate sophisticated commission programs. Each of the tiers offers a comprehensive set of analytics, reports, spreadsheets, and dashboards communicating sales, performance, and earnings information enabling sales managers and salespeople to keep abreast of their goal progress and compensation status.[8] Furthermore, such software applications facilitate sales managers in spotting trends and to identify strengths and weaknesses within the salesforce.

Advantages of Commission Plans

One advantage of straight-commission plans is that salespeople's income is linked directly to desired results and therefore may be perceived as more equitable than salary plans. In the right circumstances, a strong financial incentive can provide superior results, and commission plans provide such an incentive. Thus, such plans are likely to attract competent results-oriented salespeople and eliminate incompetent reps.

From a cost-control perspective, commissions offer further advantages. Because commissions are a variable cost, operating costs are minimized during slack selling periods. Also, working capital requirements are lessened with commission-only pay plans. Before choosing a straight-commission plan, however, the disadvantages of such plans should be considered.

Disadvantages of Commission Plans

Perhaps the most serious shortcoming of straight-commission plans is that they contribute little to company loyalty, which may mean other problems in controlling the activities of the salesforce, particularly nonselling and administrative activities. A lack of commitment may lead commission salespeople to leave the company if business conditions worsen or sales drop. Or, salespeople may neglect cultivating potentially profitable long-run customers in favor of easy sales. Also, if commissions are based on sales volume, salespeople may be encouraged to discount unnecessarily, resulting in lower profitability. Another potential problem can arise if commissions are not limited by an earnings cap, in that salespeople may earn more than their managers. Not only do managers resent this outcome, but the salespeople may not respond to direction from those they exceed in earnings.

Performance Bonuses

The third dimension of current spendable income is the **performance bonus**, either group or individual. Both types are prevalent, and some bonus plans combine them. Bonuses are typically used to direct effort toward relatively short-term objectives, such as introducing new products, adding new accounts, or reducing accounts receivable. They may be offered in the form of cash or income equivalents, such as merchandise or free travel. At CooperVision Inc., one of the world's largest contact lens manufacturers, the top 20 percent of salespeople based on performance on annual sales quotas receive a first-class vacation for themselves and a guest, with the destination changing each year.[9] Although commissions or salary may be the financial-compensation base, bonuses are used strictly in a supplementary fashion.

Advantages of Performance Bonuses

One advantage of the performance bonus is that the organization can direct emphasis to what it considers important in the sales area. In addition, sales emphasis can be changed from period to period. Bonuses are particularly useful for tying rewards to accomplishment of objectives.

Disadvantages of Performance Bonuses

One problem with the performance bonus is that it may be difficult to determine a formula for calculating bonus achievement if the objective is expressed in subjective terms (e.g., account servicing). Furthermore, if salespeople do not fully support the established objective, they may not exert additional effort to accomplish the goal.

Combination Plans (Salary plus Incentive)

The limitations of straight-salary and straight-commission plans have led to increasing use of plans that feature some combination of salary, commission, and bonus—in other words, salary plus incentive. Combination pay plans usually feature salary as the major source of salesperson income. Salary-plus-bonus and salary-plus-commission-plus-bonus plans are popular.

When properly conceived, combination plans offer a balance of incentive, control, and enough flexibility to reward important salesforce activities. For example, a company that expects its salespeople to perform a variety of activities such as gain new customers, retain key customers, establish new products in the marketplace, and maintain a balance between sales volume and profitability might use a combination plan to direct appropriate efforts toward these various objectives. The salary component could direct the salesforce toward longer-term objectives such as retaining key customers and establishing new products in the marketplace. Commissions could be paid on all sales. An annual bonus could be paid for achieving sales volume objectives. An additional bonus could be tied to profit margins achieved in each individual salesperson's territory. In such a scenario, the compensation plan is fairly simple, and the company can direct effort toward company goals. Salespeople have some earnings stability from the salary component, while also having the opportunity for upside earnings from the commission and bonuses.

One challenging aspect of the structuring combination pay plans is determining the financial combination mix, or the relative amounts to be paid in salary, commission, and bonus.

The compensation mix should be tilted more heavily toward the salary component when individual salespeople have limited control over their own performance. When well-established companies rely heavily on advertising to sell their products in highly competitive markets, the salesforce has less direct control over job outcomes. Then a salary emphasis is logical. Furthermore, if the provision of customer service is crucial as contrasted with maximizing short-term sales volume or if team selling is used, a compensation mix favoring the salary dimension is appropriate. Finally, when the time from initial customer contact to the initial sale (sales cycle) is long, a higher proportion of salary is common.

Advantages of Combination Plans

The primary advantage of combination pay plans is their flexibility. Sales behavior can be rewarded frequently, and specific behaviors can be reinforced or stimulated quickly. For example, bonuses or additional commissions could be easily added to a salary base to encourage such activities as selling excess inventory, maximizing the sales of highly seasonal products, introducing new products, or obtaining new customers. For example, rug and home accessory manufacturer Surya paid out a total of $100,000 in bonuses to four of its 60 salespeople who led the company in opening new accounts, increasing sales in existing accounts, and increasing overall sales in an annual sales contest.[10]

Combination plans can also be used to advantage when the skill and/or experience levels of the salesforce vary, assuming that the sales manager can accurately place salespeople into various categories and then formulate the proper combination for each category. This is most commonly done with sales trainees, regular salespeople, and senior salespeople, with each category of salespeople having a different combination of salary and incentive compensation.

Combination pay plans are attractive to high-potential but unproven candidates for sales jobs. College students nearing graduation, for example, might be attracted by the security of a salary and the opportunity for additional earnings from incentive-pay components.

Disadvantages of Combination Plans

As compared with straight-salary and straight-commission plans, combination plans are more complex and difficult to administer. Their flexibility sometimes leads to frequent changes in compensation practices to achieve short-term objectives. Although flexibility is desirable, each change requires careful communication with the salesforce and precise coordination with long-term sales, marketing, and corporate objectives. A common criticism of combination plans is that they tend to produce too many salesforce objectives, many of which are of the crisis resolution "firefighting" variety. Should this occur, more important long-term progress can be impeded. Furthermore, mediocre salespeople are eliminated less rapidly than they would be under a straight-commission plan.

Determining Appropriate Financial Compensation Levels

Determining the appropriate financial compensation level depends upon an understanding of the duties expected for a particular sales position. In addition, information about competitive salaries and the requirements for attracting and keeping qualified salespeople is necessary. This information can be obtained by benchmarking earnings levels of salespeople through a variety of methods including: reviewing trade publications; using salary surveys; examining Internet sites such as Indeed.com and Salary.com; and utilizing employment agents and placement firms.

In general, sales positions that are more complicated and require more skills are compensated at a higher level. While generalizations about what defines appropriate compensation levels are difficult to make, Exhibit 8.3[11] outlines conditions typically associated with higher levels of pay.

NONFINANCIAL COMPENSATION

As indicated early in this chapter, compensation for effort and performance may include nonfinancial rewards. Examples of **nonfinancial compensation** include career advancement through promotion, a sense of accomplishment on the job, opportunities for personal growth, and recognition of achievement. Sometimes, nonfinancial rewards are coupled

---

EXHIBIT 8.3 Conditions Associated with Higher Pay Levels

Higher pay levels are typically associated with:

1. Job experience, as most senior salespeople have built a record of success. Without a record of success, salespeople are likely to find another way to earn a living.
2. The importance of personal selling in the overall marketing effort.
3. The extent to which there is an expectation that salespeople sell new products into new markets. They deserve to be paid more than those who primarily service existing customers, fulfilling more of an order-taker status.
4. Higher skill levels, especially those that call for creativity and problem solving.
5. Responsibility for major accounts, where there is a high expectation that salespeople add considerable value for the customer.
6. Highly competitive markets where an intense personal selling effort is important for customer retention and growth.

with financial rewards—for example, a promotion into sales management usually results in a pay increase—so one salesperson might view these rewards as primarily financial, whereas another might view them from a nonfinancial perspective. The value of nonfinancial compensation is illustrated by the considerable number of salespeople who knowingly take cuts in financial compensation to become sales managers. The prevalence of other nonfinancial rewards in salesforce reward systems also attests to their important role.

Opportunity for Promotion

Opportunity for promotion is a highly valued reward among salespeople. Among younger salespeople, it often eclipses pay as the most valued reward.

Receiving a promotion typically involves a pay raise, but even in cases when the net dollars associated with the promotion are insignificant, some salespeople still would prefer a promotion over a simple pay raise. This is understandable, as a promotion can lead to subsequent advancement where potential earnings are much higher. For example, consider a salesperson who is promoted into product management. The pay raise may be 10 percent, but our hypothetical salesperson may give up a company car and move to a new location where the cost of living is higher. The net financial change in such circumstances could be minimal or perhaps even negative. Nonetheless, many salespeople welcome such opportunities because it puts them on track for future advancement with greater financial rewards. Given the increasing number of young to middle-aged people in the workforce, the opportunities for promotion may be limited severely in nongrowth industries. (Growth industries, such as financial services and direct sales, offer reasonably good opportunities for advancement through promotion.) Because opportunities for promotion are not easily varied in the short run, the importance of matching recruits to the job and its rewards is again emphasized. It should be noted that a promotion need not involve a move from sales into management. Some career paths may extend from sales into management, whereas others progress along a career salesperson path.

Sense of Accomplishment

Unlike some rewards, a **sense of accomplishment** cannot be delivered to the salesperson from the organization. Because a sense of accomplishment emanates from the salesperson's psyche, all the organization can do is facilitate the process by which it develops. Although organizations cannot administer sense-of-accomplishment rewards as they would pay increases, promotions, or formal recognition rewards, the converse is not true—they do have the ability to withhold this reward, to deprive individuals of feeling a sense of accomplishment. Of course, no organization chooses this result; it stems from poor management practice.

Several steps can be taken to facilitate a sense of accomplishment in the salesforce. First, ensure that the salesforce members understand the critical role they fulfill in revenue production and other key activities within the company. Second, personalize the causes and effects of salesperson performance. This means that each salesperson should understand the link between effort and performance and between performance and rewards. Third, strongly consider the practice of management by objectives or goal setting as a standard management practice. Finally, reinforce feelings of worthwhile accomplishment in communication with the salesforce.

Opportunity for Personal Growth

Opportunities for personal growth are routinely offered to salespeople. For example, college tuition reimbursement programs are common, as are seminars and workshops on such topics as physical fitness, stress reduction, and personal financial planning. Companies that offer tuition reimbursement for salespeople and other employees include Exxon mobil, General Electric, Apple, UPS, Oracle, and Chevron.[12] Interestingly, many sales job candidates think the major reward available from well-known companies is the opportunity for personal growth. This is particularly true of entrepreneurially oriented college students who hope to "learn then earn" in their own business. In a parallel development, many companies showcase their training program during recruitment and selection as an opportunity for personal growth through the acquisition of universally valuable selling skills.

Recognition

Recognition, both informal and formal, is an integral part of most salesforce reward systems. Informal recognition refers to "nice job" accolades and similar kudos usually delivered in private conversation or correspondence between a sales manager and a salesperson. Or, it might involve a thank you letter to a salesperson's family detailing the rep's accomplishments and expressing appreciation for all his or her work, or a call from the organization's president, personally thanking the rep for a big accomplishment. Informal recognition is easy to administer, costs nothing or practically nothing, and can reinforce desirable behavior immediately after it occurs. Paul Shearstone, an internationally known author and sales trainer, emphasizes the importance of recognition as a reward for sales performance:

> At the risk of making salespeople appear shallow or monolithic (they are not), recognition amongst their peers is still the quintessential motivator, whether there is an incentive program or not. The rule again, is, there is no such thing as too much recognition! Salespeople by nature gravitate to the limelight much like other performers, and so there should be no shortage of achievement and overachievement recognitions that find their way—in a timely manner—to the public's eye.[13]

Formal recognition programs have long been popular in sales organizations. The insurance industry has the Million Dollar Roundtable, and "100%" clubs for those who exceed 100 percent of their sales quota are common. The ultimate recognition for Xerox's sales elite is to be named a member of the President's Club, while salespeople at Federated Insurance strive to be a member of the Chairman's Council.

Formal recognition programs are typically based on group competition or individual accomplishments representing improved performance. Formal recognition may also be associated with monetary, merchandise, or travel awards but is distinguished from other rewards by two characteristics. First, formal recognition implies public recognition for accomplishment in the presence of peers and superiors in the organization. Second, it includes a symbolic award of lasting psychological value, such as jewelry or a plaque. Sound advice for conducting formal recognition programs is offered in Exhibit 8.4.

EXHIBIT 8.4   Guidelines for Formal Programs

Formal recognition programs have a better chance of success if sales managers

1. Remember that recognition programs should produce results well beyond the expected and that the program should make sense from a return-on-investment perspective.
2. Publicize the program before it is implemented. Build momentum for the program while it is underway with additional communiqués, and reinforce the accomplishments of the winners with postprogram communications both inside and outside the company.
3. Ensure that the celebration for winners is well conceived and executed. Consider the possibility of having customers and teammates join in with brief congratulatory testimonials or thanks.
4. Arrange for individual salespeople or sales teams to acknowledge the support of others who helped them win the award—as is the case with the Grammy Awards, for example. This builds the teamwork orientation.
5. Strive for fairness in structuring recognition programs so that winners are clearly superior performers, not those with less difficult performance goals.

As formal recognition, programs often feature lavish awards banquets and ceremonies to culminate the program and set the stage for future recognition programs. Because lavish expenditures for any salesforce activity ultimately must be well justified in this era of emphasis on productivity improvement, it is evident that many companies believe that money spent on recognition is a good investment. For more on recognition programs, see "Sales Management in the 21st Century: Recognition and Incentive Programs at Mid-States Medical Systems."

SALES EXPENSES

Most sales organizations provide full reimbursement to their salespeople for legitimate sales expenses incurred while on the job. Typical reimbursable expenses are shown in Exhibit 8.5. Selling expenses are a substantial amount in most companies, with companies spending tens of billions of dollars every year on travel and entertainment. Given the magnitude of sales expenses, it is easy to understand why most companies impose tight controls to ensure judicious spending by the salesforce.

Controls used in the sales expense reimbursement process include (1) a definition of which expenses are reimbursable, (2) the establishment of expense budgets, (3) the use of allowances for certain expenditures, and (4) documentation of expenses to be reimbursed.

SALES MANAGEMENT IN THE 21ST CENTURY

Recognition and Incentive Programs at Mid-States Medical Systems

Jamie Southward, district manager for Mid-States Medical Systems, discusses how the company uses recognition and incentive programs to achieve multiple sales goals.

Mid-States Medical Systems utilizes multiple recognition and incentive programs to drive performance and encourage salespeople to purposefully engage with customers. Presentation of the sales performance awards at the annual sales and marketing meeting provide recognition for high performing sales reps and are awarded for performance on a variety of sales-goal metrics including percent of quota achieved, total sales dollars, high gross margin producer, account retention and growth numbers, and customer satisfaction ratings. These annual recognitions are designed for high-visibility and tie to significant bonus awards along with automatic qualification for the prestigious Sales-Stars Travel Award. The travel award recognizes individual contributions toward the company-wide sales goals across the three measures of dollar sales produced over quota, overall gross margin, and customer ratings of performance. Our sales reps consider the Sales-Stars Travel Award to be the top incentive for consistent sales performance—something they diligently work toward achieving all year long. Last year's all-expenses paid trip was to Italy and this year's trip goes to Scotland. The combination of these recognition and incentive programs keeps our reps engaged and focused on performance that benefits our clients, the company, and the reps themselves.

Typical Reimbursable Expense Items   EXHIBIT 8.5

Automobile (company-leased)
Automobile (company-owned)
Mileage allowance
Other travel reimbursement
Lodging
Telephone (including mobile phone)

Entertainment
Product samples
Local promotions
Office and/or clerical expenses
Computer and related equipment

Covered expenses vary from company to company, so it is important for each company to designate which expenses are reimbursable and which are not. For example, some firms reimburse their salespeople for personal entertainment, such as the cost of movies and reading material while traveling, and others do not.

Expense budgets may be used to maintain expenses as a specified percentage of overall sales volume or profit. Expenditures are compared regularly to the budgeted amount, and expenditure patterns may change in response to budgetary pressures.

Allowances for automobile expenses, lodging, and meal costs are sometimes used to control expenditures. For example, one common practice is to reimburse personal automobile use on the job at a cents-per-mile allowance. Many firms use a per-diem (daily) allowance for meals and lodging.

Because of more stringent tax laws, extensive documentation in the form of receipts and other information concerning the what, when, who, and why of the expenditure has become standard procedure. Salespeople whose companies do not reimburse expenses must also provide such documentation to deduct sales expenses in calculating their income taxes. A typical form for documenting sales expenses is shown in Exhibit 8.6.[14]

EXHIBIT 8.6 Sales Expense Report Form

Name________________________ Week Ending________________ II_____

DAY	City and State	Lodging	Transportation		Automobile Expenses	Meals Itemize Business Meals Below			Local Taxi, Carfare, Tolls, Etc.	Entertainment	Miscellaneous Expenses	Daily Total
			Air, Rail, Etc.	Limousine Car, Rental, Etc.	Itemize Below	Breakfast	Lunch	Dinner		Itemize Below	Itemize Below	
SUN												
MON												
TUE												
WED												
THU												
FRI												
SAT												
	Totals											

Totals Expenses Paid by Employee ______

Entertainment and Business Meals

Date	Name of Person(s) Entertained Company, Title	Time and Place	Nature and Purpose of Entertainment	Amount	% of $ Allocated to Business

Itemize Below Those Expenses Charged Directly to the Company

- ☐ Deduct from My Advance
- ☐ Mail to Home Address
- ☐ Mail to Branch Office

REMARKS:

Automobile and Miscellaneous Expenses

Date	Items	Amount

Expenses Charged Directly to the Company (Air, Fare, Auto Rental, Etc.)

Date	Items	Amount

Signature

Approved

AN ETHICAL DILEMMA

You have been Jeri Snider's sales manager for more than seven years. During that time, Jeri has exhibited consistent dedication to the company, her sales team, and her customers. Her behavior has been beyond reproach—and for the previous two years, Jeri has received the Salesperson of the Year Award for the company. Besides being an outstanding performer for the company, she is a genuinely nice person with a winning personality. Looking over Jeri's latest expense report, you noticed that she had meal expenses for herself and a customer last Thursday. However, you remember making a phone call to that same customer on the very same day to follow up with some information he had requested and being informed that he was out of town for the week. Your company has very strict policies regarding business expenses.

What should you do?

a. Assume Jeri just made a simple mistake by recording the wrong date and let it go—no follow up action is required.

b. Notify Jeri and the company's accounting department that the specific meal expense is not reimbursable.

c. Discuss the situation with Jeri and ask for clarification.

The job of reporting and tracking sales expenses has become less burdensome and more cost-efficient for companies that use expense report software and Web-based programs. For example, Concur Technologies' Concur Expense Service makes it easier for salespeople to file expense reports and for sales managers to process the reports and analyze expenditures. This cloud-based application allows salespeople to easily generate reports anytime from anywhere using a computer, tablet, or smart phone. The system, which integrates with a company's back office systems, allows data to be automatically imported from a company's corporate credit card or from a photographed paper receipt. Concur's application increases accuracy and productivity while decreasing exposure to mistakes and fraud.[15] With this program, sales managers can easily audit salespeople's expenditures, focus on expenses in a particular area, and compare selling costs with selling budgets. It is also possible to track expenditures with particular hotels or rental car companies, which may enable the sales organization to negotiate more favorable rates.

The area of expense reimbursement is the cause of some ethical and legal concern in sales organizations. Certainly **expense account padding,** in which a salesperson seeks reimbursement for ineligible or fictional expenses, is not unknown. There are countless ways for an unscrupulous salesperson to misappropriate company funds. Tactics include overstating expenses, seeking reimbursement for personal expenses, inventing purchases, and filing the same expenses on separate expense reports.[16] A common ploy of expense account "padders" is to entertain friends rather than customers, then seek reimbursement for customer entertainment. Another tactic is to eat a $10 meal and report that it costs $20, since most companies do not require receipts for expenses less than $25. Others simply add a certain percentage to every expense report they file. "An Ethical Dilemma" portrays a possible problem with expense account padding.

Tight financial controls, well-publicized and enforced requirements for documentation of expenditures, an anonymous tip program, and periodic visits by highly trained financial auditors help deter expense account abuse. Although it may sound extreme, many companies have a simple policy regarding misappropriation of company funds—the minimum sanction is termination of employment, and criminal charges are a distinct possibility.

ADDITIONAL ISSUES IN MANAGING SALESFORCE REWARD SYSTEMS

In addition to the managerial issues raised thus far, four other areas of salesforce reward systems have received considerable attention: sales contests, team compensation, global considerations, and changing an existing reward system.

Sales Contests

Sales contests are temporary programs (usually lasting one sales cycle) that offer financial and/or nonfinancial rewards for accomplishing specified, usually short-term, objectives. Popular incentives include merchandise, gift certificates, cash, trendy electronics, experiential and humorous rewards, and travel. There is a long-running debate in sales management circles about whether cash or noncash incentives work best. There is no clear-cut answer, as some individuals will be more motivated by cash and others by noncash incentives. In some cases, winners who receive cash will spend the money on routine living expenses, perhaps minimizing any significant memory of their accomplishment. Those who are rewarded with trips or merchandise will likely enjoy those rewards on a guilt-free basis, since there is no alternative but to consume the award. The cash versus noncash argument for sales contests is not settled, but there is some evidence that managers prefer cash awards for increasing sales and noncash awards for a wide variety of other objectives such as motivating specific behaviors and improving teamwork, customer satisfaction, and customer loyalty.[17]

Contests may involve group competition among salespeople, individual competition whereby each salesperson competes against past performance standards or new goals, or a combination of group and individual competition. Sales contests can be instituted without altering the basic financial compensation plan.

Despite the widespread use of sales contests and the sizable expenditures for them, very little is known about their true effects. In fact, many contests are held to correct bad planning and poor sales performance, and others are held with the belief that contests must have positive effects, despite the difficulty in pinpointing these effects. There is always a concern about whether sales contests have any lasting value or simply boost short-term sales. If contests merely pull sales from a future period into the contest period, little is gained—and the expenses of running contests can be substantial.

To optimize the use of sales contests, the following guidelines are recommended.[18]

1. Minimize potential motivation and morale problems by allowing multiple winners, but do not set low expectations just so everyone can win. Salespeople should compete against individual goals and be declared winners if those goals are met.

2. Recognize that top performers will likely be motivated no matter what the incentives are. Try to structure sales contests to encourage strong efforts from the remainder of the salesforce while still appealing to the high performers.

3. Recognize that contests will concentrate efforts in specific areas, often at the temporary neglect of other areas. Plan accordingly.

4. Consider the positive effects of including nonselling personnel in sales contests to help build teamwork. Consider using team contests to enhance customer relationships.

5. Use variety as a basic element of sales contests. Vary timing, duration, themes, and rewards.

6. Ensure that sales contest objectives are clear, realistically attainable, and quantifiable to allow performance assessment and measurement of return on investment. Consider sending periodic email reminders to reps to keep them informed of their goal progress.

SALES MANAGEMENT IN THE 21ST CENTURY

Use of Sales Contests at Technology Solutions

Tom Willis, vice-president for business development at Technology Solutions, discusses how the company utilizes sales contests to provide meaningful and consistent incentives to increase sales performance.

As a regional company distributing business technology systems ranging from basic networks to more complex multi-site, integrated digital operations systems, Technology Solutions has discovered that employing a variety of different contests and reward programs over the course of the year is more effective in motivating sales performance than the approach based on annual awards at the end of the year. More individuals have the opportunity to succeed and win more times and there is no let *down if a rep misses qualifying for one, as there is another program they can shoot for. Contests are designed to encourage the sales activities needed to achieve quarterly goals and include performance-based achievements such as number of sales appointments completed in a month, gross margin generated over the quarter, new accounts gained, and total sales dollars produced. Depending on the nature of the contest, reps can win a variety of awards ranging from dinner for two at one of the metro's gourmet restaurants, tickets for family and friends to NBA games, holiday travel to NYC including 5-star hotel, restaurants, and show tickets. With multiple contests going on at any given time, our sales team stays engaged and motivated throughout the year and keeps the company on track to meet and exceed our sales goals.*

7. Prior to the contest, publicize it to build interest and excitement.

8. Provide both public (e.g., at a special event or banquet) and private (e.g., personal letter from management) recognition to the winners.

9. Encourage the winners to share their winning strategies with the salesforce.

Contests can be implemented to achieve a variety of objectives. For instance, Guardian Protection Services, the world's largest privately held security company, coordinates its sales contests for its dealer salespeople across the United States to ensure that company-wide and local priorities are addressed. At Guardian, annual contests are supplemented by monthly contests to spur extra effort toward generating new sales, improving the average selling price, and emphasizing the sale of specific products and services.[19]

The design, implementation, and administration of sales contests is made easier by companies such as Rymax Marketing Services, the largest U.S. manufacturer's representative in the incentive industry. Rymax operates worldwide, providing support and fulfillment that facilitates sales contest design, a Web-based interface that can be customized for each corporate client, and reports that allow managers and contestants to track their progress. The Rymax online catalog offers prizes from more than 200 brand-name companies, including Apple, Coach, Samsung and Nikon.[20]

It is hard to design a sales contest that will maximally motivate every member of the salesforce. Research suggests that salespeople's enthusiasm for participating in contests and their design preferences for goal type, number of winners, contest duration, and award value may vary by individual, supervisory, and sales setting characteristics.[21] Martiz Incentives offers an assessment tool for surveying the salesforce to determine how to achieve the biggest motivational effects in the most economical way.[22] Such assessment tools, in addition to input from salespeople, can be useful in designing sales contests. Postcontest feedback from salespeople and customers can also be useful in designing subsequent contests.

The precise measurement of sales contest results can also be a managerial challenge. Factors beyond the control of the salespeople can impact contest results, particularly if contests are held over a long period of time or if national or international contests are run without factoring in local market conditions. Even so, sales contests will doubtlessly continue to be a commonly used tool. By following the nine guidelines previously mentioned, sales managers can improve the odds of making justifiable investments in sales contests. For more on sales contests, see "Sales Management in the 21st Century: Use of Sales Contests at Technology Solutions."

Team Compensation

Most salespeople are still paid based on their individual performance. As mentioned throughout this textbook, however, teamwork in selling and team selling are growing in importance. As a result, many sales organizations are adjusting their compensation plans to recognize team performance. This represents a real challenge to sales managers for several reasons. Existing reward systems for individual salespeople typically are not easy to adapt to team selling situations. Salespeople who are accustomed to earning commissions based on their individual efforts may not respond enthusiastically to team-based compensation. They may be concerned that rewards for high performers might be diminished by lower-performing team members. Furthermore, it is difficult to determine an individual salesperson's contribution to overall team performance.

Given these challenges, it is easy to see that experimentation is often required to find the right compensation plan for sales teams. For instance, when salespeople with different levels of experience work as a team, commissions might be split based on experience. For example, the experienced salesperson might receive 57 percent of the commission, versus 43 percent for the less-experienced salesperson. Plans could be reviewed periodically and revised based on an individual's performance on the team. In many cases, discussion among team members determines how incentive pay is distributed. When different members have different roles it is appropriate to assign different performance metrics to each and compensate accordingly. Some companies are ranking individual team members and dividing up an incentive pool based on these rankings.

There are no easy answers for structuring team pay. In general, it is a good idea to reward both individual and team performance. Some research shows that compensation packages that reward individual and team performance are more effective than pay equality (each team member receives the same pay) and pay equity (each member is compensated according to individual performance) approaches to team compensation. Other research suggests using output-sharing incentives for teams when (1) individual efforts are affected by peer monitoring and pressures; (2) salespeople's efforts are not perfect substitutes, but rather complementary; and (3) "helping effort" is reciprocal and efficient.[23]

Sales organizations that utilize team selling are leveraging information technology to encourage and reward collaboration between sales team members and other personnel within their organizations. Sales teams can learn and share knowledge with products such as Salesforce.com's Chatter and Microsoft's Yammer. With such technology, top performers not only achieve their sales objectives, but they also routinely engage with other salespeople to orchestrate sales activities and provide expertise and resources to their colleagues.[24] For example, Microchip, a global leader in the semiconductor industry, changed its commission-based pay plan for individual salespeople to a salary-based team plan with a small commission/bonus element for team performance. After the compensation plan change, Microchip reported record growth and profitability, more collaboration between salespeople, and practically zero turnover in the salesforce.[25]

Not only do social media and business communications tools foster teamwork, they also enable sales managers to monitor individual and team contributions as an input into compensation and reward programs. For example, Terryberry, an employee recognition company, offers a social media platform called Mongo Wall that allows team members to post on the wall of other team members, make suggestions, and share resources. The platform can be filtered and searched by managers who wish to reward certain collaboration behaviors.[26]

Global Considerations

Global compensation issues are receiving more attention. In many cases, sales representation in other countries is secured through a distributor or sales agent. These situations are not so complex from a compensation management point of view because commissions or discounts from list price provide the income basis for the sellers. The compensation of native salespeople is more difficult. In many countries, political or cultural factors may have a strong influence on salesforce pay practices and preferred incentives. For example, salespeople in the United States are less often paid by straight salary than their counterparts in any other part of the world.

Furthermore, what motivates salespeople can vary from country to country. A survey of nearly 41,000 salespeople in nine countries found that only salespeople in the United States, United Kingdom, and Singapore choose money as their number-one motivator. Salespeople in Australia, Canada, Chile, New Zealand, Norway, and Sweden are more motivated by the opportunity to use their talent.[27] Given such circumstances, it may be best to localize the compensation program when dealing with native salespeople. According to Mercer's Global Compensation Strategy and Administration Survey, approximately 75 percent of multinational sales organizations use local or regional compensation plans, with 25 percent using a global approach to compensation.[28]

The compensation of expatriate salespeople presents a different set of problems.[29] Often, the company is in the position of offering additional incentives to encourage salespeople to take assignments abroad. This pattern is changing somewhat as awareness increases that overseas assignments can enhance career opportunities. Furthermore, as companies cultivate "global" employees who welcome the opportunity to experience new cultures and take advantage of learning opportunities, companies are scaling back the once-lucrative incentives for foreign-based employment. Nonetheless, arriving at equitable pay for salespeople deployed around the world requires knowledge of living costs, taxes, and other factors that are not typically dealt with by sales managers. In fact, sales managers often rely on human resource professionals to assist in global compensation planning. These professionals point out that expatriates should not lose or gain in spending power as a result of an international assignment. They also point out the importance of tying a deployment plan to the sales growth strategy and specifying the particulars of the job before addressing compensation issues. Exhibit 8.7[30] provides a list of "dos and don'ts" for developing global compensation that comes from experience gained by IBM when it revamped its global compensation scheme.

Changing the Reward System

The need to change the salesforce reward system for a given company may arise periodically as companies strive for improved performance and productivity. Changes in sales compensation are often made to bring the salesforce more in line with a shift in strategy or to maximize corporate resources. If the current plan is confusing, offers little choice, fails to drive organizational cultural initiatives, or results in unhappy salespeople,

---

DOs AND DON'Ts of Global Compensation   EXHIBIT 8.7

- Do involve reps from key countries
- Do allow local managers to decide the mix between base and incentive pay
- Do use consistent performance measures (results paid for) and emphasis on each measure
- Do allow local countries flexibility in implementation
- Do use consistent communication and training themes worldwide
- Don't design the plan centrally and dictate to local countries
- Don't create a similar framework for jobs with different responsibilities
- Don't require consistency on every performance measure within the incentive plan
- Don't assume cultural differences can be managed through the incentive plan
- Don't proceed without the support of senior sales executives worldwide

it likewise may be time for a change. Sales compensation plans may also be changed to exploit a new market opportunity. Such was the case with Installation and Service Technologies, Inc. (IST), a Kansas-based company that sells point-of-sale and wireless technologies to restaurants and retail customers across the United States.[31] When IST decided to add hardware and other tangible products to its services offerings, the company created a new sales division focused on selling products. This led sales director Matt Haselhoff to search for industry best practices in blending salary and commissions to motivate his salesforce in a fair, motivational manner. By using online resources available from Makana Motivator Express, Haselhoff was able to quickly develop and implement the new sales compensation plan. Reward systems should be closely monitored and should be changed when conditions warrant. A situation similar to the one in "An Ethical Dilemma" may warrant consideration.

Minor adjustments in reward systems can be made relatively painlessly, and sometimes even pleasurably, for all concerned parties. For example, the sales manager might plan three sales contests this year instead of the customary two, or could announce a cash bonus instead of a trip to Acapulco for those who make quota.

However, making major changes in reward systems can be traumatic for salespeople and management alike if not properly handled. Any major change in financial compensation practices is likely to produce a widespread fear among the salesforce that their earnings will decline. Because many changes are precipitated by poor financial performance by the company or inequitable earnings among salesforce members, this fear is often justified for at least part of the salesforce. It might be wise to consider how any change in compensation will affect the company's top performers and attempt to avoid a change that would hurt them.

To implement a new or modified reward system, sales managers must, in effect, sell the plan to the salesforce. To do this, the details of the plan must be clearly communicated well in advance of its implementation. Feedback from the salesforce should be encouraged and questions promptly addressed. For instance, the 260 member salesforce at Administaff formed an internal advisory board that includes top sellers as internal consultants on issues such as compensation plan changes.[32] Reasons for the change should be discussed openly, and any expected changes in job activities should be detailed.

It is recommended that, if possible, major changes be implemented to coincide with the beginning of a new fiscal year or planning period. It is also preferable to institute changes during favorable business conditions, rather than during recessionary periods.

The dynamic nature of marketing and sales environments dictates that sales managers constantly monitor their reward systems. It is not unreasonable to think that major changes could occur every few years or even more frequently.

AN ETHICAL DILEMMA

You have been hired by a copier supply company to be their new sales manager. Although it is a small multi-state company, its salesforce has typically performed well, allowing it to hold its own against much larger competitors. The former sales manager had a unique way of motivating his salesforce. Each year, all salespeople were rank ordered by number of sales dollars produced, and the bottom three performers were fired, despite having performed profitably for the company.

What should you do?

a. Keep the same system—it seems to work.

b. Change the system to an incentive award for salespeople reaching a specified sales or profitability target.

c. Continue the existing rank order system, but use a measure of profit produced rather than sales level.

GUIDELINES FOR MOTIVATING AND REWARDING SALESPEOPLE

Sales managers should realize that practically everything they do will influence sales-force motivation one way or another. The people they recruit, the plans and policies they institute, the training they provide, and the way they communicate with and supervise salespeople are among the more important factors. In addition, sales managers should realize that environmental factors beyond their control may also influence salesforce motivation. Like other managerial functions, motivating salespeople requires a prioritized, calculated approach rather than a futile attempt to address all motivational needs simultaneously. If for no other reason, the complexity of human nature and changing needs of salesforce members will prohibit the construction of motivational programs that run smoothly without periodic adjustment. Guidelines for motivating salespeople are as follows:

1. Recruit and select salespeople whose personal motives match the requirements and rewards of the job.

2. Attempt to incorporate the individual needs of salespeople into motivational programs.

3. Provide adequate job information and ensure proper skill development for the salesforce.

4. Use job design and redesign as motivational tools.

5. Concentrate on building the self-esteem of salespeople.

6. Take a proactive approach to seeking out motivational problems and sources of frustration in the salesforce.

Recruitment and Selection

The importance of matching the abilities and needs of sales recruits to the requirements and rewards of the job cannot be overstated. This is especially critical for sales managers who have little opportunity to alter job dimensions and reward structures. Investing more time in recruitment and selection to ensure a good match is likely to pay off later in terms of fewer motivational and other managerial problems.

Incorporation of Individual Needs

At the outset of this chapter, motivation was described as a complex personal process. At the heart of the complexity of motivation is the concept of individual needs. The demographics of the workforce is diverse, with individuals at different stages in their personal and work lives, each with varying interests and influences. Although there is considerable pressure and, in many cases, sound economic rationale for supporting mass approaches to salesforce motivation, there may also be opportunities to incorporate individual needs into motivational programs. When possible, individual consideration should be taken into account when motivating and rewarding salespeople. For instance, some companies, such as broadband equipment manufacturer Netopia, have turned to online incentive programs such as the portfolio of customizable programs offered by Hinda Incentives (www.hinda.com/why-hinda/rewards-portfolio) to meet the diverse needs of its resellers when attempting to motivate them. Resellers participating in the program simply log on to the customized incentives program website where they can redeem points earned by selling Netopia products for rewards from an extensive catalog of over 2,000 items ranging from digital cameras to travel certificates.[33]

Information and Skills

Salespeople must have high skill levels and be well equipped with the right information to do their jobs well. If sales managers train their people properly and give them the right information, salespeople can see how their efforts lead to the desired results. If salespeople's understanding of how their efforts produce results is consistent with that of the sales manager, reasonable goals can be set that allow performance worthy of rewards. Providing adequate information to the salesforce also enhances salesforce socialization (discussed in earlier chapters), thereby reducing role conflict and role ambiguity.

Job Design

Given the nature of sales jobs, one would expect good opportunities to stimulate intrinsic motivation without major changes in the job. Sales jobs allow the use of a wide range of skills and abilities; boredom is thus not a typical problem. And given the unique contributions of personal selling to the organization, as discussed in Chapter 2, salespeople can readily see that their jobs are critical to the organization's success. Most salespeople have considerable latitude in determining work priorities and thus experience more freedom on the job than do many other employees. Finally, feedback from sales managers or through self-monitoring is readily available. In many ways, the motivational task is easier for sales managers than for other managers. The sales job itself can be a powerful motivator.

Building Self-Esteem

Sales managers increase salesforce motivation by building salespeople's self-esteem. Positive reinforcement for good performance should be standard procedure. This may be done with formal or informal communications or recognition programs designed to spotlight good performance. When performance is less than satisfactory, it should not be overlooked but addressed in a constructive manner.

Proactive Approach

Sales managers should be committed to uncovering potential problems in motivation and eliminating them before they develop. For example, if some members of the salesforce perceive a lack of opportunity for promotion into management and are demotivated as a result, the sales manager might take additional steps to clearly define the guidelines for promotion into management and review the performance of management hopefuls in light of these guidelines. If promotion opportunities are indeed limited, the matching function of recruitment and selection again shows its importance.

SUMMARY

1. **Explain the key components of motivation: intensity, persistence, and direction.** A variety of ways exist to define motivation. Our definition includes the qualities of intensity, persistence, and direction. Intensity is the amount of mental and physical effort the salesperson is willing to expend on a specific activity. Persistence is a choice to expend effort over time, especially in the face of adversity. Direction implies that, to some extent, salespeople choose the activities on which effort is expended.

2. **Explain the difference between compensation rewards and noncompensation rewards.** Compensation rewards are those given by the organization in return for the salesperson's efforts and performance. They may include both financial and nonfinancial rewards. Noncompensation rewards are related to job design and work environment. The opportunity to be involved in meaningful, interesting work is an example of a noncompensation reward. The provision of adequate resources to do the job and a supportive management system are other examples. The focus in this chapter has been on the management of compensation rewards.

3. **Describe the primary financial and nonfinancial compensation rewards available to salespeople.** Financial compensation could include a salary component and variable pay components such as commissions and bonuses. For most salespeople, financial rewards are most important, but nonfinancial rewards also play an important role in motivating salespeople. Nonfinancial rewards include opportunities for career advancement through job promotion, a sense of accomplishment, opportunities for personal growth, and recognition. In some cases, nonfinancial rewards may be accompanied by financial rewards such as when a salesperson I promoted into management. In these instances, one salesperson might get more satisfaction out of the financial reward, while another might value the nonfinancial aspect of the reward more than the financial aspect.

4. **Describe salary, commission, and combination pay plans in terms of their advantages and disadvantages.** Straight-salary plans and straight-commission plans represent the two extremes in financial compensation for salespeople. Straight salary offers maximum control over salesforce activities but does not provide added incentive for exceptional performance. The opposite is true for straight-commission plans. The limitations of both plans have made combination plans the most popular with sales organizations. Although such plans can become too complex for easy administration, when properly conceived they offer a balance of control and incentive.

5. **Explain how to determine an appropriate financial compensation level.** In general, sales positions that are more complicated and require more skills are compensated at a higher level. Determining the appropriate financial compensation can be accomplished by benchmarking earnings levels of salespeople through a variety of methods including: reviewing trade publications; using salary surveys; examining Internet sites such as Monster.com and Salary.com; and utilizing employment agents and placement firms.

6. **Explain the fundamental concepts in sales-expense reimbursement.** Sales expenses are usually substantial. Job-related expenses incurred by salespeople are reimbursed by a large majority of sales organizations. Companies use budgets, allowances, and documentation requirements to control sales expenses.

7. **Discuss issues associated with sales contests, team compensation, global compensation, and changing a reward system.** Sales contests are used widely to achieve short-term results, but little is known about their true effects. Companies that are new to team selling may find it difficult to move from individual-based compensation to team-based compensation. It is a challenge to determine how much of each team member's pay should be based on individual performance and how much on team performance. In most team selling situations, salary is the major compensation component, although bonuses, commissions, and other team rewards can have a positive influence on motivation. Global compensation may be dependent on different cultures and other business environment factors in varying locations around the world. Sales managers often rely heavily on human resource professionals to structure global compensation plans. Changing a reward system is a delicate procedure, requiring careful communication to the salesforce, who must "buy" the new system much like a customer would buy a product.

8. **List the guidelines for motivating and rewarding salespeople.** Six managerial guidelines for motivating salespeople are as follows: First, match the recruit to the requirements and rewards of the job. Second, incorporate individual needs into motivational programs when feasible. Third, provide salespeople with adequate information and ensure proper skill development to facilitate job performance. Fourth, use job design and redesign as motivational tools. Fifth, cultivate salespeople's self-esteem. Sixth, take a proactive approach to uncovering motivational problems by trying to eliminate problems before they become serious.

UNDERSTANDING SALES MANAGEMENT TERMS

motivation
intensity
persistence
direction
intrinsic motivation
extrinsic motivation
reward system management
compensation rewards
noncompensation rewards
current spendable income
straight salary
planned earnings
salary compression
straight commission
commission base
commission rate

commission splits
commission payout event
constant rate
progressive rate
regressive rate
performance bonus
salary plus incentive
financial compensation mix
nonfinancial compensation
opportunity for promotion
sense of accomplishment
opportunities for personal growth
recognition
sales expenses
expense account padding
sales contests

DEVELOPING SALES MANAGEMENT KNOWLEDGE

1. Identify and explain the three key dimensions of motivation.

2. Distinguish between compensation rewards and noncompensation rewards.

3. Describe an optimal salesforce reward system.

4. What are the nonfinancial compensation rewards discussed in this chapter? What suggestions can you make for administering recognition rewards?

5. Evaluate straight-salary, straight-commission, and combination pay plans in terms of their advantages and disadvantages. When should each be used?

6. Refer to "Sales Management in the 21st Century: Recognition and Incentive Programs at Mid-States Medical Systems" on p. 235. How does Mid-States use recognition and incentive programs to motivate its salespeople?

7. What concerns should a sales manager have regarding the use of sales contests?

8. Refer to "Sales Management in the 21st Century: Use of Sales Contests at Technology Solutions" on p. 239. How often does Technology Solutions have sales contests? What types of incentives do they offer? Explain the rationale for the manner in which contests are conducted at Technology Solutions.

9. What challenges do sales managers face when using team-based compensation? What guidelines can sales managers follow when using team-based compensation?

10. Discuss several guidelines to improve the effectiveness of salesforce motivation and reward system management.

BUILDING SALES MANAGEMENT SKILLS

1. Assume you have been hired as the national sales manager for a newly formed electronics distributor. Your salesforce will sell directly to electronics retailers. Although the company is not widely known, it will use little other than the salesforce to promote its products in a highly competitive market. Thus, salespeople's skills are very important. Salespeople will be responsible for providing complete customer service, including handling damage claims, helping with merchandising, providing advice, and following up after the sale to ensure the customer is completely satisfied. Devise a

reward system for your salesforce, being sure to address the type of financial compensation plan you will use and why, as well as the types of nonfinancial compensation you will provide. What role will recruitment and selection play in this process? Explain.

2. Most student organizations are looking for ways to raise funds. Choose a student (or any other) organization and determine a fundraising activity that involves some form of personal selling (e.g., a raffle). Then, devise a sales contest that would be appropriate for achieving predetermined fundraising objectives. Explain your fundraiser, its objectives, the contest, and the rationale behind the contest's incentives.

ROLE PLAY

3. **Role Play**

   Situation: Read and prepare your plan for a sales contest as explained in no. 2 directly above.

   Characters: One student is the salesperson, and one is the sales manager.

   Scene: The salesperson presents the sales contest plan to the sales manager and tries to convince the sales manager to support the plan by dedicating the organization's time and/or money to the sales contest. Reverse roles and repeat the role play. After each role play, the salesperson and sales manager should discuss the salesperson's presentation and record ideas for improvement in the plan and presentation of the plan.

4. This exercise is designed to expose you to differences in compensation and motivation across salespeople and companies. Interview three salespeople (in person or via telephone or the Internet) from three companies. Provide a brief report for each salesperson indicating gender, age, experience, company, industry, compensation method, financial and nonfinancial compensation rewards, and what each believes motivates him or her to perform. Then write a summary paragraph that points to similarities and differences among the three and why these might exist. Finally, of the three, whose compensation plan would interest you the most and why?

5. Ashley Dillon, sales manager for PayWell, an automated payroll processing company, is attempting to foster teamwork in her salesforce. In particular, new salespeople often struggle to establish a customer base, and many leave their jobs during their first year of employment. PayWell compensates its sales trainees on a salary basis for three months, after which they are switched to a straight commission basis. Ashley knows that her successful senior salespeople could provide guidance to the younger salespeople, but the senior salespeople are reluctant to spend time on anything but selling. As one of the senior representatives told Ashley, "I would like to help the rookies out, but if I am not in front of customers, my commissions will drop." How can Ashley accommodate both rookie and senior salespeople to improve overall salesforce effectiveness?

6. Conduct a search using the Internet (or search for articles by some other means) to locate various incentives that might be offered to a salesforce. Explain at least three different specific incentives (e.g., an African safari trip) that could be offered to a salesforce, when and why each might be offered, and how good a motivator each might be. Attach the information that you found on the incentives to your write-up.

7. **Role Play**

   Situation: Read An Ethical Dilemma on p. 237.

   Characters: Jeri Snider, salesperson; Jeri's sales manager.

   Scene: *Location*—Sales manager's office. *Action*—Jeri's sales manager confronts her regarding meal expenses that he believes Jeri falsified on her expense report.

ROLE PLAY

MAKING SALES MANAGEMENT DECISIONS

CASE 8.1: CENTRAL ELECTRICAL SOLUTIONS

Background

Central Electrical Solutions is a market leader in the residential and commercial construction market, providing computer-controlled interfaces that allow homeowners and property managers to manage their electrical systems in an economical fashion. The company's salesforce is highly experienced, and is noted for its ability to develop sophisticated technical solutions for its customers.

Current Situation

Vince Elder, Central's sales manager, is contemplating the upcoming fourth quarter of the fiscal year and realizes he has two critical issues to deal with if Central is to meet its annual growth objectives. First, Vince has been comparing the performance of Central's top 20 key accounts this year as compared to last year. He discovered that as a group, the top 20 accounts were ahead of last year's sales figures by an impressive 15 percent. However, when he analyzed the data more closely, he found that two of the top 20 accounts were at 80 percent of last year's year-to-date sales levels. Both of the lagging accounts were in Mark Wilkerson's territory. Mark was a perennial leader among Central's senior salespeople, and his key account performance was definitely a cause for concern. Vince Elder had been aware of Mark's lackluster performance this year, and they had discussed the issue a couple of months ago, when Mark assured Vince that he would finish the year strong. Earlier today, Vince and Mark reviewed the key account situation again, and Vince came away with an uneasy feeling. He values Mark as an opinion leader among fellow salespeople and especially needed his support in introducing Central's new mobile application for its control system that would allow customers to manage electrical consumption anywhere and anytime. As Vince replayed the meeting with Mark in his head, he recalled this dialogue:

Vince: So, Mark, I really need you to bear down the fourth quarter and bring those two key accounts in over last year's sales levels.

Mark: I understand, Vince, and I will do what I can. This has been a tough year for me personally, and I think I may just need to catch my breath and get ready for next year. That knee replacement operation slowed me down a bit, and frankly, it sapped my energy for a while. My commissions are holding up OK, so I should be alright.

Vince: Mark, you became a sales leader for Central through working hard and working smart. I just hope you don't lose the edge. Are you still as hungry as you used to be?

Mark: Vince, we go back too far for you to ask a question like that. Of course I am just as hungry as ever! But I am a human being too, and right now I just need a little slack.

Vince: I just want you to reach your full potential. And I need you to help champion the roll-out of the new mobile application. You have got to help the rest of the salesforce take the mobile app over the top.

Mark: Maybe you need to find another champion. I think I'd better concentrate on getting my own act together. If we are done here, I need to get out and make some key account calls.

Questions

1. How do you suggest Elder handle Wilkerson?
2. Assess the possibility of Wilkerson becoming a champion for the roll-out of the mobile application. Is this a good idea?

Role Play

Situation: Read Case 8.1.

Characters: Vince Elder, Central Electrical Solutions sales manager, Mark Wilkerson, senior sales representative.

Scene 1: *Location*—Vince Elder's office. *Action*—Elder is unhappy with the way his last meeting with Wilkerson ended. He wants to keep pushing Wilkerson to improve his performance, but wants to do so in a positive way. Elder is meeting with Wilkerson to talk things over and hopefully move in a positive direction. Wilkerson is somewhat defensive, but has an open mind about how to proceed.

Scene 2: *Location*—Vince Elder's office. *Action*—It is year-end and Wilkerson has returned to form as a top sales representative. Unfortunately, Wilkerson seems to resent the extra pressure applied by Elder and now seems totally focused on maximizing total sales volume and thus his commissions. Before the meeting, Wilkerson tells Elder: "I am a selling machine. Spare me the rah-rah and don't ask me to be a cheerleader for any new product roll-outs." Elder doesn't like Wilkerson's current attitude, and he is determined to retain Wilkerson as a positive member of the salesforce. Elder is thinking about how noncommission rewards might be used in this case. Elder has called this meeting to lay out a plan of action and get Wilkerson's buy-in. Elder is also feeling that it will be important for him to assert his control over the situation.

CASE 8.2: RITE-WAY CLEANING PRODUCTS
Background
Rite-Way Cleaning Products has been manufacturing and selling household floor cleaning products for more than 60 years. The company offers several brands that can be used to clean a variety of floor surfaces. It stands behind all its products with a "customer satisfaction guarantee." Any consumer who is not fully satisfied with the floor cleaner on applying it properly may return it to the place of purchase and receive a refund or have the product replaced with another of equal value.

Rite-Way's products are distributed in a variety of outlets, ranging from small grocery and convenience stores to big-box stores such as Wal-Mart and Home Depot. Each customer is highly valued regardless of size. According to the company's founder, James Wyatt, "Every customer should be treated as if they are our only customer." For this reason, the company takes pride in establishing long-term customer relationships. In fact, several of the company's current customers have been distributing its products since the company was founded. The company's salesforce was built around this idea and to this day is well noted for its commitment to building strong and satisfying customer relationships.

Current Situation
Ed Riddle, Rite-Way's national sales manager, recently asked regional sales manager John Capps to coordinate a special fourth-quarter sales push to achieve projected year-end sales goals. Capps, a committed sales manager, was confident he could develop a program that would succeed. He thought a sales contest would be an excellent way to boost fourth-quarter sales in his region. By developing a

contest, he could avoid altering the current compensation package, which he believed to be satisfactory to his salespeople.

Capps has 100 salespeople in his region, about 20 percent of whom are women. The region is divided into five districts, each comprised of 20 salespeople. Rather than have all 100 salespeople compete against each other, Capps decided to have five winners, one for each district. Salespeople within each district would compete against each other, and the salesperson with the highest number of sales during the contest period would be declared the winner.

Capps recently heard about a new approach being taken by some companies to motivate their salespeople. Contest winners were awarded a trip to a fantasy baseball camp. Award winners spent a week with baseball legends who taught and coached them. The award proved to be a highly successful motivator. Capps liked this idea and decided to offer this trip to each district winner as the prize for winning the sales contest. Capps contacted the company's marketing communications group to ask them to design a set of promotional materials to be distributed to each salesperson. He then visited each district, explaining the contest rules to its salespeople. At the same time, he delivered pep talks. "Each of you has an equal chance at victory. Now is the time to seize the moment and go for the gold!"

After all the preplanning was completed, the contest finally went into effect. Most salespeople realized that they could increase their sales either by selling more to current customers or by finding new accounts. One method for increasing sales to current customers was to help them with merchandising so that they could sell more product. This seemed to work well for many salespeople. However, several concentrated on their large customers at the expense of their smaller accounts. The larger customers had much more potential and the input-to-output ratio with these customers had a much higher payoff. Several salespeople's obsession with their larger accounts got in the way of providing their smaller customers with the service they had come to expect. Some customers even threatened to take their business elsewhere. In fact, Ray's Groceries, a small but long-standing customer, was so upset with the decline in service that it dropped Rite-Way as a supplier.

Numerous salespeople got wise to the idea that they could increase their sales by loading their customers with product toward the end of the contest period. Some salespeople asked customers to purchase and take delivery of their next scheduled order early. Others offered customers special incentives if they agreed to order more product than usual. One salesperson went so far as to offer a small kickback.

In an attempt to gain new customers, some salespeople took on customers that were poor credit risks. For instance, salesman Lynn Smith knew a medium-sized hardware store in his territory was in financial trouble, so much so that the store had lost its paint supplier because of its inability to pay. Lynn figured he could enhance his sales during the contest period by taking the customer's order. If the customer was unable to pay, it would not show up until after the contest was over, and Lynn would already have these sales added to his total for the period.

About one-third of the way into the contest, Earl Jones, a sales rep in district 3, was able to land a new major account, which meant a tremendous increase in sales for him. At that point, the other salespeople in his district seemed to lose enthusiasm for the contest. As Don Eastman put it, "I don't stand a prayer of winning the contest now. The only way I would have a chance is to land a similar account. Given my present territory, that is impossible. Earl has this contest wrapped up. He might as well grab his mitt and pack his bags—he's heading for fantasy baseball camp." As the contest was drawing to a close, Capps noticed that sales had not increased nearly as much as he had anticipated. Moreover, most of the women in the salesforce did not significantly increase their sales figures. In fact, they were about the same as usual. Capps knew Riddle would want a full assessment of the contest on its completion. As he sat at his desk, he began to think about what went wrong.

Questions

1. How would you evaluate this contest? What are its pros and cons?

2. How could this contest be designed to have a better chance of success?

Role Play

Situation: Read Case 8.2.

Characters: Ed Riddle, national sales manager; John Capps, regional sales manager: Lynn Smith, salesperson.

Scene 1:   *Location*—John Capps's office. *Action*—Capps got word of Lynn Smith's tactic of taking on customers with questionable credit risk during the contest period. He is meeting with Lynn to discuss these tactics.

Scene 2:   *Location*—Ed Riddle's office. *Action*—Ed Riddle is meeting with John Capps to get a recap of his sales contest. Capps explains the pros and cons of the contest. Riddle then provides some advice for developing a sales contest in the future.

ROLE PLAY

Determining Salesforce Effectiveness and Performance

The two chapters in Part 5 focus on determining salesforce effectiveness and performance. Chapter 9 addresses the evaluation of sales organization effectiveness. Methods for analyzing sales, costs, profitability, and productivity at different sales organization levels are reviewed. Chapter 10 addresses the evaluation of salespeople's individual performance and job satisfaction. Ways of determining the appropriate performance criteria and methods of evaluation, and of using the evaluations to improve salesperson performance and job satisfaction, are discussed.

EVALUATING THE
EFFECTIVENESS OF THE
ORGANIZATION

OBJECTIVES

After completing this chapter, you should be able to

1. Differentiate between sales organization effectiveness and salesperson performance.

2. Define a sales organization audit and discuss how it should be conducted.

3. Describe how to perform different methods of sales analysis for different organizational levels and different types of sales.

4. Describe how to perform a cost analysis for a sales organization.

5. Describe how to perform an income statement analysis, activity-based costing, and return on assets managed to assess sales organization profitability.

6. Describe how to perform a productivity analysis for a sales organization.

7. Define benchmarking and Six Sigma and discuss how each should be conducted.

ACTIONABLE SALES DIAGNOSTICS: THE KEY TO EFFECTIVELY EVALUATING SALES ORGANIZATION PERFORMANCE

Sales management is responsible for more than simply coordinating and managing individual salespeople. Sales teams and individual salespeople depend on sales management seeing and understanding the big picture, assessing current strategies, and evaluating new sales opportunities. Matt Sunshine, managing partner for The Center for Sales Strategies and a sales professional with over 20 years' experience in sales and sales management, emphasizes the importance of regular and thorough sales audits that enable leaders to see their operations from all sides—a perspective that can identify bottlenecks and keep revenues climbing.

Sunshine observes that these diagnostic audits must go beyond the sales department to look at the whole company. "Sales-driven companies need every department working in the same direction, and when issues arise outside the sales team, diagnostics can identify hard-to-find issues and contribute to correcting them." Sunshine emphasizes that effective audits should follow two guidelines from established best-practice reviews applicable to virtually all business sectors. First, organizational audits require more than just a casual review. They must focus on each of the key indicators of an organization's health and well-being. These indicators include: *revenue metrics*—everything from sales dollars to margins to order sizes to product popularity matters; *competitive position*—what the organization does well contrasted with where competitors typically win; *internal structure and sales support resources*—identify and assess the capabilities of the organization in terms of enabling and supporting goals achievement; *performance metrics*—determine how the organization measures performance and the level of performance on each metric; and *customer service*—documenting and evaluating what customers are telling the organization is critical for long term success and understanding where in the organization the positive as well as the not-so-positive customer contacts are occurring.

Sunshine's second guideline is to effectively collect and analyze data across each of these areas following a three-step process to (1) recognize successes and discover roadblocks; (2) detail the observations coming from the data and diagnostics; and (3) develop recommendations for improvement. Based on his 20 years' experience, Sunshine stresses the importance of keeping the sales audit process and diagnostics actionable. "Every part of the audit process is important, but it's easy to get lost in the weeds and fail to make actionable recommendations. When sales leaders get too close to the process, they often overlook the data in favor of instinct, which can lead to wasted opportunities." He recommends incorporating these four strategies to make the most of the sales audit: keep recommendations realistic; move quickly—windows of opportunity do not remain open indefinitely; set measureable goals; and review the progress every 90 days.

Source: Matt Sunshine, "5 Steps to a Precise Internal Sales Diagnostic," *Sales & Marketing Management* (February 9, 2018), https://salesandmarketing.com/content/5-steps-precise-internal-sales-diagnostic, accessed September 7, 2018.

Assessing the success of a sales organization is difficult because so many factors must be considered. For example, the success of the sales organization must be differentiated from the success of individual salespeople (see Figure 9.1).[1] Whereas sales organization effectiveness is a function of how well the sales organization achieved its goals and objectives overall, salesperson performance is a function of how well each salesperson performed in his or her particular situation. Thus, salesperson performance contributes to, but does not completely determine, sales organization effectiveness.

FIGURE 9.1   **Sales Organization Effectiveness**

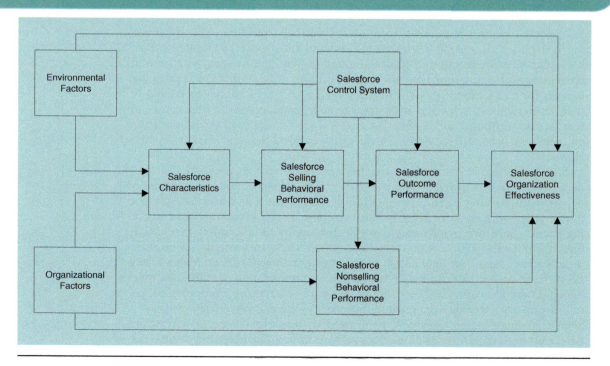

As illustrated in Matt Sunshine's discussion of the role and importance of effective sales organization audits in the opening vignette, the organizational sales audit provides sales managers with an effective tool for identifying and evaluating the capabilities of the sales unit and for guiding the development of sales strategies and action plans. The focus of the organization's evaluation is on the overall sales organization—including management levels which comprise the organization: districts, regions, territories, and individual salespeople. As emphasized by Matt Sunshine, the results from sales organization audit should be actionable and lead to strategic actions and policy changes designed to improve sales effectiveness and performance.

Evaluations of salesperson performance are confined to the individuals, not the sales organization or sales organization levels. The results of these evaluations are typically tactical. In other words, they lead a sales manager to take specific actions to improve the performance of an individual salesperson. Generally, different actions are warranted for different salespeople, depending on the areas that need improvement.

Evidence for the difference between sales organization effectiveness and salesperson performance is provided in a study of 144 sales organizations in the United States. A comparison of the more-effective and less-effective sales organizations indicated that those that were more effective had achieved much better results in many areas, compared with their less effective counterparts. For example, the more effective sales organizations generated much higher sales per salesperson ($3,988,000 versus $1,755,000) and much lower selling expenses as a percentage of sales (13 percent versus 18 percent) than the less effective sales organizations. The salespeople in the more effective organizations also outperformed salespeople in the less effective ones in several areas. However, the differences in salesperson performance were not sufficient to completely explain the differences in sales organization effectiveness. Thus, sales organization effectiveness is the result of salesperson performance as well as many other factors (e.g., sales organization structure and deployment and sales management performance).[2]

This chapter addresses the evaluation of sales organization effectiveness, and Chapter 10 addresses the evaluation of salesperson performance. Chapter 9 begins with a discussion of a sales organization audit and then describes more specific analyses of sales, costs, profits, and productivity to determine sales organization effectiveness. This is followed by a discussion of how benchmarking and Six Sigma can be used to improve sales organization effectiveness.

SALES ORGANIZATION AUDIT

Although the term *audit* is most often used in reference to financial audits performed by accounting firms, the audit concept has been extended to business functions in recent years. In Chapter 6, a **sales organization audit** was described as a comprehensive, systematic, diagnostic, and prescriptive tool. The purpose of a sales organization audit is to assess the adequacy of a firm's sales management process and to provide direction for improved performance and prescription for needed changes. It is a tool that should be used by all firms whether or not they are achieving their goals. This type of audit is the most comprehensive approach for evaluating sales organization effectiveness.

A framework for performing a sales organization audit is presented in Figure 9.2.[3] As indicated in the figure, the audit addresses four major areas: sales organization environment, sales management evaluation, sales organization planning system, and sales management functions. The purpose of the audit is to investigate, systematically and comprehensively, each of these areas to identify existing or potential problems, determine their causes, and take the necessary corrective actions. For example, after having an agency conduct an audit, Guinness was able to redesign its salesforce to improve its structure and clarity. This resulted in a more motivated, focused, efficient, and subsequently higher-performing sales organization.[4]

The sales organization audit should be performed regularly, not just when problems are evident. One of the major values of an audit is its generation of diagnostic information

FIGURE 9.2   Sales Organization Audit Framework

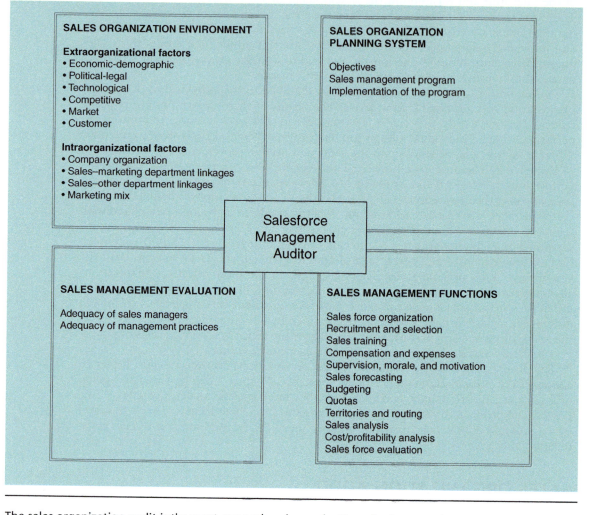

SALES ORGANIZATION ENVIRONMENT

Extraorganizational factors
• Economic-demographic
• Political-legal
• Technological
• Competitive
• Market
• Customer

Intraorganizational factors
• Company organization
• Sales–marketing department linkages
• Sales–other department linkages
• Marketing mix

SALES ORGANIZATION PLANNING SYSTEM

Objectives
Sales management program
Implementation of the program

Salesforce Management Auditor

SALES MANAGEMENT EVALUATION

Adequacy of sales managers
Adequacy of management practices

SALES MANAGEMENT FUNCTIONS

Sales force organization
Recruitment and selection
Sales training
Compensation and expenses
Supervision, morale, and motivation
Sales forecasting
Budgeting
Quotas
Territories and routing
Sales analysis
Cost/profitability analysis
Sales force evaluation

The sales organization audit is the most comprehensive evaluation of sales organization effectiveness. The audit typically provides assessments of the sales organization environment, sales management evaluation, sales organization planning system, and sales management functions.

that can help management correct problems in early stages or eliminate potential problems before they become serious. Because auditing should be objective, it should be conducted by someone from outside the sales organization. This could be someone from another functional area within the firm or an outside consulting firm.

Although outsiders should conduct the audit, members of the sales organization should be active participants. Sales managers and salespeople provide much of the information collected. Exhibit 9.1[5] presents sample questions that should be addressed in a sales organization audit. Answers typically come from members of the sales organization and from company records.

Although obviously an expensive and time-consuming process, the sales organization audit usually generates benefits that outweigh the monetary and time costs. Potential benefits resulting from an audit include, among others, increases in productivity, and sales and profits due to improvements and efficiencies in sales operations and management. This is especially true when audits are conducted regularly because the chances of identifying and correcting potential problems before they become troublesome increase with the regularity of the auditing process.

Sample Questions from a Sales Organization Audit   EXHIBIT 9.1

IV. SALES MANAGEMENT FUNCTIONS

A. Salesforce Organization

1. How is our salesforce organized (by product, by customer, by territory)?
2. Is this type of organization appropriate, given the current intraorganizational and extraorganizational conditions?
3. Does this type of organization adequately service the needs of our customers?

B. Recruitment and Selection

1. How many salespeople do we have?
2. Is this number adequate in light of our objectives and resources?
3. Are we serving our customers adequately with this number of salespeople?
4. How is our salesforce size determined?
5. What is our turnover rate? What have we done to try to change it?
6. Do we have adequate sources from which to obtain recruits? Have we overlooked some possible sources?
7. Do we have a job description for each of our sales jobs? Is each job description current?
8. Have we enumerated the necessary sales job qualifications? Have they been recently updated? Are they predictive of sales success?
9. Are our selection screening procedures financially feasible and appropriate?
10. Do we use a battery of psychological tests in our selection process? Are the tests valid and reliable?
11. Do our recruitment and selection procedures satisfy employment opportunity guidelines?

C. Sales Training

1. How is our sales training program developed? Does it meet the needs of management and sales personnel?
2. Do we establish training objectives before developing and implementing the training program?
3. Is the training program adequate in light of our objectives and resources?
4. What kinds of training do we currently provide our salespeople?
5. Does the training program need revising? What areas of the training program should be improved or deemphasized?
6. What methods do we use to evaluate the effectiveness of our training program?
7. Can we afford to train internally or should we use external sources for training?
8. Do we have an ongoing training program for senior salespeople? Is it adequate?

D. Compensation and Expenses

1. Does our sales compensation plan meet our objectives in light of our financial resources?
2. Is the compensation plan fair, flexible, economical, and easy to understand and administer?
3. What is the level of compensation, the type of plan, and the frequency of payment?
4. Are the salespeople and management satisfied with the compensation plan?
5. Does the compensation plan ensure that the salespeople perform the necessary sales job activities?
6. Does the compensation plan attract and retain enough quality sales performers?
7. Does the sales expense plan meet our objectives in light of our financial resources?
8. Is the expense plan fair, flexible, and easy to administer? Does it allow for geographical, customer, and/or product differences?
9. Does the expense plan ensure that the necessary sales job activities are performed?
10. Can we easily audit the expenses incurred by our sales personnel?

SALES ORGANIZATION EFFECTIVENESS EVALUATIONS

There is no one summary measure of sales organization effectiveness. Sales organizations have multiple goals and objectives, and thus, multiple factors must be assessed. As illustrated in Figure 9.3, four types of analyses are typically necessary to develop a comprehensive evaluation of any sales organization. Conducting analyses in each of these areas is a complex task for two reasons. First, many types of analyses can be performed to evaluate sales, cost, profitability, and productivity results. For example, a sales analysis might focus on total sales, sales of specific products, sales to specific customers, or other types of sales and might include sales comparisons to sales quotas, to previous periods, to sales of competitors, or other types of analyses. Second, separate sales analyses need to be performed for the different levels in the sales organization. Thus, a typical evaluation would include separate sales analyses for sales zones, regions, districts, and territories.

The results from one study on methods used to measure salesforce effectiveness are presented in Exhibit 9.2.[6] While many sales organizations focus on sales analysis, customer satisfaction is also heavily relied upon to determine sales organization effectiveness. This involves surveying customers to determine their level of satisfaction with the company's products, service, and salespeople, among other things. For a look at how Epic Industrial Equipment incorporates assessments of customer satisfaction into their assessment of sales organization effectiveness, see "Sales Management in the 21st Century: Epic Industrial Equipment's Evaluation of the Sales Organization includes Customer Inputs." Determining the level of customer satisfaction has become easier due to the Internet. Companies such as Maritz-CX (https://maritzcx.com) and NetReflector (www.netreflector.com) will create and administer Web-based customer satisfaction surveys for firms. Now we discuss how sales, cost, profitability, and productivity analyses can be conducted to evaluate sales organization effectiveness.

Sales Analysis

Because the basic purpose of a sales organization is to generate sales, **sales analysis** is an obvious and important element of evaluating sales organization effectiveness. The difficulty, however, is in determining exactly what should be analyzed. One key consideration is in defining what is meant by a *sale*. Definitions include a placed order, a shipped order, and a paid order. Defining a sale by when an order is shipped is probably most common.

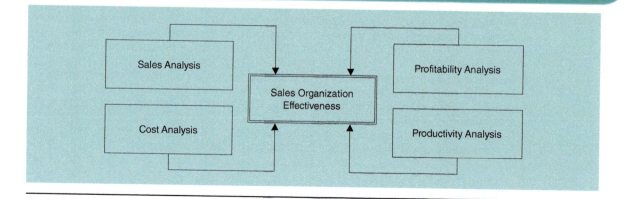

FIGURE 9.3   **Sales Organization Effectiveness Framework**

Evaluating sales organization effectiveness requires analyses of sales, cost, profitability, and productivity. Each type of analysis can be performed in several ways, should be performed at different sales organization levels, and will produce unique evaluative and diagnostic information for sales managers.

Methods Used to Measure Salesforce Effectiveness	EXHIBIT 9.2

	Percent Using
Sales results versus goal	79
Customer satisfaction	59
Profit versus goal	49
Sales manager feedback	45
Market share	39
Cost of sales	37
Sales employee feedback	28
Return on investment of sales resources	21
Other	9

SALES MANAGEMENT IN THE 21ST CENTURY

Epic Industrial Equipment's Evaluation of the Sales Organization includes Customer Inputs

Eric Nall, District Sales Manager for Epic Industrial Equipment, discusses the company's regular utilization of comprehensive sales organization audits to drive sales performance, build high-levels of customer satisfaction, and generate unmatched competitive advantage in their business sectors.

Epic Industrial is a big believer in the power of results coming from evaluations of the sales organization—a significant undertaking that is conducted annually. Similar to most sales audits, Epic's model is pretty comprehensive and gathers data along with qualitative inputs across all functions and levels of the organization. And the data *is not limited to just accounting and financial results. Structured on the 360 Assessment format, we also derive inputs from all parties to the sales process—salespeople, management, billing, finance, shipping, production, research and development, and especially our customers. The target of the evaluation is to identify what we are doing well, detail how and where we can improve, and discover untapped opportunities going forward. This level of detail in the analyses keeps us in close contact with our entire team and with our customers allowing us to better manage and deploy our sales assets across the organization and in the field. Insightful and actionable information and knowledge enabling Epic Industrial to maintain its leadership position in a highly competitive business sector.*

Regardless of the definition used, the sales organization must be consistent and develop an information system to track sales based on whatever sales definition is used.

Another consideration is whether to focus on *sales dollars* or *sales units*. This can be extremely important during times when prices increase or when salespeople have substantial latitude in negotiating selling prices. The sales information in Exhibit 9.3 illustrates how different conclusions may result from analyses of sales dollars or sales units. If just sales dollars are analyzed, all regions in the exhibit would appear to be generating substantial sales growth. However, when sales units are introduced, the dollar sales growth for all regions in 2018 can be attributed almost entirely to price increases, because units sold increased only minimally during this period. The situation is somewhat different in 2019, because all regions significantly increased the number of units sold. However, sales volume for region 2 is relatively flat, even though units sold increased. This could be caused either by selling more lower-priced products or by using larger price concessions than the other regions. In either case, analysis of sales dollars or sales units provides different evaluative information, so it is often useful to include both dollars and units in a sales analysis.

EXHIBIT 9.3   Sales Dollars versus Sales Units

	2017		2018		2019	
	Sales Dollars	**Sales Units**	**Sales Dollars**	**Sales Units**	**Sales Dollars**	**Sales Units**
Region 1	$50,000,000	500,000	$55,000,000	510,000	$62,000,000	575,000
Region 2	$55,000,000	550,000	$60,000,000	560,000	$62,000,000	600,000
Region 3	$45,000,000	450,000	$50,000,000	460,000	$56,000,000	520,000
Region 4	$60,000,000	600,000	$65,000,000	610,000	$73,000,000	720,000

Given a definition of sales and a decision concerning sales dollars versus units, many types of sales evaluations can be performed. Several alternative evaluations are presented in Figure 9.4. The critical decision areas are the organizational level of analysis, the type of sales, and the method of analysis.

Organizational Level of Analysis

Sales analyses should be performed for all levels in the sales organization for two basic reasons. First, sales managers at each level need sales analyses at their level and the next level below for evaluation and control purposes. For example, a regional sales manager should have sales analyses for all regions as well as for all districts within his or her region. This makes it possible to assess the sales effectiveness of the region and to determine the sales contribution of each district.

Second, a useful way to identify problem areas in achieving sales effectiveness is to perform a **hierarchical sales analysis,** which consists of evaluating sales results

FIGURE 9.4   **Sales Analysis Framework**

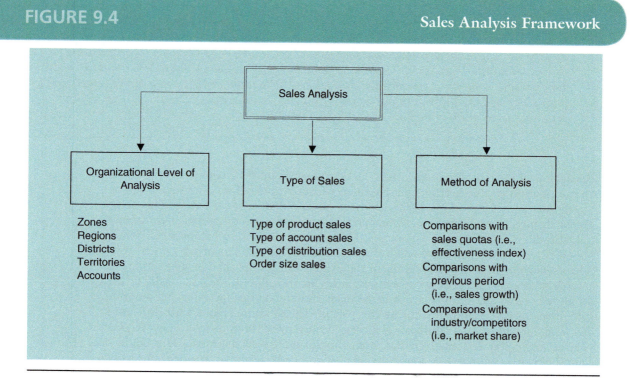

A sales analysis can be performed at a number of organizational levels and for many types of sales, and can use several methods of analysis.

throughout the sales organization from a top-down perspective. Essentially, the analysis begins with total sales for the sales organization and proceeds through each successively lower level in the sales organization. The emphasis is on identifying potential problem areas at each level and then using analyses at lower levels to pinpoint the specific problems. An example of a hierarchical sales analysis is presented in Figure 9.5.

In this example, sales for region 3 appear to be much lower than those for the other regions, so the analysis proceeds to investigate the sales for all the districts in region 3. Low sales are identified for district 4; then district 4 sales are analyzed by territory. The results of this analysis suggest potential sales problems within territory 5. Additional analyses would be performed to determine why sales are so low for territory 5 and to take corrective action to increase sales from this territory. The hierarchical approach to sales analysis provides an efficient way to conduct a sales analysis and to identify major areas of sales problems.

Type of Sales

The analysis in Figure 9.5 addresses only total firm sales at each organizational level. It is usually desirable to evaluate several types of sales, such as by the following categories:

- product type or specific products
- account type or specific accounts
- type of distribution method
- order size

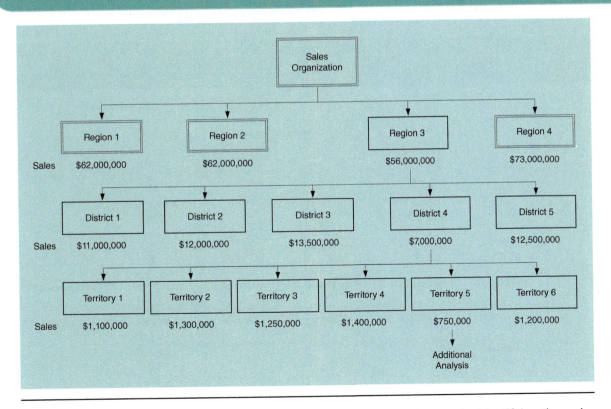

Example of Hierarchical Sales Analysis   **FIGURE 9.5**

This multistage analysis proceeds from one sales organization level to the next by identifying the major deviations and investigating them in more detail at the next lower level. In the present example, region 3 has the lowest sales, so all districts in region 3 are examined. District 4 has poor sales results, so all the territories in district 4 are examined. Additional analysis is indicated for territory 5.

The hierarchical analysis in Figure 9.5 could have included sales by product type, account type, or other type of sales at each level. Or, once the potential sales problem in territory 5 has been isolated, analysis of different types of sales could be performed to define the sales problem more fully. An example analysis is presented in Figure 9.6. This example suggests especially low sales volume for product type A and account type B. Additional analyses within these product and account types would be needed to determine why sales are low in these areas and what needs to be done to improve sales effectiveness.

The analysis of different types of sales at different organizational levels increases management's ability to detect and define problem areas in sales performance. However, incorporating different sales types into the analysis complicates the evaluation process and requires an information system capable of providing sales data concerning the desired breakdowns. "Sales Management in the 21st Century: Diversified Product Types Require Changed Sales Structure at Pfizer" illustrates the growing complexity of sales organizations consisting of diverse product types, multiple types of accounts, and specialized salesforces.

Method of Analysis

The discussion to this point has focused on the actual sales results for different organizational levels and types of sales. However, the use of actual sales results limits the analysis to comparisons across organizational levels or sales types. These within-organization comparisons provide some useful information but are insufficient for a comprehensive evaluation of sales effectiveness. Several additional types of analysis are recommended and presented in Exhibit 9.4.

Comparing actual sales results with sales forecasts and quotas is extremely revealing. A *sales forecast* represents an expected level of firm sales for defined products, markets, and time periods and for a specified strategy. Based on this definition, a sales forecast provides a basis for establishing specific *sales quotas* and reasonable sales objectives for a territory, district, region, or zone (methods for establishing sales quotas are discussed in

FIGURE 9.6   Example of Type-of-Sales Analysis by Product and Account Type

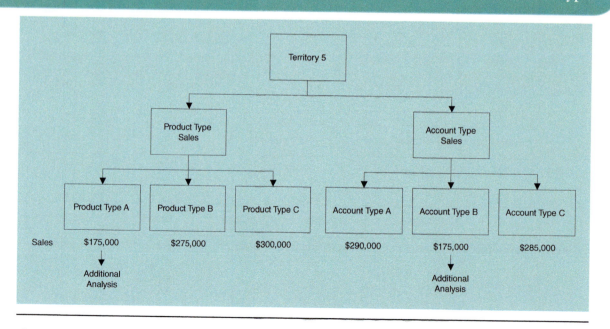

This is a continuation of the hierarchical sales analysis presented in Figure 9.5. Sales in territory 5 are analyzed by product type and account type. The analysis suggests poor sales results for product type A and account type B.

SALES MANAGEMENT IN THE 21ST CENTURY

Pfizer's Sales Structure is driven by Highly Diversified Product Types

Chris Aiken, Certified Medical Representative and Senior Professional Healthcare Representative with Pfizer, Inc. discusses the diversified portfolio of product types and increasingly complex sales organization structure at Pfizer.

Pfizer continues to move beyond a reliance on a few blockbuster medicines to a more diversified portfolio. Our global portfolio includes medicines and vaccines, as well as many of the world's best-known consumer health care products. The company has developed clear strategies and established individual business units accountable for each of these product types which include a science-based Innovative Medicines business which will now include biosimilars and a new hospital business unit for anti-infectives and sterile injectables; an off-patent branded and generic Established Medicines business operating

with substantial autonomy within Pfizer and a Consumer Healthcare business. This changed sales structure has created a company characterized by increased accountability, speed, agility, and ability to keep commitments to stakeholders by making profitable business decisions that mutually benefit our sales organization while maintaining a renewed focus on our patients.

The sales organization incorporates each of these core business types with each business type having a sales executive with clear accountability for results and charged with managing multiple levels of geographic territories and product groups. With this sales organization structure, we are able to rapidly capitalize on opportunities to advance our business by increasing support for successful new medicines, forging partnerships with key customers, entering into co-promotion and licensing agreements, investing in new technologies to add value to our core product offerings, and acquiring new products and services from outside the company.

Method of Analysis Examples   EXHIBIT 9.4

	District 1	District 2	District 3	District 4	District 5
Sales	$11,000,000	$12,000,000	$13,000,000	$7,000,000	$12,000,000
Sales quota	$11,250,000	$11,500,000	$12,750,000	$10,000,000	$11,000,000
Effectiveness index	98	104	102	70	109
Sales last year	$10,700,000	$11,000,000	$12,250,000	$6,800,000	$10,350,000
Sales growth	3%	9%	6%	3%	16%
Industry sales	$42,000,000	$42,000,000	$45,000,000	$40,000,000	$45,000,000
Market share	26%	29%	29%	18%	27%

Chapter 10). An **effectiveness index** can be computed by dividing actual sales results by the sales quota and multiplying by 100. As illustrated in Exhibit 9.4, sales results in excess of quota will have index values greater than 100, and results lower than quota will have index values less than 100. The sales effectiveness index makes it easy to compare directly the sales effectiveness of different organizational levels and different types of sales.

Another type of useful analysis is the comparison of actual results to previous periods (i.e., sales growth). As illustrated in Exhibit 9.4, this type of analysis can be used to determine sales growth rates for different organizational levels and for different sales types. Incorporating sales data for many periods makes it possible to assess long-term sales trends.

A final type of analysis to be considered is a comparison of actual sales results to those achieved by competitors (i.e., market share). This type of analysis can again be performed at different organizational levels and for different types of sales. If the comparison is extended to overall industry sales, various types of market share can be calculated. Examples of these comparisons are presented in Exhibit 9.4.

Sales analysis is the approach used most often for evaluating sales organization effectiveness. Sales data are typically more readily available than other data types, and sales results are extremely important to sales organizations. However, developing a sales analysis approach that will produce the desired evaluative information is a complex undertaking. Sales data must be available for different organizational levels and for different types of sales. Valid sales forecasts are needed to establish sales quotas for evaluating sales effectiveness in achieving sales objectives. In addition, industry and competitor sales information is also useful. Regardless of the comprehensiveness of the sales analysis, sales organizations need to perform additional analyses to evaluate sales organization effectiveness adequately.

Cost Analysis

A second major element in the evaluation of sales organization effectiveness is **cost analysis**. The emphasis here is on assessing the costs incurred by the sales organization to generate the achieved levels of sales. The general approach is to compare the costs incurred with planned costs as defined by selling budgets.

Corporate resources earmarked for personal selling expenses for a designated period represent the total **selling budget**. The key sales management budgeting task is to determine the best way to allocate these sales resources throughout the sales organization and across the different selling activities. The budgeting process is intended to instill cost consciousness and profit awareness throughout the organization, and it is necessary for establishing benchmarks for evaluating selling costs.

Selling budgets are developed at all levels of the sales organization and for all key expenditure categories. Our discussion focuses on the major selling expense categories and methods for establishing specific expenditure levels within the budget.

Firms differ considerably in how they define their selling expense categories. Nevertheless, all sales organizations should plan expenditures carefully for the major selling and sales management activities and for the different levels in the sales organization structure. The selling budget addresses controllable expenses, not uncontrollable ones. Typical selling budget expense categories are presented in Exhibit 9.5.

Both the total expenditures for each of these categories and sales management budget responsibility must be determined. Sales management budget responsibility depends on

---

EXHIBIT 9.5   Typical Selling Expense Categories in the Budget

Classification	Actual 2019	Original 2020 Budget	2nd Quarter Revision	3rd Quarter Revision	4th Quarter Revision
Compensation expenses					
Salaries					
Commissions					
Bonuses					
Total					
Travel expenses					
Lodging					
Food					
Transportation					
Miscellaneous					
Total					
Administrative expenses					
Recruiting					
Training					
Meetings					
Sales offices					
Total					

the degree of centralization or decentralization in the sales organization. In general, more centralized sales organizations will place budget responsibility at higher sales management levels. For example, if salesforce recruitment and selection take place at the regional level, then the regional sales managers will have responsibility for this budget category. Typically, the sales management activity occurs at all management levels. For example, training activities might be performed at national, zone, regional, and district levels. In this case, the budgeting process must address how much to spend on overall training and how to allocate training expenditures to the organizational levels.

The basic objective in budgeting for each category is to determine the lowest expenditure level necessary to *achieve the sales quotas*. Notice that we did not say the lowest possible expenditure level. Sales managers might cut costs and improve profitability in the short run, but if expenditures for training, travel, and so forth are too low, long-run sales and profits will be sacrificed. However, if expenses can be reduced by more effective or more efficient spending, these productivity improvements can produce increased profitability in the long run. Achieving productivity improvements has been one of the most demanding tasks facing sales managers in recent years because increases in field selling costs and extremely competitive markets have put tremendous pressure on firm profitability.

Determining expenditure levels for each selling expense category is extremely difficult. Although there is no perfect way to arrive at these expenditure levels, two approaches warrant attention: the percentage of sales method and the objective and task method.

Probably the most often used, the **percentage of sales method** calculates an expenditure level for each category by multiplying an expenditure percentage times forecasted sales. The effectiveness of the percentage of sales method depends on the accuracy of sales forecasts and the appropriateness of the expenditure percentages. If the sales forecasts are not accurate, the selling budgets will be incorrect, regardless of the expenditure percentages used. If sales forecasts are accurate, the key is determining the expenditure percentages. This percentage may be derived from historical spending patterns or industry averages. Sales management should adjust the percentage up or down to reflect the unique aspects of their sales organization.

The **objective and task method** takes an entirely different approach. In its most basic form, it is a type of zero-based budgeting. In essence, each sales manager prepares a separate budget request that stipulates the objectives to be achieved, the tasks required to achieve these objectives, and the costs associated with performing the necessary tasks. These requests are reviewed, and, through an iterative process, selling budgets are approved. Many variations of the objective and task method are used by different sales organizations.

In reality, the process of establishing a selling budget is an involved one that typically incorporates various types of analysis, many meetings, and much political maneuvering. However, the process has been streamlined in many firms through the use of computer modeling to rapidly evaluate alternative selling budgets.

After a budget has been determined, cost analysis can be performed. Examples of two types of cost analysis are presented in Exhibit 9.6. The first analysis calculates the variance between actual costs and budgeted costs for the regions in a sales organization. Regions with the largest variation, especially when actual costs far exceed budgeted costs, should be highlighted for further analysis. Large variations are not necessarily bad, but the reasons for the variations should be determined. For example, the ultimate purpose of selling costs is to generate sales. Therefore, the objective is not necessarily to minimize selling costs, but to ensure that a specified relationship between sales and selling costs is maintained. Evaluate a common budgeting challenge that sales managers must deal with in "An Ethical Dilemma."

One way to evaluate this relationship is to calculate the selling costs as a percentage of sales achieved, and then compare this percentage to a budgeted expenditure percentage. Translating actual selling costs into percentages of sales achieved provides a means for assessing whether the cost-sales relationship has been maintained, even though the actual costs may exceed the absolute level in the selling budget. This situation is illustrated by region 4 in Exhibit 9.6, where actual compensation costs exceeded budgeted costs by $300,000, yet actual costs as a percentage of sales achieved (6 percent) were no more than the budgeted expenditure percentage (6 percent).

EXHIBIT 9.6   Cost Analysis Examples

	Compensation Costs			Training Costs		
	Actual Cost	Budgeted Cost	Variance	Actual Cost	Budgeted Cost	Variance
Region 1	$3,660,000	$3,600,000	+$60,000	$985,000	$1,030,000	−$45,000
Region 2	$3,500,000	$3,700,000	−$200,000	$2,110,000	$2,040,000	+$70,000
Region 3	$3,150,000	$3,400,000	−$250,000	$830,000	$1,060,000	−$230,000
Region 4	$4,200,000	$3,900,000	+$300,000	$2,340,000	$2,160,000	+$180,000

	Compensation Costs		Training Costs	
	Actual Cost as % of Sales Achieved	Budgeted Expenditure Percentage	Actual Cost as % of Sales Achieved	Budgeted Expenditure Percentage
Region 1	6.1	6	2.9	3
Region 2	5.8	6	3.1	3
Region 3	5.4	6	2.6	3
Region 4	6.0	6	3.1	3

AN ETHICAL DILEMMA

Allegiant Medical Systems just announced their new sales performance incentive system for the coming year. As designed, this program will offer opportunities for significant monetary bonuses to each of the company's 10 regional sales organizations based on the percentage which their individual region's actual sales revenues exceed the budgeted revenues for the year. Jane Blevins, sales manager for the Southwest Region, is a highly competitive and determined that her region will win the contest. Due to the substantial expansions of several hospital systems within the Southwest Region, Jane's sales team has potential for exceptional growth in the coming year. However, Jane and her sales team are considering a plan to better assure the region wins the incentive bonus. That plan will establish a sales budget for the next year that understates the forecasted sales in a way that will make the region's year-end sales performance

look substantially better than budgeted and provide her team with a stronger chance of winning the incentive contest.

What should Jane do?

a. Continue with the plan to establish a sales budget for the next year that understates forecasted sales in a way that will make her region's performance look substantially better.

b. Establish a sales budget based on an acceptable percentage increase over the preceding year, but one that does not unrealistically count the regional hospital expansions as certainty.

c. Establish a sales budget based on the total expected sales each of her salespeople forecasts for their individual sales territories.

Sales and cost analyses are the two most direct approaches for evaluating sales organization effectiveness. Profitability and productivity analyses extend the evaluation by assessing relationships between sales and costs. These analyses can be quite complex but may provide very useful information.

Profitability Analysis

Sales and cost data can be combined in various ways to produce evaluations of sales organization profitability for different organizational levels of different types of sales. This section covers three types of **profitability analysis**: income statement analysis, activity-based costing, and return on assets managed analysis.

Income Statement Analysis

The different levels in a sales organization and different types of sales can be considered as separate businesses. Consequently, income statements can be developed for profitability analysis. One of the major difficulties in **income statement analysis** is that some costs are shared between organizational levels or sales types.

Two approaches for dealing with the shared costs are illustrated in Exhibit 9.7. The **full cost approach** attempts to allocate the shared costs to individual units based on some type of cost allocation procedure. This results in a net profit figure for each unit. The **contribution approach** is different in that only direct costs are included in the profitability analysis; the indirect or shared costs are not included. The net contribution calculated from this approach represents the *profit contribution* of the unit being analyzed. This profit contribution must be sufficient to cover indirect costs and other overhead and to provide the net profit for the firm.

An example that incorporates both approaches is presented in Exhibit 9.8. This example uses the full cost approach for assessing sales region profitability and the

Full Cost versus Contribution Approaches   EXHIBIT 9.7

Full Cost Approach		Contribution Approach	
	Sales		Sales
Minus:	Cost of goods sold	Minus:	Cost of goods sold
	Gross margin		Gross margin
Minus:	Direct selling expenses	Minus:	Direct selling expenses
Minus:	Allocated portion of shared expenses		Profit contribution
	Net profit		

Profitability Analysis Example   EXHIBIT 9.8

	Full Cost Approach	Contribution Approach		
	Region	District 1	District 2	District 3
Sales	$300,000,000	$180,000,000	$70,000,000	$50,000,000
Cost of goods sold	$255,000,000	$168,500,000	$58,500,000	$28,000,000
Gross margin	$45,000,000	$11,500,000	$11,500,000	$22,000,000
District selling expenses	$11,000,000	$5,000,000	$3,500,000	$2,500,000
Region direct selling expenses	$10,000,000	—	—	—
Profit contribution	$24,000,000	$6,500,000	$8,000,000	$19,500,000
Allocated portion of shared zone costs	$16,000,000			
Net profit	$8,000,000			

contribution approach for evaluating the districts within this region. Notice that the profitability calculations for each district include only district sales, cost of goods sold, and district direct selling expenses. A *profit contribution* is generated for each district. The profitability calculations for the region include district selling expenses, region direct selling expenses that have not been allocated to the districts, and an allocated portion of shared zone costs. This produces a net profit figure for a profitability evaluation of the region.

Although either approach might be used, there seems to be a trend toward the contribution approach, probably because of the difficulty in arriving at a satisfactory procedure for allocating the shared costs. Different cost allocation methods produce different results. Thus, many firms feel more comfortable with the contribution approach because it eliminates the need for cost allocation judgments and is viewed as more objective.

Activity-Based Costing

Perhaps a more accountable method for allocating costs is **activity-based costing (ABC)**. ABC allocates costs to individual units on the basis of how the units actually expend or cause these costs. Costs are accumulated and then allocated to the units by the appropriate drivers, factors that drive costs up or down.

Exhibit 9.9 illustrates how the profitability picture changed for a building supplies company that switched to ABC to assess distribution channel profitability.[7] Notice that with ABC, selling expenses are no longer allocated to each channel based on a percentage of that channel's sales revenues. Instead, costs associated with each activity used to generate sales for a specific channel are allocated to that channel. With ABC, a clearer picture of operating profits per channel emerges. In particular, the original equipment manufacturer channel appears to be much more profitable than the firm's prior accounting system indicates.

ABC places greater emphasis on more accurately defining unit profitability by tracing activities and their associated costs directly to a specific unit. For example, using ABC analysis, the Doig Corporation was able to lower costs by identifying which tasks added value and which ones did not. For instance, it identified which customers could be served just as well by phone, saving both reps and the company time and money.[8] As such, ABC helps foster an understanding of resource expenditures, how customer value is created, and where money is being made or lost.

Return on Assets Managed Analysis

The income statement approach to profitability assessment produces net profit or profit contribution in dollars or expressed as a percentage of sales. Although necessary and valuable, the income statement approach is incomplete because it does not incorporate any evaluation of the investment in assets required to generate the net profit or profit contribution.

The calculation of **return on assets managed (ROAM)** can extend the income statement analysis to include asset investment considerations. The formula for calculating ROAM is

$$
\begin{aligned}
\text{ROAM} = &\text{ Profit contribution as percentage of sales} \\
&\times \text{Asset turnover rate} \\
= &\text{ (Profit contribution/Sales)} \times \text{(Sales/Total assets managed)}
\end{aligned}
$$

Profit contribution can be either a net profit figure from a full cost approach or profit contribution from a contribution approach. Assets managed typically include inventory, accounts receivable, or other assets at each sales organizational level.

An example of ROAM calculations is presented in Exhibit 9.10. The example illustrates ROAM calculations for sales districts within a region. Notice that District 1 and District 2 produce the same ROAM but achieve their results in different ways. District 1 generates a relatively high profit contribution percentage, whereas District 2 operates with a relatively high asset turnover. Both District 3 and District 4 are achieving poor levels of ROAM but for different reasons. District 3 has an acceptable profit contribution

Activity-Based Costing Example   EXHIBIT 9.9

Profits by Commercial Distribution Channel (Old System)

	Contract	Industrial Suppliers	Government	OEM	Total Commercial
Annual sales (in thousands of dollars)	$79,434	$25,110	$422	$9,200	$114,166
Gross margin	34%	41%	23%	27%	35%
Gross profit	$27,375	$10,284	$136	$2,461	$40,256
SG&A allowance[a] (in thousands of dollars)	$19,746	$6,242	$105	$2,287	$31,814
Operating profit (in thousands of dollars)	$7,629	$4,042	$31	$174	$11,876
Operating margin	10%	16%	7%	2%	10%
Invested capital allowance[b] (in thousands of dollars)	$33,609	$10,624	$179	$3,893	$48,305
Return on investment	23%	38%	17%	4%	25%

Profits by Commercial Distribution Channel (New System: ABC)

	Contract	Industrial Suppliers	Government	OEM	Total Commercial
Gross profit (from previous table)	$27,375	$10,284	$136	$2,461	$40,256
Selling expenses[c] (all in thousands of dollars)					
Commission	$4,682	$1,344	$12	$372	$6,410
Advertising	132	38	0	2	172
Catalog	504	160	0	0	664
Coop advertising	416	120	0	0	536
Sales promotion	394	114	0	2	510
Warranty	64	22	0	4	90
Sales administration	5,696	1,714	20	351	7,781
Cash discount	892	252	12	114	1,270
Total	$12,780	$3,764	$44	$845	$17,433
G&A (in thousands of dollars)	$6,740	$2,131	$36	$781	$9,688
Operating profit (in thousands of dollars)	$7,855	$4,389	$56	$835	$13,135
Operating margin	10%	17%	13%	9%	12%
Invested capital[c]	$33,154	$10,974	$184	$2,748	$47,060
Return on investment	24%	40%	30%	30%	28%

[a]SG&A (selling, general and administrative expenses) allowance for each channel is 25 percent of that channel's revenues.
[b]Invested capital allowance for each channel is 42 percent of that channel's revenues.
[c]Selling expenses and invested capital estimated under an activity-based system.

percentage but very low asset turnover ratio. This low asset turnover ratio is the result of both inventory accumulations or problems in payments from accounts. District 4, however, has an acceptable asset turnover ratio, but low profit contribution percentage. This low profit contribution percentage may be the result of selling low margin products, negotiating low selling prices, or accruing excessive selling expenses.

EXHIBIT 9.10   Return on Assets Managed (ROAM) Example

	District 1	District 2	District 3	District 4
Sales	$24,000,000	$24,000,000	$24,000,000	$24,000,000
Cost of goods sold	12,000,000	12,000,000	14,000,000	14,000,000
Gross margin	12,000,000	12,000,000	10,000,000	10,000,000
Direct selling expenses	7,200,000	9,600,000	5,200,000	8,800,000
Profit contribution	4,800,000	2,400,000	4,800,000	1,200,000
Accounts receivable	8,000,000	4,000,000	16,000,000	4,000,000
Inventory	8,000,000	4,000,000	16,000,000	4,000,000
Total assets managed	16,000,000	8,000,000	32,000,000	8,000,000
Profit contribution as a percent of sales	20%	10%	20%	5%
Asset turnover	1.5	3.0	.75	3.0
ROAM	30%	30%	15%	15%

As illustrated in the preceding example, ROAM calculations provide an assessment of profitability and useful diagnostic information. ROAM is determined by both profit contribution percentage and asset turnover. If ROAM is low in any area, the profit contribution percentage and asset turnover ratio can be examined to determine the reason. Corrective action (e.g., reduced selling expenses, stricter credit guidelines, lower inventory levels) can then be taken to improve future ROAM performance.

Productivity Analysis

Although ROAM incorporates elements of productivity by comparing profits and asset investments, additional **productivity analysis** is desirable for thorough evaluation of sales organization effectiveness. Productivity is typically measured in terms of ratios between outputs and inputs. For example, as discussed in Chapter 4, one often-used measure of salesforce productivity is sales per salesperson. A major advantage of productivity ratios is that they can be compared directly across the entire sales organization and with other sales organizations. This direct comparison is possible because all the ratios are expressed in terms of the same units.

Because the basic job of sales managers is to manage salespeople, the most useful input unit for productivity analysis is the salesperson. Therefore, various types of productivity ratios are calculated on a per-salesperson basis. The specific ratios depend on the characteristics of a particular selling situation but often include important outputs such as sales, expenses, calls, demonstrations, and proposals. An example of a productivity analysis is presented in Exhibit 9.11.

Exhibit 9.11 illustrates how productivity analysis provides a different and useful perspective for evaluating sales organization effectiveness. As the exhibit reveals, absolute values can be misleading. For example, the highest sales districts are not necessarily the most effective. Although profitability analyses would likely detect this also, productivity analysis presents a vivid and precise evaluation by highlighting specific areas of both high and low productivity. Take the information concerning district 2. Although sales per salesperson is reasonable and expenses per salesperson is relatively low, both calls per salesperson and proposals per salesperson are much lower than those for the other districts. This may explain why selling expenses are low, but it also suggests that the salespeople in this district may not be covering the district adequately. The high sales may be due to a few large sales to large customers.

	District 1	District 2	District 3	District 4
Sales	$20,000,000	$24,000,000	$20,000,000	$24,000,000
Selling expenses	$2,000,000	$2,400,000	$3,000,000	$3,000,000
Sales calls	9,000	7,500	8,500	10,000
Proposals	220	180	260	270
Number of salespeople	20	30	20	30
Sales/salesperson	$1,000,000	$800,000	$1,000,000	$800,000
Expenses/salesperson	$100,000	$80,000	$150,000	$100,000
Calls/salesperson	450	250	425	333
Proposals/salesperson	11	6	13	9

Productivity Analysis Example   EXHIBIT 9.11

In any case, the productivity analysis provides useful evaluative and diagnostic information that is not directly available from the other types of analyses discussed in this module. Sales productivity and profitability are highly interrelated. However, profitability analysis has a financial perspective, whereas productivity analysis is more managerially oriented. Improvements in sales productivity should translate into increases in profitability.

Productivity improvements are obtained in one of two basic ways:

1. increasing output with the same level of input

2. maintaining the same level of output but using less input

Productivity analysis can help determine which of these basic approaches should be pursued.

IMPROVING SALES ORGANIZATION EFFECTIVENESS

Benchmarking

One popular technique for improving sales organization effectiveness is **benchmarking.** Benchmarking is an ongoing measurement and analysis process that compares an organization's current operating practices with the "best practices" used by world-class organizations. It is a tool for evaluating current business practices and finding a way to do them better, more quickly, and less expensively to better meet customer needs. Using benchmarking, Wells Fargo Home Mortgage Co., was able to consolidate its sales brochures and direct mail campaigns resulting in a savings of more than $1.4 million. It also increased sales by 102 percent using sales road maps. Rank Xerox, the British unit of Xerox, used benchmarking to increase country unit sales from 152 percent to 328 percent and improve new revenue by $200 million.[9] A research study of more than 1,600 U.S. and Canadian organizations found that those companies willing to learn from the best practices of others are more successful at improving customer satisfaction than those that are more reluctant. Perhaps this explains why such firms as IBM, AT&T, DuPont, GM, Intel, Sprint, and Xerox use benchmarking.

Figure 9.7 outlines steps in the benchmarking process. A pivotal part of this process is identifying the company or salesforce to benchmark. A literature search and personal contacts are means for identifying companies that perform the process in an exceptional manner. Winning an industry award, being recognized for functional excellence, and receiving a national quality award are three indicators of excellence. Eastman Chemical Company and IBM have used the Malcolm Baldrige National Quality Award criteria as bases on which to evaluate their salesforce, map processes leading to desired results, and focus efforts on continuously improving these processes.

FIGURE 9.7   **Benchmarking Process**

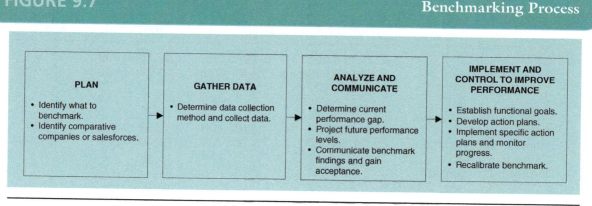

Those processes that have the greatest impact on salesforce productivity should be benchmarked. Companies such as Best Practices, LLC (www.best-in-class.com), the Benchmarking Network (www.benchmarkingnetwork.com), Sales Force Effectiveness Benchmarking Association (www.sfeba.com), and American Productivity and Quality Center (www.apqc.org) provide useful Web sites for initiating a benchmarking program.

A benchmarking study should provide several outputs. First, it should provide a measure that compares performance for the benchmarked process relative to the organization studied. Second, it should identify the organization's performance gap relative to benchmarked performance levels. Third, it should identify best practices and facilitators that produced the results observed during the study. Finally, the study should determine performance goals for the process studied and identify areas in which action can be taken to improve performance. Exhibit 9.12 provides some keys to successful benchmarking.

Six Sigma

Six Sigma, a data-driven methodology that attempts to eliminate defects in any process, provides another potentially powerful means for improving salesforce effectiveness. The word *sigma* is a mathematical term for measuring variation, with six sigma indicating a low degree of variability (3.4 mistakes per million opportunities). A form of process improvement, Six Sigma is credited with hundreds of millions of dollars of savings in several large corporations such as Allied Signal, GE, Raytheon and others. This disciplined decision-making approach aims to make processes as perfect as possible by focusing on improving processes and reducing variations through the application of the Six Sigma process as outlined in Exhibit 9.13.[10] Six Sigma can potentially be applied to any

EXHIBIT 9.12   Key to Successful Benchmarking

- Clearly identify critical activities that will improve quality or service or reduce cost.
- Properly prepare and benchmark *only one activity at a time.*
- Make sure that you thoroughly understand your own process first.
- Create a "seek, desire, and listen" environment by choosing curious and knowledgeable people for your benchmark team.
- Verify that your benchmark partner company is the best in its class, and clearly understand your partner's process.
- Provide adequate resources, not only financial, but also knowledgeable personnel.
- Be diligent in selecting the correct partner—do not use a company that may not provide advantages to you.
- Implement the benchmarking action plan.

The Steps of Six Sigma   EXHIBIT 9.13

Michael Webb, author of *Sales and Marketing the Six Sigma Way* (Kaplan, 2006) outlines steps involved in the Six Sigma process:

Define:
Begin at the beginning. What is the defect or problem you are trying to solve? Define the SIPOC (Suppliers, Inputs, Process, Outputs, Customers), and define the process itself as best you can.

Measure:
Collect data (measurements) about the process to gain a better understanding of it.

Analyze:
Try to figure out what the data is telling you. Often, you will go back and forth between the Measure and the Analyze steps to clarify your understanding of how the process really works. This becomes your hypothesis. It is essentially the expression of a theory of cause and effect for your process.
  One thing that distinguishes Six Sigma from other approaches is the genius of this insight: cause and effect can be expressed in terms of a mathematical equation:

$Y = f(x)$
Y(Output) is the f(function) of the x(process)

Improve:
After analyzing the process, you construct an experiment to prove your hypothesis. Your experiment will measurably change one of the independent variables (x)s. If your theory is correct, the result will be a measurable (and positive) change to the dependent variable (Y). If your experiment is on target, you will have reduced the instances of defects.

Control:
It does no good to learn how a process can be improved if the improvement is not institutionalized in some way so the problems do not recur. The control step is doing the things necessary to cause this to happen.

process involved in the sales organization (e.g., recruiting, selection, training, etc.) to make it better and improve salesforce effectiveness.

ETHICAL ISSUES

The value of comparing actual expenses with budgeted expenses depends on the accuracy of the expense information provided by salespeople. Although most sales organizations have prepared forms with the expense categories and instructions for salespeople, salespeople often face ethical problems in reporting their expenses. Consider the following situations:

- A salesperson has been on the road for a week and incurs laundry expenses. He knows that if he places the laundry expenses under the miscellaneous expense category in his expense report, he will have to provide receipts. He decides that he can include them under the meals category because receipts are not required for this category as long as he stays under his per-diem allowance.

- A salesperson is trying to get a customer to purchase a new product. He decides to take three individuals from the customer's firm to dinner and a basketball game, even though he knows that he has exceeded his entertainment budget for the month. He thinks about hiding these entertainment expenses in different categories in his expense report.

The decisions that salespeople make in these and similar situations affect the ability of sales managers to evaluate actual and budgeted expenses in an accurate manner. Sales

AN ETHICAL DILEMMA

A leading wholesaler of religious themed gift items and books, Trinity Merchandising is committed to their faith-based business principles. One of the company's long-standing policies does not allow alcoholic beverages to be used in any of its business activities. This includes marketing conferences and trade shows and even extends to the company's sales personnel entertaining customers. Gage Waits, sales manager for the Western Region, is discussing the recent success of salesperson Don Johnson in acquiring a substantial opening order from a national buying group along with monthly commitments over the coming year. During their discussion, Don mentions that as the result of several dinner meetings with the group's regional buying staff—where the customer's buying staff ordered wine and cocktails with their dinner—he is personally out just over $875 because of the company's policy. Don asks Gage if he could add extra mileage, over-and-beyond what he actually travels in the coming month, to his expense report that would add up to what he is out of pocket for the unreimbursed drinks.

What should Gage should do?

a. Approve Don's request to overstate his mileage in an amount that would reimburse him for the $875 in wine and cocktails his customers ordered.

b. Remind Don that company policy does not allow alcoholic beverages to be used in any business activities and that overstating his mileage would be an additional violation of company policy that should not be done for any reason. Don is simply out the $875.

c. Recognize this as a special situation that was beyond Don's control and authorize the additional $875 reimbursement for the dinner meetings and discuss strategies with Don to assist him from being put in this type of situation in the future.

managers themselves, however, may be presented with situations which present them with ethical decisions that they must deal with, as illustrated in "An Ethical Dilemma."

CONCLUDING COMMENTS

As is obvious from the discussion in this chapter, there is no easy way to evaluate the effectiveness of a sales organization. Our recommendation is to perform separate analyses of sales, costs, profitability, and productivity to assess different aspects of sales organization effectiveness. In addition, salesperson performance, which is discussed in the next chapter, must also be evaluated and considered. Each type of analysis offers a piece of the puzzle. Sales managers must put these pieces together for comprehensive evaluations. The objective underlying each of the analyses is to be able to evaluate effectiveness, identify problem areas, and use this information to improve future sales organization effectiveness.

SUMMARY

1. **Differentiate between sales organization effectiveness and salesperson performance.** Sales organization effectiveness is a summary evaluation of the overall success of a sales organization in meeting its goals and objectives in total and at different organizational levels. By contrast, salesperson performance is a function of individual salesperson performance in individual situations.

2. **Define a sales organization audit and discuss how it should be conducted.** The most comprehensive type of evaluation is a sales organization audit, which is a sys-

tematic assessment of all aspects of a sales organization. The major areas included in the audit are sales organization environment, sales management evaluation, sales organization planning system, and sales management functions. The audit should be conducted regularly by individuals outside the sales organization. It is intended to identify existing or potential problems early so that corrective action can be taken before the problems become serious.

3. **Describe how to perform different methods of sales analysis for different organizational levels and different types of sales.** Sales analysis is the most common evaluation approach, but it can be extremely complex. Specific definitions of a sale are required, and both sales dollars and units typically should be considered. A hierarchical approach is suggested as a top-down procedure to address sales results at each level of the sales organization with an emphasis on identifying problem areas. Sales analysis is more useful when sales results are compared with forecasts, quotas, previous time periods, and competitor results.

4. **Describe how to perform a cost analysis for a sales organization.** Cost analysis focuses on the costs incurred to generate sales results. Specific costs can be compared with the planned levels in the selling budget. Areas with large variances require specific attention. Costs can also be evaluated as percentages of sales and compared to comparable industry figures.

5. **Describe how to perform an income statement analysis, activity-based costing, and return on assets managed, to assess sales organization profitability.** Profitability analysis combines sales and cost data in various ways. The income statement approach focuses on net profit or profit contributions from the different sales organization levels. Activity-based costing allocates costs to individual units on the basis of how the units actually expend or cause these costs. The return on assets managed approach assesses relationships between profit contributions and the assets used to generate these profit contributions. The different profitability analyses address different aspects of profitability that are of interest to sales managers.

6. **Describe how to perform a productivity analysis for a sales organization.** Productivity analysis focuses on relationships between outputs and inputs. The most useful input is the number of salespeople, whereas relevant outputs might be sales, expenses, proposals, and so on. The productivity ratios calculated in this manner are versatile because they can be used for comparisons within the sales organization and across other sales organizations. Productivity analysis not only provides useful evaluative information but also provides managerially useful diagnostic information that can suggest ways to improve productivity and increase profitability.

7. **Define benchmarking and Six Sigma and discuss how each should be conducted.** Benchmarking is an ongoing measurement and analysis process that compares an organization's current operating practices with the "best practices" used by world-class organizations. It involves identifying the sales organization processes to be benchmarked and whom to benchmark, collecting data on the benchmarked firm, analyzing performance gaps and communicating them to the salesforce, and establishing goals and implementing plans. Six Sigma is a data-driven methodology that attempts to eliminate defects in any process. It involves defining the process problem, collecting data on the process problem, analyzing the data, determining how to improve the process and implementing a process change. Both are conducted to improve processes, thereby enhancing performance.

UNDERSTANDING SALES MANAGEMENT TERMS

sales organization audit

sales analysis

income statement analysis

full cost approach

hierarchical sales analysis
effectiveness index
cost analysis
selling budget
percentage of sales method
objective and task method
profitability analysis

contribution approach
activity-based costing (ABC)
return on assets managed (ROAM)
productivity analysis
benchmarking
Six Sigma

DEVELOPING SALES MANAGEMENT KNOWLEDGE

1. Discuss why it is important to differentiate between sales organization effectiveness and salesperson performance.

2. Discuss what is involved in conducting a sales management audit.

3. Explain how sales managers can utilize benchmarking to improve performance.

4. What is meant by a hierarchical sales analysis? Can a hierarchical approach be used in analyzing costs, profitability, and/or productivity?

5. What is the difference between the full cost and contribution approaches to income statement analysis for a sales organization? Which would you recommend for a sales organization? Why?

6. Explain how a manager evaluating the sales organization's effectiveness might reach different conclusions by analyzing sales dollars or sales units.

7. What are the two basic components of return on assets managed? How is each component calculated, and what does each component tell a sales manager?

8. Identify five different sales organization productivity ratios that you would recommend. Describe how each would be calculated and what information each would provide.

9. What purposes do benchmarking and Six Sigma serve? Discuss what is involved in each process.

10. Discuss how you think new computer and information technologies will affect the evaluations of sales organization effectiveness in the future.

BUILDING SALES MANAGEMENT SKILLS

1. Using the following information provided for the end of the current fiscal year, conduct a sales analysis to evaluate sales organization effectiveness. The company anticipated sales growth of 5 percent. Explain your findings.

	Region 1 ($000)	Region 2 ($000)	Region 3 ($000)	Region 4 ($000)
Sales	$8,100	$9,500	$8,500	$5,000
Sales quota	$8,250	$8,500	$8,150	$7,800
Sales last year	$7,850	$8,750	$8,000	$4,850
Industry sales	$23,000	$25,000	$27,000	$21,000
Previous year market share	36%	35%	30%	25%

2. Sales and cost data can be combined in various ways to produce evaluations of sales organization profitability for different organizational levels or different types of sales. Three types of profitability analysis are useful for evaluating effectiveness: activity-based costing, income statement analysis, and return on assets managed analysis. Examining Exhibit 9.9, point out differences in operating profits by commercial

distribution channel between the company's old and new (ABC) system, and explain why they differ. What would the ABC system lead you to believe regarding the effectiveness of each channel? Using the information in Exhibit 9.9 and the following information, conduct an income statement analysis and return on assets managed analysis. Explain the results of your analyses.

	Contract ($000)	Industrial Suppliers ($000)	Government ($000)	OEM ($000)
Accounts receivable	$26,578	$16,840	$72	$1,633
Inventory	$26,578	$16,840	$73	$1,634

3. Several sites are available on the Web that provide benchmarking services. One such site is Best Practices, LLC (www.best-in-class.com), a research and consulting firm that provides business insight and analysis of how world-class companies achieve exceptional economic and operational performance. Access this site and review its services.

   a. How can a company such as this be useful to a sales manager attempting to improve the sales organization?

   b. From the Best Practices, LLC home page, click on the "Products and Services" tab. Next, locate and click on "Best Practices Database" from the list of products and services and then select "Sales Leadership." You do not need to be a subscribing member to look through their database of best practices in sales leadership. Notice the different areas of sales leadership for which they provide best practices. Click on "Sales Force Effectiveness" and examine the diverse reports available. Select one that offers Free Excerpt to Non-members and read through the excerpt. Look through the other areas comprising the Sales Leadership section and some of the other free excerpts available.

      Identify two reports that might be helpful for improving a sales organization's effectiveness and briefly explain how each report's information might be used.

   c. Locate another benchmarking service on the Web. Identify its address and briefly describe its services. Compare and contrast its services to those of Best Practices, LLC.

ROLE PLAY

4. **Role Play**

   Situation: Read An Ethical Dilemma on p. 266.

   Characters: Jane, southwest region manager; Brenda, one of Jane's top salespeople

   Scene: *Location*—local restaurant for lunch. *Action*—Jane tells Brenda about her plan to understate the budgeted sales revenue targets for the southwest region in order to win the competition. Brenda is skeptical. The two discuss the pros and cons of taking this action and consider other alternatives Jane might take.

5. Using the following information, conduct a productivity analysis. Based on your analysis, do you have any concerns? Explain.

	District 1	District 2	District 3	District 4
Sales	$15,000,000	$18,000,000	$15,000,000	$18,000,000
Selling expenses	$1,500,000	$1,800,000	$2,250,000	$2,250,000
Sales calls	6,750	5,625	6,375	7,500
Proposals	165	135	195	203
Number of salespeople	15	23	15	23

MAKING SALES MANAGEMENT DECISIONS

CASE 9.1: AFFILIATED MERCHANDISING

Background

Affiliated Merchandising markets a broad mix of household goods, toys and games to retailers throughout the United States. The salesforce is organized into five regions, each comprised of five districts. A national sales manager oversees the five regional sales managers. Each regional manager is responsible for the effectiveness of his or her region, including the districts comprising their region, and is compensated according to the achievements of their region.

Current Situation

Allison Wilson is the northern region sales manager for Affiliated Merchandising. The fiscal year just ended, and Allison has compiled data to help her analyze her region's effectiveness. Although her region has had what she believes to be a very successful year, she wants to analyze each district closely. She hopes to use her analysis to identify and correct problems. Moreover, she needs to complete her analysis for her upcoming meeting with her national sales manager, Bobbi Jones. Market shares for each district were fairly sizable (30 percent, 32 percent, 34 percent, 31 percent, and 28 percent for districts 1 through 5, respectively) at the beginning of the fiscal year. Allison had expected these to remain relatively stable over the past year. The company had anticipated a sales growth of 2 percent. In addition, selling costs were budgeted at 10 percent of forecasted sales. If Allison's region did not increase sales by 2 percent and stay within the sales budget, her performance appraisal, and subsequently her compensation, would suffer. Allison knew her boss would carefully scrutinize her analysis. She hoped to be able to identify any problem areas so that she could develop solutions and implement them in the upcoming year. She was scheduled to meet with Jones in 3 days. Allison compiled the following information as shown in the table below.

	District 1 ($000)	District 2 ($000)	District 3 ($000)	District 4 ($000)	District 5 ($000)
Sales	16,400	19,000	20,900	27,500	16,800
Cost of goods sold	9,840	11,020	12,958	16,500	9,240
Compensation	1,230	1,620	1,470	2,280	1,260
Transportation	82	134	84	140	100
Lodging and meals	34	60	32	82	42
Telephone	16	20	24	28	18
Entertainment	20	16	30	24	24
Training	160	190	210	250	220
District accounts receivable	2,340	2,800	2,900	4,840	2,300
District inventory	4,000	7,000	6,400	10,500	5,000
Number of salespeople	16	18	22	24	20
Sales quota	16,200	19,500	20,500	28,250	16,600
Sales last year	15,000	18,500	20,500	27,850	16,400
Industry sales	52,904	59,376	61,472	91,667	60,000

Questions

1. What analyses should Allison perform with this data? Conduct these suggested analyses being careful to document your work and your answers.

2. What problems can you identify from your analyses?

3. What solutions would you recommend to solve these problems and improve sales effectiveness in the future? Explain why your recommendations are appropriate.

ROLE PLAY

Role Play

Situation: Read Case 9.1.

Characters: Allison Wilson, northern region sales manager; Bobbi Jones, national sales manager.

Scene: *Location*—Meeting room at Affiliated Merchandising headquarters. *Action*—Allison presents her findings from analyzing the data about the effectiveness of her salesforce. She makes a number of suggestions for solving the problems that her analysis revealed. Bobbi Jones offers several responses to her analysis and findings. He then asks Allison about the performance of her salespeople and whom, if anyone, she thinks the company should let go.

CASE 9.2: ADVANCE OFFICE TECHNOLOGY, INC.

Background

Dallas-based Advance Office Technology is a leading provider of business systems and productivity software applications. The company operates throughout the United States and is divided into five regions, each consisting of four districts with a district sales manager in charge of each one. Each sales region is overseen by a regional sales manager and a national sales manager is charged with the ultimate responsibility for the overall sales organization. Advance Office Technology's salespeople are well qualified, have college degrees, and experience in the design, sales, and operation of business productivity systems. The average tenure on the salesforce is seven years.

Current Situation

Advance Office Technology competes head on with Canon, IBM, HP, Xerox, and other major players comprising this industry and has managed to do quite well in terms of sales, profitability, and market share. In fact, Advance Office Technology has earned the reputation as a capable, innovative and aggressive competitor. Nevertheless, Jane Weathers, Advance Office Technology's president believes that the company can do much better. The following is a conversation she recently had with her national sales manager, Gage Waits.

Jane: I believe that the key to our growth lies in having a successful salesforce.

Gage: Absolutely. We have made great strides over the past three years, consistently increasing our sales volume.

Jane: Sales growth is a must. However, we need to measure up to the performance of our competition in other ways.

Gage: What do you mean?

Jane: If we want to reach the top, we have to have a salesforce that performs like those at the top. How convenient and quick is our service? How long does it take from order to delivery and setup?

Gage: I suppose we could always improve our service. However, our salespeople are well qualified and do a competent job.

Jane: What about our user training program? Can it be made more convenient for customers? Is it possible to accomplish it more quickly and less expensively without sacrificing the quality of the training?

Gage: We seem to be doing okay in this area. There haven't been a lot of complaints that I am aware of, so I assume everything is going well.

Jane: If we are going to be the best, we have to have the best salesforce. Gage, I'm counting on you to lead our salesforce to the top. I can't stress how important it is for us to have a high performing salesforce. I'd like to meet with you in two weeks to discuss your plan for addressing these issues.

Gage: Perhaps it's time to take a closer look at our sales organization. I'll do my best.

Questions

1. How could Gage use benchmarking to address Jane's concerns?

2. Outline a benchmarking study that could be used to help make Advance Office Technology's salesforce more effective.

3. What else can be done to ensure that Advance Office Technology's salesforce is performing effectively?

ROLE PLAY

Role Play

Situation: Read Case 9.2.

Characters: Jane Weathers, president; Gage Waits, national sales manager.

Scene 1: *Location*—Waits's office. *Action*—Role play the conversation between Jane and Gage as outlined in the case.

Scene 2: *Location*—Jane's office, two weeks later. *Action*—Gage is meeting with Jane to discuss his plan for improving the sales organization. He outlines his plan and Jane provides her thoughts regarding it.

EVALUATING THE PERFORMANCE OF SALESPEOPLE

OBJECTIVES

After completing this chapter, you should be able to

1. Discuss the different purposes of salesperson performance evaluations.

2. Differentiate between an outcome-based and a behavior-based perspective for evaluating and controlling salesperson performance.

3. Describe the different types of criteria necessary for comprehensive evaluations of salesperson performance.

4. Compare the advantages and disadvantages of different methods of salesperson performance evaluation.

5. Explain how salesperson performance information can be used to identify problems, determine their causes, and suggest sales management actions to solve them.

6. Discuss the measurement and importance of salesperson job satisfaction.

SALES OUTCOMES ARE IMPORTANT IN ASSESSING SALESPERSON PERFORMANCE, BUT THE KEY TO SALES PERFORMANCE IS MANAGING SALESPEOPLE AND THEIR ACTIVITIES

Customer relationship management (CRM) and its accompanying technologies and metrics have provided more data than ever before directed at managing and improving sales performance. Indeed, recent research illustrates that companies effectively utilizing CRM's advanced measurement and assessment capabilities grow sales revenue 15% faster than those that don't and see 16% more salespeople reaching quota. And yet, even with the advanced metrics from CRM systems, most sales managers continue to make the mistake of focusing solely on the outcomes of salespeople's efforts, not the quality and quantity of the effort itself.

Tom Disantis, Chief Operating Officer at Vantage Point, emphasizes the importance of utilizing the right metrics in managing the salesforce, emphasizing that "many sales organizations fall into the trap of believing that measurement of sales revenue equates to management of revenue. It doesn't. You can't manage a number; you can only manage people and their activities. That's the key to moving the revenue needle." Disantis equates a sales manager too obsessive about sales revenue numbers as comparable to a basketball coach spending the game with his eyes on just the scoreboard. "Yes the score is what matters in the end, but watching it is not going to change the outcome. If anything, it will negatively impact the outcome because if the coach is focused on the scoreboard that means he isn't focused on the only thing that can improve the score: the activities and behaviors of his players."

In order to more effectively manage the salesforce, sales leaders must break the numbers habit and make a conscious effort to refocus their attention from the scoreboard and onto the game and players. That is, to set the numbers aside and focus instead on how to best help individual sales reps succeed. This requires a change in both conversations as well as interactions to become focused on high-impact strategies and activities that will enable the sales reps to hit their targets. "Sure, revenue will be on the table, but it needs to be offset with a focus on how sales managers are supporting their sellers in executing high-impact activities. This balance will send a strong signal that while revenue is important, focusing sellers on the right activities is even more critical." Sales outcomes will always be a focus in evaluating salesperson performance. Outcomes—such as sales revenues—are easy to measure and provide the comfort of having objective numbers to analyze and compare. Still, the sales leaders who are truly making a difference in their organizations are the ones who have learned that they cannot manage outcomes such as revenue. "They can only manage the activities that lead to increased revenues. In fact, the more managers obsess about results, the less likely they are to actually achieve them."

Sources: Tom Disantis, "The Role of Metrics in Managing the Sales Force," *The Sales Operations Guide to Better Sales Management*, (2018), 18–20. Vantage Point Performance, www.VantagePointPerformance.com, accessed September 17, 2018; and "10 Underrated Sales Performance Indicators that Work," *Forbes* (July 16, 2018) www.forbes.com/sites/forbesbusinessdevelopmentcouncil/2018/07/16/10-underrated-sales-performance-indicators-that-work/#24b77084932a, accessed September 17, 2018.

Whereas Chapter 9 focused on evaluating sales organization effectiveness, this chapter examines the task of evaluating salesperson performance and job satisfaction. Evaluations of sales organization effectiveness concentrate on the overall results achieved by the different units within the sales organization, with special attention given to determining the effectiveness of territories, districts, regions, and zones, as well as identifying strategic changes to improve future effectiveness. These effectiveness assessments examine sales organization units and do not directly evaluate individuals. Nevertheless, sales managers are also responsible for the effectiveness of their assigned, individual salespeople.

Sales, like most business functions, is managed by metrics—the most common being outcomes such as revenue. As discussed by Tom Disantis in the opening vignette, the optimal evaluation of salesperson performance goes beyond simple revenue metrics to emphasize evaluation and management of the high-impact strategies and activities that enable sales reps to achieve their revenue numbers. This level of salesperson performance information enables an interactive management process designed to determine salesperson's objectives, uncover their problems, develop solutions, improve communication, and provide direction for continued development. To evaluate salesperson performance, sales managers must understand why and how performance evaluations are conducted and what should be measured, as well as how to use the information gained from these evaluations.

The purpose of this chapter is to investigate the key issues involved in evaluating and controlling the performance and job satisfaction of salespeople. The purposes of salesperson performance evaluations are discussed initially. Then, the performance evaluation procedures currently used by sales organizations are examined. This is followed by a comprehensive assessment of salesperson performance evaluation. The assessment addresses the criteria to be used in evaluating salespeople, the methods for evaluating salespeople against these criteria, and the outcomes of salesperson performance evaluations. The chapter concludes by discussing the importance and measurement of salesperson job satisfaction and relationships between salesperson performance and job satisfaction.

PURPOSES OF SALESPERSON PERFORMANCE EVALUATIONS

As the name suggests, the basic objective of salesperson performance evaluations is to determine how well individual salespeople have performed. However, the results of salesperson performance evaluations can be used for many sales management purposes:

1. To ensure that compensation and other reward disbursements are consistent with actual salesperson performance.

2. To identify salespeople who might be promoted.

3. To identify salespeople whose employment should be terminated and to supply evidence to support the need for termination.

4. To determine the specific training and counseling needs of individual salespeople and the overall salesforce.

5. To provide information for effective human resource planning.

6. To identify criteria that can be used to recruit and select salespeople in the future.

7. To advise salespeople of work expectations.

8. To motivate salespeople.

9. To help salespeople set career goals.

10. To relate salesperson performance to sales organization goals.

11. To enhance communications between salesperson and sales manager.

12. To improve salesperson performance.

These diverse purposes affect all aspects of the performance evaluation process. For example, performance evaluations for determining compensation and special rewards should emphasize activities and results related to the salesperson's current job and situation. Performance evaluations for the purpose of identifying salespeople for promotion into sales management positions should focus on criteria related to potential effectiveness as a sales manager and not just current performance as a salesperson. To be effective, sales performance reviews should also be action-oriented and tied to real-time selling activities. "Sales Management in the 21st Century: Addvance Medical utilizes Continuous Performance Evaluation to drive Improved Sales Performance and Employee Satisfaction." describes the use of a continuous performance evaluation process that occurs naturally as part of the sales manager's coaching and feedback.

SALESPERSON PERFORMANCE EVALUATION APPROACHES

It would be impossible to describe in detail all the performance evaluation approaches used by sales organizations. However, it is possible to catalog a number of general observations which provide a glimpse into current practices in evaluating salesperson performance.

1. Most sales organizations evaluate salesperson performance annually, although many firms conduct evaluations semiannually or quarterly. Recently, there has been a growing trend toward the use of more frequent performance reviews and even continuous reviews that flow out of the coaching and feedback relationships between sales manager and salesperson.

SALES MANAGEMENT IN THE 21ST CENTURY

Addvance Medical utilizes Continuous Performance Evaluation to drive Improved Sales Performance and Employee Satisfaction

James Richardson, Sales Director for the Western District of Addvance Medical, discusses the company's method for utilizing continuous performance reviews rather than the traditional end-of-year review in practice at many organizations.

Addvance Medical is coming up on its 23rd anniversary as a leading supplier of medical equipment and supplies and we learned a long time ago that the backward looking, end-of-the-year performance reviews did not provide many—if any—positive outcomes related to either performance improvement or employee satisfaction. We still do the one-on-one review of the previous year's results—but its intention is to set the stage looking forward to the coming year and even the second year

out. The year-end review establishes a baseline for each salesperson and their territory within the dynamic and changing context of what is going on in their territory in terms of competition, customers, and market conditions. That data and information is utilized to establish sales goals and action plans going forward which feed into the organization's model of continuous performance review. Sales managers provide ongoing coaching and feedback to each salesperson. It is a collaborative process that is continuing—it never stops! It allows for and encourages shorter and more targeted coaching reviews of performance, sales activities, and action plans—reviews that are relevant to the immediate situation and thus generate improvements to plans and activities which empower our salespeople to be more productive in the field. Addvance has invested in this model of continuous performance reviews for over 10 years—a model that has enabled the company to meaningfully increase sales, market share, and employee satisfaction every year.

---

2. Most sales organizations use combinations of input and output criteria that are evaluated by quantitative and qualitative measures. However, emphasis seems to be placed on outputs, with evaluations of sales volume results the most popular.

3. Sales organizations that set performance standards or quotas tend to enlist the aid of salespeople in establishing these objectives. The degree of salesperson input and involvement does, however, appear to vary across firms.

4. Many sales organizations assign weights to different performance objectives and incorporate territory data when establishing these objectives.

5. Most firms use more than one source of information in evaluating salesperson performance; client and peer feedback are some of the common sources of information.

6. Most salesperson performance evaluations are conducted by the field sales manager who supervises the salesperson. However, some firms involve the manager above the field sales manager in the salesperson performance appraisal.

7. Most sales organizations provide salespeople with a written copy of their performance review and have sales managers discuss the performance evaluation with each salesperson. These discussions typically take place in an office, although sometimes they are conducted in the field.

Although performance appraisal continues to be primarily a top-down process, changes are taking place in some companies leading to the implementation of a broader-based assessment process. An increasingly popular assessment technique, dubbed **360-degree feedback,** involves performance assessment from multiple raters, including sales managers, internal and external customers, team members, and even salespeople themselves. As part of its 360-degree review, sales managers at Knowledgepoint, a human resources software provider, solicit feedback from coworkers in areas such as rapport with clients, time management, and presentation skills when evaluating salespeople.

Keys to an Effective 360-Degree Feedback System   EXHIBIT 10.1

1. Ensure that participants willingly provide honest feedback by distributing the feedback instrument confidentially, aggregating responses by rating source, having rating forms sent directly to the person or group organizing the data, and including feedback from at least three respondents in each rater group (e.g., customers, coworkers, team members). Allow participants some input in selecting raters.
2. Explain to all participants how the data will be used.
3. Ensure that the data sources remain confidential, so those being rated do not know specifically who did the rating.
4. Verify that the data are accurate. The assessment tools used to gather the data should be reliable and valid.
5. Ensure that subjects can use the data to improve their performance. Present the feedback from the different groups (perspectives). It should be in a format that is easy to use and interpret. Compare feedback from others with one's own perceptions. Feedback should be linked to development tools and processes.
6. Determine how the system will affect the organization overall and systematically evaluate its effectiveness.
7. Do not rely exclusively on 360-degree feedback. Timely feedback concerning day-to-day performance is important.

Among its many benefits, 360-degree feedback helps managers better understand customer needs, detect barriers to success, assess developmental needs, create job involvement, reduce assessment bias, and improve performance. Because this evaluation method tends to make employees feel valued, they stay with the organization longer. However, when using the process, keep in mind that bias may still exist. Individuals may be less forthright in giving feedback and less accepting of feedback from others if they believe it will have damaging consequences. Furthermore, top salespeople tend to underestimate their performance, while bottom performers overestimate.[1] Also, other ratings and self-ratings tend to differ significantly most of the time.[2] Thus, it may be best to use feedback in conjunction with other appraisal techniques. Exhibit 10.1 provides keys to implementing an effective 360-degree feedback system.[3] To facilitate this evaluation process, many organizations are utilizing web-based applications to distribute and collect multiple evaluations. Companies such as Trakstar Performance Appraisal

Software (www.trakstar.com/) and Qualtrics 360 (www.qualtrics.com/employee-experience/360-degree-feedback/) are recognized providers of customized 360-degree performance appraisal services.

Another evaluation approach that moves away from the traditional top-down appraisal is referred to as **performance management**. This approach involves sales managers and salespeople working together on setting goals, giving feedback, reviewing, and rewarding. With this system, salespeople create their own development plans and assume responsibility for their careers. The sales manager acts as a partner in the process, providing feedback that is timely, specific, regular, solicited, and focused on what is within the salesperson's control to change. Salespeople are compensated on the value of their contributions to the organization's success. To facilitate the review process, sales managers may want to use software applications, such as Performance Now Enterprise Edition, which provide a framework for implementing a comprehensive performance management system.

Performance management ultimately focuses on improving salesperson performance by finding new and better ways to satisfy customers. A study of 437 U.S. companies in 58 industries reported that companies following a performance management approach had greater financial and productivity performance relative to other companies in their industry.[4]

The typical approach to performance evaluation incorporates four distinct stages. In stage one, the sales manager and salesperson discuss the salesperson's evaluation, which is based on feedback from multiple sources, such as the manager, customers, team members, and the salesperson. This discussion should include activities and performance across the entire period and not focus on the most recent item that was very successful or possibly a failure. During stage two, the sales manager rates the salesperson according to predetermined criteria or standards of performance in order to determine whether the salesperson is above or below expectations. In stage three, the salesperson's performance is reviewed relative to his or her previous performance evaluation to ascertain accomplishments in performance and areas that need improvement. It is important that the evaluation include both the good and the bad. A review that focuses only on the positive aspects of performance is only half a review. If the evaluation does not assist salespeople in identifying and understanding what they can do to further improve performance, the entire team and sales organization will pay the price in terms of continued substandard performance. The final stage focuses on improving the system and the salesperson's development and future performance. During this stage, the sales manager and salesperson work together to specify resources, structure, and training needed for performance improvements. Mutual agreement is reached regarding objectives, degree, and type of improvement and the action plan. It's not enough to simply provide guidance on how to improve. The action plan lays out a roadmap to improvement and lets the salesperson know exactly what he or she needs to do to measure up and provides a way to develop needed skills through coaching, seminars, and other means.[5]

Despite the approach taken, several key decisions concerning the appraisal process must be made. The remainder of this chapter addresses the key decision areas and alternative methods for developing comprehensive evaluation and control procedures.

KEY ISSUES IN EVALUATING AND CONTROLLING SALESPERSON PERFORMANCE

A useful way to view different perspectives for evaluating and controlling salesperson performance is presented in Exhibit 10.2. An **outcome-based perspective** focuses on objective measures of results with little monitoring or directing of salesperson behavior by sales managers. By contrast, a **behavior-based perspective** incorporates complex and often subjective assessments of salesperson characteristics and behaviors with considerable monitoring and directing of salesperson behavior by sales managers.

Perspectives on Salesperson Performance Evaluation	EXHIBIT 10.2

Outcome-Based Perspective	**Behavior-Based Perspective**
• Little monitoring of salespeople • Little managerial direction of salespeople • Straightforward, objective measures of results	• Considerable monitoring of salespeople • High levels of managerial direction of salespeople • Subjective measures of salesperson characteristics, activities, and strategies

The perspectives that a sales organization might take toward salesperson performance evaluation and control lie on a continuum. The two extremes are the outcome-based and behavior-based perspectives.

The outcome-based and behavior-based perspectives illustrated in Exhibit 10.2 represent the extreme positions that a sales organization might take concerning salesperson performance evaluation. Although our earlier review of current practice indicates a tendency toward an outcome-based perspective, most sales organizations operate somewhere between the two extreme positions. However, emphasis on either perspective can have far-reaching impacts on the salesforce and important implications for sales managers. Several of these key implications are presented in Exhibit 10.3. See how placing too much focus on outcomes may lead to undesirable behavior as illustrated in "An Ethical Dilemma."

On balance, these implications provide strong support for at least some behavior-based evaluations in most selling situations, including internationally. Research finds a positive relationship between behavior-based control and salesperson outcome performance, and sales organization effectiveness. In the absence of any behavior-based measures and limited monitoring and direction from sales management, salespeople are likely to focus on the short-term outcomes that are being evaluated. The process of obtaining the desired outcomes may be neglected, causing some activities that produce short-term results (e.g., selling pressure, unethical activities) to be emphasized and activities related to long-term customer relationships (e.g., customer orientation, post-sale service) to be minimized.

Outcome-Based versus Behavior-Based Implications	EXHIBIT 10.3

The more behavior-based (versus outcome-based) a salesperson performance evaluation is,

- The more professionally competent, team-oriented, risk-averse, planning-oriented, sales-support-oriented, and customer-oriented salespeople will be.
- The more intrinsically and recognition-motivated salespeople will be.
- The more committed to the sales organization salespeople will be.
- The more likely salespeople will be to accept authority, participate in decision making, and welcome management performance reviews.
- The lower the need for using pay as a control mechanism.
- The more innovative and supportive the culture is likely to be.
- The more inclined salespeople are to sell smarter rather than harder.
- The better salespeople will perform on both selling (e.g., using technical knowledge, making sales presentations) and nonselling (e.g., providing information, controlling expenses ethically) behavioral performance dimensions.
- The better salespeople will perform on outcome (e.g., achieving sales objectives) performance dimensions.
- The better the sales organization will perform on sales organization effectiveness dimensions (e.g., sales volume and growth, profitability, and customer satisfaction).
- The greater salespeople's job satisfaction will be.

AN ETHICAL DILEMMA

Troy Wells, sales manager for Trident Manufacturing, is reviewing the year-end sales reports for each of his salespeople. Trident offers salespeople a significant annual bonus based on a combination of (a) the percentage of their individual sales revenue over budget and (b) the annual gross profit percentage for each salesperson. In looking through the reports, Troy has noticed an unusually high spike in December gross profit percentages on the report for Cari Ellington. This anomaly corresponds with information Troy has received about several of Cari's customers calling in about their volume discounts not being reflected on recent invoices resulting in over-priced purchases. Those missing discounts could be the cause for the sudden increase in Cari's gross margin numbers. The accounting department has made the corrections and re-invoiced the customers. However, Troy is curious about the discounts being left off so close to year-end—meaning that any corrections impact next year's revenue and gross profit numbers and not the year under review. Cari has sold for Trident for 5 years and does not make this kind of mistake. Troy is concerned that Cari might have purposefully not entered the sales discounts in order to inflate her gross profit and qualify for a larger bonus.

What should Troy do?

a. Terminate Cari's employment for attempting to pad her gross profit performance. This type of performance cannot be tolerated.

b. Based on Cari's excellent record over five years with the company, assume this was just a mistake and not do anything at this time. After all, accounting has corrected the invoices for the customers and those revised invoices will also correct Cari's initially overstated gross profit numbers. Everything is taken care of.

c. Meet with Cari and discuss the customer calls concerning the missing discounts on several sales invoices. Ask for Cari's explanation of what might have happened and what could be done to prevent the errors going forward.

A reasonable conclusion from this discussion is that sales organizations should use both outcome-based and behavior-based measures when evaluating salesperson performance. Hybrid approaches incorporating both outcome-based and behavior-based measures place considerable emphasis on the following: supervision; evaluation of attitude, effort, and quantitative results; and complete, accurate paperwork. However, the relative emphasis on outcome-based and behavior-based measures depends on environmental, firm, and salesperson considerations. Limited research finds that behavior-based control is emphasized when the selling environment is uncertain, the salesforce is small, outputs and the cost of measuring them are inadequate, means for measuring behaviors are available, products are less complex, the percentage of routine activities is high, and salespeople are more educated. In addition, when formalization is high, outcome-based control can reduce its negative impact on role ambiguity and organizational commitment. Establishing the desired emphasis should be the initial decision in developing a salesperson performance evaluation and control system. Once this emphasis has been established, the sales organization can then address the specific criteria to be evaluated, the methods of evaluation, and how the performance information will be used. Regardless of the relative emphasis, however, some research suggests that greater control leads to higher levels of salesperson job satisfaction, organizational commitment and job performance, and lower levels of role stress.[6]

Criteria for Performance Evaluation

The typical salesperson job is multidimensional. Salespeople normally sell multiple products to diverse customers and perform a variety of selling and nonselling activities. Therefore, any comprehensive assessment of salesperson performance must include multiple criteria.

FIGURE 10.1   Dimensions of Salesperson Performance Evaluation

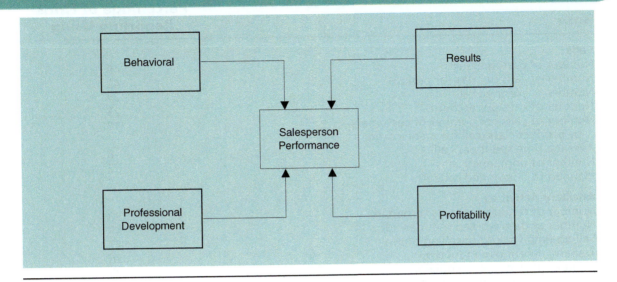

A comprehensive evaluation of salesperson performance should incorporate criteria from these dimensions. Sales organizations using a behavior-based perspective would focus on behavioral and professional development criteria, whereas those using an outcome-based perspective would emphasize results and profitability criteria.

Although the specific criteria depend on the characteristics of a given selling situation and the performance evaluation perspective, the four performance dimensions illustrated in Figure 10.1 should be considered: behavioral and professional development (behavior-based perspective) and results and profitability (outcome-based perspective). Regardless of the specific evaluative criteria chosen, it is important that salespeople know and understand the criteria to achieve desired performance. Moreover, sales managers should explain the rationale underlying the use of specific criteria. They may even want to let salespeople help in determining the evaluation criteria. When salespeople believe that the criteria upon which they are being evaluated is appropriate, they are likely to be more satisfied with their job.

Behavior

The behavioral dimension consists of criteria related to activities performed by individual salespeople. The emphasis is on evaluating exactly what each salesperson does. These **behavioral criteria** should not only address activities related to short-term sales generation but should also include nonselling activities needed to ensure long-term customer satisfaction and to provide necessary information to the sales organization. Examples of typical behavioral criteria are presented in Exhibit 10.4.[7]

As might be expected, most sales organizations focus on the number of sales calls made as the key behavioral criterion. However, other activities are also important to at least some sales organizations. At Motorola, for instance, customer satisfaction is measured to determine goal achievement. Part of salespeople's compensation at IBM is based on customer satisfaction. When salespeople's rewards are based on a customer satisfaction rating, salespeople are likely to demonstrate a higher level of customer service activity. This helps to explain research that finds that when buyers rate salespeople highly, they tend to give the salesperson's organization higher performance ratings.

Salespeople have the most control over what they do, so evaluations of their performance should include some assessment of their behaviors. Interestingly, foreign subsidiaries of U.S.–based multinationals appear to rely more heavily than U.S. firms on behavioral

---

EXHIBIT 10.4 Behavioral Criteria

Base	Percentage of Firms Reporting Using
Calls	
Number of customer calls	48
Number of calls per day (or period)	42
Number of planned calls	24
Number of calls per account	23
Number of calls per number of customers— by product class (call frequency ratio)	18
Average time spent per call	8
Number of unplanned calls	7
Planned to unplanned call ratio	3
Ancillary Activities	
Number of required reports turned in	38
Number of days worked (per period)	33
Selling time versus nonselling time	27
Training meetings conducted	26
Number of customer complaints	25
Number of formal presentations	22
Number of quotes	21
Percentage of goods returned	17
Number of dealer meetings held	17
Number of service calls made	15
Number of formal proposals developed	15
Advertising displays set up	13
Number of demonstrations conducted	12
Dollar amount of overdue accounts collected	10
Number of letters/phone calls to prospects	9

---

criteria for evaluating salesperson performance. This may be because behavior-based systems have been found to be better than compensation at promoting selling techniques among salespeople in other cultures, particularly Europe.[8] As discussed in Exhibit 10.3, the use of behavior-based criteria will also facilitate the development of a professional, customer-oriented, committed, and motivated salesforce.

Professional Development

Another dimension of considerable importance in evaluating the performance of individual salespeople relates to professional development. **Professional development criteria** assess improvements in certain characteristics of salespeople that are related to successful performance in the sales job. For example, if product knowledge is critical in a particular selling situation, then evaluations of the product knowledge of individual salespeople over various periods should be conducted. Examples of professional development criteria are presented in Exhibit 10.5.[9]

Many sales organizations incorporate multiple professional development criteria into their salesperson performance evaluations. This is appropriate, because salespeople have control over the development of personal characteristics related to success in their selling situation. The professional development criteria introduce a long-term perspective into the process of salesperson performance evaluation. Salespeople who are developing professionally are increasing their chances of successful performance over the long run. Although the professional development and behavioral criteria might be combined into one category, the preferred practice is to keep them separate to reflect their different perspectives.

Professional Development Criteria EXHIBIT 10.5	
Base	**Percentage of Firms Reporting Using**
Communication skills	88
Product knowledge	85
Attitude	82
Selling skills	79
Initiative and aggressiveness	76
Appearance and manner	75
Knowledge of competition	71
Team player	67
Enthusiasm	66
Time management	63
Judgment	62
Cooperation	62
Motivation	61
Ethical/moral behavior	59
Planning ability	58
Pricing knowledge	55
Report preparation and submission	54
Creativity	54
Punctuality	49
Resourcefulness	49
Knowledge of company policies	48
Customer goodwill generation	41
Self-improvement efforts	40
Care of company property	39
Degree of respect from trade and competition	38
Use of promotional materials	37
New product ideas	35
Use of marketing/technical backup teams	33
Good citizenship	22

Results

The results achieved by salespeople are extremely important and should be evaluated. Examples of **results criteria** used in salesperson performance evaluations are listed in Exhibit 10.6.[10]

A potential problem with the use of results criteria in Exhibit 10.6 is that the overall results measures do not reflect the territory situations faced by individual salespeople. The salesperson with the highest level of sales may have the best territory and may not necessarily be the best performer in generating sales. In fact, some research shows that rewards for achieving results have a negative effect on performance and satisfaction because salespeople may view the rewards as arbitrary if the goals are beyond their control. Aside from the impossible task of developing territories that are exactly equal, the only way to address this potential problem is to compare actual results with standards that reflect the unique territory situation faced by each salesperson. These standards are generally called sales quotas.

A **sales quota** represents a reasonable sales objective for a territory, district, region, or zone. Because a sales forecast represents an expected level of firm sales for a defined geographic area, time period, and strategy, there should be a close relationship between the sales forecast and the sales quota. Any of the several forecasting approaches discussed in Appendix 4 might be used to develop sales forecasts that are translated into sales quotas.

Accurate sales forecasts are critical for establishing valid sales quotas at all sales organization levels. To increase the accuracy of sales forecasts and subsequently quotas, they should be developed quarterly, particularly in highly dynamic environments.

EXHIBIT 10.6   Results Criteria

Base	Percentage of Firms Reporting Using
Sales	
Sales volume in dollars	79
Sales volume to previous year's sales	76
Sales volume by (versus) dollar quota	65
Percentage of increase in sales volume	55
Sales volume by product or product line	48
Sales volume by customer	44
Amount of new account sales	42
Sales volume in units	35
Sales volume to (versus) market potential	27
Sales volume by customer type	22
Sales volume to physical unit quota	9
Sales volume per order	7
Sales volume per call	6
Sales volume by outlet type	4
Percentage of sales made by telephone or mail	1
Market Share	
Market share achieved	59
Market share per quota	18
Accounts	
Number of new accounts	69
Number of accounts lost	33
Number of accounts buying the full line	22
Dollar amount of accounts receivable	17
Number of accounts (payment is) overdue	15
Lost account ratio	6

Although forecasts provide the basis for developing quotas, they must be adjusted to determine each individual's quota. Exhibit 10.7 shows results of a survey indicating the relative importance placed on various factors by sales managers when assigning sales quotas.[11] Research suggests that salesperson performance can be enhanced by assigning more challenging quotas to experienced salespeople who have demonstrated exceptional competence or to novices who quickly exhibit high potential. Likewise, performance may be enhanced by setting fair, consistent, and realistic quotas and by explaining to salespeople the rationale behind the quota assignment.[12]

Although it varies from company to company, some research indicates that a majority of companies require salespeople to achieve 100 percent or more of quota to be considered a strong performer. Over 26 percent of the respondents in this research claimed that achieving 111 percent or more of quota is necessary to be considered a strong performer. However, most companies (72 percent) consider salespeople who make 90 percent or less of quota to be average performers.[13] As seen in Exhibit 10.8, this research also found that sales managers often work closely with salespeople to improve their performance when they fail to achieve quota.[14]

Profitability

A potential problem with focusing on sales results is that the profitability of sales is not assessed. Salespeople can affect profitability in two basic ways. First, salespeople have an impact on gross profits through the specific products they sell and/or through the prices they negotiate for final sale. Thus, two salespeople could generate the same level of sales dollars and achieve the same sales/sales quota evaluation, but one salesperson could

Elements Important in Assigning Sales Quotas	EXHIBIT 10.7	
Statement	**Mean[1,2]**	**Rank**
Concentration of businesses within the sales representative's territory is important in determining the amount of quota.	1.82	1
The geographical size of territory is important in determining the amount of quota.	1.95	2
Growth of businesses within the sales representative's territory is important in determining the amount of quota.	2.11	3
Commitment by the sales manager to assisting the sales representative is important in determining the amount of quota.	2.23	4
Complexity of products sold is important in determining the amount of quota.	2.50	5
The sales representative's past sales performance is important in determining the amount of quota.	2.54	6
Extent of product line is important in determining the amount of quota.	2.59	7
The financial support (e.g., compensation) a firm provides sales representatives is important in assigning quota.	2.76	8
The relationship of your product line is important in determining the amount of quota.	2.82	9
The amount of clerical support given to a sales representative is important in determining the amount of quota.	3.13	10

[1]The rating scale and weights used to rate the importance of each statement were as follows: 1 strongly agree; 2 agree; 3 neutral; 4 disagree; and 5 strongly disagree.
[2]The responses numbered 186.

Examples of Managerial Actions Resulting from Failure to Achieve Assigned Quota				EXHIBIT 10.8	
	Percentage Agreement				
Action to Salesperson	**Strongly Disagree**	**Disagree**	**Neutral**	**Agree**	**Strongly Agree**
Nothing	12.7	38.2	18.5	25.4	5.2
Informal reprimand to do better	9.2	16.1	19.0	47.1	8.6
A stern verbal warning	10.7	30.5	23.4	29.7	5.7
Sales manager works closely with salesperson to improve	7.6	7.0	17.4	48.8	19.2
Formal probation	12.2	34.9	24.4	22.1	6.4

produce more gross profits by selling higher margin products and/or maintaining higher prices in sales negotiations.

Second, salespeople affect net profits by the expenses they incur in generating sales. The selling expenses most under the control of salespeople are travel and entertainment expenses. Therefore, two salespeople could generate the same levels of total sales, the same sales/sales quota performance, and even the same levels of gross

EXHIBIT 10.9 Profitability Criteria

Base	Percentage of Firms Reporting Using
Sales	
Net profit dollars	69
Gross margin per sales (a percentage of sales)	34
Return on investment	33
Net profit as a percent(age) of sales	32
Margin by product category	28
Gross margin (in dollars)	25
Margin by customer type	18
Net profit per sale	14
Return on sales cost	14
Net profit contribution	—
Order(s)	
Number of orders secured	47
Average size of order secured	22
Order-per-call ratio (a.k.a. batting average)	14
Number of orders canceled	11
Net orders per repeat order	10
Number of canceled orders per orders booked	4
Selling Expense	
Selling expense versus budget	55
Total expenses	53
Selling expense to sales	49
Average cost per call	12
Selling expense to quota	12
Expenses by product category	7
Expenses by customer type	3

profits, but one salesperson could contribute more to net profits through lower travel and entertainment costs. Examples of **profitability criteria** are listed in Exhibit 10.9.[15]

Sales organizations are increasingly incorporating profitability criteria into their salesperson performance evaluations. The most frequently used profitability criterion is net profit dollars. Selling expenditures relative to budget is also heavily emphasized. The need to address profitability criteria is especially important during a slow-growth, competitive environment in which sales growth is so difficult and productivity and profitability so important.

Comment on Criteria

Conducting a comprehensive evaluation of salesperson performance typically requires consideration of behavioral professional development, results, and profitability criteria. Each set of criteria tells a different story as to how well salespeople have performed and provides different diagnostic information for control purposes. Michael Maretich, Global Sales Manager for the Stepan Company, explains the company's unique and highly effective sales performance evaluation system in "Sales Management in the 21st Century: Tri-State Chemical uses Automated Multiple Factor Assessments to Provide Real-Time Feedback to Salespeople and Sales Managers." This ongoing performance evaluation is integrated into sales managers' coaching of individual salespeople and incorporates multiple performance criteria and real-time feedback for performance improvement.

Tri-State Chemical uses Automated Multiple Factor Assessments to Provide Real-Time Feedback to Salespeople and Sales Managers

Vernon Bates, Sales Manager for Tri-State Chemical, provides insight into the company's successful use of a comprehensive and multi-factor model for evaluating salespeople.

Tri-State employs a multi-factor model for evaluating salespeople. While it does incorporate an extensive set of evaluations, the entire process is individualized for each salesperson. The four categories we evaluate for each salesperson are sales effort and activities, sales outcomes, profit production, and professional development. The category for sales effort and activities includes number of customer calls completed as well as calls made to non-customers, number of presentations made, number of proposals and quotes presented, and number of customer demonstrations and training sessions presented. Sales outcomes assess sales related accomplishments: dollar and unit sales volume generated, percent of quota by product group, ratio of new accounts gained compared to accounts lost, and customer reported level of satisfaction with the salesperson using the "Net Promoter Score." The profit production category assesses each salesperson's gross margin on sales dollars, average order size in dollars and units, and selling expense ratios. Evaluation of professional development takes into account number of training meetings the salesperson has completed—some of these can be completed online, timeliness in submitting sales reports, and customer ratings of the salesperson's level of selling skills, technical product knowledge, and enthusiasm. The process is fully automated and each salesperson—and their manager—has access to real-time dashboards and reports detailing performance on each measure at any time throughout the sales year. This level of detail and real-time information enable Tri-State's sales managers and salespeople to collaborate on action plans and has resulted in increased sales performance along with enhanced salesperson engagement and satisfaction.

Performance Evaluation Methods

Sales managers can use a number of different methods for measuring the behaviors, professional development, results, and profitability of salespeople. Ideally, the method used should have the following characteristics.

- *Job relatedness:* The performance evaluation method should be designed to meet the needs of each specific sales organization.
- *Reliability:* The measures should be stable over time and exhibit internal consistency.
- *Validity:* The measures should provide accurate assessments of the criteria they are intended to measure.
- *Standardization:* The measurement instruments and evaluation process should be similar throughout the sales organization.
- *Practicality:* Sales managers and salespeople should understand the entire performance appraisal process and should be able to implement it in a reasonable amount of time.
- *Comparability:* The results of the performance evaluation process should make it possible to compare the performance of individual salespeople directly.
- *Discriminability:* The evaluative methods must be capable of detecting differences in the performance of individual salespeople.
- *Usefulness:* The information provided by the performance evaluation must be valuable to sales managers in making various decisions.

Designing methods of salesperson performance evaluation that possess all these characteristics is a difficult task. As indicated in Exhibit 10.10, each evaluative method has certain strengths and weaknesses. No single method provides a perfect evaluation.

EXHIBIT 10.10   Comparison of Performance Evaluation Methods

Evaluation Criteria

Performance Evaluation Method	Job-Relatedness	Reliability	Validity	Standardization	Practicality	Comparability	Discriminability	Usefulness
Graphic rating/checklist	Very good	Good	Good	Very good	Very good	Very good	Poor	Good
Ranking	Poor	Poor	Poor	Very good	Poor	Good	Excellent	Poor
Objective-setting/MBO	Very good	Good	Good	Poor	Good	Poor	Good	Poor
Behaviorally Anchored Rating Scale (BARS)	Very good	Good	Good	Poor	Good	Poor	Poor	Good

---

Therefore, it is important to understand the strengths and weaknesses of each method so that several can be combined to produce the best evaluative procedure for a given sales organization.

Graphic Rating/Checklist Methods

Graphic rating/checklist methods consist of approaches in which salespeople are evaluated by using some type of performance evaluation form. The performance evaluation form contains the criteria to be used in the evaluation as well as some means to provide an assessment of how well each salesperson performed on each criterion. An example of part of such a form is presented in Exhibit 10.11.

EXHIBIT 10.11   Graphic Rating/Checklist Example

1. Asks customers for their ideas for promoting business
   Almost Never   1   2   3   4   5   Almost Always   N/A
2. Offers customers help in solving their problems
   Almost Never   1   2   3   4   5   Almost Always   N/A
3. Is constantly smiling when interacting with customers
   Almost Never   1   2   3   4   5   Almost Always   N/A
4. Admits when he/she doesn't know the answer, but promises to find out
   Almost Never   1   2   3   4   5   Almost Always   N/A
5. Generates new ways of tackling new or ongoing problems
   Almost Never   1   2   3   4   5   Almost Always   N/A
6. Returns customers' calls the same day
   Almost Never   1   2   3   4   5   Almost Always   N/A
7. Retains his or her composure in front of customers
   Almost Never   1   2   3   4   5   Almost Always   N/A
8. Delivers what he or she promises on time
   Almost Never   1   2   3   4   5   Almost Always   N/A

This method is popular in many sales organizations. It is especially useful in evaluating salesperson behavioral and professional development criteria. As part of its assessment process, Eastman Chemical Company asks its customers to evaluate their satisfaction with the company by using a rating scale. As evident from Exhibit 10.12, Eastman's salespeople are responsible for several behavior-based performance factors.[16] Rating methods have been developed to evaluate all the important salesperson performance dimensions. There are even employee-appraisal software programs, such as Reviewsnap, available to assist in the review process. The customizable program asks users to rate employees by goals, development plans, and competencies.[17]

As evident from Exhibit 10.10, graphic rating/checklist methods possess many desirable characteristics, especially in terms of job-relatedness, standardization, practicality, and comparability. The reliability and validity of these methods, however, must be continually assessed and the specific rating scales improved over time.

The major disadvantage of graphic rating/checklist methods is in providing evaluations that discriminate sufficiently among the performances of individual salespeople or among the performances on different criteria for the same salesperson. For example, some sales managers may be very lenient in their evaluations; they may try to play it safe and give all salespeople ratings around the average. In addition, when evaluating an individual salesperson, some sales managers are subject to a *halo effect,* meaning that their evaluations on one criterion affect their ratings on other criteria.

The advantages of graphic rating/checklist methods clearly outweigh the disadvantages. However, care must be taken to minimize potential sales management biases when the evaluation forms are completed, and continuous attention to reliability and validity issues is necessary.

Ranking Methods

Otherwise similar to graphic rating/checklist methods, **ranking methods** rank all salespeople according to relative performance on each performance criterion rather than evaluating them against a set of performance criteria. Companies such as Ford, General Electric, and Microsoft use ranking methods. Many approaches might be used to obtain the rankings. An example of a ranking approach in which salespeople are compared in pairs concerning relative communication skills is presented in Exhibit 10.13.

Ranking methods provide a standardized approach to evaluation and thus force discrimination as to the performance of individual salespeople on each criterion. The process of ranking forces this discrimination in performance. Despite these advantages, ranking methods have many shortcomings, as indicated in Exhibit 10.10. Of major concern are the constraints on their practicality and usefulness. Ranking all salespeople against each performance criterion can be a complex and cognitively difficult task. The ranking task can be simplified by using paired-comparison approaches like the one presented in Exhibit 10.13. However, the computations required to translate the paired comparisons into overall rankings can be extremely cumbersome.

Even if the evaluative and computative procedures can be simplified, the rankings are of limited usefulness. Rank data reveal only relative ordering and omit any assessment of the differences between ranks. For example, the actual differences in the communication skills of salespeople ranked first, second, and third may be small or large, but there is no way to tell the degree of these differences from the ranked data. In addition, information obtained from graphic rating/checklist methods can always be transformed into rankings, but rankings cannot be translated into graphic rating/checklist form. Despite their limitations, many companies find forced rankings to be an effective way to identify and reward core competencies. However, given their limitations, it is suggested that ranking methods for salesperson performance evaluations be used as a supplement to other methods.

Objective-Setting Methods

The most common and comprehensive goal-setting method is **management by objectives (MBO)**. Applied to a salesforce, the typical MBO approach is as follows:

EXHIBIT 10.12 Eastman Chemical Company Customer Satisfaction Survey

Importance: Rate the importance of each statement (your buying criteria) by asking, "Would I place additional business with a supplier who improved performance in this category from 'average' to 'outstanding'?"

Performance: Rate Eastman performance and your best "other supplier" on each criteria.

Importance
5—Definitely Would
4—Probably Would
3—Uncertain
2—Probably Would Not
1—Definitely Would Not
N/A—Not Applicable

Performance
5—Outstanding
4—Good
3—Average
2—Fair
1—Poor
N/A—Not Applicable

	Importance	Eastman	Best Other Supplier
Product			
1. Product Performance: Supplier provides a product that consistently meets your requirements and performance expectations.			
2. Product Mix: Supplier offers a range of products that meets your needs.			
3. Packaging: Supplier has the package type, size, and label to meet your needs.			
4. New Products: Supplier meets your needs through timely introduction of new products.			
5. Product Availability: Supplier meets volume commitments and is also fair and consistent during times of restricted supply.			
6. Product Stewardship: Supplier provides information about the transportation, storage, handling, use, recycling, disposal, and regulation of products and product packaging.			
Service			
7. Order Entry: Supplier has a user-friendly system to place orders that is flexible and responsive to routine order changes as well as urgent or special requests.			
8. Delivery: Supplier consistently delivers the right product on time and in satisfactory condition.			
9. Technical Service: Supplier provides timely technical support through training, information, problem solving, and assistance in current and new end-use applications.			
10. Sharing Information: Supplier is a resource for product, market, industry, and company information that helps you better understand business issues.			
11. New Ideas: Supplier offers new ideas that add value to your business.			

Eastman Chemical Company Customer Satisfaction Survey (*continued*)   EXHIBIT 10.12

	Importance	Performance	
		Eastman	Best Other Supplier
Pricing/Business Practices			
12. Pricing Practices: Supplier is consistent with the marketplace in establishing pricing practices.			
13. Paperwork: Supplier provides clear and accurate paperwork and business documents that meet your needs.			
14. Commitment to total quality management: Supplier exhibits strong commitment to total quality management in all aspects of their business.			
15. Responsiveness: Supplier listens and responds to your business needs in a timely manner.			
Relationship			
16. Integrity: Supplier is credible, honest, and trustworthy.			
17. Dependability: Supplier follows through on agreements.			
18. Supplier Contact: Supplier is easy to contact and provides the right amount of interface with the appropriate personnel.			
19. Problem Solving: Supplier provides empowered employees to solve your problems.			
Supplier Commitment			
20. Industry Commitment: Supplier exhibits a strong commitment to your industry.			
21. Regional Commitment: Supplier has the appropriate resources in place in your region to provide products and services needed.			
22. Customer Commitment: Supplier is strongly committed to helping your business be successful.			

1. Mutual setting of well-defined and measurable goals within a specified time period

2. Managing activities within the specified time period toward the accomplishment of the stated objectives

3. Appraisal of performance against objectives

As with all the performance evaluation methods, MBO and other goal-setting methods have certain strengths and weaknesses (see Exhibit 10.10). Although complete reliance on this or any other goal-setting method is inadvisable, the incorporation of some goal-setting procedures is normally desirable. This is especially true for

---

EXHIBIT 10.13 Ranking Method Example

Performance Criterion: Communication Skills

	Much Better	Slightly Better	Equal Better	Slightly Better	Much Better	
Jane Haynes	X	___	___	___	___	Ron Castaneda
Ron Castaneda	___	X	___	___	___	Bill Haroldson
Bill Haroldson	___	___	X	___	___	Jane Haynes

EXHIBIT 10.14 Quota Evaluation Example

Salesperson	Actual Quota	Weight	Weighted Performance	Index	Performance
Laura					
Sales	600,000	3	552,000	92	276
Gross profits	150,000	6	180,000	120	720
Demonstrations	200	4	250	125	500
Overall performance					115
David					
Sales	700,000	3	710,000	101	303
Gross profits	170,000	6	174,000	102	612
Demonstrations	200	4	200	100	400
Overall performance					101
Kendra					
Sales	550,000	3	650,000	118	354
Gross profits	140,000	6	100,000	71	426
Demonstrations	180	4	150	82	332
Overall performance					86

---

performance criteria related to quantitative behavioral, professional development, results, and profitability criteria. Absolute measures of these dimensions are often not very meaningful because of extreme differences in the territory situations of individual salespeople. The setting of objectives or quotas provides a means for controlling for territory differences through the establishment of performance benchmarks that incorporate these territory differences.

Quotas can be established for other important results criteria and for specific behavioral, professional development, and profitability criteria. Each type of quota represents a specific objective for a salesperson to achieve during a given period. Actual performance can be compared with the quota objective and a performance index calculated for each criterion being evaluated. The individual performance indices can then be weighted to reflect their relative importance and combined to produce an overall performance index. An example of this procedure is shown in Exhibit 10.14.

This example illustrates an evaluation of Laura, David, and Kendra on sales, gross profit, and demonstration quotas. The unequal weights reflect that the firm is placing the most importance on gross profits, followed by demonstrations and then sales. Laura has performed the best overall, but she did not reach her sales quota for this period.

David has performed reasonably well on all criteria. Kendra's situation is interesting in that she performed the best on the sales quota but poorly overall due to low performance indices for gross profits and demonstrations. Perhaps she is concentrating too much on short-term sales generation and not concerning herself with the profitability of sales or the number of product demonstrations. In any case, the use of quotas provides an extremely useful method for evaluating salesperson performance and highlighting specific areas in which performance is especially good or especially poor.

Behaviorally Anchored Rating Scales

The uniqueness of **behaviorally anchored rating scales (BARS)** is due to its focus on trying to link salesperson behaviors with specific results. These behavior-results linkages become the basis for salesperson performance evaluation in this method.

The development of a BARS approach is an iterative process that actively incorporates members of the salesforce. Salespeople are used to identify important performance results and the critical behaviors necessary to achieve those results. The critical behaviors are assigned numbers on a rating scale for each performance result. An example of one such BARS rating scale is presented in Figure 10.2.

The performance result in this example is achieving cooperative relations with sales team members. Seven behaviors have been assigned numbers on a 10-point rating scale to reflect the linkages between engaging in the behavior and achieving the result. This scale can then be used to evaluate individual salespeople. For instance, the example rating of 5.0 in the figure suggests that the salesperson occasionally supports the sales team on problems encountered in the field and thus achieves only a moderate amount of cooperation with sales team members.

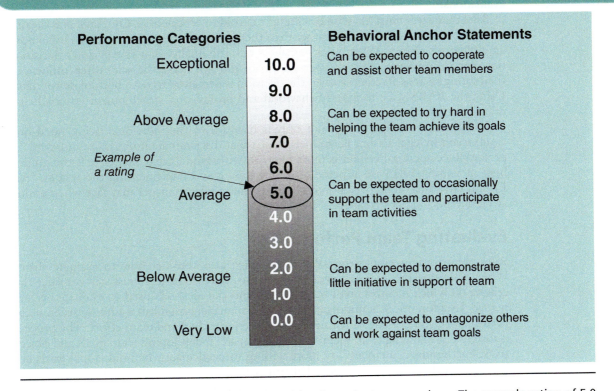

Evaluating: Cooperation with Other Sales Team Members   FIGURE 10.2

This scale evaluates a salesperson's cooperation with other sales team members. The example rating of 5.0 suggests a moderate level of cooperation in which the salesperson gives only occasional support to the sales team.

As indicated in Exhibit 10.10, the BARS approach rates high on job relatedness. This is because of the rigorous process used to determine important performance results and critical salesperson behaviors. The results and behaviors identified in this manner are specific to a given selling situation and directly related to the job of the salespeople being evaluated. Research indicates that positive feedback about sales behaviors has a greater impact on salesperson behavior than positive output feedback, perhaps because it gives salespeople direction for improving selling. The really unique aspect of BARS is the focus on linkages between behaviors and results. No other approach incorporates this perspective.

In sum, the basic methods for evaluating salesperson performance include graphic rating/checklist methods, ranking methods, objective-setting methods, and BARS methods. Each approach has specific strengths and weaknesses that should be considered. Combining different methods into the salesperson performance evaluation process is one way to capitalize on the strengths and minimize the weaknesses inherent in each approach.

Performance Evaluation Bias

Sales managers must be careful to avoid bias when assessing salespeople. For instance, sales managers tend to give more favorable performance ratings to those with whom they have closer personal relationships and less favorable performance ratings to those with whom they maintain formal role-defined relationships. Similarly, sales managers are more likely to discount internal responsibility while bolstering external explanations when appraising salespeople with whom they work well and are socially compatible. In addition, these salespeople are less likely to receive coercive feedback. Sales managers also tend to rate individuals in more difficult territories higher in ability and performance than those in less difficult territories. Furthermore, supervisors are more likely to rate those who are better at impression management (the ability to shape and manage a self-image that positively influences others), which tend to be males, more favorably when using subjective evaluations.

Sales managers must likewise be careful to avoid **outcome bias.** Outcome bias occurs when the outcome of a decision rather than the appropriateness of the decision influences an evaluator's ratings. When sales managers rate the quality of a salesperson's decision, outcome information (e.g., salesperson did or did not make the sale) often influences their ratings across all criteria when the decision is perceived to have been inappropriate. Using the BARS scale to assess behavioral and professional development criteria helps reduce outcome bias.

Performance evaluation bias not only is harmful to the individual being rated but could result in legal action. Personnel actions that discriminate unfairly are unlawful. A performance appraisal system is more likely to withstand a legal challenge if the guidelines in Exhibit 10.15 are adhered to in developing and implementing the system. "An Ethical Dilemma" illustrates potential difficulties a sales manager may face when evaluating salesperson performance.

Evaluating Team Performance

Sales organizations employing sales teams must also consider how to evaluate them. When designing the appraisal process for teams, sales managers must still consider the criteria on which members will be evaluated and the methods used to evaluate performance. In addition, it is important that sales managers establish a link between team performance and positive outcomes to promote individual and team effort. The process is fostered by allowing team members to participate in developing team goals and objectives. Furthermore, members are more willing to participate when individual goals are linked to team goals. Individual and group assignments necessary for reaching goals should be prioritized to help the team better manage its time.

Generally, the team as a whole should be evaluated, in addition to assessing individual member performance. Team performance can be measured by team members as well

Guidelines for Withstanding Discriminatory Appraisal Lawsuits   EXHIBIT 10.15

- Conduct reviews at least once a year, preferably more often.
- Base the appraisal system on a thorough job analysis that identifies the important duties or elements of job performance.
- Base the appraisal system on behaviors or results, not vague or ambiguous salesperson traits or characteristics.
- Observe salespeople performing their work.
- Train performance raters how to use the system, including proper use of the rating forms.
- Use the same rating form, that measures specific criteria, for all salespeople.
- Fill out the rating form *honestly*. Sales managers are asking for trouble if they allow salespeople to think their performances are satisfactory if they are not.
- Address both the salesperson's strengths and weaknesses.
- Carefully document appraisals and their rationale. Both the sales manager and salesperson should sign and date the evaluation after the meeting.
- Develop with the salesperson a plan of action and specific goals for the coming months.
- Bring in a third party for sensitive evaluation meetings.
- Never make reference to a legally protected class of which the salesperson is a member (e.g., racial or religious origin, gender, age).
- Have higher-level managers or human resource managers review appraisals.
- Develop a formal appeal mechanism or system that provides an avenue of appeal to salespeople who are dissatisfied with their evaluations.
- Provide performance counseling, guidance, and/or training to help poor performers improve their performance.

AN ETHICAL DILEMMA

Jason Singley is a District Manager for ENCO Distributing and is responsible for evaluating the performance of each of the 11 salespeople in his district. These annual performance appraisals play a large part in each of the salesperson's bonus and future promotion opportunities. Susan Carr, the company's National Sales Director, recently dropped by Jason's office and encouraged him to look favorable on one of his salespeople, Debra Green, during her upcoming performance appraisal. From that discussion, Jason understands that a regional sales management position has opened up in another district and suspects that Debra may be in line for the promotion—particularly if her performance evaluation is good. While Debra is a good salesperson, her performance has not exactly been outstanding. Jason's dilemma is further complicated by one of his other salespeople—a consistent top performer quarter after quarter—actually being a strong candidate for the promotion to

the sales manager position, although Jason would hate to lose him.

What should Jason do?

a. Follow the National Sales Director's suggestion and complete a favorable performance appraisal for Debra Green setting her up for the promotion.

b. Explain to the National Sales Director how the other salesperson is a better candidate for the promotion.

c. Both salespeople are very good salespeople and losing either of them for the promotion would negatively impact Jason's district sales performance. Jason should submit good performance reviews for both salespeople, but assure that the reviews are not strong enough to get them promoted. That way he can keep both of them in his district.

EXHIBIT 10.16 Teamwork Effectiveness and Measurement

ORCA TECHNOLOGIES, INC.
TEAMWORK EFFECTIVENESS EVALUATION

TEAM MEMBER BEING EVALUATED: **Bart Waits**

Team Communication	Never	Always
1. Listens effectively		1 2 3 4 ⑤
2. Is open-minded and receptive to ideas of others		1 2 ③ 4 5
3. Is organized in written and verbal communication		1 2 3 4 ⑤
4. Initiates and participates in discussions		1 2 ③ 4 5
5. Responds promptly to requests		1 2 3 4 ⑤
6. Confirms important communication in writing		1 2 3 ④ 5

Major Communication Strength:

Positive Suggestion for Improving Communication Skills:

Team Productivity	Never	Always
1. Is industrious and effectively uses time		1 2 ③ 4 5
2. Meets targets and deadlines		1 ② 3 4 5
3. Produces accurate and quality work		1 2 3 ④ 5
4. Organizes and plans effectively		1 2 ③ 4 5
5. Focuses on high-priority projects		1 2 ③ 4 5
6. Stays within team budgets		1 ② 3 4 5

Major Productivity Strength:

Positive Suggestion for Improving Productivity Skills:

Team Relationships	Never	Always
7. Is sensitive to the needs of other team members		1 2 3 4 ⑤
8. Is supportive of and concerned for other members		1 2 3 4 ⑤
9. Is flexible and cooperates with team members		1 2 3 ④ 5
10. Is dependable and keeps commitments		1 2 3 ④ 5
11. Is pleasant and maintains a positive attitude		1 2 3 4 ⑤
12. Is patient and maintains control		1 2 ③ 4 5

Major Relationship Strength:

Positive Suggestion for Improving Relationship Skills:

as by the sales manager. Exhibit 10.16 provides an example of a multidimensional approach team members can use to evaluate teammates' critical skills and behaviors. The measurement allows sales managers to develop a composite performance appraisal, merging each team member's viewpoint. The process helps strengthen teams, enhance morale, and contribute to a healthy working climate. In addition, the team and its members must be evaluated against predetermined performance criteria. Exhibit 10.17 outlines a process for measuring team performance.

For sales managers, it is important to note that less than effective team performance is often not the fault of individual team members, but of management. The commitment and support of top management has significant weight as a key determinant of a team's achievement. This commitment includes appropriate use of teams, provision of start-up support and training, enabling cross-team communication, and establishing accountability for team performance.

Steps for Measuring Team Performance   EXHIBIT 10.17

1. Develop team and individual performance standards and measures that will be used to gauge the level of performance achieved.
2. Map the standards and measures to relevant individual and team-level activities that will contribute to the achievement of the team.
3. Define the terminology precisely and review the criteria with team members to ensure both awareness and understanding.
4. Integrate inputs from management and team members to develop relative importance weights for the performance standards.
5. Decide how to collect the data and track performance for each standard and feed this information back to the team.
6. Take action based on the evaluations in order to recognize and reward appropriately.

Using Performance Information

Using different methods to evaluate the behavior, professional development, results, and profitability of salespeople provides extremely important performance information. The critical sales management task is to use this information to improve the performance of individual salespeople, sales teams, and the overall operations of the sales organization. Initially, it should be used to determine the absolute and relative performance of each salesperson. These determinations then provide the basis for reward disbursements, special recognition, promotions, and so forth.

The second major use of this performance information is to identify potential problems or areas in which salespeople need to improve for better performance in the future. If salespeople are evaluated against multiple criteria, as suggested in this chapter, useful diagnostic information will be available. The difficulty exists in isolating the specific causes of low performance areas. A framework for performing this analysis is given in Figure 10.3.

The first step in this analysis is to review the performance of each salesperson against each relevant criterion and summarize the results across all salespeople being supervised. The purpose of this step is to determine whether there are common areas of low performance. For example, the situation is different when most salespeople are not meeting their sales quotas than when only one or two salespeople are not meeting their sales quotas.

Once the poor performance areas have been identified, the sales manager must work backward to try to identify the cause of the poor performance. Merely determining that most salespeople did not meet their sales quotas is not sufficient to improve future performance; the sales manager must try to uncover the reason for this poor performance. The basic approach is to try to answer the question, "What factors affect the achievement of this performance dimension?" For instance, in regard to achieving sales quotas, the key question is, "What factors determine whether salespeople achieve their sales quotas?" All the factors identified should be reviewed to isolate the cause of any poor performance. Several factors that might cause poor performance in different areas are presented in Exhibit 10.18.

After identifying the potential causes of poor performance, the sales manager must determine the appropriate action to reduce or eliminate the cause of the problem so that performance will be improved in the future. Examples of potential management actions for specific problems are also presented in Exhibit 10.18.

Consider again poor performance on sales quota achievement. Assume that intense review of this problem reveals that salespeople not meeting sales quotas also do not make many product demonstrations to prospects. This analysis suggests that if salespeople were to make more product demonstrations, they would be able to generate more sales and thus achieve their sales quotas. The sales management task is to determine what

FIGURE 10.3 — Framework for Using Performance Information

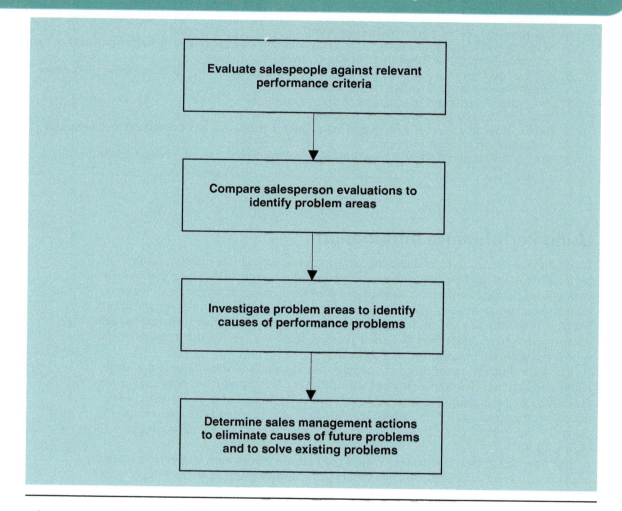

Sales managers need to be able to use the information provided by salesperson performance evaluations in a diagnostic manner. The basic diagnostic approach is to determine problem areas, identify the causes of these problems, and take appropriate action to eliminate the causes and to solve problems that are already present, thus improving future salesperson performance.

management actions will lead to more product demonstrations by salespeople. Possible actions include more training on product demonstrations, direct communication with individual salespeople about the need for more product demonstrations, or some combination of these or other management actions.

This discussion highlights the thought processes that sales managers need to use to identify performance problems, isolate the causes of these problems, and determine the appropriate management actions necessary to solve the problems and improve future salesperson performance. Using this approach successfully requires that sales managers have a detailed understanding of the personal selling and sales management processes and relationships. Such an understanding is essential for them to be able to determine the causes of performance problems and identify the appropriate management actions to solve these problems.

Our discussion and examples have emphasized problems affecting many salespeople. The same basic approach can be used for performance problems that are unique to one individual salesperson. In fact, many sales organizations use performance reviews as a means for a sales manager to meet with each salesperson, analyze the salesperson's

Sample Problems, Causes, and Management Actions   EXHIBIT 10.18

Performance Problems	Potential Causes	Sales Management Actions
Not meeting sales or other results quotas	Sales or other results quotas incorrect; poor account coverage; too few sales calls	Revise sales or other results quotas; revise effort allocation; redesign territories; develop motivational programs; provide closer supervision
Not meeting behavioral quotas	Behavioral quotas incorrect; too little effort; poor quality of effort	Revise behavioral quotas; develop motivational programs; conduct training programs; provide closer supervision
Not meeting profitability quotas	Profitability quotas incorrect; low gross margins; high selling expenses	Revise profitability quotas; change compensation; develop incentive programs; provide closer supervision; conduct training programs
Not meeting professional development quotas	Professional development quotas incorrect; inadequate training	Revise professional development quotas; conduct training programs; provide closer supervision; develop motivational programs; change hiring practices

performance on each criterion, and suggest ways to improve future performance. These performance reviews provide one means for communicating the *performance feedback* that is so important to salespeople. Performance feedback is also an important determinant of salesperson job satisfaction, which is discussed next.

SALESPERSON JOB SATISFACTION

In addition to evaluating salesperson performance, sales managers should be concerned with the **job satisfaction** of salespeople. Research results have consistently found relationships between salesperson job satisfaction and turnover, absenteeism, motivation, and organizational commitment. Salespeople who are satisfied with their job tend to stay with the firm and work harder than those who are not satisfied.

Other research has investigated relationships between salesperson performance and salesperson satisfaction. This research has produced conflicting findings concerning the direction of the relationship between performance and satisfaction. In other words, it has not been established whether achieving high performance causes salesperson satisfaction or whether salesperson satisfaction determines salesperson performance. However, there is some evidence that salespeople's job satisfaction has a positive effect on customer satisfaction.[18] It is clear, however, that sales managers should be concerned with both the performance and satisfaction of their salespeople. Of importance to sales managers is how salesperson satisfaction might be measured and then how this satisfaction information might be used.

Measuring Salesperson Job Satisfaction

Because job satisfaction is based on individual perceptions, measures of salesperson satisfaction must be based on data provided by individual salespeople. In addition, there are many different aspects of a salesperson's job, and these different areas should be

EXHIBIT 10.19   Sample Questions from Revised INDSALES Scale

Component	Total Number of Items	Sample Items
The job	4	My work gives me a sense of accomplishment. My job is exciting.
Fellow workers	4	My fellow workers are selfish. My fellow workers are pleasant.
Supervision	4	My sales manager really tries to get our ideas about things. My sales manager keeps his or her promises.
Company policy and support	4	Top management really knows its job. Management is progressive.
Pay	4	My pay is low in comparison with what others get for similar work in other companies. I'm paid fairly compared with other employees in this company.
Promotion and advancement	4	My opportunities for advancement are limited. I have a good chance for promotion.
Customers	4	My customers are loyal. My customers are trustworthy.

incorporated into the satisfaction evaluation. Fortunately, a scale for evaluating the job satisfaction of salespeople, termed INDSALES, has been developed, validated, and revised. Portions of the revised scale are presented in Exhibit 10.19.[19,20]

On this scale, salespeople indicate their level of agreement with statements concerning their particular sales job. These statements are designed to measure their satisfaction in seven general areas: satisfaction with the job, fellow workers, supervision, company policy and support, pay, promotion and advancement, and customers. Answers to the specific questions for each area are summed to produce a separate satisfaction score for each job dimension. These individual job dimension scores can then be summed to form an overall salesperson satisfaction score. Sales managers can then view the dimensional or overall satisfaction scores for each salesperson or for specified groups of salespeople.

Using Job Satisfaction Information

INDSALES provides extremely useful evaluative and diagnostic information. Because sales managers can evaluate the degree of salesperson satisfaction with specific aspects of the sales job, areas in which satisfaction is low can be investigated further by looking at the individual questions for that dimension. For example, if salespeople tended to express dissatisfaction with the supervision they were receiving, management could investigate the answers to the specific questions designed to evaluate the supervision dimension (see Exhibit 10.19). The sales manager in this example might find that most salespeople responded negatively to the statement, "My sales manager really tries to get our ideas about things." The sales manager could then try to increase salesperson satisfaction by using a more participative management style and trying to incorporate salesperson input into the decision-making process.

One useful approach is to perform separate analyses of salesperson satisfaction for high-performing and low-performing salespeople. Research results suggest that there may be important differences in job satisfaction between high performers and low performers. Not incorporating these differences could lead sales managers to make changes that would tend to reduce the turnover of low performers but not of high performers.

Research has also found an important relationship between salesperson satisfaction and performance feedback. Interestingly, negative output feedback does not lower satisfaction with supervisors, whereas negative behavioral feedback appears to improve satisfaction marginally. This suggests salespeople are open to feedback that helps improve their sales performance. Further support for this finding comes from studies showing that sales managers' leadership and role-modeling behaviors positively affect salespeople's job satisfaction. This suggests a sales manager can become an effective leader by doing many of the activities involved in performance appraisal: providing feedback on what salespeople need to improve; offering recognition and rewards in a manner that acknowledges individuals and teams; and helping and supporting salespeople in developing their talents and careers. Carefully evaluating salesperson performance and satisfaction, identifying problem areas, and solving these problems is really what sales management is all about.

SUMMARY

1. **Discuss the different purposes of salesperson performance evaluations.** Performance evaluations can serve many different purposes and should be designed with specific purposes in mind. They may serve to determine appropriate compensation and other reward disbursements, to identify salespeople who should be promoted or fired, to determine training and counseling needs, to provide information for human resource planning to identify criteria for future recruitment and selection of salespeople, to advise salespeople of work expectations, to motivate salespeople, to help salespeople set career goals, to tie individual performance to sales organization goals, to enhance communications, and to ultimately improve salesperson performance.

2. **Differentiate between an outcome-based and a behavior-based perspective for evaluating and controlling salesperson performance.** An outcome-based perspective focuses on objective measures of results, with little monitoring or direction of salesperson efforts by sales managers. By contrast, a behavior-based perspective focuses on close supervision of salesperson efforts and subjective measures of salesperson characteristics, activities, and strategies. The perspective taken by a sales organization will affect salespeople and has important implications for sales management.

3. **Describe the different types of criteria necessary for comprehensive evaluations of salesperson performance.** The multifaceted nature of sales jobs requires that performance evaluations incorporate multiple criteria. Although the specific criteria depend on the characteristics of a particular selling situation, comprehensive evaluations of salesperson performance require that four dimensions be addressed: behavioral, professional development, results, and profitability criteria. Addressing each of these areas is necessary to get a complete picture of salesperson performance and to produce the diagnostic information needed to improve future performance.

4. **Compare the advantages and disadvantages of different methods of salesperson performance evaluation.** Sales managers can use four basic methods to evaluate salesperson behaviors, professional development, results, and profitability: graphic rating/checklist methods, ranking methods, objective-setting methods, and behaviorally anchored rating scales (BARS). Each method has certain strengths and weaknesses that must be understood and can be compensated for by using other methods in combination. Special attention should be directed toward developing performance benchmarks or quotas that reflect the unique characteristics of each territory.

5. **Explain how salesperson performance information can be used to identify problems, determine their causes, and suggest sales management actions to solve them.** The suggested approach is to first identify areas of poor performance, then work backward to try to identify the cause by asking, "What factors affect the achievement of this performance dimension?" Finally, the most effective sales management action to remove the cause of the problem and improve future performance must be determined. Examples of possible actions are given in Exhibit 10.18.

6. **Discuss the measurement and importance of salesperson job satisfaction.** Dissatisfied salespeople tend to be absent more, leave the firm more, and work less hard than satisfied salespeople. The INDSALES scale can be used to measure salesperson satisfaction in total and for specific job dimensions. Analysis of the satisfaction with individual job dimensions can be used to determine appropriate action to increase salesperson job satisfaction.

UNDERSTANDING SALES MANAGEMENT TERMS

360-degree feedback	profitability criteria
performance management	graphic rating/checklist methods
outcome-based perspective	ranking methods
behavior-based perspective	management by objectives (MBO)
behavioral criteria	behaviorally anchored rating scales (BARS)
professional development criteria	outcome bias
results criteria	job satisfaction
sales quota	

DEVELOPING SALES MANAGEMENT KNOWLEDGE

1. Discuss the different purposes of an evaluation of salesperson performance and how each purpose affects the performance evaluation process.

2. Characterize the salesforce of a firm that uses an outcome-based perspective for evaluating salespeople.

3. Why should sales managers pay more attention to behavioral criteria when evaluating salespeople?

4. Compare and contrast the graphic rating/checklist and ranking methods for evaluating salesperson performance.

5. Consider the different types of ethical issues that sales managers might encounter in the process of conducting sales performance evaluations. List three of these ethical issues and explain how sales managers might effectively avoid and/or deal with each one.

6. Discuss the importance of using different types of quotas in evaluating and controlling salesperson performance.

7. What is unique about the BARS method for evaluating salesperson performance?

8. Explain the strengths and weaknesses of using the management by objectives (MBO) approach as a sales performance evaluation method.

9. Why should sales managers be concerned with the job satisfaction of salespeople?

10. How can evaluations of salesperson performance and satisfaction be used by sales managers?

BUILDING SALES MANAGEMENT SKILLS

1. Develop a method that can be used to evaluate salespeople's performance in the following areas: communication skills, attitude, initiative and aggressiveness, appearance and manner, knowledge of competition, enthusiasm, cooperation, and time management. Explain any advantages and/or disadvantages associated with your measurement method.

2. Using the following scale (1 to 5, with 1 being "strongly disagree" and 5 "strongly agree") and the statements in Exhibit 10.19, interview three salespeople and determine the level of job satisfaction of each. Explain areas of dissatisfaction and offer suggestions for improving satisfaction.

3. Following is an evaluation of salesperson Sally from the XYZ Corporation that was filled out by her sales manager. The company requires all its sales managers to use this form when evaluating salespeople.

   The following scale was used: Almost Never   1   2   3   4   5   Almost Always

	Sally's Score
Asks customers for their ideas for promoting business	2
Offers customers help in solving their problems	1
Is constantly smiling when interacting with customers	4
Admits when she does not know the answer, but promises to find out	4
Generates new ways of tackling new or ongoing problems	1
Returns customers' calls the same day	2
Retains her composure in front of customers	5
Delivers what she promises on time	1
Remains positive about the company in front of customers	5
Knows the design and specification of company products	4
Knows the applications and functions of company products	2
Submits reports on time	2
Maintains company specified records that are accurate and complete	2
Uses expense accounts with integrity	3
Uses business gift and promotional allowances responsibly	3
Controls costs in other areas of the company (order processing and preparation, delivery, etc.) when taking sales orders	3

   Identify any problems that you see with Sally and make suggestions for improving her performance. In your analysis, be sure to consider the reasons why Sally may be doing a poor job in some of these areas. How could information like this be used to improve the performance of the sales organization?

ROLE PLAY

4. **Role Play**

   Situation: Look at the evaluation of Sally from question 3. Identify problems you see with Sally.

   Characters: Brandon, sales manager; Sally, salesperson.

   Scene: *Location*—Brandon's office. *Action*—Brandon is discussing Sally's performance evaluation with her. He makes suggestions for improvements. Sally does not take the suggestions well. She becomes upset. She believes that Brandon is biased against her because she is a woman and lets him know this in no uncertain terms. In fact, she threatens to bring a lawsuit against him.

ROLE PLAY

5. **Role Play**

Situation: Read An Ethical Dilemma on p. 303.

Characters: Jason, district sales manager; Susan, national sales director and Jason's boss.

Scene: *Location*—Jason's office. *Action*—Susan is paying a visit to Jason to solicit his thoughts about Debra Green. She is very excited about Debra and makes suggestions about how she might be evaluated. Jason discusses his thoughts about Debra and suggests who he thinks would make a good candidate for the sales management position opening up next month.

6. Use the Internet to search for two performance evaluation software packages. You may want to Google "performance evaluation software" or "performance appraisal software." Provide the name of the software package and the company that provides it. Then, list the pros and cons of using each software package to help sales managers evaluate salespeople. Finally, of the two software packages you evaluated, if you were a sales manager, which would you choose to use and why?

MAKING SALES MANAGEMENT DECISIONS

CASE 10.1: MIDCON STEEL

Background

Tim Barnes is a district sales manager for Midcon Steel, a major fabricator and distributor of a wide variety of steel components for the commercial construction industry. Prior to joining Midcon, Tim was a salesperson for one of Midcon's major competitors and has some 14 years of experience in the steel sector. He was recruited and hired by Midcon largely because of his philosophy on personal selling. Tim's philosophy is customer-oriented and based on three premises. First, to succeed in sales requires the proper attitude. That is, a salesperson should have a positive, forward-looking, and cooperative attitude. Second, a salesperson should show initiative. Tim believes "that things don't happen until you take the right actions to make them happen." Third, salespeople should be aggressive, but never manipulative or unethical. Tim is convinced that honest and ethical behaviors lead to long-term, trusting relationships between buyers and sellers.

Current Situation

Tim is preparing for the process of a year-end evaluation of his salespeople. When the year began, he met with each salesperson to explain the criteria on which their performance would be judged. In a collaborative process, three sales performance quotas were established, including a sales dollar quota, new account quota, and sales call quota. The relative importance of each of these quotas was determined by the following weighting system: a weight factor of 4 for new accounts, 3 for sales dollars generated, and 2 for sales calls. It was also explained to the salespeople that their performance would also be evaluated by the number of customer complaints received and by the extent to which they submitted required reports. Finally, salespeople would be judged on their ability to meet customer needs. This includes sales reps' ability to suggest ideas for growing the business, helping customers solve problems, finding answers to customer questions not readily known, returning customers' calls, and delivering what is promised.

At a recent leadership seminar, Tim learned about the 360-degree performance appraisal process that involves getting feedback from multiple sources. Tim thought this would be an ideal way to evaluate his salespeople and decided he would have each salesperson give a questionnaire to a customer, a sales team member, and a member of Midcon's customer service unit to evaluate that salesperson's performance. Each questionnaire contained the following questions: (1) How often did you have contact with this salesperson over the course of the year? (2) Were you able to work closely with this salesperson to satisfy your needs? (3) Overall, how would you evaluate this salesperson's performance? (4) How satisfied are you with this salesperson? The questionnaire was to be signed by the respondent and returned to the salesperson who would then submit it to Tim for review. Tim figured that if he noticed something in the responses he did not like, he would discuss it with the salesperson. Tim thought that evaluating quota achievement would be a fairly straightforward process and that he could easily determine discrepancies and make salespeople aware of their shortcomings.

Questions

1. Assess Tim's use of 360-degree feedback for performance appraisal. Can you make any suggestions for improving this process?

2. What do you think about the type of feedback Tim is willing to provide his salespeople? How do you suggest the performance feedback be handled?

3. What can Tim do to ensure that his salespeople make efforts to improve their performance in the areas he deems important?

Role Play

ROLE PLAY

Situation: Read Case 10.1.

Characters: Tim Barnes, district sales manager; James Wall, regional sales manager.

Scene: *Location*—James Wall's office. *Action*—Wall is meeting with Tim to review how things have been going for him during his first year at Midcon. Tim explains his performance review process to Wall. Wall makes some suggestions for improving Tim's appraisal methods and performance feedback.

CASE 10.2: ROTA-MOLD
Background

Rota-Mold produces custom extruded and molded plastic parts for use by other manufacturers as components in producing automobiles and trucks, household tools and small appliances, and children's toys. Based in Chicago, Rota-Mold has been in business for over 30 years and is recognized as a leader in the industry. The company does business throughout North America and employs 160 salespeople. Its sales organization consists of three regions with four districts in each region. There are three regional sales managers and twelve district sales managers.

Last year, Jeremy Sutton was promoted to district sales manager at Rota-Mold. He had been a salesperson with a competing firm for five years prior to joining Rota-Mold two years ago. Jeremy was dissatisfied with the work environment at his previous employer, so when he arrived at Rota-Mold, he was eager to take on new challenges with a company he viewed as progressive.

Current Situation

As Jeremy reflected on his first year as district sales manager, he was concerned. His district had experienced higher-than-expected turnover among his salespeople during the year, and he was puzzled. In his opinion, Rota-Mold offered excellent pay and benefits, a cooperative work environment, a challenging and rewarding job, strong company support, and opportunity for promotion.

Although Jeremy was very satisfied at Rota-Mold, he began to believe that his salespeople might not be as happy. As a salesperson, he had noticed that dissatisfied colleagues' job performance often suffered. However, his salespeople's performance on the whole was not significantly down. Like many salesforces, his salespeople's performances ranged from less than average to outstanding. Nevertheless, he knew the importance of being satisfied. It was job dissatisfaction that led to his departure from his previous job.

In an attempt to measure the level of job satisfaction among his salespeople, Jeremy administered INDSALES to his salesforce. When the results were tabulated, he was surprised to find several areas in which salespeople expressed dissatisfaction. Salespeople seemed to be dissatisfied with their pay, thinking that it was low in comparison with what others were getting for similar work in other companies. Much to his dismay, Jeremy's salespeople seemed to be dissatisfied with him. They thought that he did not attempt to solicit their ideas about things and did not live up to his promises.

Salespeople also expressed their dissatisfaction with the promotion policy, believing that it was unfair. They did not think that promotion was based on ability. Although Jeremy was satisfied with the company's training program, his salespeople were not. Finally, salespeople did not believe they were receiving adequate support from the home office. Although Jeremy was surprised and disappointed at the level of dissatisfaction among his salespeople, he was glad he took steps to analyze their job satisfaction. He was eager to take steps to bring about greater satisfaction. Jeremy decided to draw up plans for improving satisfaction and present them to his boss at their meeting scheduled for next week.

Questions

1. What steps can Jeremy take to increase the level of satisfaction among his salespeople?

2. Rather than examining overall salesforce job satisfaction, what might be a more useful approach to examining salesforce job satisfaction with INDSALES?

3. What do you perceive the relationship to be between job satisfaction and turnover at Rota-Mold?

Role Play

ROLE PLAY

Situation: Read Case 10.2.

Characters: Jeremy Sutton, district sales manager; Alex Wilson, regional sales manager and Jeremy' boss; Sharon Ames, member of Jeremy's salesforce.

Scene 1:   *Location*—Wilson's office. *Action*—Jeremy explains to Wilson his plans for improving satisfaction amongst his salespeople. Wilson provides his reaction, including his assessment of Jeremy's method for determining salesforce job satisfaction.

Scene 2:   *Location*—in the car en route to a sales call. *Action*—Jeremy is accompanying one of his salespeople, Sharon Ames, on a sales call. He asks Sharon why his salespeople think he does a poor job soliciting their ideas and following through on promises and how she thinks he could improve in these areas. Sharon provides her thoughts and ideas.

360-degree feedback An assessment technique that involves performance assessment from multiple raters.

A

absorption training A method of sales training that involves furnishing trainees or salespeople with materials that they peruse without opportunity for immediate feedback and questioning.

account targeting strategy The classification of accounts within a target market into categories for the purpose of developing strategic approaches for selling to each account or account group.

achieving congruence The process of matching the capabilities of a sales recruit with the needs of the organization.

achieving realism The process of giving a sales recruit an accurate portrayal of the sales job.

activity-based costing (ABC) A method that allocates costs to individual units on the basis of how the units actually expend or cause these costs.

ADAPT A questioning methodology that can lead to productive interactions with buyers. ADAPT suggests that questions be used to **A**ssess the buyer's situation, **D**iscover their needs, **A**ctivate the buying process, **P**roject the impact of having the buyer solve a problem or realize an opportunity, and make a **T**ransition to the sales presentation or next step in the buying process.

adaptive selling The ability of a salesperson to alter their sales messages and behaviors during a sales presentation or as they encounter different sales situations and different customers.

AIDA An acronym for the various mental states the salesperson must lead their customers through when using mental states selling: **a**ttention, **i**nterest, **d**esire, and **a**ction.

amoral management A form of management in which management is neither moral nor immoral, but decisions lie outside the sphere to which moral judgments apply.

apathetics A salesperson who is low on commitment to the organization and low on involvement in his or her selling job.

assessment center Centers that offer a set of well-defined procedures for using techniques such as group discussions, business game simulations, presentations, and role-playing exercises for the purpose of employee selection or development.

B

background investigation A reference check on the job candidate that can help verify the true identity of the person and possibly confirm his or her employment history.

behavior approach A category of research that tries to uncover what makes an effective leader. It seeks to catalog behaviors associated with effective leadership.

behavior-based perspective A perspective that incorporates complex and often subjective assessments of salesperson characteristics and behaviors with considerable monitoring and directing of salesperson behavior by sales managers.

behavioral criteria Criteria for performance evaluation that emphasize exactly what each salesperson does.

behavioral simulations A method of sales training in which trainees portray specified roles in staged situations.

behaviorally anchored rating scales (BARS) A performance evaluation method that links salesperson behaviors with specific results.

benchmarking An ongoing measurement and analysis process that compares an organization's current operating practices with the "best practices" used by world-class organizations.

bottom-up forecasting approaches A forecasting approach that consists of different methods for developing sales forecasts for individual accounts; these forecasts are then combined by sales managers into territory, district, region, zone, and company forecasts.

breakdown approach An approach used for calculating salesforce size that assumes an accurate sales forecast is available, which is then "broken down" to determine the number of salespeople needed to generate the forecasted level of sales.

business consultant A role the salesperson plays in consultative selling where he or she uses internal and external (outside the sales organization) sources to become an expert on the customer's business. This role also involves educating customers on the sales firm's products and how these products compare with competitive offerings.

business marketing A marketing situation in which business is the target market.

business strategy An organizational strategy level that must be developed for each strategic business unit (SBU) in the corporate family, defining how that SBU plans to compete effectively within its industry.

business unit portfolio A firm's portfolio of their SBUs.

buying center The many individuals from a firm who participate in the purchasing process.

buying needs Buying behavior that can be personal and organizational. The organizational purchasing process is meant to satisfy the needs of the organization; however, the buying center is made up of individuals who want to satisfy individual needs.

Buying Power Index (BPI) A market factor calculated for different areas by the equation $BPI = (5I + 2P + 3R) \div 10$ where I = Percentage of U.S. disposable personal income in the area, P = Percentage of U.S. population in the area, and R = Percentage of U.S. retail sales in the area.

buying process Organizational buyer behavior that consists of several phases: Phase 1 is recognition of problem or need; Phase 2 is determination of the characteristics of the item and the quantity needed; Phase 3 is description of the characteristics of the item and quantity needed; Phase 4 is search for and qualification of potential sources; Phase 5 is acquisition and analysis of proposals; Phase 6 is evaluation of proposals and selection of suppliers; Phase 7 is selection of an order routine; Phase 8 is performance feedback and evaluation.

C

career fair An event in which several employers are brought together in one location (physically or virtually) for recruiting purposes.

candor Salespeople must communicate with candor, or honesty, to build trust-based relationships with customers. Acting otherwise can ruin a business relationship, perhaps forever.

centralization The degree to which important decisions and tasks in an organization are performed at higher levels in the management hierarchy.

change agent A key role played by salespeople as they stimulate sales cycles and help customers reach buying decisions as soon as reasonably possible. By being a catalyst for change, salespeople are involved in diffusion of innovation and can have a positive impact on economic cycles.

channel conflict Occurs when the interests of different channels are not consistent.

classroom / conference training Sales training that features lectures, demonstrations, and group discussion with expert trainers serving as instructors.

coaching A leadership function in which a sales manager concentrates on continuous development of salespeople through supervisory feedback and role modeling.

code of ethics A written code of ethical business behavior that members of an association are urged to adhere to.

coercive power Power in an interpersonal relationship that is based on a belief that one party can remove rewards and provide punishment to affect behavior.

cognitive feedback Information about how and why the desired outcome is achieved.

commission base Commission pay based on sales volume or some measure of profitability.

commission payout event Commission pay that is given when the order is confirmed, shipped, billed, paid for, or some combination of these events.

commission rate Commission pay in which a percentage of the commission earned is paid to the salesperson.

commission splits Commission pay that is divided between two or more salespeople or between salespeople and the employer.

communications agent A key role performed by salespeople who are involved in two-way communications between their customers and their employers. This exchange of information has economic and strategic value for both customers and sales organizations.

compensation rewards Organizational rewards that are given in return for acceptable performance or effort.

competitive knowledge Knowledge of a competitive product's strengths and weaknesses in the market.

conflicts of interest Job conflicts that place the salesperson in a position that could violate customer demands to benefit the company, or that could violate company policy to benefit customer demands.

constant rate A commission rate in which the salesperson is paid a constant percentage of what he or she sells.

consultative selling The process of helping customers reach their strategic goals by using the products, services, and expertise of the sales organization.

contingency approach A category of research that tries to uncover what makes an effective leader and recognizes the importance of the interaction between situational factors and other factors.

continued affirmation An example of stimulus response selling in which a series of questions or statements furnished by the salesperson is designed to condition the prospective buyer to answering "yes" time after time, until, it is hoped, he or she will be inclined to say "yes" to the entire sales proposition.

contribution approach An approach to determining an organization's profitability that only uses direct costs, not indirect or shared costs; net contribution is calculated from this approach.

corporate citizens A salesperson who is highly committed to the organization, but who does not strongly identify with his or her selling role.

corporate mission statement A statement that provides direction for strategy development and execution throughout the organization.

corporate strategy An organizational strategy level that consists of decisions that determine the mission, business portfolio, and future growth directions for the entire corporate entity.

cost analysis The assessment of costs incurred by the sales organization to generate the achieved levels of sales.

current spendable income Money provided in the short term that allows salespeople to pay for desired goods and services.

customer compatibility Refers to the customer's perception that a salesperson is a good person to do business with. Personal characteristics such as a pleasant personality can enhance compatibility, but professionalism and making it easy for the customer to do business with the selling firm also determine compatibility.

customer knowledge Information relating to customers' needs, buying motives, buying procedures, and personalities.

customer orientation A customer orientation can be demonstrated through behaviors such as determining the buyer's unique needs before recommending a purchase, preventing and correcting problems, and sincere listening during sales calls.

customer relationship management (CRM) A business strategy to select and manage the most valuable customer relationships. It requires a customer-centric business philosophy and culture to support effective marketing, sales, and service processes.

customer survey A survey intended to define customer expectations.

customer value The customer's perception of what they receive (e.g., products, services, information) in exchange for what they give up (e.g., time, effort, and money). Customer value is influenced by the buyer's situations, needs, and priorities.

customer value agent A key role of salespeople which includes creating, communicating, delivering, and continually increasing customer value.

D

decision model An analytical approach to the allocation of selling effort in which mathematical formulations are used to achieve the highest level of sales for any given number of sales calls and to continue increasing sales calls until their marginal costs equal their marginal returns.

decomposition method Method for developing company forecasts by breaking down previous company sales data into four major components: trend, cycle, seasonal, and erratic events.

Delphi method A structured type of jury of executive opinion method that involves selection of a panel of managers from within the firm who submit anonymous forecasts for each account.

dependability Salespeople demonstrate dependability by simply doing what they say they will do. Dependability is essential for building customer trust.

detailer A salesperson in the pharmaceutical industry working at the physician level to furnish valuable information regarding the capabilities and limitations of medications in an attempt to get the physician to prescribe their product.

differentiation strategy A type of generic business strategy. It involves the creation of something perceived industrywide as being unique and provides insulation against competitive rivalry because of brand loyalty and resulting lower sensitivity to price.

diffusion of innovation The process whereby new products, services, and ideas are distributed to the members of society.

direction Salespeople choose where their efforts will be spent among various job activities.

distributors channel Middlemen that take title to the goods that they market to end users.

E

economic stimuli Something that stimulates or incites activity in the economy.

effectiveness index A type of sales analysis that can be computed by dividing actual sales results by the sales quota and multiplying by 100.

employee referral programs Interorganizational programs in which existing employees are used as sources for recruiting new salespeople because they have a good understanding of the type of person sought for a sales position.

ethical leadership communicates and models ethical behavior, listens to and balances employee interests in making fair decisions, and judges success by how results are obtained to promote ethical behavior in the salesforce.

expense account padding Expense reimbursement in which a salesperson seeks reimbursement for ineligible or fictional expenses.

expert power Power in an interpersonal relationship that is based on the belief that a person has valuable knowledge or skills in a given area.

exponential smoothing A type of moving averages method that weights company sales in the most recent year differently than company sales in the past years.

extensive problem solving The lengthy decision-making process to collect and evaluate purchase information in new task-buying situations.

extrinsically motivated Motivation occurring when salespeople are rewarded by others.

F

farmers Sometimes referred to as order-takers, these salespeople try to increase sales with existing customers.

financial compensation mix The relative amounts to be paid in salary, commission, and bonus.

financial contributor A key role played by salespeople as they produce revenue for their organizations and improve profitability by enhancing sales organization productivity.

forecast A prediction for a future period; forecasts provide the basis for making sales management decisions.

full cost approach An approach that deals with shared costs in an organization by allocating the shared costs to individual units based on some type of cost allocation procedure that results in a net profit figure.

functional specialization Term used to describe a salesforce in which salespeople specialize in a required number of selling activities.

G

generic business strategies The most popular of classification schemes used in developing a business unit strategy. These generic strategies are low cost, differentiation, or niche.

geographic specialization Term used to describe a salesforce whose salespeople are typically assigned a geographic area and are responsible for all selling activities to all accounts within the assigned area.

global account management (GAM) A type of major account organization that serves the needs of major customers with locations around the world.

government organizations Federal, state, and local government agencies.

graphic rating/checklist methods Approaches in which salespeople are evaluated by using some type of performance evaluation form.

H

hierarchical sales analysis A way to identify problem areas in achieving sales effectiveness that consists of evaluating sales results throughout the sales organization from a top-down perspective.

hunters Salespeople who focus on gaining new customers; these salespeople increase market share for their companies by adding new customers. Hunters may also be called order-getters and pioneers.

hybrid sales organization A sales organization structure that incorporates several of the basic structural types; the objective of a hybrid structure is to capitalize on the advantages of each type while minimizing the disadvantages.

I

immoral management A form of management in which management decisions, actions, and behavior imply a positive and active opposition to what is ethical.

income statement analysis A type of profitability analysis that studies the different levels in a sales organization and different types of sales.

incremental approach An approach used for calculating salesforce size that compares the marginal profit contribution with the marginal selling costs for each incremental salesperson.

independent representatives Independent sales organizations that sell complementary, but noncompeting, products from different manufacturers; also called manufacturers' representatives or reps.

industrial distributors Sales channel middlemen who take title to the goods they market to end users.

influence strategies A type of communication strategy sales managers can use on their salesforce that can be based on threats, promises, persuasion, relationships, and manipulation.

initial interviews Brief interviews used to screen job applicants in order to replace a review of resumes or application forms.

initiation to task The degree to which a sales trainee feels competent and accepted as a working partner.

institutional stars A salesperson who is highly committed to the organization and highly involved in his or her selling job.

institutions Public and private organizations.

integrated marketing communication (IMC) The strategic integration of multiple marketing communication tools in the most effective and efficient manner.

integrative meeting A sales meeting in which several sales and sales management functions are achieved.

intensity The amount of mental and physical effort put forth by the salesperson.

intensive interviews Interviews conducted to get an in-depth look at a job candidate.

interviewer bias Something that occurs when an interviewer allows personal opinions, attitudes, and beliefs influence judgments about a job candidate.

intrinsically motivated Motivation occurring when salespeople find their jobs inherently rewarding.

J

job analysis The process of investigating the tasks, duties, and responsibilities of the job.

job application form A form job applicants fill out designed to gather all pertinent information and exclude unnecessary information.

job description A written summary of the job.

job involvement A strong attachment by the salesperson to the job itself.

job preview The process of giving a sales recruit an idea of what the sales job constitutes and how the job is performed.

job qualifications The aptitude, skills, knowledge, personal traits, and willingness to accept occupational conditions necessary to perform the job.

job rotation The exposure of the sales trainee to different jobs.

job satisfaction A salesperson's happiness with his or her job.

job security Job reward in which the salesperson feels comfortable that his or her job will last.

jury of executive opinion method A bottom-up forecasting approach in which the executives of the firm use their expert knowledge to forecast sales to individual accounts.

L

Leader–Member Exchange (LMX) model A sales leadership model that focuses on the salesperson–sales manager dyad as a reciprocal influence process.

leadership The use of influence with other people through communication processes to attain specific goals and objectives.

legitimate power Power in an interpersonal relationship that is associated with the right to be a leader, usually as a result of designated organizational roles.

limited problem solving The decision-making process that occurs in a modified rebuy buying situation that involves collecting additional information and making a change when purchasing a replacement product.

line sales management Sales management position that is part of the direct management hierarchy within the sales organization. Line sales managers have direct responsibility for a certain number of subordinates and report directly to management at the next highest level in the sales organization.

lone wolf A salesperson who is often enthusiastic about his or her selling job (high involvement), but who is not bound to his or her organization (low commitment).

long-term ally A role the salesperson plays in consultative selling where he or she supports the customer, even when an immediate sale is not expected.

low-cost strategy A type of generic business strategy. It involves aggressive construction of efficient-scale facilities, vigorous pursuit of cost reductions from experience, tight cost, and overhead control, usually associated with high relative market share.

M

major account organization A type of market specialization based on account size and complexity; an organization that handles major accounts, or large, important accounts.

major account selling The development of specific programs to serve a firm's largest and most important accounts.

management by objectives (MBO) A performance evaluation method that involves the (1) mutual setting of well-defined and measurable goals within a specified time period, (2) managing activities within the specified time period toward the accomplishment of the stated objectives, and (3) appraisal of performance against objectives.

management levels The number of different hierarchical levels of sales management within the organization.

manipulation An influence strategy that involves sales managers controlling circumstances to influence the target of influence.

market bonus A one-time payment given upon hiring that recognizes an existing imbalance in the supply and demand in a given labor market to entice a sales recruit to join the organization.

market factor method Method for breaking down company forecasts that involves identifying one or more factors that are related to sales at the zone, region, district, territory, or account levels and using these factors to break down the overall company forecast into forecasts at these levels.

market specialization Term used to describe a salesforce that assigns salespeople specific types of customers and are required to satisfy all needs of these customers.

marketing mix A marketing offer designed to appeal to a defined target market.

marketing strategy An organizational strategy level that includes the selection of target market segments and the development of a marketing mix to serve each target market.

mental states selling An approach to personal selling that assumes that the buying process for most buyers is essentially identical and that buyers can be led through certain mental states, or steps, in the buying process; also called the formula approach.

mentor A coach or sales trainer who observes and informs sales trainees on how to improve their sales performances.

merchandiser Sales support personnel who support the retail sales effort by setting up point-of-purchase displays, rotating stock, and keeping store personnel informed about new products and sales promotions.

misrepresentation Something that occurs when incorrect information is given about a job to entice a sales recruit into taking that job.

missionary salespeople Salespeople who usually work for a manufacturer but may also be found working for brokers and manufacturing representatives. Sales missionaries are expected to "spread the word" to convert noncustomers to customers.

modified rebuy buying situation A situation that exists when an account has previously purchased and used the product.

moral management A form of management in which management activity conforms to a standard of ethical, or right, behavior.

motivation A measurement of an individual's intensity, persistence, and direction.

moving averages Method for developing company forecasts by calculating the average company sales for previous years.

multilevel selling A variation of team selling in which the emphasis is to match functional areas between the buying and selling firms.

N

national account management (NAM) A type of major account organization that focuses on meeting the needs of specific accounts with multiple locations throughout a large region or entire country.

need satisfaction selling An approach to selling based on the notion that the customer is buying to satisfy a particular need or set of needs.

needs assessment A process performed to compare the specific performance-related skills, attitudes, perceptions, and behaviors required for salesforce success with the state of readiness of the salesforce.

new task buying situation A situation in which an organization is purchasing a product for the first time.

niche strategy A type of generic business strategy. It involves service of a particular target market, with each functional policy developed with this target market in mind. Although market share in the industry might be low, the firm dominates a segment within the industry.

noncompensation rewards Organizational rewards that include factors related to the work situation and wellbeing of each salesperson.

nonfinancial compensation Job rewards that include career advancement through promotion, sense of accomplishment on the job, opportunities for personal growth, recognition of achievement, and job security.

O

objective and task method A type of zero-based budgeting in which each sales manager prepares a separate budget request that stipulates the objectives achieved, the tasks required to achieve these objectives, and the costs associated with performing the necessary tasks.

observation The process in which sales managers monitor their salespeople during field selling activities.

on-the-job training (OJT) Sales training that puts the trainee into actual work circumstances under the observant eye of a supportive mentor or sales manager.

opportunities for personal growth Job reward such as college tuition reimbursement programs and seminars and workshops on such topics as physical fitness, stress reduction, and personal financial planning.

opportunity for promotion Job reward in which a salesperson obtains a higher job position on the organizational chain.

order-getters Salespeople who actively seek orders, usually in a highly competitive environment.

order-takers Salespeople who specialize in maintaining existing business.

organizational commitment A psychological bond to an organization or a bond demonstrated through behavior over time.

original equipment manufacturers (OEM) Organizations that purchase products to incorporate into products.

outcome bias The prejudice that occurs when the outcome of a decision rather than the appropriateness of the decision influences an evaluator's ratings.

outcome feedback Information about whether a desired outcome is achieved.

outcome-based perspective A perspective that focuses on objective measures of results with little monitoring or directing of salesperson behavior by sales managers.

P

percentage of sales method A method of cost analysis that calculates an expenditure level for each category by multiplying an expenditure percentage times forecasted sales.

performance bonus A type of current spendable income used to direct effort toward relatively short-term objectives.

performance management An approach that involves sales managers and salespeople working together on setting goals, giving feedback, reviewing, and rewarding.

performance testing A method used to determine sales training needs that specifies the evaluation of particular tasks or skills of the salesforce.

persistence The salesperson's choice to expend effort over time, especially when faced with adverse conditions.

personal selling Personal communication with an audience through paid personnel of an organization or its agents in such a way that the audience perceives the communicator's organization as being the source of the message.

persuasion An influence strategy in which sales managers use expert and referent power to imply that the target of influence must first change his or her attitudes and intentions to produce a subsequent change in behavior.

pioneers Salespeople who are constantly involved with either new products, new customers, or both. Their task requires creative selling and the ability to counter the resistance to change that will likely be present in prospective customers.

planned earnings An advantage of fixed salaries in which management can predict easily what individuals will be paid.

planning activities The first step in the salesperson recruitment and selection process; they include (1) conducting a job analysis, (2) establishing job qualifications, (3) completing a written job description, (4) setting recruitment and selection objectives, and (5) developing a recruitment and selection strategy.

planning and control unit The first step in territory design; an entity that is smaller than a territory.

portfolio models An analytical approach to the allocation of selling effort where each account served by a firm is considered as part of an overall portfolio of accounts; therefore, accounts within the portfolio represent different situations and receive different levels of selling effort attention.

private employment agency An external source for recruiting salespeople in which a fee is charged by the agency that is paid by the employer or the job seeker, as established by contract before the agency begins work for either party.

problem-solving selling An extension of need satisfaction selling that goes beyond identifying needs to developing alternative solutions for satisfying these needs.

product knowledge Knowledge about a product's benefits, applications, competitive strengths, and limitations.

product specialization Term used to describe a salesforce that assigns salespeople selling responsibility for specific products or product lines.

productivity analysis A form of analysis that is measured in terms of ratios between outputs and inputs.

professional development criteria Criteria for performance evaluation that assess improvements in certain characteristics of salespeople that are related to successful performance on the sales job.

professional organizations Professional organizations sales executives join to establish a network of colleagues who have common interests.

profitability analysis An analysis that combines sales and cost data to produce a measure of how profitable an organization is.

profitability criteria Criteria for performance evaluation that assess the profitability of sales.

progressive rate A commission rate in which the percentage a salesperson is paid increases as he or she reaches prespecified selling targets.

promises An influence strategy in which sales managers can use reward power to achieve desired behaviors.

R

ranking methods Approaches in which salespeople are evaluated according to a relative performance on each performance criterion rather than evaluating them against a set of performance criteria.

recognition Job reward that can be informal such as "nice job" accolades, or formal such as group competition or individual accomplishments representing improved performance.

recruitment The second step in the salesperson recruitment and selection process; it is the procedure of locating a sufficient number of prospective job applicants.

recruitment and selection strategy A plan formulated after the recruitment and selection objective have been set that requires the sales manager to consider the scope and timing of recruitment and selection activities.

referent power Power in an interpersonal relationship that is based on the attractiveness of one party to another.

regressive rate A commission rate in which the percentage a salesperson is paid declines at some predetermined point.

relationship strategy A determination of the type of relationship to be developed with different account groups.

relationships An influence strategy containing two types of influence processes: one based on referent power that builds on personal friendships, or feelings of trust, admiration, or respect; the other based on legitimate power over another party by virtue of position in the organizational hierarchy.

resellers Organizations that purchase products to sell.

results criteria Criteria for performance evaluation that assess the results achieved by salespeople.

return on assets managed (ROAM) A calculation that can extend the income statement analysis to include asset investment considerations.

revenue producers Something that brings in revenue or income to a firm or company.

reward power Power in an interpersonal relationship that stems from the ability of one party to reward the other party for a designated action.

reward system management The selection and use of organizational rewards to direct salespeople's behavior toward the attainment of organizational objectives.

role definition A salesperson's understanding of what tasks are to be performed, what the priorities of the tasks are, and how time should be allocated among the tasks.

role playing A method of sales training in which one trainee plays the role of the salesperson and another trainee acts as the buyer; role playing is videotaped or performed live for a group of observers, who then critique the performance.

routinized response behavior The process in which a buyer is merely reordering from the current supplier.

S

salary compression A narrow range of salaries in a salesforce.

salary plus incentive Payment plans for salespeople that feature some combination of salary, commission, and bonus pay.

sales analysis An important element in evaluating sales organization effectiveness in which the organization studies its sales progress.

sales channel strategy The process of ensuring that accounts receive selling effort coverage in an effective and efficient manner.

sales contests Temporary programs that offer financial and/or nonfinancial rewards for accomplishing specified, usually short-term, objectives.

sales dialogue Business conversations which take place over time as salespeople attempt to initiate, develop, and enhance relationships with customers.

sales expenses Expenses incurred while on the job that include travel, lodging, meals, entertainment of customers, telephone, and personal entertainment.

sales leadership Activities that influence others to achieve common goals for the collective good of the sales organization and the company.

sales management Activities related to the planning, implementation, and control of the sales management process.

sales meeting A gathering of salespeople, sales managers, and sometimes other business functions to achieve specific objectives, such as salesperson motivation, recognition, or training.

sales organization audit A comprehensive, systematic, diagnostic, and prescriptive tool used to assess the adequacy of a firm's sales management process and to provide direction for improved performance and prescription for needed changes.

sales process A series of interrelated steps beginning with locating qualified prospective customers. From there, the salesperson plans the sales presentation, makes an appointment to see the customer, completes the sale, and performs post-sale activities.

sales productivity The ratio of sales generated to selling effort used.

sales professionalism Common elements of sales professionalism include the use of customer-oriented, truthful, non-manipulative sales strategies and tactics to satisfy the long-term needs of customers and the selling firm. Sales professionalism also requires that salespeople work from a dynamic, ever-changing knowledge base.

sales quota A reasonable sales objective for a territory, district, region, or zone.

sales supervision Activities related to working with subordinates on a day-to-day basis.

sales support personnel A firm's personnel whose primary responsibility is dissemination of information and performance of other activities designed to stimulate sales.

sales techniques Fundamental procedures salespeople can follow to make sales.

sales trainer A mentor for salespeople in their organization who provides advice and information for improving sales performance.

sales training media Communications and computer technology used in the sales training process.

sales training objectives Objectives sales managers set during sales training that force the manager to define the reasonable expectations of sales training.

salesforce audit A systematic, diagnostic, prescriptive tool that can be employed on a periodic basis to identify and address sales department problems and to prevent or reduce the impact of future problems.

salesforce composite method A bottom-up forecasting approach that involves various procedures by which salespeople provide forecasts for their assigned accounts, typically on specially designed forms or electronically via computer.

salesforce deployment Important sales management decisions involved in allocating selling effort, determining salesforce size, and designing territories.

salesforce socialization The process by which salespeople acquire the knowledge, skills, and values essential to perform their jobs.

salesforce survey A survey in which sales managers monitor their salesforce in an attempt to isolate sales training needs.

salesperson competence Salesperson competence, or expertise, is an important dimension required to build customer trust. Customers expect salespeople to know what they are doing and to get answers if they don't already know the answer.

selection The third step in the salesperson recruitment and selection process; it is the process of choosing which candidates will be offered the job.

self-management An individual's effort to control certain aspects of his or her decision making and behavior.

selling budget Corporate resources earmarked for personal selling expenses for a designated period.

selling strategy Involves the planning of sales messages and interactions with customers. Selling strategy can be defined at three levels: for a group of customers, i.e., a sales territory; for individual customers; and for specific customer encounters, referred to as sales calls.

sense of accomplishment Job reward that emanates from the salesperson's psyche.

sexual harassment Lewd remarks, physical and visual actions, and sexual innuendos that make individuals feel uncomfortable.

single factor models An analytical approach to the allocation of selling effort in which the typical procedure is to classify all accounts on one factor and then to assign all accounts in the same category the same number of sales calls.

Six Sigma A data-driven methodology that attempts to eliminate defects in any process.

span of control The number of individuals who report to each sales manager.

SPIN selling A problem solving approach to selling that assesses the customer's Situation, determines a customer Problem, analyses the Implications of those problems, and proposes a solution (Need payoff).

specialization A concept in which certain individuals in an organization concentrate on performing some of the required activities to the exclusion of other tasks.

staff sales management Sales management position that does not directly manage people, but is responsible for certain functions (e.g., recruiting and selecting, training) and is not directly involved in sales-generating activities.

stimulus response selling An approach to selling in which the key idea is that various stimuli can elicit predictable responses from customers. Salespeople furnish the stimuli from a repertoire of words and actions designed to produce the desired response.

straight commission A form of payment in which salespeople are paid by commission only.

straight rebuy buying situation A situation wherein an account has considerable experience in using the product and is satisfied with the current purchase arrangements.

straight salary A form of payment in which salespeople are paid one set salary.

strategic account organization Represents a type of market specialization based on account size and complexity.

strategic business unit (SBU) A single product or brand, a line of products, or a mix of related products that meets a common market need or a group of related needs, and the unit's management is responsible for all (or most) of the basic business functions.

strategic orchestrator A role the salesperson plays in consultative selling in which he or she arranges the use of the sales organization's resources in an effort to satisfy the customer.

stress interview An interview designed to put job candidates under extreme, unexpected, psychological duress for the purpose of seeing how they react.

supervision The day-to-day control of the salesforce under routine operating conditions.

survey of buyer intentions method A bottom-up forecasting approach that asks individual accounts about their purchasing plans for a future period and translates these responses into account forecasts.

T

target market A specific market segment to be served.

task-specific self-esteem The feeling salespeople have about themselves relating to performing and accomplishing job-related duties; high levels have been linked to improved performance and job satisfaction.

team selling The use of multiple-person sales teams in dealing with multiple-person buying centers of their accounts.

telemarketing A sales channel that consists of using the telephone as a means for customer contact to perform some of or all the activities required to develop and maintain account relationships; also called telesales.

territory A designated area that consists of whatever specific accounts are assigned to a specific salesperson.

threats An influence strategy in which a manager might specify a desired behavior and the punishment that will follow if the behavior is not achieved.

time and territory management (TTM) Salesperson's training to teach salespeople how to use time and efforts for maximum work efficiency.

top-down forecasting approaches A forecasting approach that consists of different methods for developing company forecasts at the business unit level that are then broken down by sales managers into zone, region, district, territory, and account forecasts.

total quality management (TQM) An approach that incorporates a strong customer orientation, a team-oriented corporate culture, and the use of statistical methods to analyze and improve all business processes, including sales management.

trade shows A typically industry-sponsored event in which companies use a booth to display products and services to potential and existing customers.

trait approach A category of research that attempts to determine the personality traits of an effective leader.

transactional selling Sales approaches that advocate putting pressure on the customer to "say yes" rather than truly satisfy the customer's needs. Transactional selling focuses on maximizing the outcomes of individual transactions rather than on longer-term relationships with customers.

transformational leadership A sales leadership model in which the leaders are charismatic, inspirational, and driven by a sense of mission.

trust-based relationship selling In contrast to transactional selling, trust-based relationship selling seeks to initiate, develop, and enhance long-term customer relationships by earning customer trust, focusing on customer needs, and having the salesperson play a key role in building the value received by the customer.

trust-building To be successful at trust-building with their customers, salespeople should demonstrate five key attributes: customer orientation; competence or expertise; dependability; candor or honesty; and compatibility.

U

users Organizations that purchase products and services to produce other products and services.

W

workload approach An approach used for calculating salesforce size that first determines how much selling effort is needed to cover the firm's market adequately and then calculates the number of salespeople required to provide this amount of selling effort.

Chapter 1

[1]"The 500 Largest Sales Forces in America," *Selling Power* (October 2017): 24–40.

[2]Michael Moorman, Torsten Bernewitz, Marshall Solem, and Ty Curry, "Building a Customer-Focused Growth Engine: Establishing Sales Force Effectiveness Priorities," *Selling Power* (Special Edition 2012): 6.

[3]Tim Riesterer, "Is the 57% Statistic An Urban Legend?" salesandmarketing.com (January 26, 2017): 1–2; Nicholas Toman, Brent Adamson, and Cristina Gomez, "The New Sales Imperative," *Harvard Business Review* (March–April 2017): 119–125.

[4]Nigel Piercy, "Evolution of Strategic Sales Organizations in Business-to-Business Markets," *Journal of Business & Industrial Marketing* (May 25, 2010): 349–359; Kenneth Le Meunier-Fitzhugh and Tony Douglas, *Achieving a Strategic Sales Focus* (Oxford, United Kingdom: Oxford University Press, 2016).

[5]Byron Matthews and Tamara Schenk, *Sales Enablement* (Hoboken, New Jersey: John Wiley & Sons, 2018); Scott Santucci, "Good Growth Ahead," *Selling Power* (February 2018): 18–19; Scott Santucci and Elay Cohen, "A Strategic Imperative," *Selling Power* (June 2018): 28–29.

[6]Heather Baldwin, "Rx for Success," *Selling Power* (July/August/September 2012): 10–11.

[7]Heather Baldwin, "Cost Consciousness," *Selling Power* (July/August/September 2013): 10–11.

[8]Erik Charles, "In the Age of AI, Training Is More Critical Than Ever," salesandmarketing.com (July 26, 2018): 1–3; Raju Vegesna, "How Sales Reps Can Stop Worrying and Learn to Love AI," salesandmarketing.com (August 3, 2018): 1–3; Henry Canaday, "The Future is in Your . . . AI Software," *Selling Power* (April 2018): 22–23.

[9]Selling Power Editors, "Maximize Web Leads, Virtually," *Selling Power* (February 2017): 5.

[10]Laurence Minsky and Keith A. Quesenberry, "How B2B Sales Can Benefit from Social Selling," hbr.org (November 10, 2016): 1–6.

[11]Michael Labate, Kirsten Boileau, and Phil Lurie, "Three Ways Salespeople at SAP Are Winning with Social Selling." *Selling Power* blog (April 3, 2017): 1–3.

[12]Maria Valdivieso de Uster, "The Seven Biggest Trends Upending Sales Today," from the Salesforce.com blog at www.salesforce.com/quotable/articles/biggest-sales-trends (accessed September 23, 2018).

[13]"Running Up the Down Escalator: 2017 CSO Insights World Class Sales Practices Report," from the CSO Insights blog at www.csoinsights.com/wp-content/uploads/sites/5/2017/08/2017-World-Class-Sales-Practices-Summary-Report.pdf (accessed September 13, 2018).

[14]Norman Behar, "How to Create a World-Class Sales Organization," from the Sales Readiness Group blog at www.salesreadinessgroup.com/blog/creating-a-world-class-sales-organization (accessed September 20, 2018).

[15]Kylee Lessard "Five Traits that Separate the Best Sales Managers," from the LinkedIn blog at https://business.linkedin.com/sales-solutions/blog/sales-leaders/2018/02/5-traits-that-separate-the-best-sales-managers-, February 20, 2018.

[16]"Running Up the Down Escalator."

[17]"BMC: Connecting with a New, Broader Set of Decision-Makers," from the LinkedIn home page at https://business.linkedin.com/sales-solutions/case-studies/technology/bmc (accessed September 30, 2018).

[18]Brian Williams, "Great Salespeople Think Like Entrepreneurs," from the Brevet Group blog at https://blog.thebrevetgroup.com/salespeople-entrepreneurs-part2 (accessed October 2, 2018).

[19]This section is synthesized from Javier Marcos Cuevas, "The Transformation of Professional Selling: Implications for Leading the Modern Sales Organization," *Industrial Marketing Management*, 69 (February 2018): 198–208; The Miller Heiman Group, "What are the Top 12 Sales Best Practices You Should Follow?" www.millerheimangroup.co.uk/blog/what-are-the-top-12-sales-best-practices-you-should-follow (accessed September 10, 2018); Michael Caccavale, "Five Best Practices For Sales Enablement," *Forbes* magazine online, at www.forbes.com/sites/forbesagencycouncil/2018/02/13/five-best-practices-for-b2b-sales-enablement/#724f6f134c16, February 23, 2018; and William C. Moncrief, "Are Sales as We Know It Dying . . . or Merely Transforming?" *Journal of Personal Selling & Sales Management*, 37 (December 2017): 271–279.

*All efforts were made to secure permissions for all materials not created by the authors. Anyone with a concern should contact the publisher.

[20]Hannah Grove, Kevin Sellers, Richard Ettenson, and Jonathan Knowle, "Selling Solutions Isn't Enough," *MIT Sloan Management Review* (Fall 2018, August 1, 2018) online at https://sloanreview-mit-edu.ezproxy2.library.colostate.edu/article/selling-solutions-isn't-enough.

[21]Gabe Larson, "12 Leadership Tips from the Most Influential Sales Pros" from the Inside Sales blog at https://blog.insidesales.com/sales-leadership/sales-leadership-tips, April 12, 2018; Claire McConnachie, "The Top-7 Characteristics of a Successful Sales Manager," from the Salesforce Search blog at www.salesforcesearch.com/blog/the-top-7-characteristics-of-a-successful-sales-manager, February 21, 2017; Daniel J. Goebel, Dawn Deeter-Schmelz, and Karen Norman Kennedy, "Effective Sales Management: What Do salespeople Think?" *Journal of Marketing Development and Competitiveness*, 7 (May 2013): 11–22; and Dan Thompson, "The Straightforward Truth about Effective Sales Leadership," www.saleshacker.com/5-habits-of-highly-effective-sales-leaders, April 28, 2017.

[22]"Top Habits of Highly Effective Sales Managers," from the Sales Drive, LLC blog at https://salesdrive.info/7-daily-habits-of-highly-effective-sales-managers, Nov. 3, 2017; Larson, "12 Leadership Tips"; Forbes Business Development Council, "Eight Essential Qualities Every Great Sales Manager Needs," *Forbes* online at www.forbes.com/sites/forbesbusinessdevelopmentcouncil/2017/10/20/eight-essential-qualities-every-great-sales-manager-needs/#3a3f080027d3, October 2017; and McConnachie, "The Top-7 Characteristics of a Successful Sales Manager."

Chapter 2

[1]The definition of marketing according to the American Marketing Association as shown at www.marketingpower.com (accessed March 26, 2014).

[2]"The Largest Sales Forces in America," *Selling Power* (2017).

[3]"Tyco National Account Manager Position Description," as it appeared on www.firesecurity.taleo.net/careersection (accessed April 16, 2014).

[4]Thomas N. Ingram, Raymond W. LaForge, Charles H. Schwepker, Jr., Ramon A. Avila, and Michael R. Williams, *Sell*, 5th ed. (Stamford, CT: Cengage Learning, 2017).

[5]John E. Swan and Johannah Jones Nolan, "Gaining Customer Trust: A Conceptual Guide for the Salesperson," *Journal of Personal Selling & Sales Management*, 5 (November 1985): 39–48.

[6]Carew International "Do the Right Thing," *Message from the Mentor*, November 1, 2012.

[7]Chally Group Worldwide, "How to Select a Sales Force That Sells," http://chally.com/how-to-select-a-sales-force-that-sells/ (accessed April 10, 2014).

[8]Robert F. Gwinner, "Base Theory in the Formulation of Sales Strategy," *MSU Business Topics* (Autumn 1968): 37; Mack Hanan, *Consultative Selling*, 7th ed. (New York: American Management Association, 2004).

[9]Neil Rackham, *SPIN Selling* (New York: McGraw-Hill Book Company, 1988).

[10]Kevin J. Corcoran, Laura J. Petersen, Daniel B. Baitch, and Mark F. Barrett, *High Performance Sales Organizations* (Chicago: Richard D. Irwin, 1995): 44.

[11]Hanan, p. 5.

[12]Information compiled from www.indeed.com (accessed August 22, 2018).

[13]Geoffrey James, "The Consultative Approach to Selling," *Selling Power* (March/April 2010): 29–32.

[14]Thomas N. Ingram, "Future Themes in Sales and sales Management: Complexity, Collaboration, and Accountability," *Journal of Marketing Theory and Practice* (Fall 2004): 1–11; Thomas N. Ingram, Raymond W. LaForge, William B. Locander, Scott B. MacKenzie, and Philip M. Podsakoff, "New Directions in Sales Leadership Research," *Journal of Personal Selling & Sales Management*, 25 (Spring 2005): 137–154.

[15]"2014 Gold Stevie Award Winner: DHL Freight Forwarding, Bonn, Germany, Cigdem Wondergem, Global Head of Sales Training," The Stevie Awards for Sales & Customer Service, www.stevieawards.com/pubs/sales/awards/426_2940_24874.cfm (accessed April 18, 2014).

[16]Mathew Sweezey, "5 Keys to Sales and Marketing Alignment," *ClickZ*, January 23, 2014, www.clickz.com/clickz/column/2324296/5-keys-to-sales-and-marketing-alignment (accessed April 13, 2014); Christine Crandell, "Sales and Marketing Alignment Begins with the Customer," *Forbes*, April 5, 2013, www.forbes.com/sites/christinecrandell/2013/04/05/sales-and-marketing-alignment-begins-with-the-customer/.

Chapter 3

[1]Betsy Cummings, "Getting Reps to Live Your Mission," *Sales & Marketing Management* (October 2001): 15.

[2]Matt Murray, "GE Says It Will Combine Appliances, Lighting Units," *Wall Street Journal Online* (August 30, 2002): 1–2.

[3]Robert Schoenberger, "GE Finds Merger Pays Off in Profits," *The Courier-Journal* (September 13, 2003): F1–F2.

[4]Michael E. Porter, *Competitive Strategy* (New York: The Free Press, 1980): 34.

[5]Madhubalan Viswanathan and Eric M. Olson, "The Implementation of Business Strategies: Implications

for the Sales Function," *Journal of Personal Selling & Sales Management* (Winter 1992): 45.

⁶Adapted from John F. Tanner, Jr., Michael Ahearne, Thomas W. Leigh, Charlotte H. Mason, and William C. Moncrief, "CRM in Sales-Intensive Organizations: A Review and Future Directions," *Journal of Personal Selling & Sales Management* (Spring 2005): 169–170.

⁷Alex R. Zablah, Danny N. Bellenger, and Wesley J. Johnston, "An Evaluation of Divergent Perspectives on Customer Relationship Management: Towards a Common Understanding of an Emerging Phenomenon," *Industrial Marketing Management* 33 (2004): 475–489.

⁸Lisa Gschwandtner, "It's All About Strategy," *Selling Power* (January/February 2010).

⁹Darrell K. Rigby, Frederick F. Reichheld, and Phil Schefter, "Avoid the Four Perils of CRM," *Harvard Business Review* (February 2002): 101–110.

¹⁰Julia Chang, "CRM at Any Size," *Sales & Marketing Management* (August 2004): 33–34; "John Deere Would Have Been Proud," *Sales & Marketing Strategies and News* (May 2004): 22–23.

¹¹Henry Canaday, "Three Ways Sales and Marketing Can Collaborate to Boost Revenue," *Selling Power* (January/February 2012).

¹²Michael V. Copeland, "Best Buy's Selling Machine," *Business 2.0* (July 2004): 93–102.

¹³Adapted from Dominique Rouzies, Erin Anderson, Ajay K. Kohli, Ronald E. Michaels, Barton A. Weitz, and Andris A. Zoltners, "Sales and Marketing Integration: A Proposed Framework," *Journal of Personal Selling & Sales Management* (Spring 2005): 113–122.

¹⁴Ernest Waaser, Marshall Dahneke, Michael Pekkarinen, and Michael Weissel, "How You Slice It: Smarter Segmentation for Your Sales Force," *Harvard Business Review* (March 2004): 105–111.

¹⁵Henry Canaday, "Segmenting Customers for Profit," *Selling Power* (October 2007): 111–112.

¹⁶Reported in Chad Kaydo, "You've Got Sales," *Sales & Marketing Management* (October 1999): 30.

¹⁷*Ibid.*, 34.

¹⁸Mike McCue, "Solutions That Make a Difference," *Sales & Marketing Management* (October 2007): 19–21.

¹⁹Henry Canaday, "A Cool Duo," *Selling Power* (September 2007): 76–80.

²⁰Andy Cohen, "Herman Miller," *Sales & Marketing Management* (July 1999): 60.

²¹Louise Lee, "It's Dell vs. the Dell Way," *Business Week* (March 6, 2002): 61–62; Jack Ewing, "Where Dell Sells with Brick and Mortar," *Business Week* (October 8, 2007): 78.

²²Henry Canaday, "Independent Rep's Comp," *Selling Power* (January/February 2001): 79.

²³Adapted from Harold J. Novick, "The Case for Reps vs. Direct Selling: Can Reps Do It Better?" *Industrial Marketing* (March 1982): 90–98; "The Use of Sales Reps," *Small Business Report* (December 1986): 72–78.

²⁴Tricia Campbell, "Who Needs a Sales Force Anyway?" *Sales & Marketing Management* (February 1999): 13.

²⁵Adapted from Michael D. Hutt, Wesley J. Johnston, and John R. Rouchelto, "Selling Centers and Buying Centers: Formulating Strategic Exchange Patterns," *Journal of Personal Selling & Sales Management* (May 1985): 34. Used with permission.

²⁶Adam Bluestein, "In-Your-Face-Selling," *INC. Magazine* (November 2006): 35–36.

²⁷Jeffrey L. Josephson, "Is Inbound Marketing Right for B2B?" SalesAndMarketing.com, January 31, 2014, http://salesandmarketing.com/content/inbound-marketing-right-b2b.

²⁸Eilene Zimmerman, "Making the Dysfunctional Functional," *Sales & Marketing Management* (September 2004): 30–31.

²⁹Henry Canaday and Gerhard Gschwandtner, "The Name's the Game," *Selling Power* (October 2007): 80–82.

³⁰Christopher Palmer, "Giving the Booth a Boost," *Business Week* (April 16, 2007): 12; Trade Shows in the United States, https://10times.com/USA/trade shows (accessed September 18, 2018).

³¹Megan Sweas, "High-Tech Trade Shows," *Sales & Marketing Management* (February 2004): 12.

³²Deborah L. Vence, "Trade Show Magic," *Marketing News* (November 11, 2002): 4.

Chapter 4

¹Dave Kahle, "How Sharp Is Your Sales Structure?" *American Salesman* 58(8) (2013): 8–14.

²Reported in "Structuring the Sales Organization," in *Sales Manager's Handbook,* ed. John P. Steinbrink (Chicago: The Dartnell Corporation, 1989): 90.

³See Robert W. Ruekert, Orville C. Walker, Jr., and Kenneth J. Roering, "The Organization of Marketing Activities: A Contingency Theory of Structure and Performance," *Journal of Marketing* (Winter 1985): 13, for a more complete presentation of structural characteristics and relationships. The discussion in this section borrows heavily from this article.

⁴Steven W. Martin, "Is Your Sales Organization Good or Great?" *HBR Blog Network,* February 25, 2013, http://blogs.hbr.org/2013/02/is-your-sales-organization-goo/.

⁵*Ibid.,* 20–21.

[6]From David W. Cravens, *Strategic Marketing,* 7th ed. (New York: McGraw-Hill): 541. Reprinted by permission of The McGraw-Hill Companies.

[7]Andris A. Zoltners, Prabhakant Sinha, and Sally E. Lorimer, "Match Your Sales Force Structure to Your Business Life Cycle," *Harvard Business Review* (July/August 2006): 81–89.

[8]Maurie Cushman, "Geographic Sales Territories—Pros and Cons," *Aspen Grove Investments,* August 17, 2013, http://aspengroveinvestments.com/geographic -sales-territories-pros-and-cons/.

[9]Christian Homburg, John P. Workman, Jr., and Ove Jensen, "Fundamental Changes in Marketing Organization: The Movement Toward a Customer-Focused Organizational Structure," *Journal of the Academy of Marketing Science* (Fall 2000): 459–478.

[10]Keith Regan, "Yahoo Reshuffles Ad Sales Unit from Top Down," *E-Commerce Times* (June 25, 2007): 1–3.

[11]George S. Yip and Audrey J.M. Bink, "Managing Global Accounts," *Harvard Business Review* (September 2007): 103–111.

[12]Adapted from Benson P. Shapiro and Rowland T. Moriarity, *Organizing the National Account Force* (Cambridge, MA: Marketing Science Institute, April 1984): 1–37.

[13]John P. Workman, Jr., Christian Homburg, and Ove Jensen, "Intraorganizational Determinants of Key Account Management Effectiveness," *Journal of the Academy of Marketing Science* (Winter 2003): 3–21.

[14]Marji McClure, 'Major Opportunities," *Selling Power* (July/August 2006): 34–37.

[15]From David W. Cravens and Raymond W. LaForge, "Salesforce Deployment," in *Advances in Business Marketing,* ed. Arch G. Woodside (1990): 76.

[16]Raymond W. LaForge, David W. Cravens, and Clifford E. Young, "Improving Salesforce Productivity," *Business Horizons* (September/October 1985): 54. Copyright © 1985 by the Foundation for the School of Business at Indiana University. Reprinted by permission.

[17]Robert C. Dudley and Das Narayandas, "A Portfolio Approach to Sales," *Harvard Business Review* (July/August 2006): 16–18.

[18]See Raymond W. LaForge, David W. Cravens, and Clifford E. Young, "Using Contingency Analysis to Select Effort Allocation Methods," *Journal of Personal Selling & Sales Management* (August 1986): 23, for a summary of productivity improvements from decision model applications.

[19]Andy Cohen, "Profits Down? Time to Add to Your Headcount," *Sales & Marketing Management* (August 2002): 15.

[20]Scott Hensley, "As Drug-Sales Teams Multiply, Doctors Start to Tune Them Out," *Wall Street Journal Online* (June 12, 2003): 1–4.

[21]Arlene Weintraub, "The Doctor Won't See You Now," *Business Week* (February 5, 2007): 30–32.

[22]Betsy Wiesendanger, "Temp Reps," *Selling Power* (May 2004): 68–71.

[23]LaForge, Cravens, and Young, "Improving Salesforce Productivity," 57.

[24]Ken Grant, David W. Cravens, George S. Low, and William C. Moncrief, "The Role of Satisfaction with Territory Design on the Motivation, Attitudes, and Work Outcomes of Salespeople," *Journal of the Academy of Marketing Science* (Spring 2001): 165–178.

Chapter 4 APPENDIX

[1]Naresh Sadarangani and John A. Gallucci, "Using Demand Drivers for a Collaborative Forecasting Success," *The Journal of Business Forecasting* (Summer 2004): 12–15.

[2]For other classification schemes and more detailed discussion of individual forecasting methods, see John T. Mentzer and Mark A Moon, *Sales Forecasting Management: A Demand Management Approach* (Thousand Oaks, CA: Sage Publications, 2005). For more on the Delphi technique, see Victoria Story, Louise Hurdley, Gareth Smith, and James Saker, "Methodological and Practical Implications of the Delphi Technique in Marketing Decision-Making: A Re-Assessment," *The Marketing Review* (2001): 487–504; Harry R. White, *Sales Forecasting: Timesaving and Profit-Making Strategies That Work* (Glenview, IL: Scott, Foresman and Company, 1984): 6; David M. Georgoff and Robert G. Murdick, "Manager's Guide to Forecasting," *Harvard Business Review* (January/February 1986): 113; J. Scott Armstrong, Roderick J. Brodie, and Shelby McIntyre, "Forecasting Methods for Marketing: Review of Empirical Research," *International Journal of Forecasting* 3 (1987): 355.

[3]See John T. Mentzer, "Forecasting with Adaptive Extended Exponential Smoothing," *Journal of the Academy of Marketing Science* (Fall 1988): 62, for discussion and examples of different exponential smoothing methods.

[4]Mark Barash, "Eliciting Accurate Sales Forecasts from Market Experts," *Journal of Business Forecasting* (Fall 1994): 24.

[5]Kenneth B. Kahn and John T. Mentzer, "The Impact of Team-based Forecasting," *Journal of Business Forecasting* (Summer 1994): 18.

[6]Norton Paley, "Welcome to the Fast Lane," *Sales & Marketing Management* (August 1994): 65.

[7]Dianne Ledingham, Mark Kovac, and Heidi Locke Simon, "The New Science of Sales Productivity," *Harvard Business Review* (September 2006): 124–133.

[8]These and other recommendations are available in Robin T. Peterson, "Sales Force Composite Forecasting—An Exploratory Analysis," *Journal of Business Forecasting* (Spring 1989): 23; James E. Cox, Jr., "Approaches for Improving Salespersons' Forecasts," *Industrial Marketing Management* 18 (1989): 307.

[9]For a review and more complete discussion of this approach, see Adrian B. Ryans and Charles B. Weinberg, "Territory Sales Response," *Journal of Marketing Research* (November 1979): 453; Adrian B. Ryans and Charles B. Weinberg, "Territory Sales Response Models: Stability over Time," *Journal of Marketing Research* (May 1987): 229. For specific examples of regression analysis used to establish territory sales quotas, see David W. Cravens, Robert B. Woodruff, and James C. Stamper, "An Analytical Approach for Evaluating Sales Territory Performance," *Journal of Marketing* (January 1972): 31; David W. Cravens and Robert B. Woodruff, "An Approach for Determining Criteria of Sales Performance," *Journal of Applied Psychology* (June 1973): 240.

[10]From "A Market Response Model for Sales Management Decision Making" by Raymond LaForge and David Cravens. Copyright © 1981 by Pi Sigma Epsilon. From *Journal of Personal Selling & Sales Management* (Fall/Winter 1981–1982): 14. Reprinted with permission of M.E. Sharpe, Inc.

[11]Adapted from Adrian B. Ryans and Charles B. Weinberg, "Territory Sales Response Models: Stability over Time," *Journal of Marketing Research* (May 1987): 231, published by the American Marketing Association.

[12]John T. Mentzer and Mark A Moon, *Sales Forecasting Management: A Demand Management Approach* (Thousand Oaks, CA: Sage Publications, 2005).

[13]Zuhaimy Haji Ismail and Maizah Hura Ahamad, "Delphi Improves Sales Forecasts: Malaysia's Electronic Companies' Experience," *Journal of Business Forecasting* (Summer 2003): 22–29.

[14]See Benito E. Flores and Edna M. White, "A Framework for the Combination of Forecasts," *Journal of the Academy of Marketing Science* (Fall 1988): 95, for an examination of different combination approaches.

[15]John T. Mentzer and Mark A. Moon, *Sales Forecasting Management: A Demand Management Approach* (Thousand Oaks, CA: Sage Publications, 2005).

Chapter 5

[1]Michael Munson and W. Austin Spivey, "Salesforce Selection That Meets Federal Regulation and Management Needs," *Industrial Marketing Management* 9 (February 1980): 12.

[2]http://www.census.gov. Accessed May 10, 2018.

[3]Rene Darmon, "Where Do the Best Sales Force Profit Producers Come From?" *Journal of Personal Selling & Sales Management* 3 (Summer 1993): 17.

[4]Fred Yager, "Five Tips for Hiring the Right Candidate," *Dice*, http://resources.dice.com/report/the-cost-of-bad-hiring-decisions/ (accessed February 1, 2018).

[5]Presentation by Daniel Mahurin, District Marketing Manager with Federated Mutual Insurance, October 15, 2013.

[6]Herbert Greenberg and Patrick Sweeney, *How to Hire and Develop Your Next Top Performer: The Qualities That Make Salespeople Great*, 2nd ed. (New York: McGraw-Hill Company, 2013.)

[7]Fred Yager, "Five Tips for Hiring the Right Candidate," *Dice*, http://resources.dice.com/report/the-cost-of-bad-hiring-decisions/ (accessed February 1, 2018).

[8]Georgia Chao, Anne O'Leary-Kelly, Samantha Wolf, Howard Klein, and Philip Gardner, "Organizational Socialization: Its Content and Consequences," *Journal of Applied Psychology* 79 (October 1994): 730.

[9]John Sullivan, "Ouch, 50% Of New Hires Fail! 6 Ugly Numbers Revealing Recruiting's Dirty Little Secret," www.ere.net/ouch-50-of-new-hires-fail-6-ugly-numbers-revealing-recruitings-dirty-little-secret (accessed February 1, 2018).

[10]Taken from "Position Details—Sales Associate," position description at https://careers.fastenal.com/details/309671 (accessed February 2, 2018).

[11]Frank Cespedes and Daniel Weinfurter, "The Best Ways to Hire Salespeople," (November 2, 2015), https://hbr.org/2015/11/the-best-ways-to-hire-salespeople (accessed May 10, 2018).

[12]Benson Smith, "Taller Is Better," *Gallup Management Journal* (June 9, 2005). David Mayer and Herbert Greenberg, "What Makes a Good Salesman," *Harvard Business Review*, 84 (July/August 2006): 164–71.

[13]https://vimeo.com/227053905 (accessed July 8, 2019).

[14]Richard McFarland, Joseph Rode and Tasadduq Shervani, "A Contingency Model of Emotional Intelligence in Professional Selling," *Journal of the Academy of Marketing Science* (January 2016), 108–118.

[15]John S. Hill and Meg Birdseye, "Salesperson Selection in Multinational Corporations: A Study," *Journal of Personal Selling & Sales Management* 9 (Summer 1989): 39.

[16]Phillip R. Cateora, Mary Gilly, John Graham and R. Bruce Money, *International Marketing*, 17th ed. (New York, NY: McGraw-Hill Education, 2016); Erika Rasmusson, "Can Your Reps Sell Overseas? How to Make Sure They Have What It Takes," *Sales & Marketing Management* 150 (February 1998): 110.

[17]Position description taken from Monster, https://job-openings.monster.com/Professional-Sales-Piscat

away-NJ-US-Xerox-Authorized-Agent-Program/ 11/192873711 (accessed February 2, 2018).

[18]This ad appeared in *Selling Power* (August/September 2013).

[19]Adapted from *Industrial Marketing Management* (March 1995), 24: 135–144, "Guidelines for Managing an International Sales Force" by Earl Honeycutt and John Ford. Copyright © 1995, with permission from Elsevier.

[20]"Why Employee Referrals are the Best Source of Hire," research by Jobvite.com, https://theundercov errecruiter.com/infographic-employee-referrals-hire (accessed March 8, 2018).

[21]Interview with Patrick Cunningham, District Marketing Manager with Federated Mutual Insurance, November 3, 2010.

[22]Recruiterbox, "Employee Referral Program Tips that Actually Work!" https://recruiterbox.com/blog/ employee-referral-program-tips-that-actually-work (accessed March 8, 2018); Andy Bargerstock and Hank Engel, "Six Ways to Boost Employee Referral Programs," *HR Magazine* 39 (December 1994): 72; Kathryn Tyler, "Employees Can Help Recruit New Talent," *HR Magazine* 41 (September 1996): 57.

[23]Fay Hansen, "Recruitment & Staffing," *Workforce Management*, 85 (June 26, 2006): 59–61.

[24]Darmon, "Where Do the Best Sales Force Profit Producers Come From?"

[25]Martha Frase-Blunt, "Make a Good First Impression," *HR Magazine* 49 (April 2004): 80–84.

[26]Drawn from: "A Guide to Attracting Talent: Writing Effective Online Recruitment Adverts," www.jvp group.co.uk/news/article/d3898f04-13d8-42b5-9ecf-313f32cecb34 (accessed March 8, 2018); "Focus on . . . Writing for Online Recruitment," *Personnel Today* (November 1, 2005): 36; Technojobs, "Writing and Online Recruitment Job Advert," www.technojobs .co.uk/info/recruiter-guides/writing-an-online -recruitment-job-advert.phtml (accessed September 8, 2010); Tracey Bowyer, "How to Write an Effective Online Employment Advertisement," Host Careers, www.hostcareers.com/index.php?page=en_ Effective+Ad (accessed September 15, 2010); Susan Wareham, "How to Write an Effective Recruitment Advertisement," Ezine Articles (June 25, 2010), http://ezinearticles.com/7How-to-Write-an -Effective-Recruitment-Advertisement&id=4553621 (accessed September 8, 2010).

[27]"Using Social Media for Talent Acquisition," www. shrm.org/hr-today/trends-and-forecasting/research-and-surveys/pages/social-media-recruiting-screen ing-2015.aspx (accessed March 8, 2018).

[28]Alison Doyle, "Guide to How Companies Recruit Employees," www.thebalance.com/how-do-compani es-recruit-employees-2062874 (accessed March 8, 2018).

[29]Lain Ehmann, "Too Good to Fail," *Selling Power* (September/October 2010): 74–75.

[30]Brian Westfall, "How Fortune 500 Companies Engage Talent on Twitter," https://www.softwaread vice.com/resources/how-fortune-500-companies-engage-talent-on-twitter-update (accessed March 9, 2018).

[31]Gillian Flynn, "E-Recruiting Ushers in Legal Dangers," *Workforce* 81 (April 2002): 70–72; Judith Marshall, "Don't Rely Exclusively on Internet Recruiting," *HR Magazine* 48 (November 2003): 24. Alex Johnson, "Lack of computer skills foils many job-seekers," MSNBC.com (July 29, 2010), www.msnbc .msn.com/id/33106445/ (accessed September 8, 2010).

[32]Steven G. Rogelberg, *Encyclopedia of Industrial and Organizational Psychology*, 2 (Thousand Oaks, CA: Sage, 2007): 666–670.

[33]Michael S. Cole, Hubert S. Field, William F. Giles and Stanley G. Harris, "Recruiters' Inferences of Applicant Personality Base on Resume Screening: Do Paper People Have a Personality?" *Journal of Business Psychology*, 24 (2009): 5–18.

[34]Flynn, "E-Recruiting Ushers in Legal Dangers."

[35]*Ibid*.

[36]"Recruiting Chatbots Won't Take Your Job, But They May Make It Easier," Gregory Lewis, August 21, 2017 from https://business.linkedin.com/talent-solutions/blog/future-of-recruiting/2017/how-recruiting-chatbots-work-and-what-recruiters-and-candidates- (accessed May 8, 2018).

[37]William Cron, Greg W. Marshall, Jagdip Singh, Rosann L. Spiro, and Harish Sujan, "Salesperson Selection, Training, and Development: Trends, Implications, and Research Opportunities," *Journal of Personal Selling & Sales Management*, 25 (Spring 2005): 123–136.

[38]Samantha McLaren, "9 Ways AI Will Reshape Recruiting (and How You Can Prepare)," February 12, 2018 at https://business.linkedin.com/talent-solutions/blog/future-of-recruiting/2018/9-ways-ai-will-reshape-recruiting-and-how-you-can-prepare (accessed May 5, 2018).

[39]Interview with Patrick Cunningham, District Marketing Manager with Federated Mutual Insurance, November 3, 2010.

[40]"Interviewing the Candidate," Sales Consultants International, Inc., Cleveland, OH. All reasonable efforts were made to contact the publisher for permission to use this guide. If any copyright holder takes issue with its use please contact the publisher.

[41]Diane Arthur, *Fundamentals of Human Resources Management: A Practical Guide for Today's HR Professional* (2015), 5th ed., [place of publication not identified], AMA Self-Study.

[42]Source: Mary Dowd, "List of Interview Questions About Integrity (May 7, 2018), http://work.chron.com/list-interview-questions-integrity-6082.html (accessed May 10, 2018); Lisa McQuerrey, "How to Interview a Person About Ethics," http://work.chron.com/interview-person-ethics-5685.html (accessed May 10, 2018); Chitra Reddy, "Top 11 Interview Questions to Assess Honesty," https://content.wisestep.com/interview-questions-assess-honesty (accessed May 10, 2018); Dpma Dezibe. "How to Interview to Uncover a Candidate's Ethical Standards," https://hiring.monster.com/hr/hr-best-practices/recruiting-hiring-advice/interviewing-candidates/interview-questions-to-ask-candidates.aspx (accessed May 10, 2018); Pinnacle, "5 Interview Questions to Help You Hire Ethical Employees," https://pinnacle.jobs/blog/5-interview-questions-to-help-you-hire-ethical-employees (accessed May 10, 2018); "Honest or Not? 10 Questions to Spot Ethical Applicants," (May 2013), http://ala-apa.org/newsletter/2013/05/14/honest-or-not-10-questions-to-spot-ethical-applicants (accessed May 10, 2018).

[43]Wesley J. Johnson and Martha C. Cooper, "Industrial Sales Force Selection: Current Knowledge and Needed Research," *Journal of Personal Selling & Sales Management* 1 (Spring/Summer 1981): 49.

[44]Greg W. Marshall, Miriam B. Stamps, and Jesse N. Moore, "Preinterview Biases: The Impact of Race, Physical Attractiveness, and Sales Job Type on Preinterview Impressions of Sales Job Applicants," *Journal of Personal Selling & Sales Management* 18 (Fall 1998): 21; Thomas E. Ford, Frank Gambino, Hanjoon Lee, Edward Mayo and Mark A. Ferguson, "The Role of Accountability in Suppressing Managers' Preinterview Bias against African-American Sales Job Applicants," *Journal of Personal Selling & Sales Management,* 24 (Spring 2004): 113–124.

[45]G. Stoney Alder and Joseph Gilbert, "Achieving Ethics and Fairness in Hiring: Going beyond the Law," *Journal of Business Ethics,* 68 (Spring 2006): 449–464.

[46]Henry Canaday, "Begin with the Best," *Selling Power* (March 2006): 90–93.

[47]For more on these see Peter Schulman, "Applying Learned Optimism to Increase Sales Productivity," *Journal of Personal Selling & Sales Management,* 19 (Winter 1999): 31–37; Sarah Maxwell, Gary Reed, Jim Saker and Vicky Story, "The Two Faces of Playfulness: A New Tool to Select Potentially Successful Sales Reps," *Journal of Personal Selling & Sales Management,* 25 (Summer 2005): 215–229; Seymour Adler, "Personality Tests for Salesforce Selection: Worth a Fresh Look," *Review of Business* 16 (Summer/Fall 1994): 27.

[48]Dawn R. Deeter-Schmelz and Jane Z. Sojaka, "Personality Traits and Sales Performance: Exploring Differential Effects of Need for Cognition and Self-Monitoring," *Journal of Marketing Theory & Practice,* 15 (Spring 2007): 145–157; Daniel H. Pink, *To Sell is Human* (2012), New York, NY: Penguin Group.

[49]Henry Canaday, "Smart Selection," *Selling Power* (April/May/June 2013): 42–43.

[50]William Cron, Greg W. Marshall, Jagdip Singh, Rosann L. Spiro and Harish Sujan, "Salesperson Selection, Training, and Development: Trends, Implications, and Research Opportunities," *Journal of Personal Selling & Sales Management* 25 (Spring 2005): 123–136.

[51]Based on Samual J. Maurice, "Stalking the High-Scoring Salesperson," *Sales & Marketing Management* (October 7, 1985): 63; George B. Salsbury, "Properly Recruit Salespeople to Reduce Training Cost," *Industrial Marketing Management* 11 (April 1982): 143; Richard Kern, "IQ Tests for Salesmen Make a Comeback," *Sales & Marketing Management* (April 1988): 42.

[52]Chally Group, "Chally Case Studies," www.chally.com/results/case-studies/cardinal-health/ (accessed October 15, 2013).

[53]Newsweek staff, "Inside the Head of an Applicant," (February 20, 2005), www.newsweek.com/inside-head-applicant-122389 (accessed May 10, 2018).

[54]William Cron, Greg W. Marshall, Jagdip Singh, Rosann L. Spiro and Harish Sujan, "Salesperson Selection, Training, and Development: Trends, Implications, and Research Opportunities," *Journal of Personal Selling & Sales Management,* 25 (Spring 2005): 123–136.

[55]E. James Randall, Ernest F. Cooke, and Lois Smith, "A Successful Application of the Assessment Center Concept to the Salesperson Selection Process," *Journal of Personal Selling & Sales Management* 5 (May 1985): 53.

[56]Eleanor Beaton, "Digital Drivers," *Profit,* 27 (May 2008): 32–33.

[57]Alex Howland, Ronald Rembisz, Tiffani Wang-Jones, Sherilin Heise, and Sheldon Brown, "Developing a Virtual Assessment Center," 67 (June, 2015): 110–126.

[58]Presentation by Daniel Mahurin, District Marketing Manager with Federated Mutual Insurance, October 15, 2013.

[59]Marty Nemko, "Earn an MBA in 3 Minutes," *Kiplinger's Personal Finance,* 60 (October 2006): 93.

[60]Henry Canaday, "Two Steps to Better Sales Hiring," *Selling Power* (July/August/September 2013): 70.

[61]"Background/Reference Checks May Provide Defense to Discrimination Suit," *Fair Employment Practices Guidelines* (December 1, 2003): 4–5.

[62]J.T. O'Donnell, "85 Percent of Job Applicants Lie on Resumes. Here's How to Spot a Dishonest Candidate," Inc., www.inc.com/jt-odonnell/staggering-85-of-job-applicants-lying-on-resumes-.html (accessed May 10, 2018).

[63]Larry Besnoff and Arthur Cohen, "Hazardous Hires," *Waste Age*, 38 (April 2007): 106–110; William J. Woska, "Legal Issues for HR Professionals: Reference Checking/Background Investigations," *Public Personnel Management*, 36 (Spring 2007): 79–89.

[64]*How to Select a Sales Force That Sells*, 3rd ed. (Dayton, OH: The HR Chally Group, 1998): 14. Reprinted with kind permission from HR Chally Group for the 9th edition. All reasonable efforts were made to contact the publisher for permission to use this for the 10th edition. If any copyright holder takes issue with its use please contact the publisher.

[65]William J. Woska, "Legal Issues for HR Professionals: Reference Checking/Background Investigations," *Public Personnel Management* 36 (Spring 2007): 79–89.

[66]Reuters, "The Facts About Drug Testing During the Hiring Stage," (April 1, 2009), www.reuters.com/assets/print?aid=USTRE5305E120090401 (accessed September 24, 2010).

[67]Gatewood and Feild, *Human Resource Selection*.

[68]W.E. Patton III and Ronald King, "The Use of Human Judgement Models in Sales Force Selection Decisions," *Journal of Personal Selling & Sales Management* 12 (Spring 1992): 1.

[69]G. Stoney Alder and Joseph Gilbert, "Achieving Ethics and Fairness in Hiring: Going Beyond the Law," *Journal of Business Ethics* 68 (Spring 2006): 449–464. Source: U.S. Equal Employment Opportunity Commission, "Laws Enforced by EEOC: The Genetic Information Nondiscrimination Act of 2008," www.eeoc.gov/laws/statutes/index.cfm (accessed October 21, 2015); Diane Arthur, *Fundamentals of Human Resources Management: A Practical Guide for Today's HR Professional* (2015), 5th ed. [place of publication not identified], AMA Self-Study.

[70]C. David Shepherd and James Heartfield, "Discrimination Issues in the Selection of Salespeople: A Review and Managerial Suggestions," *Journal of Personal Selling & Sales Management* 11 (Fall 1991): 67.

[71]G. Stoney Alder and Joseph Gilbert, "Achieving Ethics and Fairness in Hiring: Going Beyond the Law," *Journal of Business Ethics* 68 (Spring 2006): 449–464.

[72]"Interviewing Job Applicants: Watching What You Say," *Fair Employment Practices Guidelines* (July 2005): 1–3.

[73]Munson and Spivey, "Salesforce Selection," 15.

[74]For more discussion of what information should not be sought in a job interview, see John P. Steinbrink, ed., *The Dartnell Sales Manager's Handbook,* 14th ed. (Chicago: The Dartnell Corporation, 1989): 820; Shepherd and Heartfield, "Discrimination Issues."

[75]Jon M. Hawes, "How to Improve Your College Recruiting Program," *Journal of Personal Selling & Sales Management* 9 (Summer 1989): 51; Alison Doyle, "What is a Stress Interview?" (January 1, 2018), www.thebalancecareers.com/what-is-a-stress-interview-2062108 (accessed May 10, 2018).

[76]Adapted from "What Would You Do?" *Sales & Marketing Management* 154 (March 2002): 64.

Chapter 6

[1]Alan J. Dubinsky, Roy D. Howell, Thomas N. Ingram, and Danny N. Bellenger, "Salesforce Socialization," *Journal of Marketing* 50 (October 1986): 195.

[2]Mark W. Johnston, A. Parasuraman, Charles M. Futrell, and William C. Black, "A Longitudinal Assessment of the Impact of Selected Organizational Influences on Salespeople's Organizational Commitment during Early Employment," *Journal of Marketing Research* 27 (August 1990): 341.

[3]Jeffrey K. Sager, "How to Retain Salespeople," *Industrial Marketing Management* 19 (May 1990): 155.

[4]Judy A. Siguaw, Gene Brown, and Robert E. Widing II, "The Influence of the Market Orientation of the Firm on Sales Force Behavior and Attitudes," *Journal of Marketing Research* 31 (February 1994): 106.

[5]Federated Insurance Marketing Representative brochure, www.federatedinsurance.com/ws/cs/groups/external/@fedins/@general/documents/media/prod_557610.pdf (accessed May 22, 2018).

[6]Gilbert A. Churchill, Jr., Neil M. Ford, Steven W. Hartley, and Orville C. Walker, Jr., "The Determinants of Salesperson Performance: A Meta-Analysis," *Journal of Marketing Research* 22 (May 1985): 117.

[7]Brainshark, "2016 CSO Insights Sales Enablement Optimization Study," www.brainshark.com/sites/default/files/cso-insights-2016-sales-enablement-optimization-study.pdf (accessed May 22, 2018).

[8]Henry Canaday, "Begin with the Best," *Selling Power* (March 2006): 90–93. See also Howard Stevens and Theodore Kinni, *Achieve Sales Excellence* (Avon, MA: Platinum Press, 2007).

[9]Maureen Hrehocik, "The Best Sales Force," *Sales & Marketing Management,* 159 (October 2007): 22–27.

[10]CSO Insights, "2017 CSO Insights World-Class Sales Practices Report," Miller Heiman Group (2017), www.csoinsights.com/wp-content/uploads/sites/5/2017/08/2017-World-Class-Sales-Practices-Report.pdf (accessed June 6, 2018).

[11]Byron Matthews and Tamara Schenk, *Sales Enablement* (2018), John Wiley & Sons: Hoboken, New Jersey, 15–16.

[12]Christine Comaford, "Salespeople Are Burning Out Faster Than Ever—Here's Why," *Forbes* online, www.

forbes.com/sites/christinecomaford/2016/06/18/how-leaders-can-engage-retain-top-sales-talent/#593533645cbb (accessed May 22, 2018).

[13]ATD Research, "2016 State of Sales Training," www.td.org/research-reports/2016-state-of-sales-training (accessed May 22, 2018).

[14]Vijay Lakshmi Singh, Ajay K. Manrai and Lalita A. Manrai, "Sales Training: A State of the Art and Contemporary Review," *Journal of Economics, Finance and Administrative Science*, 20 (2015): 54–71.

[15]Source: Jim Dickie, "Sales Training: Is it Worth It?" https://trainingindustry.com/magazine/issue/sales-training-is-it-worth-it (accessed May 22, 2018).

[16]Ashraf M. Attia, Earl D. Honeycutt, Jr. and Mark P. Leach, "A Three-Stage Model for Assessing and Improving Sales Force Training and Development," *Journal of Personal Selling & Sales Management* 25 (Summer 2005): 253–68.

[17]See Alan J. Dubinsky and Richard W. Hansen, "The Sales Force Management Audit," *California Management Review* 24 (Winter 1981): 86.

[18]Joseph O. Rentz, C. David Shepherd, Armen Tashchain, Pratibha A. Dabholkar, and Robert T. Ladd, "A Measure of Selling Skill: Scale Development and Validation," *Journal of Personal Selling & Sales Management* 22 (Winter 2002): 13–21.

[19]Betsy Cummings, "Wake Up, Salespeople!" *Sales & Marketing Management* 154 (June 2002): 11.

[20]C. David Shepherd, Stephen B. Castleberry, and Rick E. Ridnour, "Linking Effective Listening with Salesperson Performance: An Exploratory Investigation," *Journal of Business & Industrial Marketing* 12 (Fall 1997): 315.

[21]Bhaswati Bhattacharyya, "What Sales Training in 2017 Needs to Include," Sales Hacker, www.saleshacker.com/sales-training-2017-needs-include (accessed May 25, 2018).

[22]Sales Management Association, "Salesperson Learning Preferences," (2017), 1–32, www.allego.com/assets/2017-Salesperson-Learning-Preferences-Report_Allego.pdf (accessed May 24, 2018).

[23]Salesforce Research, "State of Sales," https://a.sfdcstatic.com/content/dam/www/ocms/assets/pdf/misc/state-of-sales-report-salesforce.pdf (accessed May 24, 2018).

[24]William Cron, Greg W. Marshall, Jagdip Singh, Rosann L. Spiro and Harish Sujan, "Salesperson Selection, Training, and Development: Trends, Implications, and Research Opportunities," *Journal of Personal Selling & Sales Management* 25 (Spring 2005): 123–136.

[25]Howard Stevens and Theodore Kinni, *Achieve Sales Excellence* (Avon, MA: Platinum Press, 2007).

[26]Sales Management Association, "Salesperson Learning Preferences," (2017), 1–32, www.allego.com/assets/2017-Salesperson-Learning-Preferences-Report_Allego.pdf (accessed May 24, 2018).

[27]Marc Hequet, "Product Knowledge: Knowing What They're Selling May Be the Key to How Well They Sell It," *Training* (February 1988): 18.

[28]Alan J. Dubinsky and Thomas N. Ingram, "A Classification of Industrial Buyers: Implications for Sales Training," *Journal of Personal Selling & Sales Management* 2 (Fall/Winter 1981–1982): 49.

[29]Julia Chang, "Multicultural Selling," *Sales & Marketing Management* 155 (October 2003): 26.

[30]Victoria Davies Bush and Thomas N. Ingram, "Adapting to Diverse Customers: A Training Matrix for International Marketers," *Industrial Marketing Management* 25 (September 1996): 373; Strout, Brewer, and Kaydo, "Are Your Salespeople Tech Savvy?"

[31]"Snapshot: Global Etiquette Dos and Don'ts" Forbes online (March 18, 2010), www.forbes.com/2010/03/18/business-travel-etiquette-forbes-woman-leadership-global_slide (accessed May 24, 2018).

[32]Harish Sujan, Barton A. Weitz, and Mita Sujan, "Increasing Sales Productivity by Getting Salespeople to Work Smarter," *Journal of Personal Selling & Sales Management* 8 (August 1988): 9.

[33]Scott A. Inks and Amy J. Morgan, "Technology and the Sales Force: Increasing Acceptance of Sales Force Automation," *Industrial Marketing Management* 30 (June 2001): 463–472; Robert C. Erffmeyer and Dale A. Johnson, "An Exploratory Study of Sales Force Automation Practices: Expectations and Realities," *Journal of Personal Selling & Sales Management* 21 (Spring 2001): 167–175.

[34]Mark P. Leach, Annie H. Liu and Wesley J. Johnston, "The Role of Self-Regulation Training in Developing the Motivation Management Capabilities of Salespeople," *Journal of Personal Selling & Sales Management* 25 (Summer 2005): 269–281.

[35]Colette A. Frayne and J. Michael Geringer, "Self-Management Training for Improving Job Performance: A Field Experiment Involving Salespeople," *Journal of Applied Psychology* 85 (June 2000): 361–372.

[36]Jared F. Harrison, ed., *The Sales Manager as a Trainer* (Orlando, FL: National Society of Sales Training Executives, 1983): 7.

[37]Sarah Boehle, "Global Sales Training's Balancing Act," *Training* 47 (January 2010): 29–31.

[38]Source: Aja Frost, "The 25 Best Sales Training Programs for Every Budget and Team," https://blog.hubspot.com/sales/best-sales-training-programs; Norman Behar, "6 Traits of an Effective Corporate Sales Training Program," www.salesreadinessgroup.com/blog/effective-corporate-sales-training-program; Jonathan Dawson, "7 Guidelines for Selecting Sales Training Programs," (March 21, 2016), http://sell

chology.com/training/guidelines/; Norman Behar, "How to Choose the Best Sales Training Company," www.salesreadinessgroup.com/blog/choosing-the-best-sales-training-company; "How to Select a Sales Firm Dedicated to Treating On-The-Field Success and Sales Performance," https://brooksgroup.com/sales-resources/choosing-a-sales-training-company; "Training Companies – Selecting the Right One: A Guide for Comparing Training Companies," www.aps-online.net/training_companies.htm (all accessed May 30, 2018).

³⁹Mark Magnacca, "A Guide to Millennial Learning," *Training* (January 4, 2018), https://trainingmag.com/guide-millennial-learning (accessed June 6, 2018).

⁴⁰Kevin Hallenbeck, "The Role of Sales Mentor: It Can Provide Rewards for Both the Salesperson and Sales Manager that Can Last a Lifetime" (February 19, 2016), *New Hampshire Business Review*, p. 9.

⁴¹Michelle Marchetti, "The Case for Mentors," *Sales & Marketing Management* 156 (June 2004): 16.

⁴²Julian Birkinshaw and Jordan Cohen, "Make Time for Meaningful Work," *Businessline*, October 15, 2013.

⁴³Forbes Business Development Council, "13 Winning Sales Training Techniques," Forbes online (April 20, 2018), https://www.forbes.com/sites/forbesbusinessdevelopmentcouncil/2018/04/20/13-winning-sales-training-techniques/#392738426d10 (accessed June 7, 2018).

⁴⁴Thomas Brashear, Danny Bellenger, James Boles and Hiram Barksdale, Jr., "An Exploratory Study of the Relative Effectiveness of Different Types of Sales Force Mentors," *Journal of Personal Selling & Sales Management* 26 (Winter 2006): 7–18.

⁴⁵ASTD Staff, "Leading Sales Organizations Provide More Training," *T+D* (February 2013): 22.

⁴⁶Celemi, "Celemi Apples & Oranges. Version: Manufacturing—Sales," https://celemi.com/ready-made-solutions/apples-oranges/manufacturing-sales (accessed June 7, 2018).

⁴⁷Paradigm Learning, "Zodiak®: Sales Professionals," www.paradigmlearning.com/products-and-services/zodiak-game-of-business-finance-and-strategy/zodiak-sales-professionals.aspx (accessed December 19, 2013).

⁴⁸Kevin Glover and Connie Muray, "Simulations for Selling Success," *T+D* (January 2012): 80.

⁴⁹Betsy Morris, "Real World if Finding New Uses for Virtual Reality," *Wall Street Journal* (June 6, 2017): B4.

⁵⁰For guidelines for enhancing role playing, see "Skills," *Personal Selling Power* (January/February 1995): 54. Also see Colin Gabler and Raj Agnihotri, "Sales Role Play . . . Take Two . . . Action! Using Video Capture Technology to Improve Student Performance," *Journal of the Academy of Business Education*, Vol. 19 (Spring 2018): 95–105; Thomas N. Ingram, "Guidelines for Maximizing Role-Play Activities," in *Proceedings,* National Conference in Sales Management, Dallas, TX, 1990.

⁵¹Federated Insurance, "Training & Development," www.federatedinsurance.com/wstest/fi/Careers/TrainingDevelopment/index.htm (accessed December 17, 2013).

⁵²Henry Canaday, "Students of the Marketplace," *Selling Power* (November/December 2010): 25–27.

⁵³Marty Rosenheck, "The Modern Medicine Show," *Chief Learning Officer*, 9 (June 2010): 46–48.

⁵⁴See for example www.saleshacker.com/best-sales-podcasts (accessed June 7, 2018).

⁵⁵Henry Canaday, "Students of the Marketplace," *Selling Power* (November/December 2010): 25–27.

⁵⁶Byron Matthews and Tamara Schenk, *Sales Enablement* (2018), John Wiley & Sons: Hoboken, New Jersey, 95.

⁵⁷Jim Day, Sandy Dick, and Tori Eggleston, "Sales Training at Cisco Systems Goes Digital-and-Interactive," *Velocity*, Q1 (2010): 13–16; Kate Day and Lisa Maria Fedele, "Learning at the Speed of Life," *T+D* (June 2012): 60–63. See also www.cisco.com/c/en/us/about/careers/working-at-cisco/students-and-new-graduate-programs/sales-associates-program.html.

⁵⁸ASTD Staff, "Leading Sales Organizations Provide More Training," *T+D* (February 8, 2013): 22.

⁵⁹Doug Harward, "Key Trends 2014," *Training Industry Magazine* (Winter, 2014): 25–28.

⁶⁰Marty Rosenheck, "The Modern Medicine Show," *Chief Learning Officer* 9 (June 2010): 46–48.

⁶¹Lawrence Grafton, "How Dell Revitalized Corporate Communications with Video," Streaming Media (May, 2014), p. WP77+, http://link.galegroup.com/apps/doc/A375817867/AONE?u=cent1000&sid=AONE&xid=bb86a116 (accessed June 1, 2018).

⁶²http://remaxshowcase.com/rsn.htm (accessed June 8, 2018).

⁶³Kathy Chin Leong, "Video E-Mail Goes Corporate," *Computerworld (*March 21, 2005): 23–24.

⁶⁴Heather Baldwin, "The Five-Minute Training Trend," *SellingPower.Com Sales Management Newsletter* (June 14, 2006), www.sellingpower.com/html_newsletter/PrintNewsletter/?NLID=537.

⁶⁵Richard Castle, "Mobile Learning: Is Your Content Fit for Purpose," *Training & Development* (April 2013): 22–23; Debbie Williams, "5 Tips for Designing Effective Visual eLearning Content" (January 19, 2018), www.topyx.com/lms-blog/5-instructional-design-tips-for-the-beginner-elearning-administrator (accessed June 8, 2018); Samantha Ferns, "How to Design Fantastic M-Learning With 9 Guidelines" (Feburary 16, 2017), www.infoprolearning.com/blog/9-guidelines-to-design-fantastic-mobile-learning-mlearning (accessed June 8, 2018).

[66]Brandon Hall, "Five Approaches to Sales Training," *Chief Learning Officer* (November 2010): 18.

[67]Michele Marchetti, "Tapping Top Talent," *Sales & Marketing Management* 156 (August 2004): 14.

[68]Jim Day, Sandy Dick, and Tori Eggleston, "Sales Training at Cisco Systems Goes Digital-and-Interactive," *Velocity* Q1 (2010): 13–16; Megan Dobransky and Nikki Vanry, "Instructor-led Training vs. eLearning," (March 1, 2017), www.edgepointlearning.com/blog/instructor-led-training-vs-elearning (accessed June 8, 2018).

[69]*Ibid*; Marc Ratcliffe, "7 Tips for Virtual Training Success," www.td.org/newsletters/atd-links/7-tips-for-virtual-training-success (accessed June 8, 2018). David Maxfield, "Virtual VS. Classroom Training" (July 26, 2016), https://trainingmag.com/virtual-vs-classroom-training (accessed June 8, 2018).

[70]Brandon Hall Group Research Team, "Training Budget Benchmarks and Optimizations for 2017" (December, 2016), www.litmos.com/wp-content/uploads/2016/12/BHG-training-budget-benchmarks-report-2017.pdf (accessed June 8, 2018). All reasonable efforts were made to contact the publisher for permission to use this table. If any copyright holder takes issue with its use please contact the publisher.

[71]"The Fractured State of Enterprise Sales Enablement and Training," www.allego.com/resources/fractured-state-enterprise-sales-enablement-training-infographic (accessed June 7, 2018).

[72]Sarah Boehle, "Global Sales Training's Balancing Act," *Training* 47 (January 2010): 29–31.

[73]Ashraf Attia, Asri Jantan, Nermine Atteya and Rana Fakhr, "Sales Training: Comparing Multinational and Domestic Companies," *Marketing Intelligence & Planning*, Vol 32 (Issue 1, 2014): 124–138.

[74]Mark Magnacca, "A Guide to Millennial Learning," *Training* (January 4, 2018), https://trainingmag.com/guide-millennial-learning (accessed June 6, 2018).

[75]Malcom S. Knowles, *Self-Directed Learning: A Guide for Learners and Teachers* (New York: Association Press, 1975).

[76]Andrew B. Artis and Eric G. Harris, "Self-Directed Learning and Sales Force Performance: An Integrated Framework," *Journal of Personal Selling & Sales Management* (Winter 2007): 9–24.

[77]Jared Fuller, "10 sales Training Techniques for Sales Managers," https://blog.pandadoc.com/10-sales-training-techniques-for-sales-managers (accessed June 7, 2018); Mark Magnacca, "A Guide to Millennial Learning," *Training* (January 4, 2018), https://trainingmag.com/guide-millennial-learning (accessed June 6, 2018).

[78]Bhaswati Bhattacharyya, "What Sales Training in 2017 Needs to Include," Sales Hacker, www.saleshacker.com/sales-training-2017-needs-include (accessed May 25, 2018).

[79]Mike Schultz, "The Seven Keys for Training for Maximum Impact," *T+D* (March 2013): 52–57.

[80]Jon M. Hawes, Stephen P. Hutchens, and William F. Crittenden, "Evaluating Corporate Sales Training Programs," *Training and Development Journal* 36 (November 1982): 44.

[81]Donald L. Kirkpatrick, 1976. "Evaluation of Training" in *Training and Development Handbook*, ed. Robert L. Craig (1976), USA: McGraw-Hill Book Company, p. 18–27.

[82]Mark P. Leach and Anie H. Liu, "Investigating Interrelationships among Sales Training Evaluation Methods," *Journal of Personal Selling & Sales Management* 23 (Fall 2003): 327–339.

[83]Kate Day and Lisa Maria Fedele, "Learning at the Speed of Life," *T+D* (June 2012): 60–63.

[84]Ashraf M. Attia, Earl D. Honeycutt Jr. and Mark P. Leach, "A Three-Stage Model for Assessing and Improving Sales Force Training and Development," *Journal of Personal Selling & Sales Management* 25 (Summer 2005): 253–268.

[85]Melone and Summy, "Sales Training 101: Best Practices for Keeping Pace with Rapid Change in Selling," presentation at the National Conference in Sales Management, April 5, 2002.

[86]Charles Gottenkieny, "Proper Training Can Result in Positive ROI," *Selling* (August 2003): 9.

[87]For more on how to assess the return on investment of sales training, see Clive Shepherd, "Assessing the ROI of Training," www.fastrak-consulting.co.uk/tactix/features/tngroi/tngroi.thm (accessed January 7, 2014).

[88]Mark Magnacca, "Where's the Return? A Look at Modern Ways to Efficiently Track Sales Training ROI," SellingPowerBlog (December 18, 2017), http://blog.sellingpower.com/gg/2017/12/wheres-the-return-a-look-at-modern-ways-to-efficiently-track-sales-training-roi.html (accessed June 1, 2018).

[89]David McGeough, "Measuring ROI," *Training* (March/April 2011): 27.

[90]Jared Fuller, "10 sales Training Techniques for Sales Managers," https://blog.pandadoc.com/10-sales-training-techniques-for-sales-managers (accessed June 7, 2018).

[91]The Sales Educators, *Strategic Sales Leadership: Breakthrough Thinking for Breakthrough Results* (Mason, OH: Thomson, 2006): 81.

[92]Sources: Brian Fravel, "6 Training Reinforcement Tips for Sales Success" (June 6, 2017), https://trainingindustry.com/blog/sales/6-training-reinforcement-tips-for-sales-success (accessed June 8, 2018); The Sales Readiness Group, "Maximizing the Effectiveness of Sales Training" (2012): 1–6.

[93]"Training: S&MM Pulse," *Sales & Marketing Management* 158 (July/August 2006): 21.

[94]Alan J. Dubinsky, Marvin A. Jolson, Ronald E. Michaels, Masaaki Kotabe, and Chae Un Lim, "Ethical Perceptions of Field Sales Personnel: An Empirical Assessment," *Journal of Personal Selling & Sales Management* 12 (Fall 1992): 9; Karl A. Boedecker, Fred W. Morgan, and Jeffrey J. Stoltman, "Legal Dimensions of Salespersons' Statements: A Review and Managerial Suggestions," *Journal of Marketing* 55 (January 1991): 70.

[95]Scott Inks, Ramon Avila, and Joe Chapman, "A Comparison of Buyers' and Sellers' Perceptions of Ethical Behaviors Within the Buyer-Seller Dyad," *Marketing Management Journal* (Spring 2004): 117–128.

[96]To learn more about a technique for using cases for ethical sales training, see John A. Weber, "Business Ethics Training: Insights from Learning Theory," *Journal of Business Ethics,* 70 (2007): 61–85.

[97]Melone and Summy, "Sales Training 101: Best Practices for Keeping Pace with Rapid Change in Selling."

[98]Boedecker et al., "Legal Dimensions of Salespersons' Statements."

[99]Sean Valentine, "Ethics Training, Ethical Context, and Sales and Marketing Professionals' Satisfaction with Supervisors and Coworkers," *Journal of Personal Selling & Sales Management* 29 (January 2009): 227–42.

Chapter 7

[1]The figure and discussion are adapted from Thomas N. Ingram, Raymond W. LaForge, William B. Locander, Scott B. MacKenzie, and Philip M. Podsakoff, "New Directions for Sales Leadership Research," *Journal of Personal Selling & Sales Management* (Spring 2005).

[2]Karen Flaherty, "Understanding the Relationship Between the Role of the Salesperson and the Role of the Sales Manager," in *The Oxford Handbook of Strategic Sales and Sales Management,* eds. David W. Cravens, Kenneth Le Meunier-Fitzhugh, and Nigel F. Piercy (Oxford, England: Oxford University Press, 2011): 51–76.

[3]Philip M. Podsakoff, Scott B. MacKenzie, Robert H. Moorman, and Richard Fetter, "Transformational Leader Behaviors and Their Effects on Followers' Trust in Leader, Satisfaction, and Organizational Citizenship Behaviors," *Leadership Quarterly* (1990): 107–142.

[4]Christian Schmitz and Shankar Ganesan, "Managing Customer and Organizational Complexity in Sales Organizations," *Journal of Marketing,* Vol. 78 (November 2014): 59–77.

[5]Source: Douglas Grisaffe, Rebecca VanMeter and Lawrence Chonko, "Serving First for the Benefit of Others: Preliminary Evidence for a Hierarchical Conceptualization of Servant Leadership," *Journal of Personal Selling & Sales Management*, Vol. 36 (March, 2016): 40–58.

[6]Daniel Goleman, "Leadership That Gets Results," *Harvard Business Review* (March–April 2000): 78–90; Daniel Goleman, Richard Boyatzis, and Annie McKee, *Primal Leadership: Realizing the Power of Emotional Intelligence* (Boston: Harvard Business School Press, 2002); Fernando Jaramillo, Douglas B. Grisaffe, Lawrence B. Chonko, and James A. Roberts, "Examining the Impact of Servant Leadership on Sales Force Performance," *Journal of Personal Selling & Sales Management* (Summer 2009): 257–275.

[7]Jay Mulki, Barbara Caemmerer and Githa Heggde, "Leadership Style, Salesperson's Work Effort and Job Performance: The Influence of Power Distance," *Journal of Personal Selling & Sales Management,* Vol. 35 (March, 2015): 3–22.

[8]Rosemary R. Lagace, "An Exploratory Study of Trust between Sales Managers and Salespersons," *Journal of Personal Selling & Sales Management* 11 (Spring 1991): 49; David Strutton, Lou E. Pelton, and James R. Lumpkin, "The Relationship between Psychological Climate and Salesperson–Sales Manager Trust in Sales Organizations," *Journal of Personal Selling & Sales Management* 13 (Fall 1993): 1; Karen E. Flaherty and James M. Pappas, "The Role of Trust in Salesperson–Sales Manager Relationships," *Journal of Personal Selling & Sales Management* 20 (Fall 2000): 271–278; Howard J. Klein and Jay S. Kim, "A Field Study of the Influence of Situational Constraints, Leader–Member Exchange, and Goal Commitment on Performance," *Academy of Management Journal* 41 (February 1998): 88.

[9]Charles Schwepker, Jr. "Psychological Ethical Climate, Leader–member Exchange and Commitment to Superior Customer Value: Influencing Salespeople's Unethical Intent and Sales Performance," *Journal of Personal Selling & Sales Management,* 37 (March, 2017): 72–87; Charles Schwepker, Jr. and Megan Good "Reducing Salesperson Job Stress and Unethical Intent: The Influence of Leader-Member Exchange Relationship, Socialization and Ethical Ambiguity," *Industrial Marketing Management,* Vol. 66 (2017): 205–218.

[10]Karen Flaherty, "Understanding the Relationship Between the Role of the Salesperson and the Role of the Sales Manager," in *The Oxford Handbook of Strategic Sales and Sales Management,* eds. David W. Cravens, Kenneth Le Meunier-Fitzhugh, and Nigel F. Piercy (Oxford, England: Oxford University Press, 2011): 51–76.

[11]Based on John French, Jr. and Bertram Raven, "The Bases of Social Power," in *Studies in Social Power,* ed. D. Cartwright (Ann Arbor, MI: The University of Michigan Press, 1959).

[12]Interview with Marty Reist, June 15, 2008.

[13]Adapted from Gerhard Gschwandtner, "Personal PR Strategies for Creating Power and Influence" in *Personal Selling Power* (October 1990): 20; Rebecca Newton, "Three Ways To Increase Your Personal Power At Work, Forbes Online (September 6, 2016), www.forbes.com/sites/rebeccanewton/2016/09/06 /three-ways-to-increase-your-personal-power-at-work/#6b4358a610a7 (accessed June 11, 2018); Elaine Bailey, "& Ways to Improve Your Personal Power and Influence as a Leader" (October 24, 2012), www.elainebaileyinternational.com/wordpress/20 12/10/7-ways-to-improve-your-personal-power-and-influence-others (accessed June 11, 2018).

[14]This discussion of influence strategies is largely based on Madeline E. Heilman and Harvey Hornstein, *Managing Human Forces in Organization* (Homewood, IL: Irwin, 1982): 116.

[15]Henry Canaday, "Selling the New SunGard Way," *Selling Power* (October/November/December 2013): 27–31; "50 Best Companies to Sell For," Selling Power (October/November/December 2013): 35.

[16]Jerome A. Colletti and Mary S. Fiss, "The Ultimately Accountable Job: Leading Today's Sales Organization," *Harvard Business Review* 84, 7/8 (July–August 2006): 125–131.

[17]Henry Canaday, "Tactical Gains," *Selling Power* (October/November/December 2012): 60–61.

[18]Matt Brown, "Tips for Communicating Effectively with Sales Teams," *Sales & Marketing Management* online (June 5, 2017), https://salesandmarketing. com/content/tips-communicating-effectively-sales-teams (accessed June 13, 2018).

[19]Henry Canaday, "A Socially Salable World," *Selling Power* (April/May/June 2012): 46–50.

[20]Mark C. Johlke, Dale F. Duhan, Roy D. Howell, and Robert W. Wilkes, "An Integrated Model of Sales Managers' Communication Practices," *Journal of the Academy of Marketing Science* 28 (Spring 2000): 263–277.

[21]Patricia Fripp, "9 Things Sales Leaders Need to Know about Communication," *Selling Power* online (October 15, 2015), http://salesleadership blog.sellingpower.com/2015/10/15/9-things-sales-leaders-need-to-know-about-communication (accessed June 12, 2018); Marcel Schwantes, "Need to Motivate a Team" (January 18, 2017), www.inc. com/marcel-schwantes/first-90-days-communica tion-habits-all-leaders-need-to-motivate-a-team.html (accessed June 12, 2018); John Hall, "3 Things Leaders With Impressive Communication Skills Always Do" (August 13, 2017); www.inc.com/john-hall/3-things-leaders-with-impressive-communica tion-ski.html (accessed June 12, 2018).

[22]Molly Buccini, "Sales Statistics: 6 Coaching Facts Every Sales Leader Needs to Hear," Brainshark, (August 3, 2016), https://www.brainshark.com/ ideas-blog/2016/august/sales-statistics-coaching-for-sales-leaders (accessed June 13, 2018).

[23]Brainshark, "The B2BSales Coaching Challenge: How Technology Can Help," www.brainshark.com/ sites/default/files/the-case-for-b2b-sales-coaching. pdf (accessed June 13, 2018).

[24]Byron Matthews and Tamara Schenk, *Sales Enablement*, Hoboken, NJ: Wiley & Sons (2018).

[25]The Sales Readiness Group, "5 Hallmarks of High Impact Sales Organizations," 2017 Sales Management Research Report (2017), https://cdn2. hubspot.net/hubfs/275587/offers/research-consid eration-salesmanagement-2017.pdf (accessed June 13, 2018).

[26]Heather Baldwin, "Talk to Me," *Selling Power* (January/February/March 2012): 10–13.

[27]Heather Baldwin, "Coaching Ops," *Selling Power* (July/August/September 2013): 23–25.

[28]Heather Baldwin, "Talk to Me," *Selling Power* (January/February/March 2012): 10–13.

[29]Miller Heiman Group, webinar entitled "What Does the Future of Sales Look Like?" https://go. millerheimangroup.com/2017-Q3-SalesEnablement-WB-FutureofSalesWebinarRecording-OWB-TOFU-EN_02.TY-Page.html (accessed May 15, 2018).

[30]Compiled from Barry J. Farber, "Sales Managers: Do Yourself a Favor," *Personal Selling Power* (April 1990): 33; "First Train Them, Then Coach Them," *Sales & Marketing Management* (August 1987): 64–65; Stuart R. Levine, "Performance Coaching," *Selling Power* (July/August 1996): 46; Bill Cates, "A Coach for All Reasons," *Selling Power* (June 1996): 64–65; Selling Power Editors, "Ten Ways to Make Every Moment You Spend with a Salesperson Count," *Selling Power* online, (September 5, 2017), www.sellingpowe r.com/2017/09/05/13186/offers/ten-ways-to-make-every-moment-you-spend-with-a-salesperson-count (accessed June 13, 2018).

[31]Joshua Miller, "14 Coaching Principles All Managers Should Practice" (July 5, 2015), www.linkedin.com/ pulse/14-coaching-principles-all-managers-should-practice-joshua-miller (accessed June 13, 2018).

[32]Source: Kevin Higgins, "The Key to Motivational Sales Meetings," BusinessChief.com, www.businesschief.com/leadership/3596/The-key-to-motivational-sales-meetings (accessed June 18, 2018).

[33]Mark McMaster, "Sales Meetings Your Reps Won't Hate," *Sales & Marketing Management* 153 (May 2001): 63–67.

[34]Compiled from John Treace, "5 Tips for Better Sales Meetings," *Inc.* online (October 2, 2012), www.inc. com/john-treace/5-tips-for-better-sales-meetings. html (accessed June 14, 2018); Mark Hunter, "10 tips for running a successful sales meeting," Agile CRM blog (January 24, 2018), https://www.agilecrm. com/blog/10-tips-running-successful-sales-meeting (accessed June 14, 2018); Tony Smith, "How to Run a

Productive Sales Meeting [7 Tips]," The Brooks Group website (July 31, 2017), https://brooksgroup.com/sales-training-blog/how-run-productive-sales-meeting-7-tips (accessed June 14, 2018).

35 3M Visual Systems Division, "Six Secrets to Holding a Good Meeting." Copyright © Minnesota Mining and Mfg. Co. Reproduced for 9th edition by permission. All reasonable efforts were made to contact the publisher for permission to use this list for this edition (10th ed.). If any copyright holder takes issue with its use please contact the publisher.

36 John D. Hansen and Robert J. Riggle, "Ethical Salesperson Behavior in Sales Relationships," *Journal of Personal Selling & Sales Management* (Spring 2009): 151–166.

37 Archie B. Carroll, "In Search of the Moral Manager," *Business Horizons* 30 (March/April 1987): 12. Copyright © 1987 by the Foundation for the School of Business at Indiana University. Reprinted by permission.

38 "Sales & Marketing Creed: The International Code of Ethics for Sales & Marketing." Reprinted by permission of SMEI, www.smei.org.

39 O.C. Ferrell, Mark W. Johnston, and Linda Ferrell, "A Framework for Personal Selling and Sales Management Ethical Decision Making," *Journal of Personal Selling & Sales Management* (Fall 2007): 291–299.

40 Charles H. Schwepker, Jr. and David J. Good, "Transformational Leadership and Its Impact on Sales Force Moral Judgment," *Journal of Personal Selling & Sales Management* (Fall 2010): 299–317; Thomas N. Ingram, Raymond W. LaForge, and Charles H. Schwepker, Jr., "Salesperson Ethical Decision Making: The Impact of Sales Leadership and Sales Management Control Strategy," *Journal of Personal Selling & Sales Management* (Fall 2007): 301–315; Charles Schwepker, Jr., "Improving Sales Performance Through Commitment to Superior Customer Value: The Role of Psychological Ethical Climate," *Journal of Personal Selling & Sales Management*, 33 (Fall, 2013): 389–402.

41 Michael Brown and Linda Trevino, "Ethical Leadership: A Review and Future Directions," *The Leadership Quarterly*, 17 (2006): 595–616.

42 Charles Schwepker, Jr., "Influencing the Salesforce through Perceived Ethical Leadership: The Role of Salesforce Socialization and Person-Organization Fit on Salesperson Ethics and Performance," *Journal of Personal Selling & Sales Management*, 35 (December, 2015): 292–313; Charles Schwepker, Jr. and Thomas Ingram, "Ethical Leadership in the Salesforce: Effects on Salesperson Customer Orientation, Commitment to Customer Value and Job Stress," *Journal of Business & Industrial Marketing*, 31 (2016): 914–27.

Chapter 8

1 Data from U.S. Department of Labor, Bureau of Labor Statistics, "May 2013 National Occupational Employment Statistics," www.bls.gov/oes/current/oes_nat.htm (accessed May 1, 2014).

2 Steven P. Brown, Kenneth R. Evans, Murali K. Mantrala, and Goutam Challagalla, "Adapting Motivation, Control, and Compensation Research to a New Environment," *Journal of Personal Selling & Sales Management* 25 (Spring 2005): 155–167.

3 Ruth Kanfer, "Work Motivation: Theory, Practice, and Future Directions," in *The Oxford Handbook of Organizational Psychology*, ed. Steve W.J. Kozlowski (Oxford, United Kingdom, 2012): 455–460.

4 Thomas Steenburgh and Michael Ahearne, "Motivating Salespeople: What Really Works," *Harvard Business Review* 90 (July/August 2012): 71–75.

5 Tim Houlihan, "Don't Show me the Money: The Truth About What Motivates High Performance," Sales & Marketing Management, White Paper Series (June 30, 2017).

6 Jeanne Greenberg and Herbert Greenberg, *What It Takes to Succeed in Sales: Selecting and Retaining Top Producers* (Homewood, IL: Dow-Jones Irwin, 1990): 112.

7 "Sales Compensation Changes, with Mixed Salary Levels," *Bloomberg BNA* (May 2013): 1–2.

8 http://corecommissions.com/products (accessed September 5, 2018).

9 "Seeing the CEO and the Sites: Planners Search for the Right Mix of Team-Building Events and Unstructured Time," *Sales and Marketing Management* (October 4, 2013), www.salesandmarketing.com/content/seing-ceo-and-sites.

10 "Surya Awards Winners in Sales Force Contest with $100K in Prizes," *Home Textiles Today* (October 22, 2012): 20.

11 The Sales Educators, *Strategic Sales Leadership: Breakthrough Thinking for Breakthrough Results* (Mason, OH: Thomson, 2006).

12 Affordable Colleges Online, "Fortune 500 Companies Picking Up the Tuition Tab," www.affordablecollegesonline.org/financial-aid/top-company-college-tuition-reimbursement-programs/ (accessed April 20, 2014).

13 Paul Shearstone, "Creating Sales Incentive Programs that Work, Part 2," http://sbinfocanada.about.com/cs/marketing/a/incentiveprogps_2.htm (accessed May 2, 2014).

14 Sample expense report from Expensable.com, http://www.expensable.com/products/expense-report-sample.htm (accessed January 3, 2011).

[15] Concur Technologies, www.concur.com/search.html? q=default&p=www.concur.com/solutions/exp/default. htm (accessed January 5, 2011).

[16] Automatic Data Processing, "Tricks Employees Use to Pad Their Expenses," www.adp.com/tools-and-res ources/newsletters/~/media/CBC4D674B62 F4990A3F67C209C579012.ashx (accessed April 12, 2014).

[17] The Forum for People Performance Management and Measurement, "Match Employee Awards to Specific Organizational Objectives for Optimal Success," Executive White Paper, www.performance forum.org/Match_Employee_Awards_to_Specific_ Organizational_Objectives.64.0.html (accessed January 3, 2011).

[18] William H. Murphy, "Sales Contest Research: Business and Individual Difference Factors Affecting Intentions to Pursue Contest Goals," *Industrial Marketing Management* 8 (January 2009): 109–118; Noah Lim, Michael J. Ahearne, and Sung H. Ham, "Designing Sales Contests: Does the Prize Structure Matter?" *Journal of Marketing Research* 46 (June 2009): 356–371; Jason Garrett and Srinath Gopalakrishna, "Customer Value Impact of Sales Contests," *Journal of the Academy of Marketing Science* 38 (December 2010): 775–786; F. Juliet Poujol and John F. Tanner, Jr., "The Impact of Contests on Salespeople's Orientation: An Application of Tournament Theory," *Journal of Personal Selling & Sales Management* 30 (Winter 2010): 33–46; Barbara Scofidio, " This Is Your Motivation Strategy?" *Corporate Incentives and Meetings* (March 2010): 13–16; Scott Ladd, "May the Force Be with You," *HR Magazine* (September 2010): 105–107; The Forum for People Performance Management and Measurement, "Making the Case for Sales Incentives to the Tune of 10 Percent ROI," Executive White Paper, www.performanceforum. org/Making_the_Case_for_Sales_Incentives.66.0. html (accessed January 4, 2011).

[19] "Security Dealers Share the Best & the Worst of Sales Contests," *SDM Magazine* (October 14, 2010), www.sdmmag.com/articles/security-dealers-share- the-best-the-worst-of-sales-contests.

[20] Rymax Marketing Services, "MaxSite Catalog," www.rymaxinc.com/Maxsite/Homepage/Default. aspx (accessed February 15, 2014).

[21] William H. Murphy, Peter A. Dacin, and Neil M. Ford, "Sales Contest Effectiveness: An Examination of Sales Contest Design Preferences of Field Sales Forces," *Journal of the Academy of Marketing Science* 32 (Spring 2004): 127–143.

[22] Maritz, "Maritz Motivation," www.maritz.com/ About-Maritz/Our-Businesses/Motivation.aspx. (accessed January 15, 2014).

[23] Steven P. Brown, Kenneth R. Evans, Murali K. Mantrala, and Goutam Challagalla, "Adapting Motivation, Control, and Compensation Research to a New Environment," *Journal of Personal Selling & Sales Management,* 25 (Spring 2005): 155–167.

[24] Sarah Sluis, "Sales Management Tools and Trends to Watch: Transform Sales With Technology," *Customer Relationship Management* (February 2014): 29–32.

[25] Brent Adamson, Matthew Dixon, and Nicholas Toman, "Why Individuals No Longer Rule on Sales Teams," *HBR Blog Network,* January 9, 2014, http:// blogs.hbr.org/2014/01/why-the-individual-no-lon ger-rules-in-sales/.

[26] Alex Palmer, "Taking Employee Recognition Mobile," Incentive, April 25, 2014, www.incentivema g.com/News/Industry/Articles/Taking-Employee- Recognition-Mobile/.

[27] John F. Tanner, Jr. and George Dudley, "International Differences—Examining Two Assumptions about Selling," reported in *Baylor Business Review* (Fall 2003): 44–45.

[28] Fay Hansen, "Currents in Compensation and Benefits," *Compensation and Benefits Review,* 40 (May/June 2008): 5–6.

[29] Xavier Baeten, "Global Compensation and Benefits Management: The Need for Communication and Coordination," *Compensation and Benefits Review,* 42 (September/October 2010): 392–402; Thomas Shelton, "Global Compensation Strategies: Managing and Administering Split Pay for an Expatriate Workforce," *Compensation and Benefits Review,* 40 (January/February 2008): 56–60.

[30] From "Global Gamble," by Michele Marchetti, *Sales & Marketing Management* 148 (July 1996): 64–69. Copyright © VNU Business Media Inc. Reprinted by permission.

[31] Sales & Marketing Management's SSM, "Fast-track Motivation: Makana Motivator Case Study," (July 31, 2010), www.salesandmarketing.com/article /fast-track-motivation-makana-motivator-case-study.

[32] Betsy Cummings, "Hearing Them Out," *Sales & Marketing Management* 157 (January 2005): 10.

[33] Hinda Incentives Rewards Portfolio, www.hinda. com/why-hinda/rewards-portfolio (accessed August 28, 2018).

Chapter 9

[1] Adapted from David W. Cravens, Thomas N. Ingram, Raymond W. LaForge, and Clifford E. Young, "Behavior-Based and Outcome-Based Salesforce Control Systems," *Journal of Marketing* 57 (October 1993): 47–59. Reprinted by permission of American Marketing Association.

[2] David W. Cravens, Thomas N. Ingram, Raymond W. LaForge, and Clifford E. Young, "Hallmarks of Eff- ective Sales Organizations," *Marketing Management* 1 (March 1992): 56.

[3]From "The Sales Force Management Audit" by Alan J. Dubinsky and Richard W. Hansen. Copyright © 1981, by The Regents of the University of California. Reprinted from the *California Management Review*, 24(2). By permission of The Regents.

[4]Meridian's, http://www.meridianise.com/Testimonials.htm (accessed July 3, 2007).

[5]From Dubinsky and Hansen, "The Sales Force Management Audit."

[6]From "Measuring Sales Effectiveness," by Geoffrey Brewer, *Sales & Marketing Management* 152 (October 2000): 136. Copyright © VNU Business Media Inc. Reprinted by permission.

[7]Reprinted by permission of *Harvard Business Review*. From "Measure Costs Right: Make the Right Decisions," by Robin Cooper and Robert S. Kaplan (September/October 1988): 96–103. Copyright © 1988 by the Harvard Business School Publishing Corporation, all rights reserved.

[8]Bridget McCrea, "A-B-C, Easy as 1-2-3," *Industrial Distribution* 92 (October 2003): H1–H4.

[9]Best Practices LLC Web site, http://www3.best-in-class.com/bestp/domrep.nsf/pages/716AD479AB1F512C85256DFF006BD072!OpenDocument (accessed June 27, 2007).

[10]Michael J. Webb, "Do You Know the Answers to These Questions?" Sales Performance Consultants, question 4. Available at http://www.salesperformance.com/FAQ.aspx (accessed July 6, 2007). Copyright © 2004 Sales Performance Consultants, Inc. Used by permission.

Chapter 10

[1]Fernando Jaramillo, Francois A. Carrillat, and William B. Locander, "Starting to Solve the Method Puzzle in Salesperson Self-Report Evaluations," *Journal of Personal Selling & Sales Management* 23 (Fall 2003): 369–377.

[2]Fernando Jaramillo, Francois A. Carrillat, and William B. Locander, "A Meta-Analytic Comparison of Managerial Ratings and Self-Evaluations," *Journal of Personal Selling & Sales Management* 25 (Fall 2005): 315–328.

[3]Adapted from Allan Church, "First-Rate Multirater Feedback," *Training & Development* 49 (August 1995): 42–43; and Scott Wimer and Kenneth M. Nowack, "13 Common Mistakes Using 360-Degree Feedback," *Training & Development* 52 (May 1998): 69–78; Bret J. Becton and Mike Schraeder, "Participant Input into Rater Selection: Potential Effects on the Quality and Acceptance of Ratings in the Context of 360-Degree Feedback," *Public Personnel Management* 33 (Spring 2004): 23–32.

[4]Helen Rheem, "Performance Management: A Progress Report," *Harvard Business Review* (March/April 1995): 11.

[5]Adapted from SellingPower Online, "Performance Review Basics," *SellingPower Sales Management Newsletter* (January 5, 2004); SellingPower Online, "Talking About Employee Performance," *SellingPower Sales Management Newsletter* (March 17, 2003).

[6]David W. Cravens, Greg W. Marshall, Felicia G. Lassk, and George S. Low, "The Control Factor," *Marketing Management* 13 (January/February 2004): 39–44.

[7]Donald Jackson, Jr., John Schlacter, and William Wolfe, "Examining the Bases Utilized for Evaluating Salespeople's Performance," *Journal of Personal Selling & Sales Management* 15 (Fall 1995): 57–65.

[8]Dominique Rouzies and Anne Macquin, "An Exploratory Investigation of the Impact of Culture on Sales Force Management Control Systems in Europe," *Journal of Personal Selling & Sales Management* 23 (Winter 2003): 61–72.

[9]Jackson, Schlacter, and Wolfe, "Examining the Bases Utilized for Evaluating Salespeople's Performance."

[10]*Ibid.*

[11]From "Selling and Sales Management in Action," by David J. Good and Robert W. Stone. Copyright © 1991 by Pi Sigma Epsilon. From *Journal of Personal Selling & Sales Management*, 11(3) (Summer 1991): 57–60. Reprinted with permission of M.E. Sharpe, Inc.

[12]Charles H. Schwepker, Jr. and David J. Good, "Understanding Sales Quotas: An Exploratory Investigation of Consequences of Failure," *Journal of Business & Industrial Marketing* 19 (2004): 39–48.

[13]David J. Good and Charles H. Schwepker, Jr., "Sales Quotas: Critical Interpretations and Implications," *Review of Business* 22 (Spring 2001): 32–36.

[14]*Ibid.*

[15]Jackson, Schlacter, and Wolfe, "Examining the Bases Utilized for Evaluating Salespeople's Performance."

[16]Eastman Chemical Company, "Checking Customer Value through Continual Improvement" survey.

[17]https://www.reviewsnap.com/features/performance-management-software (accessed September 7, 2018).

[18]Christian Homburg and Ruth M. Stock, "The Link between Salespeople's Job Satisfaction and Customer Satisfaction in a Business-to-Business Context: A Dyadic Analysis," *Journal of the Academy of Marketing Science* 32 (Spring 2004): 144–158.

[19]For a complete discussion of the scale, see Gilbert A. Churchill, Jr., Neil M. Ford, and Orville C. Walker, Jr., "Measuring the Job Satisfaction of Industrial Salesmen," *Journal of Marketing Research* (August 1974): 254. For validation support, see Charles M. Futrell, "Measurement of Salespeople's Job Satisfaction: Convergent and Discriminant Validity of Corresponding INDSALES and Job

Descriptive Index Scales," *Journal of Marketing Research* (November 1979): 594; Rosemary Lagace, Jerry Goolsby, and Jule Gassenheimer, "Scaling and Measurement: A Quasi-Replicative Assessment of a Revised Version of INDSALES," *Journal of Personal Selling & Sales Management* 13 (Winter 1993): 65. See also Sarath A. Nonis and S. Altan Erdem, "A Refinement of INDSALES to Measure Job Satisfaction of Sales Personnel in General Marketing Settings," *Journal of Marketing Management* 7 (Spring/Summer 1997): 34.

[20]James M. Comer, Karen A. Machleit, and Rosemary R. Lagace, "Psychometric Assessment of a Reduced Version of INDSALES," *Journal of Business Research* 18 (1989): 295–296. Reprinted by permission of Elsevier Science.

Note: All references to figures and exhibits have been indicate with an "f" or "e" after the page number.